Hate Crime in the Media

Recent Titles in Crime, Media, and Popular Culture

Black Demons: The Media's Depiction of The African American Male
Dennis Rome

Cybercrime: Criminal Threats from Cyberspace
Susan W. Brenner

Death Row Women: Murder, Justice, and the New York Press
Mark Gado

Famous American Crimes and Trials
Edited by Frankie Y. Bailey and Steven Chermak

Killer Priest: The Crimes, Trial, and Execution of Father Hans Schmidt
Mark Gado

Media Representations of September 11
Edited by Steven Chermak, Frankie Y. Bailey, and Michelle Brown

Public Executions: The Death Penalty and the Media
Christopher S. Kudlac

Scottsboro and Its Legacy: The Cases that Challenged American Legal and Social Justice
James R. Acker

Hate Crime in the Media

A History

Victoria Munro

Crime, Media, and Popular Culture
Frankie Y. Bailey and Steven Chermak, Series Editors

 PRAEGER

AN IMPRINT OF ABC-CLIO, LLC
Santa Barbara, California • Denver, Colorado • Oxford, England

Library of Congress Cataloging-in-Publication Data

Munro, Victoria.
  Hate crime in the media : a history / Victoria Munro.
    pages cm — (Crime, media, and popular culture)
  Includes bibliographical references and index.
    ISBN 978–0–313–35622–3 (hardback : alk. paper) — ISBN 978–0–313–35623–0 (ebook) 1. Hate crimes—United States. 2. Mass media and culture—United States. I. Title.
  HV6773.52.M86   2014
  070.4′49364150973—dc23   2014004390

ISBN: 978–0–313–35622–3
EISBN: 978–0–313–35623–0

18 17 16 15 14   1 2 3 4 5

This book is also available on the World Wide Web as an eBook.
Visit www.abc-clio.com for details.

Praeger
An Imprint of ABC-CLIO, LLC

ABC-CLIO, LLC
130 Cremona Drive, P.O. Box 1911
Santa Barbara, California 93116-1911

This book is printed on acid-free paper ∞

Manufactured in the United States of America

Contents

Series Foreword   vii

Acknowledgments   xi

Chapter 1. Introduction: Creating the Other   1

Chapter 2. Making Enemies Abroad and at Home: Hate and War   23

Chapter 3. Unwelcome Hordes: Immigrants and Hate   65

Chapter 4. The Color of Hate: Race, Space, and Place   105

Chapter 5. Sinners, Fanatics, and Terrorists: The Religious Other   151

Chapter 6. Personal Space and Identity: Hate and the Lesbian, Gay,
   Bisexual, and Transgender Community   181

Chapter 7. The Language of Hate: Hate Speech, Hate Talk, and the
   First Amendment   211

Chapter 8. Conclusion: Reframing the Other   237

Index   249

About the Author   253

Series Foreword

We are pleased to introduce this volume as the latest entry in Praeger's interdisciplinary series on crime, media, and popular culture. This series provides a home for scholars who are engaged in research on crime and mass media issues. The authors in this series tackle tough, often "hot button" issues related to the pervasiveness of media in our lives and the nature of social discourse. Ranging across many broad themes, the books in this series have explored topics including high-profile criminal cases, media coverage of 9/11, surveillance, and racial stereotypes.

In this volume, Victoria Munro focuses on hate crime in the media. Since the first contacts between racial/ethnic groups on the North American continent, the clash of cultures and belief systems has provided fertile ground for stereotyping of Others. These stereotypes were used as the rationales for dominance, control, and exploitation of land and labor. The evolving social, political, and economic institutions of the colonies and later the United States created and institutionalized inequities. In the United States and elsewhere in the world, fear and loathing of those who were different and who were "in the way of progress" was expressed both in political and social discourse and in physical aggression.

In the nineteenth century, mass media in the United States came into its own with the proliferation of print and, later, visual media. The themes of popular culture were echoed and expanded in the pages of the "penny press," "dime novels," and other publications aimed at working-class audiences. By the end of the century, photographers were capturing images of the lives of the "other half" who occupied the tenements of the cities. The arrival of migrants (African Americans from the rural South) and a new wave of European immigrants

(Irish fleeing the potato famine) in the cities of America brought conflicts not only among these two groups who were competing for jobs, but with white "nativists" who viewed both groups with disdain. By the early twentieth century, the influx of Polish and Italian immigrants from eastern Europe who neither spoke English nor were Protestant spurred the expansion of the anti-immigration policies that were first applied to the Chinese in the late nineteenth century. These policies sometimes worked to the advantage of Africans Americans who left the South during the "Great Migration" of African Americans between the two world wars. But for black Americans, the process of assimilation was even more treacherous than for the foreign newcomers. By the early twentieth century, all of these groups had experienced the power of mass media as a vehicle for the proliferation of negative stereotypes. The caricatures of racial/ethnic groups in newspapers, pulp fiction, films, radio, and advertising reinforced the negative perceptions held by those who were deciding if these racial/ethnic minorities could be assimilated into the American mainstream. In the pages of popular fiction, in newspapers, and in films, vigilante groups such as the Ku Klux Klan sometimes emerged as defenders of white dominance, white womanhood, and the status quo.

In this volume, Munro provides the historical context for understanding hate and bias-related acts in American society, from individual acts of violence to the treatment of designated enemies during times of war. As she documents, race/ethnicity has been only one of the forms of "otherness" that has inspired acts of violence. To the extent that white, male, Protestant, heterosexual has been normative in American society, those of other gender, religion, and sexuality have been subject to suspicion, discrimination, and bias-related aggression. Munro's analysis of the role of media in public discourse illustrates how the struggle for "space" and "place" by these other Americans has been viewed.

In her introduction to this volume, Munro provides an overview of cases that have been important in the formation of policies dealing with hate- or biased-related crimes. At the same time, she makes the point that these crimes are not a phenomenon of the past. Like war, which generates hate-based crimes on a larger scale, individual bias-related crimes are not easily eradicated because they depend on often irrational beliefs. In the chapters that follow, Munro explores the past and the present of such violence and its depiction in the media.

In her final chapter, before offering her conclusions, Munro examines the language of hate that supports the stigmatization of others. As she notes, this language has become so much a part of American culture that it is often used casually and dismissed as "only joking." This language has entered the discourse of both traditional and "new media" forums found on the Internet. In the context of the First Amendment "free speech" protections, the debate continues about language as the equivalent of a physical assault on the target.

The relevance of Munro's volume to contemporary life is illustrated by the frequent appearance in the media of stories about cases of violence directed toward individuals and groups that are identified as Others by the aggressors. In these cases, the media report the questions posed by law enforcement and the public about whether such acts rise to the level of "hate crimes." As this foreword is being written, cases in the news include assaults and murder. The media also report on acts of bullying that cause victims emotional distress and are sometimes factors in suicides by victims.

In this volume, Munro offers valuable insight into the often tragic consequences of hate in America and the various roles played by media in portraying, maintaining, and/or challenging the roots of hate.

Frankie Y. Bailey and Steven Chermak,
Series Editors

Acknowledgments

I have had background support from a variety of people that has enabled me to (finally!) complete this book. I would like to acknowledge:

— my parents who raised me to see humanity and not categories and hierarchies, and for providing me with a sense of humor
— my sister, Maggie, for picking up all my dropped pieces, supporting me always, loving me and keeping me sane
— George Lipsitz for providing me a chance to explore, question, and debate different perspectives and frames, and for his humanity
— Frankie Y. Bailey and Steven Chermak for believing in me, starting me on this journey, and supporting my efforts
— Phyllis Mahan and Patricia Jones-Whyte, my fellow writers (both of whom finished their projects before I did!) for their support, understanding and gentle pushes . . . you kept me from total submersion in the Brea Tar Pits!
— John Carlis for his wise advice even if I didn't manage to follow it and for his sense of humor
— my publisher, particularly Beth Ptalis, who stuck with me and continued to push me to completion
— Toby, the other half of my brain and partner in crime for always being there
— my big sister Lee for her support, encouragement, and love even from afar
— Cathy, who has always been there for me and is forever part of my family
— my other parents, Kay and Jim Keane, for their never-ending love and support
— my band mates, especially Steve who got me started, Bob and Hutch who always check in, and Katie and Laurel . . . just because
— Kelsey and Christopher for their continuing support

And last but never least, my children, Meg, Colin, and Ian, for their many special attributes, their love, and their peculiar notions of support . . . "Mom, you're never going to finish this are you?"

1

Introduction: Creating the Other

Michael Burzinski, 29, was murdered in July 1994 in Houston, Texas because he was gay. Followed from a nightclub by four young men, he was hit on the head as he unlocked his car, forced into the back, beaten in the face with the butt of a gun, and driven to an ATM where he was robbed of $400. He was then shot in the back of the head. The four charged with his killing were Demarco McCullum, Terrance Perro, Decedrick Gainous, and Christopher Lewis. McCullum, who told the others during the attack that Burzinski had to die because he knew their names (then proceeded to say their names to Burzinski), later told his friends he "felt like a judge" because he had killed someone.

The defendants told the police they had decided to rob a homosexual, as they had been told homosexuals "had money and were easy targets." They waited outside a nightclub in a known gay area of Houston and chose Burzinski as their victim. McCullum was found guilty of capital murder in November 1995 and sentenced to death. Gainous was convicted of capital murder and received a life sentence. Perro was convicted of aggravated robbery and sentenced to life. Lewis was convicted of aggravated robbery and sentenced to 15 years.

An article at the time stated, "McCullum, the Aldine Mustangs' quarterback last year, and Gainous, a defensive back, both graduated this spring and were to have reported Tuesday to Tyler Junior College, where each had earned a football scholarship."[1] Articles about the case focused attention on the four youths and their high school football careers. Descriptions of the perpetrators included statements such as: "one of the state's top 20 running backs," "the Aldine Mustangs' quarterback last year," "earned football scholarships to Tyler Junior College," and "Perro, a wide receiver who caught 15 passes for 398 yards last season . . ."[2]

Burzinski, on the other hand, was described in terms of his sexuality: "who was openly homosexual"[3] and "a native of Toledo, Ohio, is openly homosexual."[4] In all the articles, Burzinski was framed primarily as a man who was openly homosexual; he was never treated as an interesting subject or a sympathetic victim. This dehumanization of Burzinski was countered by considerable details that humanized the perpetrators: they were star football players, responsible students—well-known and well-liked, friendly to people and "cracked jokes." As the execution of Demarco McCullum approached in 2004, this trend continued with talk about his lost football career and college plans. The press described McCullum as "full of promise," an inmate of "model behavior," who possessed "athletic gifts."[5] "A former football hero and celebrity at Aldine High School was executed Tuesday evening for killing a man 10 years ago."[6]

Three intertwining elements surround the publicity for this case, and how they interact gives some idea of a hierarchy that exists in American culture. The victim was gay, and homosexuality is often relegated to a low position on the scale of worth. The perpetrators were Black, another category typically given low status, but in this case their status was raised due to the lower status of the victim. The third element is sports, which has high status, and the defendants were primarily raised to a higher status by their participation in sports and the media's framing of them as star athletes. The media could have framed them with the prevalent "Black as criminal" frame but in opposition to the lower framing of the victim as "homosexual," chose to fall back on the "Black as athlete" frame, a stereotypical framing in itself but less harmful than the criminal stereotype.

The stereotype that gays have money and are easy targets (resting on stereotypes about masculinity) has led to numerous assaults and deaths. In Burzinski's death, his killers admitted to believing this to be the case and chose their victim accordingly. ". . . [P]ublished reports have noted that gay men earn more on average than their heterosexual counterparts. According to newspaper reports, a man convicted in the 1993 execution-style slaying of a gay Tyler (Texas) man said he targeted gays to rob partly because he believed they carry a good deal of money."[7] Law professor Joseph Broadus (George Mason University) testified before Congress in 1994 and helped defeat the Employment Non-Discrimination Act by identifying homosexual households as "elite" and therefore not in need of special legislation. According to Broadus, those in the average gay household earn twice as much as the national average.[8]

In 1992, Colorado amended its constitution to prevent state and local governments from extending civil rights protections specifically to gay men, lesbians, and bisexuals. The constitution was challenged four years later in the U.S. Supreme Court, which struck it down as "born of animosity" toward gays. Professor James Woodard testified in court that the median annual household income for gays and lesbians was 40 percent higher than for heterosexual households, and therefore gays and lesbians needed no special protections. Justice

Scalia, writing the dissent, determined that such testimony was evidence that gays had disproportionate political power as a result of their higher income, and that gave Colorado voters the right to rein in their power through legislation.

Recent studies, however, are in disagreement with this testimony. A 2012 Gallup poll determined that the lesbian, gay, bisexual and transgender (LGBT) population tends to have lower levels of income and education than the general population: "Among those who report income, about 16% of LGBT-identified individuals have incomes above $90,000 per year, compared with 21% of the overall adult population. Additionally, 35% of those who identify as LGBT report incomes of less than $24,000 a year, significantly higher than the 24% for the population in general. These findings are consistent with research showing that LGBT people are at a higher risk of poverty."[9] This research includes the recently published study finding that even taking poverty rates during the latest recession into account, lesbian, gay, and bisexual Americans have remained more likely to be poor than heterosexual Americans.[10]

In this book, I look at the creation of groups as Other in American culture and how the mediated versions of these groups connect to hate crimes against them. By Other, I speak of the construction of certain groups based on attributes such as race, ethnicity, religion, and sexual identity as different from the dominant group in American society. For example, if the dominant group is heterosexual, then the creation of homosexuals as innately different and hierarchically lower creates them as Other, as "not us." This creation serves to contain those defined as Other in subordinate positions politically, economically, and socially and makes them a target for discrimination and hate-based actions.

From assumptions about group characteristics such as "gays are wealthy" to hate crimes against "Muslim-looking" people, the images we create of marginalized groups and the stereotypes we believe about them have contributed throughout our history to an enormous number of hateful acts. We would like to believe that hate crimes are the acts of individual evil or ill people; in reality, our cultural creations of Other lead to circumstances that foster many levels of biased behaviors, not just by individuals, but by group actions and even by institutions such as law enforcement agencies that should be protecting those who are vulnerable. In *Documenting the Hate*, which reported on bias incidents in New York City between January 1992 and June 1993, Dennis Deleon, New York's commissioner of human rights, stated: "We issue denunciations while rarely looking at our feet, planted firmly in the traditions where the bigotry that caused the violence has taken root. All perpetrators of bias incidents are our children, raised with the unchallenged slanders and stereotypes that populate our media, our schools, our conversations and our hearts."[11]

My goal in this book is to look at some of these stereotypes in our culture and take note of the traditions of hate that have been part of American culture since the beginning of our country. Along with the images, I look at the results, the hate crimes committed against Othered Americans or those we come in conflict with during war. The importance of mediated images can be clearly illustrated by the hate crimes that took place directly after the Oklahoma City bombing in 1995 as the media talked about the incident as characteristic of "Muslim terrorists." Those deemed to be Muslim suffered at the hands of their fellow Americans due to the framing of the incident by the media; in reality, no Muslim was involved in the attack at all.

Discourse analysis "aims primarily to illustrate and describe the relationship between textual and social processes. In particular, it is concerned with the politics of representation—the manifest political consequences of adopting one mode of representation over another."[12] Discourse analysis focuses on language as constitutive, as "structures of signification that construct social realities, particularly in terms of defining subjects and establishing their relational positions within a system of signification."[13] Much rests on the constitution of subjects: their authority to speak and act, what are considered legitimate forms of knowledge and legitimate political practices, and "importantly, common sense within particular social groups and historical settings . . ."[14] Discourse functions to give legitimacy to some while excluding and silencing other subjects and competing discourses. My goal in this book is to analyze some particular discourses surrounding the creation of Others in American history and culture, and what those creations have meant in terms of hate crimes toward these groups. By looking both historically and currently at our framing, I hope to provide a critical eye on our current practices. The media plays a vital role in this process, choosing some victims as noteworthy while ignoring others, and framing perpetrators in limited ways such as focusing on the actions of White supremacists when in reality most hate crimes are not committed by these groups. The frames tell us who is worthy of concern, and they focus our fears and our efforts in very limited ways while maintaining the current hegemony in America today.

Before discussing how I frame my analysis, a look at the growth of laws specifically created to deal with the phenomenon of hate crime forms an important backdrop to my discussion. The creation of federal and state hate crime laws has been political and contentious, and the debate over the need for these laws and their efficacy in dealing with bias-based incidents continues today.

CIVIL RIGHTS ACTS OF 1964 AND 1968

Although the history of the United States is littered with bodies, including thousands of Black people lynched and killed in recent centuries, it was the death of two young White men and one Black man in 1964 that produced the final impetus for passage of the Civil Rights Act and for federal investigation into civil rights violations, including hate crimes. James Chaney, Andrew Goodman, and

Michael Scherer came to Mississippi in the summer of 1964 as part of the Freedom Summer campaign to register Black voters. With the help of local police, the three were kidnapped and murdered by a local Ku Klux Klan group in June 1964. The Federal Bureau of Investigation (FBI) investigation into the murders, called Mississippi Burning or MIBURN, "became the largest federal investigation ever conducted in Mississippi."[15] The role of the FBI in investigating hate crimes increased once the Civil Rights Act passed in July 1964 and as a result of the MIBURN investigation.

The Civil Rights Act of 1964 outlawed discrimination against racial, ethnic, national, and religious groups as well as women. On paper at least, it ended racial segregation in schools, public accommodations, and places of employment, and inequities in voter registration requirements, although it retained some of the requirements making it difficult for Black Americans to be eligible to vote. Title IX of the act made it easier to move civil rights cases out of state courts and into federal courts when the state court venues included segregationist judges and/or all-White juries. The act covered victims who were attempting to participate in different federally protected activities that included voting, applying for employment or being employed, serving as a juror, running for elected office, taking advantage of public places, or attending school.

The 1968 Civil Rights Act, considered by some as the first modern hate crime legislation, allows federal prosecution of anyone who injures, intimidates, or interferes with another person (or attempts to do so) by force or threat of force because of the person's race, color, religion, or national origin. In general, the 1968 Civil Rights Act added prohibitions on housing discrimination —including the sale, rental, or financing of housing—to the activities covered by the 1964 act. The 1968 act included prohibitions against "threatening, intimidating or interfering with persons in their enjoyment of a dwelling because of the race, color, religion, sex, handicap, familial status, or national origin of such persons, or of visitors or associates of such persons."[16] Many current hate crimes take place in victims' neighborhoods and revolve around anti-integration stances regarding housing. At least by law, the 1968 act prohibits such behavior.

YUSUF HAWKINS

On August 23, 1989, a 16-year-old Black youth named Yusuf Hawkins was shot and killed by a 19-year-old Italian American in the Bensonhurst section of New York City. Hawkins and three of his friends came to Bensonhurst that evening to look at a used car advertised in the newspaper. They were confronted by a mob of White teenagers with baseball bats who were waiting for a group of Blacks and Hispanics supposedly coming to "kick their asses." In the end, the

mere fact of Black skin was enough to condemn Hawkins to death from two bullets fired point-blank into his chest.[17]

The Bensonhurst incident, as it came to be known, grew to far greater significance
than the murder of one individual by another. The killing was a "bias incident," a
new designation used by the New York police department for crimes committed on
the basis of racial or other bias. Hawkins was killed because he was Black and had
ventured unknowingly into a neighborhood that did not welcome outsiders.

National attention remained on the arrest and trial of the perpetrators in large
part due to the protests and counterprotests that sprang from the case. Involvement
of leaders such as the Reverend Al Sharpton and Louis Farrakhan, and the bringing
of protests into Bensonhurst resulted in bitter invective from both sides. There were
numerous scenes in the newspapers and on television of faces contorted with hatred,
fingers pointed in anger, and symbolic gestures such as the watermelons hoisted by
Bensonhurst youth to taunt and belittle Black Americans.

While the Bensonhurst incident drew national attention to race relations
between Black and White Americans, it also added a chapter to the increasing
number of hate crimes singled out in the news. New York City during the
1980s was the setting for many of these cases, and the response from the media
and the general population was heightened by the numerous political aspirations
of some of the main actors. The prevalence of these nationally known bias cases
led to federal hate crime legislation being passed at the end of the decade.

Yusuf Hawkins and his friends watched *Mississippi Burning*, a film about the
1964 Goodman, Chaney, and Scherer murders, before going to look at the used
car. After taking the subway to Bensonhurst, they walked along the sidewalk
toward the address where the used car was for sale. The four ran into a group
of young White men gathered on the sidewalk with baseball bats and golf clubs.

Keith Mondello, a 19-year-old of Italian/Jewish background, had had some
sort of relationship with Gina Feliciano, a high school dropout and crack addict
who lived with her mother over the corner store. She brought Black and Hispanic
friends to the block, which was not looked upon kindly by the neighborhood.
Mondello told her to stop bringing "niggers and spics" around, or there would
be trouble. August 23, 1989, was Gina's eighteenth birthday. She told Keith
and Sal "the Squid" (one of the store's owners) that her Black and Hispanic
friends were coming to "beat the shit out of all of yez."[18] The rumor was that
she was bringing in 20 or so friends. Mondello, Sal, and others gathered a group
together to combat the intruders, arming themselves with baseball bats, a favorite
neighborhood weapon. Unknown to this mob, Gina, seeing the group gathering
outside her apartment, called her friends and canceled. When Yusuf Hawkins
and his friends arrived, they walked right into the middle of this tension. While
some in the White group realized that the four young Black men weren't the
"right" group, 19-year-old Joey Fama did not waste time asking questions—he

ran up and shot Yusuf and then ran away. The shots entered Yusuf's chest, and he died soon afterward.

Fama was fairly representative of the working-class White youth in Bensonhurst. "They are fiercely protective of their turf and will fight for their tiny fiefdoms with fists, feet, bats, knives, and even guns. The play-actors who aren't really certifiable criminals are sometimes the most dangerous in turf-war situations, because their sense of social insecurity makes them feel they have more to prove than the others, so they'll go the extra distance."[19]

The New York City Police Department (NYPD) Bias Incident Investigation Unit was given the Bensonhurst case. "In a report published for the National Institutes of Justice, Bias Crime and the Criminal Justice Response (1989), bias crimes and hate groups are described as very much on the rise. The study found an increased frequency of incidents committed by loosely knit neighborhood groups, usually made up of young White males."[20] At the time of Hawkins's death, New York State had a discrimination statute that could enhance prison sentences, but little else to differentiate the treatment of a hate crime offender. Yusuf Hawkins's killing was the 314th case investigated by the NYPD Bias Unit in 1989. Perceived to be more heavy-handed, the precinct detectives were also acquainted with some of the families of those charged and were more sympathetic to the suspects than the Bias Unit appeared to be. Some precinct detectives even told family members that they would not have charged their son if it had been up to them. "But a disingenuous approach by local investigators to cases where race is a factor was one reason the Bias Unit was formed to begin with."[21]

In addition to the racial tensions, Bensonhurst made the Bias Unit's job more difficult with its adherence to the code of silence. The police found it hard to get people to talk about their neighbors, particularly in a mob-invested neighborhood such as Bensonhurst where people were afraid of repercussions if they talked. Numerous witnesses ended up in protective custody before the trial was over, and some reported receiving threatening phone calls. In 2005, Joseph D'Angelo, a witness in the case against mobster John Gotti (a resident of Bensonhurst), admitted that he had lied to police about Yusuf Hawkins's murder and that he had also pressured a woman who knew many details about the killing not to talk to the police. "It's part of the mob. That's what we do, we lie to the police." On August 23, 1989, D'Angelo had called his friend Joseph Serrano to Bensonhurst because of the supposed impending attack by Blacks and Hispanics. Serrano was the one who brought Joey Fama with him to the gathering.[22]

MEDIA RESPONSE

In the Bensonhurst case, Black men ventured into a predominantly White neighborhood. The print media used descriptions of various neighborhoods to provide contextual details and more importantly, explanations of why the events happened as they did. The majority of descriptors applied to Bensonhurst included the notion of enclave and insularity. Described as a "working-class neighborhood" and a "down-at-the-heels ethnic White neighborhood," it was pointed out repeatedly that Bensonhurst was a transplant straight out of Italy, a foreign enclave in the middle of New York, and this "specialized culture" was presented as a reason behind the actions of the young men involved in the crime. In addition, the papers pointed to White ethnics' fear in the then depressed job market that they would be replaced by others, particularly Blacks, and Bensonhurst's strong sense of turf.

At a time when Ronald Reagan and George H. W. Bush were creating a fear of the Black man and denigrating the Black working force with statements about "welfare queens" and images of Black youths on drugs, the already insecure White working class looked at young Black males as the ultimate threat. In addition, the concern over a girl from the neighborhood dating Black men put the threat on another front as well, one with a long history of emotional responses. The clear racism of the neighborhood was described in mitigating terms by the press: it was "understandable" due to the insular and traditional nature of the "enclave," because of the fear of economic insecurity by the working-class population, because of their protectiveness over "their" women, and because of the traditions of "macho bonding exercises" that create a mob out of a group of White teenagers. Gina Feliciano, the young woman who threatened to bring in Blacks to "kick some ass," almost more than Joseph Fama, was held responsible for the incident.

The press compared Hawkins's neighborhood to Bensonhurst; both were "socially and exclusively homogenous places where outsiders automatically draw residents' attention."[23] The well-kept homes, flowers, and religious statues of Bensonhurst were contrasted with Hawkins's neighborhood. "Down the street [from Hawkins's house] at the corner of Alabama Avenue, where sunflowers droop over the weeds of an empty lot and a burned-out building provides cover for drug transactions and the voices of LL Cool J and other rappers fill the air, a half-dozen neighborhood youths were tossing a basketball at a make-shift hoop on a telephone pole."[24] Although Hawkins himself was not a drug user, by implication he represented a neighborhood defined in ultimately stereotypical terms by empty lots, drugs, rap music, and basketball.

The press seemed to remove any idea of individual responsibility from those involved except for that assigned Gina Feliciano and pointed out that "stereotypes and cultural precepts act to define young Black men as dangerous, and therefore, somehow legitimate victims of assault."[25] In addition, the press pointed to a new generation of racism, that of the young White working class that had been wrenched by the economic dislocations of the 1980s and who had no memory of the civil rights struggles of the 1960s and 1970s. The Reagan administration's arguments that White males were being mistreated, particularly in the workforce, coupled with media portrayals that fueled old fears, were creating negative feelings toward Blacks in White ethnic areas such as Bensonhurst. Many cited statistics on Black involvement in crime, pointing to an understanding of why the neighborhood's fear of Blacks might be justified. All this in the face of neighborhood reaction from Bensonhurst that included screams of "niggers go home," labels of "mulignans" (a corruption of the Italian for eggplants, a reference to Black skin), and the waving of watermelons at Black protesters marching through the neighborhood.

The more conservative press took to highlighting what they saw as Black racism, particularly as personified by Al Sharpton. This version pointed out that Blacks and Hispanics "more and more, are making New York a frightening place to live."[26] By justifying neighborhoods' fears of Black crime, the press created an understanding for the public as to why the White neighborhood reacted as it did to Black intruders. Some felt that "Black revolutionaries" were leading the marches through Bensonhurst merely to incite violence. A more conservative analysis denied that Bensonhurst was a racial attack since it was primarily an argument over a woman.

What was not mentioned in the typical write-ups on the case were the ironies in the posturing of Bensonhurst residents against the high rate of Black crime and their own fears, against the backdrop of the involvement of many in the neighborhood in organized crime. "While people who live on the quiet side streets complain about how crack-crazed Blacks are ruining the city of New York, the guys in the suits map new strategies for smuggling drugs and guns into the five boroughs and how they will invest the profits into legitimate businesses."[27]

HATE CRIME STATISTICS ACT, 1990

In April 1990, in part a response to the growing number of bias cases like the one in Bensonhurst, Congress passed the Hate Crime Statistics Act, which requires the attorney general to collect data about hate crimes. The task of collecting, compiling, and managing the data was given to the FBI, who assigned it to the Uniform Crime Reporting (UCR) Program. The first report came out in 1992. The act required the collection of data each calendar year regarding crimes "that manifest evidence of prejudice based on race, religion, sexual orientation, or ethnicity." While federal data collection is mandated, participation at the local and state levels is voluntary, which immediately limits the overall picture provided by the statistics. The purpose of the act was to enable the government and law enforcement agencies at all levels to get a better handle on the breadth and depth of hate crimes in the country, including frequency, location, offender characteristics, victim characteristics, and types of crimes committed.

Thanks in part to the legacy of Jesse Helms, the Hate Crime Statistics Act also includes language stemming from Senator Helms's strong antigay bias. "Nothing in this Act shall be construed, nor shall any funds appropriated to carry out the purpose of the Act be used, to promote or encourage homosexuality."[28] Gregory Herek, a leading expert on anti-LGBT hate crime, points to the impact of Helms's antigay bigotry, including his helping to prevent effective AIDS prevention programs for gay and bisexual men, which in all probability caused many deaths, and the power that one politician can have in maintaining a heterosexist (or racist or sexist) society, particularly when combined with an unwillingness on the part of other politicians to challenge this stance.

While the LGBT population has been fighting uphill political battles for equality, they have been the victims of hate crimes that range from property crimes to simple assaults to especially violent assaults and murders. Several studies compare victims of heterosexual murders to those of LGBT murders. The homicides of male homosexual and bisexual victims were more violent and frequently showed evidence of overkill, which Herek describes as "wounding far beyond what would be required to cause a victim's death."[29] Scotty Joe Weaver, a young (18) gay man from Alabama, was murdered by his two roommates and one of their friends. He was beaten, cut, and strangled. Once dead, his body was placed face up on the ground, and the murderers then urinated on him and set him on fire. Gordon Church was murdered in Utah by two men who slashed his neck, attached his testicles to a car battery, and repeatedly shocked him, kicked him in the face and head, raped him with a tire iron that punctured his liver and other internal organs, and then beat him over the head with the tire iron.[30] ". . . [O]verkill and related forms of brutality may indicate the extent to which sexual minorities are dehumanized in the minds of perpetrators. When attackers regard their victims as less than human, they're unlikely to feel any inhibition about brutalizing them. Such denigration can ultimately be traced to the stigma that is attached to homosexuality in our culture."[31] Many hate crimes against LGBT people never make it into the statistics, as a number of states choose not to include protections for the LGBT community in their hate crime laws. Media treatment of LGBT victims is partially responsible for the unwillingness of the public and the legal system to protect this population.

MATTHEW SHEPARD

On the night of October 6, 1998, twenty-one-year-old Matthew Shepard was attacked in Laramie, Wyoming, because he was gay. Picked up in the Fireside Lounge on the campus of the University of Wyoming by two men who pretended to be gay, Matthew was driven out of town, where he was beaten, robbed, and left tied to a fence outside of town in near freezing weather. He was discovered 18 hours later by a bicyclist who at first thought he was a scarecrow. Shepard died six days later from severe brain injuries.

The media attention to the Shepard case was immediate, widespread, and persistent. It was used to push for passage of the Hate Crimes Prevention Act, a bill that would broaden the definition of hate crimes to include assaults on gays as well as women and people with disabilities. This bill, initiated in 2001, had been tied up precisely because the inclusion of gays was so controversial. As *Time* magazine pointed out, Shepard's death created a challenge for Republicans who needed to condemn the killing while at the same time continue to condemn homosexuality. On both sides of the issue of LGBT equality and rights, political groups had been forming and gathering strength since the 1980s. The Human Rights Campaign was founded in 1980 to work for equality for lesbian, gay, bisexual and transgender Americans. On the right, Focus on the Family (founded in 1977) and the Family Research Council (founded in 1981) were promoting "traditional family values" and lobbying against LGBT rights, bringing strong opposition to the normalizing of LGBT people and the creation and protection of their rights.

Matthew Shepard's killers, Aaron McKinney and Russell Henderson, were caught quickly. McKinney was convicted of first-degree felony murder and second-degree murder, aggravated robbery, and kidnapping, and sentenced to two consecutive life sentences with no chance of parole. Henderson pleaded guilty to felony murder and received the same sentence.

The depiction of Matthew Shepard by the media had much to do with who he was and the political use that could be made from his death. Shepard was presented as the youth he was, small and helpless looking, as nonthreatening an individual as possible. His position tied to the fence was even likened to a crucifixion by some media sources. He became the perfect representation of a nonthreatening face for homosexuality to be juxtaposed against the predatory disease-ridden pedophiles that the religious right created and condemned. "The point of this iconography is to divest Shepard of any maturity, any manhood, any adult sexuality—for that matter, any true humanity. It is literally to infantilize him, to turn him into a symbol that is at once pitiful and utterly unthreatening to the stereotypes that still burden most homosexual men, stereotypes that continue to weaken our self-confidence and self-respect."[32]

While one side argued the need for extending national hate crime laws to include homosexuals, the other argued that hate crime penalty enhancements privileged some Americans above others and were unnecessary: McKinney and Henderson were caught, convicted, and sentenced very quickly with no such legislation in place, as Wyoming had no state hate crime laws, and gays were not included in federal legislation at the time.

"Four major points emerged from the community-wide debate and discussion: The media were intrusive; they projected an unsubstantiated and unfair portrait of Wyoming as a 'hate state'; they relentlessly linked Shepard's murder to the fact that Wyoming had no hate crime law; and they overtly promoted hate crime legislation as a necessary response to the death."[33] Assigning guilt beyond the immediate killers took place from both ends of the political spectrum and was represented in media originating from these camps. The culture of Laramie specifically, and Wyoming in general, was blamed for fostering hate toward gays. This blame led to solutions of legislation (hate crime laws specifically) and further education regarding gay humanity and rights. Blaming McKinney and Henderson as depraved individuals, anomalies rather than representatives, denied the need for structural change regarding the place of the LGBT population in America and allowed others to continue to believe that our current laws were enough to protect all Americans equally.

THE MATTHEW SHEPARD AND JAMES BYRD, JR., HATE CRIMES PREVENTION ACT, 2009

Even with all the publicity and political rhetoric that ensued after Shepard's murder, the Matthew Shepard and James Byrd, Jr., Hate Crimes Prevention Act was not signed into law until President Obama did so in October 2009, thirteen years after it was first introduced. In addition to broadening the protected groups, the law also allows the federal government to provide assistance to states for the investigation and prosecution of hate crimes, particularly in states that do not have their own hate crime legislation. Another provision of the bill allows for state and local law enforcement training. Although originally passed by the Senate in 2007, it faced a veto from then president Bush, who felt hate crime legislation for the LGBT community was unnecessary, and Democrats removed it from the rest of the Department of Defense bill to which it was attached. The bill was named for Matthew Shepard and for James Byrd Jr.

James Byrd Jr., a Black man, was brutally murdered in 1998 by three men, two of whom were White supremacists. The murder took place in Jasper, Texas, on June 7. The three offered Byrd a ride home and then took him to a remote road outside of town, where they proceeded to beat him, urinate on him, and chain him by his ankles to their pickup truck. He was dragged for three miles down the road, probably conscious, until his body hit a culvert, which severed his right arm and his head. After leaving countless pieces of torn flesh behind, the three murderers deposited what was left of Byrd's body in front of a Black church. All three perpetrators were caught, convicted, and sentenced. One has been executed; the other two remain in prison.

The Matthew Shepard and James Byrd, Jr., Hate Crimes Prevention Act expanded already existing federal hate crime laws to apply to crimes motivated by a victim's actual or perceived gender, sexual orientation, gender identity, or disability and removed the stipulation that victims had to be engaged in federally protected activities. In addition, it gave federal authorities a greater mandate to carry out hate crime investigations that local law enforcement agencies chose not to pursue themselves. It also added hate crimes based on gender and gender identity to the categories covered under the Hate Crimes Statistics Act so that the FBI would now be required to collect statistics on these hate crimes as well.

STATE HATE CRIME LAWS

Hate Crime Laws: A Practical Guide provides international benchmarks for drafting hate crime legislation, including answering important questions about the purpose and practice of hate crime laws. The publication establishes the two required elements of a hate crime: it must be a criminal offense, and it must be committed with a particular motivation, in this case, bias. "This means that the perpetrator intentionally chose the *target* of the crime because of some *protected characteristic*."[34]

Hate crimes are distinct from other crimes in that the victims are chosen by what they are rather than who they are, thus creating a target group from which any interchangeable member can stand in for the chosen victim and widening the impact of the offense beyond the immediate target. "Hate crimes . . . can damage the fabric of society and fragment communities."[35] While the individual victim may be impacted physically and/or psychologically, those that share the victim's characteristics may also be impacted psychologically. Therefore, symbolically, hate crime laws serve to let those in the margins know that they are an important part of the larger society and that acts of hatred against them will not be tolerated. From a practical point of view, passing hate crime legislation improves awareness of and response to hate crimes and makes data collection more effective.

In answer to the argument that hate crime laws discriminate in that they appear to protect some groups over others, the guide responds that these offenses can occur against majority communities as well and that hate crime legislation protects groups of people from bias based on categories that are not exclusive: ethnicity (which does not specify any particular ethnic group), race (again, any race, including White), or religion, for example. "Rather, laws protect all individuals defined by the generic version of that characteristic."[36] While some argue that a power differential is necessary to commit a hate crime, I would agree with the guide; when a victim is chosen by the category to which he or she belongs, and the category is protected, it is a hate crime regardless of the relative positions the perpetrator and victim hold in society. In reality, the vast majority of hate crimes are perpetrated against those in marginalized positions by White Americans, and therefore the focus has been and should remain primarily on this manifestation of hate. That should not preclude the charging of a hate crime when the victim is chosen because he or she is White, for example, and this type of hate crime continues to be prosecuted in the United States.

State hate crime laws are formulated in a variety of different ways throughout the United States. Some create new offenses with bias or hate as a required element of the offense. Others add enhanced penalties to already existing offenses when the element of bias can be proven. While substantive offenses (those created specifically as hate or bias offenses) help create the symbolic benefits of hate crime legislation, they can also be harder to prosecute because they require proof of the bias motivation to convict. The penalty enhancement is easier to implement but may not receive the same public recognition (and therefore symbolic effect) as charging a perpetrator with a hate crime.[37]

Sarah Soule and Jennifer Earl found patterns in the processes by which states adopted hate crime legislation and what some of the important factors have been in determining these patterns. By 1995, thirty-seven states had passed some type of criminal law dealing with hate crimes. Soule and Earl found that the per capita income level of a state, the regional media attention to hate crimes, the percentage of the state's legislators who are Democrats, and whether the state had already adopted either civil legislation to redress hate crimes or a data collection response to hate crimes all affected the likelihood of passing a criminal law. While a higher per capita income, increased media attention, and a higher number of Democrats all contributed to an increase in passage of criminal laws dealing with hate crimes, prior passage of civil or data collection responses decreased the passage of criminal hate crime legislation, as these responses deflected the need for stronger anti–hate crime measures. In addition, the authors found that states that exclude certain groups (e.g., those based on sexual orientation) from an initial hate crime law were less likely in the future to pass protections for these groups.[38]

U.S. hate crime law is still evolving as arguments continue over which groups should be protected and what is required of different law enforcement and training bodies. Most jurisdictions protect race, ethnicity, and religion. Some have added sexual orientation. Other common inclusions are gender, age, and physical disability. Currently, 15 states have laws that address hate crimes based on sexual orientation and gender identity, while 15 more include sexual orientation but not gender identity. Five states currently have no state hate crime laws at all, and Wyoming remains one of these. Washington and Oregon were the first states to pass hate crime legislation, in 1981, although California's statute, passed in 1987, is considered by most legal scholars to be the original hate crime statute.[39]

"Hate crimes do not occur in a vacuum; they are a violent manifestation of prejudice, which can be pervasive in the wider community."[40] Dennis Deleon, New York City's Commissioner of Human Rights in the 1990s, points to the cyclical nature of hate crime; an event occurs that receives wide publicity and following that event, revenge hate crimes and then retaliatory hate crimes occur.

Following the incident with Rodney King in Los Angeles and the acquittal of the police in the case, anti-White assaults jumped dramatically. Following the terrorist attack on September 11, 2001, the number of hate crimes against those perceived as Arab and/or Muslim rose significantly, just as they had after the Oklahoma City bombing. "Social acceptance of discrimination against particular groups is an important factor in causing hate crimes to increase. Hence, although hate crimes can be committed against members of the majority population, it is the most marginalized communities who are disproportionately victims of hate crimes."[41]

Cogan provides a response to the argument that hate crime laws are discriminatory and unnecessary, pointing out that an historical hierarchy has existed in crime, as all crimes have not been treated equally. For example, degrees of murder depend on intent and motivation. Hate crimes have a greater impact not only on the individual victims,[42] but on the communities to which these victims belong and the larger group that shares the targeted characteristic. Few, if any, would argue about the widespread emotional and psychological impact of the terrorist attacks on September 11, 2001, that spread far beyond the individual victims who were killed. Hate crimes are a "form of intimidation not only for the victim but all members of the group targeted."[43] Hate crime categories are not specific; thus, the group "race" encompasses not only Black Americans but White as well, and other categories do not discriminate among ethnicities, disabilities, or religions. Cogan cites limitations to hate crime legislation such as the fact that these laws are "enforced by a criminal justice system—police, prosecutors, and judges—which itself is plagued with institutional racism, sexism, and homophobia."[44] She expresses concern with the validity of data collected showing that in Florida, Whites were the largest category of hate crime victims and that FBI data showed disproportionate arrest rates for Black Americans for committing hate crimes.

Hate crimes function as a boundary keeping those deemed Other in their subordinate place by fear of violent consequences. In much the same way as terrorists do, perpetrators of hate crimes terrorize entire groups by their attacks on representative members, as the group understands that the victim chosen could be any one of them as symbolic of perceived threat. Mainstream America does not recognize prejudice the way it used to now that there is a Black president and more visible Black participation in the media, in politics, in entertainment and sports, and in academics than in the past. Many do not acknowledge that discrimination is still an important issue today. "We would like to presume that hatred reflects a sick, pathological fringe element that has little, if anything, to do with the dominant American culture." This type of thinking allows us to frame ourselves as blameless while it is "them" who are guilty.[45]

Polls have shown Americans to have a distorted view of the percentage of the U.S. population that is Black, Latino, or Jewish. "According to a recent Gallup national survey, the average American estimates that 30 percent of the population of the United States is Black (actually, the figure for those who regard themselves as Black or African-American is about 12 percent); that 25 percent of all Americans are Latino (actually the figure is close to 13 percent); and that 15 percent of our population is Jewish (actually the figure is only 2 percent maximum)."[46] The misperceptions contribute to how Americans define their world and how they react to it. Levine and McDevitt point out that stereotypes can justify the commission of hate crimes in the minds of the perpetrators since they provide dehumanized images of particular individuals, making it easier to treat them as "not us."

Brian Levin argues that punishing hate crime is consistent with the aims of our criminal justice system. Through past decades of Supreme Court decisions, as well as evolving state laws, we are developing constitutional and increasingly effective legal responses to "punish conduct that is objectively more dangerous to victims and society."[47] *R.A.V. vs. St. Paul* (1992) struck down a statute as overbroad because it punished speech (symbolic speech in this case) that evoked anger or resentment. "Four of the justices supported the position that it was constitutional to punish expression whose severity went beyond just offending someone. Because threats and so-called fighting words were traditionally held to be unprotected by the First Amendment, these justices maintained that it was permissible for the government to selectively punish bigoted speech within these categories on the basis of content of the idea expressed."[48] *Wisconsin vs. Mitchell* (1993) upheld the constitutionality of penalty enhancement laws (in this case applied to Black perpetrators of a hate crime against a White victim). Levin argues that the greater harm done by hate crimes justifies the enactment of hate crime legislation and the enhancement of penalties. "In comparison to crime generally, hate crimes are seven times as likely to involve attacks against persons. Hate crime assaults are twice as likely to cause injury and four times as likely to involve hospitalization than do assaults in general."[49] Hate crimes often involve multiple offenders attacking a single victim, and offenders often commit a series of attacks rather than just one.

Carolyn Petrosino argues for the inclusion of historical events as hate crimes even though these events occurred well before such a designation existed. She uses the idea of intrinsic justice rather than our current legal definitions of what constitutes hate crimes to compare past events in American history to hate events now, finding some real similarities as well as some differences. Petrosino defines hate crimes as the victimization of minorities due to their racial or ethnic identity by members of the majority, adding to this definition a consideration of whether the legal authorities at the time of the crime would have responded in the same way had the victims been White Anglo-Saxon Protestants. She points to the fact that "the normative values of past eras . . . denied personhood to victims"[50] while the government and other authorities played a direct role in allowing or even encouraging acts against marginalized groups. "There are many parallels between historical and present-day hate crimes. The most apparent similarity is the presence of White racism in American culture."[51] Petrosino concludes that historical hate crimes were shaped by the forces and current normative values of their time. She cautions that modern hate crimes have the potential to do greater harm due to access to weapons of mass destruction and notes the convergence of hate crimes with domestic terrorism.

I agree with Petrosino's assessment that historical events could, and in retrospect should, be classified as hate crimes due to the nature of the motivation behind the events, the targets of the hate, and the damage done. I do not limit this consideration to racial and ethnic minorities, however, as Americans have been targeted for other reasons such as religion, sexual identification, and their relationship to the United States in terms of their definition as enemy or as immigrants.

HATE, SPACE, AND PLACE

I have chosen the idea of space as a central organizing point for my discussion of hate in the media and American culture. Hate crimes are very often tied to contested spaces, whether these are the literal spaces of country, state, neighborhood, church, school, and public amenities or the more figurative spaces surrounding relationships and marriage, sexual orientation and self-image, and ideology. This is an arbitrary choice but one that makes sense because contestations over literal and figurative space are the places where images of the Other are created and most viciously disputed. I start with the largest contestation over physical space and ideology, war, and move from there to the other end of the spectrum, cultural wars over representation, naming, and imagined space.

Wars are fought over territory, resources, and ideology. The creation of the enemy Other is a particularly telling one in terms of the lengths to which we go to dehumanize and denigrate those deemed enemy. Three particular wars in American history show both similarities and differences in how we have created our enemies in public and the treatment we have given those seen as representative of this enemy Other. The first is the war over possession of the territory now known as the United States with the native peoples who originally occupied this land. Both historically and currently, the media created an enemy Other, so different from "us" that at times their extermination seemed a national policy. The second war is the war against Asian peoples, waged during World War II with the Japanese and during the Vietnam War with the Vietnamese who, both as enemies and allies, were considered lesser and Other. The third war is the recent one we have waged against those in Iraq and Afghanistan who are the current enemy Other.

Immigration involves the movement of non-Americans into the physical space of the United States. Throughout American history, there have been times when immigrants have been welcomed to help grow the emerging country and as a workforce in times of need. There have also been periods of intense nativism during which the incoming immigrants were seen as so Other as to necessitate banning them from our shores. At different times in the past, we have imagined and created various incoming immigrant groups as lesser peoples deserving of limited, if any, rights to American benefits, institutions, and citizenship. The first group that I consider is the Chinese who, particularly in the nineteenth and early twentieth centuries, were the focus of political activity that resulted in the Chinese Exclusion Act. They were also victims of violence as various places in the western United States worked to expel them. The next group, the Italians, also came in increasing numbers during the nineteenth and early twentieth centuries. Although it seems counterintuitive by today's standards, this group was originally imagined and created as non-White, which demonstrates how the "commonsense" configuration of a particular time may really be understood only from the perspective of history. Italians, too, were the focus of much negative media attention and the victims of hate crimes that included lynchings. Finally, I consider immigrants from our southern neighbor, Mexico. Although Mexican people have been coming to the United States for centuries, our current contentious battles over immigration center primarily on this group, and their creation in the past as racial Other and in the present as criminal Other, as well as their high rates of hate crime victimization, make them an essential element in a discussion over national space and place.

Although biologically based racial distinctions do not actually exist, this historical categorization is at the basis of many creations of Other and contestations over space and place. I use the idea of race to discuss the spaces allowed Black Americans in our society. Hate crimes against Black Americans from the earliest days of slavery through Reconstruction, Civil Rights, and now have been legion. As much if not more than any group in our history, Black Americans have born the brunt of our creation of a dehumanized Other who is the then logical and accepted victim of hate crimes. Contestations over American space from sharing neighborhoods to public spaces such as hotels, restaurants, and theaters, to rights such as voting, serving on juries, and being elected to public office, to rules of etiquette and demeanor when confronting the dominant population, have all resulted in the creation of a dehumanized Other and the promulgation of vicious hate crimes. For this reason, my chapter on race focuses on this one particular group.

The fourth space I discuss is that surrounding religion and the arguments over whose version of religious ideology is correct and allowable. Throughout our history, we have designated a number of groups as religious Others, and this continues today with the current pervasive denigration of Muslims. Irish Catholics arrived in the nineteenth century and were deemed Other not only for their initially assigned non-White status, but also for their Catholicism. This anti-Catholic strain has continued into the twentieth century in groups such as the

Ku Klux Klan during the 1920s and the presidential elections in 1928 and 1960. Although violence against Jews has not been as large a part of American history as it has been in other countries, the creation of the Jewish Other and hate crimes against Jews are still ongoing strains in our culture. Finally, our creation of the Muslim Other and the rise of hate crimes against this group, particularly since September 11, 2001, continue today.

The fifth and most personal space that I consider is how we define ourselves in terms of sexual orientation and gender identity. The space considered here is literal in terms of rights to places such as participation in the military, groups like the Boy Scouts of America, or legal marriage and its benefits. It is also figurative in terms of how we see ourselves and create our own identities. It includes contested spaces such as restrooms labeled "Men" or "Women" and notions of what a "man" or a "woman" really is or what we determine it should be. Some of the most vicious hate crimes are committed over contestations that have to do with sexual identity, and hate crime laws in this area have been the site for argument, invective, and demeaning categorizations.

My final chapter concerns language, media, and hegemony in American culture. Through language, inequities in power relationships are created and played out. As the dominant culture appropriates symbols belonging to others, the power to name oneself and determine public image can be lost. Words traditionally used to degrade Native Americans appear as sport team names. Public figures speak of those created as Other in derogatory words through the media. The whole issue of hate speech, what it is and whether it should be regulated when weighed against our First Amendment rights, continues to be debated. The use of the label "politically correct" to ridicule and end debates about multiculturalism is another area where contestations over the spaces in our media occur. Who gets to define the public images of each group? What will we allow in the public media in terms of disrespect and hate-filled speech? What is the appropriate response to hate speech, whether it is actual words or symbolic speech such as burning crosses or hanging nooses? America—unlike Canada, Britain, France, and Germany, for example—allows our public media to provide access to hate-filled speech because of the First Amendment. How is this contrasted to equal protection rights under the Constitution?

Throughout these chapters on space and hate, I will be discussing the presentation of hate and hate crimes in the American media from the images we have created of groups framed as Other to the presentation of perpetrators and victims when hate crimes occur that receive media attention. Coupled with this is my concern that the continued focus on individual perpetrators as representative of hate in America takes away from the more imbedded structural forms of hate that maintain the status quo in our society. When we normalize the creation of enemy Others in our midst and their treatment as second-class citizens by our institutions, we allow hate to exist and continue.

NOTES

1. S. K. Bardwell and Lydia Lum, "Four Aldine teen-agers held in Montrose slaying," *Houston Chronicle*, August 17, 1994, 1.

2. Ibid.

3. S. K. Bardwell and T. J. Milling, "Slaying victim's kin offers cash for info in possible hate crime," *Houston Chronicle*, August 4, 1994, 31.

4. Bardwell and Lum, "Four Aldine teen-agers."

5. Dale Lezon, "Killer who's to die this week had a football future," *Houston Chronicle*, November 8, 2004.

6. Dale Lezon, "Former high school football star put to death," *Houston Chronicle*, November 10, 2004.

7. Bardwell and Lum, "Four Aldine teen-agers," 29.

8. Broadus, Joseph. 1994. Testimony. Employment Non-Discrimination Act of 1994: Hearing of the Committee on Labor and Human Resources, United States Senate, One Hundred Third Congress, second session, on S. 2238 to prohibit employment discrimination on the basis of sexual orientation, 29 July. Washington: U.S. Government Printing Office.

9. Gary J. Gates and Frank Newport, "Special report: 3.4% of U.S. adults identify as LGBT," *Gallup*, October 18, 2012, http://www.gallup.com/poll, accessed 8/22/13.

10. M. V. Lee Badgett, Laura E. Dursy, and Alyssa Schneebaum, *New Patterns of Poverty in the Lesbian, Gay, and Bisexual Community* (Williams Institute, UCLA School of Law, June 2013).

11. New York City Commission on Human Rights, *Documenting the Hate: A Report on Bias Incidents in New York City from January 1992 to June 1993*, New York City Commission on Human Rights, New York, November 1993, 1.

12. Richard Jackson, "Constructing enemies: 'Islamic terrorism' in political and academic discourse," *Government and Opposition* 42, no. 3, 2007, 395.

13. Ibid., 396.

14. Ibid.

15. FBI, "Hate Crime-Overview," www.fbi.gov/about-us/investigate/civilrights/hate_crimes/overview, accessed 9/5/13.

16. Legal Information Institute, *Title VII of the Civil Rights Act of 1968*, Cornell University Law School, http://www.law.cornell.edu/cfr/text/7/1901.203, accessed 9/5/13.

17. See for example, John DeSantis, *For the Color of His Skin: The Murder of Yusuf Hawkins and the Trial of Bensonhurst* (New York: Pharos Books, 1991).

18. Ibid., 59.

19. Ibid., 46–47.

20. Ibid., 86.

21. Ibid., 126.

22. Julia Preston, "Gotti witness tells of role in bias attack in Brooklyn," *New York Times*, August 19, 2005. Accessed January 20, 2006, from the *New York Times* archives.

23. Michael Kaufman, "Despair comes twice to a Brooklyn family," *New York Times*, August 26, 1989, A26.

24. M. A. Farber, "In son's slaying, a father finds his mission," *New York Times*, September 28, 1989, B12.

25. Howard French, "Hatred and social isolation may spur acts of racial violence, experts say," *New York Times*, September 4, 1989, A31.

26. Lorrin Anderson, "Cracks in the mosaic," *National* Review, June 25, 1990, 38.

27. DeSantis, *For the Color of His Skin*, 48.

28. 1990 Hate Crime Statistics Act, Sec.2, b.

29. Gregory Herek, "Overkill in Alabama: All the rage," *Beyond Homophobia*, September 13, 2007. www.beyondhomophobia.com/blog/category/hate-crimes, accessed September 4, 2013.

30. *Trends in Hate*, November 21, www.trendsinhate.com/hatedates/NovemberHate Dates/November21.html, accessed September 4 ,2013.

31. Herek, "Overkill in Alabama."

32. Andrew Sullivan, "Afterlife," *New Republic*, November 22, 1999. http://igfculture watch.com/1999/11/22/afterlife/, accessed November 8, 2013.

33. Robert O. Blanchard, "The 'hate state' myth," Reasononline, http://reason.com/archives/1999/05/01/the-hate-state-myth, accessed 11/08/2013.

34. Italics in original. OSCE Office for Democratic Institutions and Human Rights (ODIHR), *Hate Crime Laws: A Practical* Guide (Warsaw, Poland, 2009), 16. http://www.osce.org/odihr/36426 (accessed September 4, 2013).

35. Ibid., 17.

36. Ibid., 32.

37. Ibid., 33–36.

38. Sarah A. Soule and Jennifer Earl, "The enactment of state-level hate crime law in the United States: Intrastate and interstate factors," *Sociological Perspectives* 44, no. 3 (2001): 281–305.

39. Tom Streissguth, *Hate Crimes* (New York: Facts on File, Inc., 2003), 51.

40. OSCE Office for Democratic Institutions and Human Rights, *Hate Crime Laws*, 21.

41. Ibid., 20.

42. See, for example, G. M. Herek, J. R. Gillis, and J. C. Cogan, "Psychological correlates of hate crime victimization among lesbian, gay, and bisexual adults," *Journal of Consulting and Clinical Psychology* 67, no. 6 (1999): 945–951.

43. Jeanine C. Cogan, "Hate crime as a crime category worthy of policy attention," *American Behavioral Scientist* 46 September 1, 2001): 178.

44. Ibid., 182.

45. Jack Levin and Jack McDevitt, *Hate Crimes Revisited: America's War on Those Who Are Different* (Cambridge, MA: Westview, 2002), 46.

46. Ibid., 34.

47. Brian Levin, "Hate Crimes: Worse by Definition," *Journal of Contemporary Criminal Justice* 15, no. 1 (February 1999): 6.

48. Ibid., 9.

49. Ibid., 15.

50. Carolyn Petrosino, "Connecting the past to the future: Hate crime in America," *Journal of Contemporary Criminal Justice* 15, no. 1 (February 1999): 24.

51. Ibid., 34.

2

Making Enemies Abroad
and at Home: Hate and War

War, typically exemplified by a nationally created, nationally hated Other, contributes to hate crimes on the largest scale. War is accompanied by differences of social, political, and economic ideology, religion, race, or other fundamental identity traits. Conflict is often couched in extremes: good versus evil, a struggle for "our" way of life, a struggle for survival. Those deemed Others are described in extremes too, thereby providing "us" the emotional incentive and psychological ability to exterminate the threat posed by "them." The line between violent acts of war and violent acts that go beyond what is appropriate during war can blur, spilling over to civilians and even our own citizens; however, some of these acts are clearly outside the boundaries of acceptability and are hate crimes.

A cultural study of American wars shows similarities in the depictions of three Others (Native Americans, Asians, and Arabs) and how those designated as enemies have been created, perceived, and treated abroad and at home. Images of such Others can begin long before and persist long after a war, resting firmly on decades, if not centuries, of accumulated images, metaphors, misinformation, and public rhetoric and debate. These images, enabled by widely available cultural texts and ever-increasing technological means to disperse information and opinion worldwide, foster our willingness to accept war as a solution to conflict and to accept hate crimes against our own citizens as symbolic representatives of enemy Others.

Generally, identifying a common enemy, a hegemonic device of social control, reinforces dominant values based on differences in age, race, ethnicity, religion, culture, or appearance. Merskin claims, "There is a standard repertoire of propagandistic words and images that serves to dehumanize the 'other' as part of the construction of an enemy image in the popular imagination and thus makes a retaliatory backlash against human beings seem logical and natural."[1] This repertoire appears in times of crisis: defining the enemy as lacking what we most value and deeming the enemy system evil in opposition to "our" good system. It involves zero-sum thinking: what is positive for us must be negative for them and vice versa. Thus if "we" are human, "Once an individual is constructed as an outsider, this person is no longer thought of as having humanity."[2] Such dehumanizing, believed necessary in war for cohesion with fellow soldiers and for creating public support, provides justification for killing and other acts of violence. To avoid collateral damage done by misplaced anger both abroad and at home, we must separate individuals with no responsibility from the larger conflict during a war. Maintaining a realistic perspective on the context in which war occurs, which means maintaining a realistic perspective on American aggression at home and elsewhere, is essential in providing a less sweeping creation of the enemy. The animosity felt by our enemies is not created from nothing but exists as the result of past and present American actions and attitudes; we create animosity by treating others as inferior and disregarding the rights of those seen to stand in the way of our economic, political, and social desires.

Common threads arising in war include dehumanizing the enemy by the creation of a faceless mass rather than individuals with equal humanity to us; our resulting ability to kill large numbers, including unarmed women, children, and the elderly; our ability to torture prisoners; and our ability to regard the enemy as prey. Since our earliest conflicts, the belief that the only good "fill in the blank" enemy is a dead one has been integral to wartime thinking. Daily "success" in the Vietnam War was measured in enemy body counts on the evening news. Wartime anger may be brought to bear on anyone representing the enemy, even to the extent of misidentification. Hate crimes can have as their victims those who personify our culturally created enemy; the accuracy of this identification does not matter to the angry perpetrator. Responsibility for these creations is built into the structure of our media, our politics, and our culture.

LANGUAGE OF WAR

In *War Without Mercy*, John Dower illustrates that a nationally created enemy is not just an American phenomenon, but a feature of war.[3] Dower looked not only at America's creation of the Japanese enemy during World War II, but at Japan's creation of the American enemy. Each side considered the other as subhuman and a threat to its own survival. Using a variety of popular culture texts and media sources, Dower demonstrates the strength of wartime images and words in creating a hated enemy from both an American and a Japanese perspective.

He compares these creations with the brutality unleashed by each side against an enemy considered less than human.

Language creates its own reality and is not merely reflective of an objective reality. Through choice of language, use of metaphor, descriptive choices in naming and describing others, and the parameters we set on our discussions, language has the power to define, create, and persuade. Metaphors equate one object or idea with another, linking them in our minds. "Instead of viewing Muslims as people who have been symbolically portrayed as animals, then, they begin in our minds to become animals."[4] Our understanding of the world is tied to our language, which relies on cultural signs and symbols to create meaning, taking the unknown and likening it to the familiar to provide a framework for understanding. This all too often creates misunderstandings or false understandings and an attempt to force differences into our own cultural constraints. We understand reality in part through metaphors; metaphors describing Others contribute to the treatment these people receive. They also create barriers to solving problems since disagreement is often couched in such extreme ways as to preclude a more reasonable solution than violence.

In *Faces of the Enemy*, Sam Keen looks at how cultures degrade those they hate in words and images. "In the beginning we create the enemy. Before the weapon comes the image. We *think* others to death and then invent the battle-axe or the ballistic missiles with which to actually kill them. Propaganda precedes technology."[5] Propaganda has long been an instrument of war aimed at mobilizing hatred while preserving friendship with allies and demoralizing the enemy. Convincing us that the enemy is evil provides justification for whatever actions are deemed necessary to win, including extermination.

Propaganda includes not only what is said, but also what is not, turning the enemy into a few representational images while ignoring the complex realities of a whole people. Permeating our culture during war through the mass media and now social media as well, propaganda can become so ingrained in daily images and words as to be virtually invisible. The more recent technology of the Internet and the cell phone allows for speedy dissemination of information, misinformation, comment, and countercomment and contributes minute by minute to this environment.

Often ignoring the role the United States has had in creating these enemies, media representations provide a limited version of conflict and the enemy Other. Native Americans, who were slaughtered by the thousands, were believed to deserve their fate as retribution for harm done to immigrant Europeans, a view that conveniently ignored the invasion of native lands, the decimation of their populations through war, disease and murder, and the treatment of tribal peoples as obstacles in the way of European desires rather than equal human beings with rights and desires of their own. Prior to World War II, the treatment of Asian immigrants and our relationship with Japan were again conveniently ignored as Americans were shocked and surprised by the attack on Pearl Harbor. More recently, the attacks of September 11, 2001, did not happen in a vacuum but were at least in partial response to the decades of outright conflict, and those more insidiously ingrained in cultural battles, with Arab and Muslim peoples.

Using three representational conflicts, this chapter includes a discussion of enemy images in the media during times of war and hate crimes following these creations. The images themselves, lacking depth and any understanding of difference, contribute to an atmosphere that fosters hate. While fueling animosity toward others, they preclude more rational thought and less violent solutions to conflict.

NATIVE AMERICANS

The nobility of the Redskin is extinguished, and what few are left are a pack of whining curs who lick the hand that smites them. The Whites, by law of conquest, by justice of civilization, are masters of the American continent, and the best safety of the frontier settlements will be secured by the total annihilation of the few remaining Indians.[6]

Barbara Perry notes, "It was the image of Natives as savages and wild men that allowed their persecution. Drawing on the emerging notions of social Darwinism, Europeans in the Americas constructed Native Americans as less than human. Some went as far as to characterize them as consorts of the Devil."[7] As Europeans arrived on the American continents, they viewed the landscape and its inhabitants through the blinders of ethnocentrism. With a belief that God was on their side and a desire for land, gold, and power, those indigenous to the Americas were created as obstacles to be removed or at the very least, changed into useful artifacts. Native Americans were imagined from the earliest times as nonhuman or as lesser humans. As the "noble savage," they were a part of nature like the animals of the forest. As merely "savage," they were considered backward, ignorant, and inferior. Equated with evil and sin, killing every one of them could be considered "not merely warfare but the cleansing of sin itself."[8]

As Europeans settled on the American continents, their needs and wants determined how they defined and subsequently dealt with Native Americans. As settlers needing food and safety, they developed friendly relationships with some of the tribes they encountered. In some places, at least, there was the understanding that tribes possessed sovereignty over the land and were to be treated as nations, albeit as lesser ones. As Europeans became established in greater numbers and needed more land, they defined Native Americans as savages, backward, and uncivilized, providing justifications to take their land and move or exterminate them. Tribes were moved westward and then on to reservations;

if any valuable resources were discovered, Native Americans were defined (child-like/in need of supervision, warlike/in need of containing and controlling) to provide encroaching settlers an ideology that allowed them to contain the tribes in smaller and smaller areas or get rid of them entirely. Even now, as tribal people retain some of the rights granted them by the many (broken) treaties, controversies arise when these rights come in conflict with the dominant culture. The continuing fishing rights controversies in Wisconsin, Minnesota and other states are examples of this.

Indians are either completely denied as ever having existed, or we are used, like building materials, to construct the façade of conquest, a place to house the Doctrine of Discovery. But we are never human beings, never wronged human beings with our own honor, pride, integrity and existence who are capable of great deeds, and surviving with joy.[9]

In the south, the Spanish destroyed a majority of Native Americans they encountered. In the north, the English and French did the same. Columbus, after reading a proclamation in Spanish to whatever natives he encountered, regardless of the fact that none could understand him, claimed land for Spain. Should any Native Americans object, the proclamation stated:

I certify to you that, with the help of God, we shall powerfully enter into your country and shall make war against you in all ways and manners that we can, and shall subject you to the yoke and obedience of the Church and of Their Highnesses. We shall take your wives and your children, and shall make slaves of them, and as such shall sell and dispose of them as Their Highnesses may command. And we shall take your goods, and shall do you all the mischief and damage that we can, as to vassals who do not obey and refuse to receive their lord and resist and contradict him.[10]

In encounter after encounter, Columbus and his men killed and mutilated large numbers of indigenous people. On the island of Hispaniola, for example, four years after Columbus's arrival in 1492, a third to half of the Native Americans had died or been killed. Women and children were enslaved, and numerous people were taken back to Europe to show off as plunder from the New World (a majority died on the way or shortly after arriving in Europe). Because native religious beliefs were not in the realm of the familiar to the Christian Europeans, Native Americans were created as having no religion. "They should be good and intelligent servants, for I see that they say very quickly everything that is said to them; and I believe they would become Christians very easily, for it seemed to me that they had no religion."[11]

The vital importance of these conflicting worldviews and the ability of the Europeans to deny Native American humanity and culture because their differences did not fit preconceived notions on so many levels, led to war crimes in the past and continue to contribute to hate crimes today.

EXAMPLES OF WAR (HATE) CRIMES

In the 1650s, Dutch colonists brought back eighty decapitated Indian heads from a massacre and used them as kickballs in the streets of New Amsterdam. In 1711, the Virginia
house of Burgesses appropriated 20,000 pounds "for extirpating [sic] all Indians without
distinction of Friends or Enemies." An English traveler in the northern colonies casually
recorded in his diary, in 1760, that "some People have an Indian's Skin for a Tobacco
Pouch," while a Revolutionary War soldier campaigning against the Iroquois could note
with equal dispassion that he had been given a pair of boot-tops made from the freshly
skinned legs of two enemy braves.[12]

Much has been written on the violent encounters between Native Americans
and the waves of settlers moving across the continent. These include battles
fought between opponents as well as more heinous attacks on the unarmed and
unresisting of both sides. For the purposes of this discussion, the examples here,
whether labeled war crimes or large-scale hate crimes, depict some of the worst
treatments of Native American peoples as a commentary on the results of creating a dehumanized enemy.

In February 1643, after seeking protection from Dutch settlers in New
Amsterdam, New York, the Wecquaesgeek tribe was attacked by soldiers and
freemen. While soldiers, with permission and encouragement from Governor
Kieft, attacked one group of Wecquaesgeek, another was attacked by the freemen. Although the attackers were told to kill "only" the men, between 80 and
120 Native Americans, men, women, and children were massacred. "Young children, some of them snatched from their mothers, were cut in pieces before the
eyes of their parents, and the pieces were thrown into the fire or into the water;
other babes were bound on planks and then cut through, stabbed and miserably
massacred, so that it would break a heart of stone . . ."[13]

On the night of February 25, 1860, a small group of men from Eureka,
California, took boats across the bay to an island where the Wiyot tribe had gathered. The Wiyots ". . . were a small tribe of sedentary people who wove basketry
skullcaps, traveled in redwood canoes, fished for trout, salmon, and shellfish."
They used Indian Island for their annual ritual of renewal even as more and
more White settlers moved into the area and the town of Eureka. As the Wiyots
slept,

The Whites landed on a deserted part of the island and slipped silently through the
cypress groves. When they reached the Wiyot village, they went methodically from
hut to hut, killing every Indian they found. They killed indiscriminately, men, women,
and children. Mostly they killed with hatchets and Bowie knives. Those who fled were
slaughtered in the mud and surf. Others clumped instinctively, helplessly together
and were hacked to death where they stood. A mile away in Eureka, people heard the
Wiyots die.[14]

The night's toll on the tribe left 60 to 70 dead. "Another two hundred or more were massacred simultaneously on the south spit of the Humboldt bay and at the mouth of the Eel River, in what were presumably coordinated attacks designed to exterminate the Wiyots at a single stroke."[15]

The infamous Sand Creek massacre took place on November 29, 1864, in Colorado. Black Kettle's band of Cheyenne settled at Sand Creek with the assurance that they would be under the protection of Fort Lyon. However, Major Scott Anthony, the commanding officer at Fort Lyon, and Colonel John Chivington decided to attack the band. Governor Evans of Colorado had raised a "hundred-day troop" with permission from the War Department and did not want these men to go to waste. They were "raised to kill Indians and they must kill Indians."[16] Black Kettle had put an American flag as well as a White flag on his tepee to indicate that he was friendly to the United States. Ignoring these signs, the army attacked the village, killing hundreds of men, women, and children indiscriminately. "Chivington's instructions to his boys were simple: 'Kill and scalp all, big and little; nits make lice.' "[17] Robert Bent, the son of a White man and a Cheyenne woman, wrote of what he saw that day at Sand Creek. He watched soldiers shoot unarmed women and children. He saw a woman cut open with her unborn child lying at her side. "I saw the body of White Antelope with the privates cut off, and I heard a soldier say he was going to make a tobacco pouch out of them. I saw one squaw whose privates had been cut out . . . I saw a little girl who had been hid in the sand. Two soldiers drew their pistols and shot her, and then pulled her out of the sand by the arm."[18] Although the majority of those killed were women and children, Chivington praised his men for a job well done, and the headline in the *Rocky Mountain News* read "All Acquitted Themselves Well." The troops exhibited the scalps they had taken and displayed the children taken captive. After Sand Creek, Governor Evans sent a proclamation to the citizens of Colorado telling them to hunt hostile Indians and destroy them wherever they were found.

The massacre at Wounded Knee occurred on December 29, 1890. Big Foot, bringing his band of Lakota to the Pine Ridge reservation in South Dakota, also flew a White flag over his wagon. The U.S. cavalry met his band and led them to Wounded Knee Creek, where in the process of disarming them, one of the band shot off a rifle. The troops opened fire on all, including the women and children who had been grouped in a separate area from the men.

The 7th Cavalry had a splendid record, but all witnesses agree that from the moment it opened fire, it ceased to be a military unit and became a mass of infuriated men intent only on butchery. Women and children attempted to escape by running up the dry ravine, but were pursued and slaughtered——there is no other word—by hundreds of maddened soldiers, while shells from the Hotchkiss guns, which had been moved to permit them to sweep the ravine, continued to burst among them. The line of bodies was afterward found to extend for more than two miles from camp—and they were all women and children.[19]

More than 150 Lakota were killed. Souvenir hunters collected not only the material artifacts of the Native Americans, but parts of their bodies as well. Leonard Wright Colby, a brigadier general in the Nebraska National Guard, even took a live baby (Zintkala Nuni) from her dead mother's arms after the Wounded Knee massacre as a souvenir, removing her from her tribe and condemning her to a short life caught between two cultures.

Over the centuries, Native American bodies have been the site for souvenirs of conquest: skin used to make objects (reins for horses, leggings or bags for people), scalps and noses to prove the number of dead, and scalps and heads as trophies of war. Private parts were routinely cut off and sometimes kept by the conquerors. Native bones have ended up in museums and are only now beginning to be returned to the tribes for proper burial. This taking of enemy body parts is an ongoing practice of war when the enemy has been created as a lesser or nonhuman entity.

PRESIDENTIAL RHETORIC

Shifts in the dominant paradigms for dealing with Native Americans occurred over time and are exemplified by some specific examples of presidential rhetoric. During the presidency of Thomas Jefferson, the boundaries of the country had not yet been tapped, and the tribes were considered to have a degree of sovereignty over their traditional lands. During the years of Andrew Jackson's presidency, as the eastern part of the United States became increasingly crowded, Jackson forcefully removed any native "obstacles" east of the Mississippi to lands further west. In the time of Theodore Roosevelt, when the United States stretched from coast to coast, most tribes were confined to reservations as assimilationists attempted to turn them into replicas of White citizens (albeit without the same rights and privileges) and find means to deprive them of land and treaty rights. Official policies illustrated the role(s) delegated to Native Americans, and presidential rhetoric provided strong national statements of the place held by native peoples in American culture.

Thomas Jefferson's view of Native Americans was both paternalistic and patronizing. "We are now your fathers; and you shall not lose by the change."[20] On paper, he treated with them as a lesser but sovereign group, assuring them, "We, indeed, are always ready to buy land; but we will never ask but when you wish to sell . . ."[21] Jefferson considered Native Americans a barbarous people, lesser beings than the peoples of Europe. He likened Native Americans to animals in terms of their growth rate and the survival of their young; in his 1781 State of Virginia speech, he stated that the Native American "meets death with more deliberation, and endures torture with a firmness unknown almost to religious enthusiasm with us." The idea that there are lesser peoples who do not feel the same emotional and physical pains as those more advanced (White) is a common belief in creating a subhuman Other. U.S. military officials made similar statements about the Japanese during World War II.

Andrew Jackson was a strong proponent of the policy of removal, relocating all tribes east of the Mississippi to lands west of the river. The Indian Removal Act of 1830 was passed during Jackson's second year in office. As a precursor to his election as president and one source of the popularity that got him elected, Jackson fought in numerous battles against Native Americans such as the Creek War (1813–1814), which included the infamous Battle of Horseshoe Bend. President Jackson was "[t]he same Andrew Jackson who had supervised the mutilation of 800 or so Creek Indian corpses—the bodies of men, women, and children that he and his men had massacred—cutting off their noses to count and preserve a record of the dead, slicing long strips of flesh from their bodies to tan and turn into bridle reins."[22] Jackson encouraged the practice of killing all women and children to eradicate future generations and the removal of all powers from tribal leaders to ensure subservience to the U.S. government.

Jackson referred to Native Americans as savages and argued that no reasonable man could want this country left in the hands of the Native Americans who lacked, in his view, civilization and religion. "They have neither the intelligence, the industry, the moral habits, nor the desire of improvement which are essential to any favorable change in their condition. Established in the midst of another and a superior race, and without appreciating the causes of their inferiority or seeking to control them, they must necessarily yield to the force of circumstances and ere long disappear."[23]

Jackson's process of removal did not go according to original plans (peaceful removal with support for those who volunteered to go while those who chose to remain could do so), and the removal process culminated a number of years later with the Trail of Tears, the forcible removal of the Cherokee to Oklahoma during which more than 4,000 died from cold, disease, and hunger.

Theodore Roosevelt embodied many of the prevailing ideas about Native Americans at the beginning of the twentieth century, believing them savages, childlike, and in need of the guidance of the more "civilized" White nations. Like Jackson, Roosevelt was clear that the land in North America would be wasted on a nomadic people. "To recognize the Indian ownership of the limitless prairies and forests of this continent—that is, to consider the dozen squalid savages who hunted at long intervals over a territory of 1,000 square miles as owning it outright—necessarily implies a similar recognition of the claims of every White hunter, squatter, horse thief, or wandering cattleman."[24] Roosevelt's ideas on land ownership led him to support allotment, the breaking up of tribally held reservation lands into individually owned allotments (usually the least desirable areas under consideration). The Dawes Allotment Act was passed in 1887 and had an immediate effect on tribal land and customs. Allotment was considered essential to the assimilation of Native Americans into mainstream society and allowed "excess" tribal lands to be sold to non–Native Americans. While many spoke of the benefits of assimilating the tribes by moving them from land held in common to individual ownership, in reality, the result was the loss of huge amounts of land to White buyers and a serious weakening of tribal structures.

Roosevelt believed that the tribes benefited far more than they suffered by the incursion of Europeans on the American continent, and he dismissed the atrocities perpetrated against the tribes as a few incidents of occasional mistreatment. "But we must not, because of occasional wrong-doing, blind ourselves to the fact that on the whole the White administrator and the Christian missionary have exercised a profound and wholesome influence for good in savage regions."[25] Roosevelt went on to say, "Of course the best that can happen to any people that has not already a high civilization of its own is to assimilate and profit by American or European ideas, the ideas of civilization and Christianity . . ."[26]

Since his days as governor of New York, Roosevelt believed in a four-pronged approach to assimilating Native Americans. This included Christianizing them by sending missionaries to the reservations, compulsory education (including forbidding students to speak their own languages and punishing those who did), turning tribally held land into individual allotments, and in return for all of this, rewarding those who assimilated with United States citizenship.[27] When not discussing assimilation, Roosevelt spoke for extermination. "I don't go so far as to think that the only good Indians are dead Indians, but I believe nine out of every ten are, and I shouldn't like to inquire too closely into the case of the tenth. The most vicious cowboy has more moral principle than the average Indian."[28]

STEREOTYPES IN AMERICAN MEDIA AND POPULAR CULTURE

"The image of the Indian in dramatic, violent, and exotic terms was incorporated in the reports of missionaries and soldiers, in philosophic treatises, in histories, and in the first American bestsellers, the captivity narratives of the seventeenth and eighteenth centuries."[29] How Native Americans were popularly defined in political rhetoric, military propaganda, news reports during the years of conflict with different tribes, art (paintings, photographs, sculptures), and novels fostered a particular ideology that resulted in their treatment in war as vermin to be exterminated and in peace as lesser humans to be contained, controlled, and molded into acceptable citizens. Continued reliance on those definitions and images has contributed to hate crime incidents throughout history up to the present, from those who exterminated the hundreds of Wiyots in California or Lakota at Wounded Knee to more individual examples in recent times.

Our current media make contributions daily to the past store of images of Native Americans, perpetuating early and mistaken beliefs. These include toys, cultural practices such as children playing "cowboys and Indians," movies, books, sports team mascots and rally cries, news reports, and school and college curricula. The many Native American customs, languages, religions, and other cultural attributes have been distilled into a generic representation based on the elements of native cultures best known through the publicity surrounding wars with the European American settlers.

Barbara Perry, who has done extensive work on hate crimes and Native Americans, states, "One of the themes underlying my conceptualization of hate crime is that it is legitimated and accompanied by an array of facilitative mechanisms, such as stereotypes, language, legislation, and job segregation. It is apparent, for example, that stereotyping Native Americans as savages, or criminalizing their rituals, or excluding them from citizenship, have served to maintain their stigmatized outsider identity."[30]

A generic and enduring Native American image based on wars with Plains cultures sustains the creation of native peoples as barbaric and savage. John C. Ewers discusses the historical development of the generic Plains Indian as the stereotypical Native American.[31] Precedents for this generic Plains identity include the works of painters such as George Catlin, novels by those like James Fennimore Cooper, widespread reporting on the Plains wars, and the popularity of the Wild West shows. The shows travelled eastward and across the ocean, spreading this particular image far and wide.

With television, movies, storybooks and nonfiction texts, toys, and games as their sources, past images and stereotypes with dominant themes of hostility and war continue to be the primary staples for American children. "Mary Gloyne Byler (Cherokee) analyzed 600 children's books about Native Americans. She found depersonalization, ridicule, derision, inauthenticity, and stereotyping in the vast majority. Native people were treated in patronizing ways, portrayed as fantasy, set in an unidentified past, or juxtaposed with animals."[32] Even icons of American literary culture such as the books written by Laura Ingalls Wilder contribute to these images.

I would not want my child to read *Little House on the Prairie*. I would shield him from the slights she slings upon his ancestors. They appear in her book only as beggars and thieves, and she adds injury to insult by comparing the Osages—who turned Thomas Jefferson's head with their dignity and grace—to reptiles, to garbage or scum (depending on the definition of the word she actually uses). Mrs. Wilder assigns them descriptive adjectives that connote barbarism, brutality, and bloodthirstiness, and makes much ado about their odor.[33]

Native Americans are often unnamed and anonymous generic representatives of what is understood to be native peoples. As Hirschfelder points out, "The device of repeatedly referring to people in this impersonal and anonymous way, and then reinforcing the anonymity with illustrations that are nondescript, creates the impression that one is not dealing with full-fledged human beings."[34] He goes on to say:

A more direct assault is made upon the humanity of American Indians by the use of key words and phrases which trigger negative and derogatory images. Words such as savage, buck, squaw and papoose do not bring to mind the same images as do the words man, boy, woman and baby. Descriptions of half-naked, hideously-painted creatures brandishing tomahawks or scalping knives, yelping, howling, grunting, jabbering, or snarling are hardly conducive to a sympathetic reaction to the people so described.[35]

Following earlier media, film provided a new channel through which to spread the same limited, stereotypical roles of a generic and violent Plains culture. "The Hollywood Indian is a mythological being who exists nowhere but within the fertile imaginations of its movie actors, producers, and directors. The preponderance of such movie images has reduced native people to ignoble stereotypes."[36]

In film, Native languages have been disregarded, created as grunts or bird and animal imitations, and have only recently appeared as legitimate languages in movies like *Dances with Wolves*. Native Americans in film have been constructed as a savage presence in opposition to civilized White Americans. White women and children are portrayed in jeopardy, but not Native American women and children, who were killed in far greater numbers. "Through the star system and a variety of other narrative and nonnarrative devices, viewers of Westerns are normally encouraged to grieve over White deaths and generally to rejoice in Indian deaths."[37]

While recent films have tried to present a more balanced perspective of Native Americans, using native actors, writers, and directors, the array of past films is still available through rentals, the Internet, and television. Important questions to consider in the treatment of any group in film include questions of perspective and control, questions of portrayal and choice of actor, and the historical era and viewpoint. In many films, protagonist Native Americans are those who help White settlers and assimilate into White society while the villains are those who fight for cultural autonomy and their traditional way of life. Clearly this limited representation serves the hegemony of the dominant culture while defining those outside its borders as wrong.

MODERN HATE CRIMES

"I see hate crimes nested within a matrix of social processes that have long produced and reproduced the subordinate status of Native Americans in the United States."[38] As did past practices of colonization, modern hate crime functions to oppress and segregate Native Americans. Barbara Perry equates the term "ethnoviolence" with hate crime, pointing out that past practices of genocide against Native Americans resulted in violence toward both groups of and individual

Native Americans. Historically, genocide was coupled with ethnocide, the deculturing of the different nations, including the removal of all possible customs (clothing, hairstyle, language, subsistence patterns, religious practices) and replacing them with those of the dominant culture. Native cultures were defined as lacking the traits contained in the dominant culture rather than having a legitimate and different culture of their own.

> The disempowerment of Native Americans along with their construction as the deviant Other provide the context for anti-Indian violence. The former makes them vulnerable targets, the latter legitimate targets, all of which has been well documented.[39]

As Perry explains, "It is within the cultural realm that we find the justifications for inequities, and for hate crime, for these processes are predicated on legitimating ideologies and images that mark the Other, and the boundaries between self and Other, in such a way as to normalize the corresponding inequities."[40] The preponderance of negative images in the popular culture and media, the mediated view of Native Americans, is well ingrained in American culture at this point.

Historically, Native Americans have been defined from the outside, with definitions born from the ethnocentric view of those in power, and these definitions led to their containment physically as well as boundaries surrounding their (lack of) rights as citizens. "Thus it is important to note the role hate crime plays in punishing those Others who have attempted to overstep their boundaries by assuming they, too, are worthy of first-class citizenship. This is especially evident at the localized points of contact where Whites feel their identity, or safety, or sense of proprietorship threatened by unwelcome intrusions of people of color."[41] This has been true historically; as settlers arrived and moved across the continent, the points of contact with Native Americans became the places where wars and hate crimes occurred and where identities and rights were disputed. Now the figurative borders between the treaty rights held by tribes and the demands of the larger society, and the more literal borderlands along reservations, are areas of conflict with and violence from the dominant culture. The controversy in Wisconsin over spearfishing rights in the 1990s, which led to a pattern of violence against the Wisconsin tribes, provides a clear example of the first. "Attackers fired shots, lobbed rocks and pipe bombs at them, and created dangerous waves that rocked their boats while they were out on the water."[42] The town of Farmington, New Mexico, near the Navajo reservation provides a clear illustration of the second type of borderland, a site of repeated violent attacks on the Navajo people.

Treaty Rights and Hate Groups

In Washington State in the 1960s, Native Americans held fish-ins to protect their treaty rights to hunt and fish on traditional sites. Local tribes like the

Nisqually were joined by others, including celebrities (e.g., Marlon Brando), church leaders, and those with experience from the Black civil rights movement. Early publicity sided with the White fishermen and the government, falling back on common stereotypes with headlines such as "Skagits on the Warpath?" and cartoons like the one labeled "Redmen Want Powwow With Great White Father (Rosellini)." Rosellini was the governor of Washington State at the time. "The public, media-driven image of Native Americans as anti-conservation, selfish, violent, even anarchic, was difficult for the natives to combat."[43] Local Whites fought against the native protesters, even shooting at them with rifles and shotguns. Native activist Hank Adams was shot in the stomach at one fish-in. State law enforcement, "egged on and helped by the citizens and vigilantes, clubbed Indian people, slapped them in handcuffs, threw them in jail."[44] As the decade played out, support began to move more toward the Native Americans and away from the state. The result of these protests was a court battle that culminated in the 1974 *Boldt* decision granting Native Americans the right to take up to 50 percent of the harvestable fish and to have an equal part in the management of the fishing industry through the creation of a tribal fisheries commission. "However, the decision increased the violent opposition of the other groups who were most affected by it—the White commercial and sport fishermen."[45]

Anti–Native American groups such as ICERR (Interstate Congress for Equal Rights and Responsibilities), S/SPAWN (Salmon-Steelhead Preservation Action for Washington Now), and PARR (Protect Americans Rights and Resources) exist in response to continued tribal treaty rights to natural resources. As native nations assert their legal treaty rights to hunt and fish on nonreservation lands, conflicts occur with these organizations as well as sports enthusiasts and local White property and business owners. The Anishinaabe in northern Wisconsin have repeatedly asserted their rights to spearfish in nonreservation lakes. Court decisions have upheld these rights, but that does not protect the bands from violence. "Since 1983 anti-Indian leaders have charged that the Chippewa treaties are invalid and that unregulated Indian hunting and fishing would kill all the deer and fish and destroy the tourist industry."[46] However, in the early 1990s, Native Americans on average harvested 24,968 walleye per year opposed to an estimated sport harvest of 320,000 and an average of 215 musky per year compared to an annual sport harvest of 9,454.[47] In a content analysis of 45 newspaper articles and four television newscasts on the spearfishing controversy in Wisconsin, Daniel Perkins showed that the structure of the news stories, including prominence given opposing viewpoints; authority given representatives of the opposing sides, including who was on camera (White business owners) and who was paraphrased (representatives of the Anishinaabe people); and the relative weight given the impact of the events, all worked to enforce the hegemony of the state. ". . . [N]one of the 45 articles assessed the State's arguments in this matter but rather presented them at face value. What were continually questioned were the motives of the Native Americans and the reasoning the Native Americans presented."[48] The structure of the news directed readers' attention toward a conclusion that reinforced the hegemony of the state and the views and structures of the nonnative society. While the conflict between the Anishinaabe and surrounding business owners was the central theme, the fact that the Anishinaabe took fewer fish than their rightful kill and yearly restocked the lakes was never stated. The Great Lakes Indian Fish and Wildlife Commission, which represents the tribes, planted 450,000 fingerling walleyes in the lakes during the year of the reported protests. In any case, the Anishinaabe were positioned negatively, their "greed" depicted in contrast to the economic woes of the surrounding business owners.

The *Voigt* decision in 1983 (U.S. Court of Appeals for the Seventh Circuit) determined that Wisconsin had no right to regulate fishing on Anishinaabe reservations and guaranteed the Anishinaabe the right to hunt and fish off reservation without being bound by state regulations. However, "[w]hen the Anishinaabe (Chippewa) started to fish the way they had been guaranteed by the treaties, and which the courts had just reaffirmed, they were assaulted on a daily basis. The locals, assisted by skinheads, members of the Aryan Nation and the KKK, called them timber niggers, welfare warriors, and spear chuckers."[49] Bumper stickers stated "Save a Spawning Walleye, Spear a Squaw." Native Americans had their tires slashed, were run off the road, and were threatened. White backlash against the Anishinaabe treaty rights created an atmosphere of hate conducive to the commission of hate crimes, and hate crimes occurred.

RESERVATION BORDERLANDS

I never killed one. Least I don't think so. I know there was one time we threw one in the back of a pickup and were takin' him out into the hills to do a number on him, and he come to and jumped out. Musta known what he was headed for and figured that was better. I don't know why. We was doin' about fifty, sixty. We could see him bouncin' down the road behind us. We didn't go back and check him out, so I don't know how bad he was hurt. But it wouldn't have surprised me if he was history.[50]

In a 1999 study, Barbara Perry interviewed 72 Native Americans in the towns bordering the Navajo reservation in the western United States and found that the majority had either been victims of hate crimes themselves or knew someone who had been. Incidents ranged from name-calling and shoving to assaults with knives and lighter fluid.[51]

The town of Farmington, New Mexico, on the border of the reservation, has been the site of numerous instances of violence against the Navajo over past decades. In 1974, three Navajo men were beaten, tortured, and murdered by three White teenage boys (ages 15 and 16) who ended up serving short sentences in the local reform school. The resulting protests from the Navajo put Farmington on the map as an area of cultural conflict. In 1975, the U.S. Civil Rights Commission reported on the climate and culture of racial hatred in Farmington, pointing out problems of police prejudice against natives and systematic economic discrimination. A follow-up report 30 years later stated that while the climate in Farmington was somewhat improved, there were still significant problems such as police bias and a lack of Navajo representation in local government.[52]

In response to the 1974 murders, Farmington mayor Marlo Webb stated that it was "just high school students rolling drunks, and all the drunks were Navajo" to bolster his claim that these were not hate crimes. However, it was clear that anti-Navajo sentiment ran high in the area. "Subsequently, the Justice Department sued the county hospital for refusing to treat Navajos in its emergency room, and the U.S. Equal Opportunity Commission sued the city for employment discrimination."[53] In 2002, Webb continued to demonstrate his cultural sensitivity. " 'They've culturally not come in to join what we call modern society,' the mayor said of his Navajo neighbors. 'They're not, they haven't been educated to do it. They're not equipped to do it. They're very backward.' "[54]

In researching his book on the Farmington murders, Rodney Barker interviewed Farmington youth to determine their underlying racial attitudes. "That was what we did on Friday and Saturday nights: Drive around lookin' for drunk Indians to roll. 'Subs,' we called 'em, as in subhumans. They weren't hard to find, they were everywhere. Lyin' in the alleys shit-faced. Weavin' down the side streets lookin' for a place to flop. Staggerin' along the highway on their way back to the rez. GodDAMN, you'd say. Let's kick some Indian ass."[55] The young speaker's brother collected "trophy buckles" from the Indians he rolled (belt buckles). The speaker himself started rolling Indians when he was in the eighth grade. "They had no self-respect and we had no respect for them either. About all they were good for was buyin' booze."[56] Common activities perpetrated against the Navajo included robbery, assault, stranding (giving someone a ride and then dumping them away from town), tear gassing, and even murder.

Unfortunately, the assaults and murders of the Navajo continue in the Farmington area. "They kill you with their eyes first, then pick a secluded spot to beat you up."[57] In 2000, a 36-year-old Navajo woman was offered a ride home by two young Farmington men. She was taken to a deserted area, stabbed, chased down as she ran, and then killed with a sledgehammer. The same two men had earlier killed another Navajo; they had beaten him with a shovel, gouged out his eyes, and mutilated his genitals. Bobby Fry, one of the murderers, stated that he hates the Navajo, calling them "guts" and "trogs," and bragging about "rolling Indians."[58] In June 2006, a 47-year-old Navajo man was offered a ride by three White teenagers who then drove him to the edge of town and beat him while saying, "Die Nigger—just die!" The police report of this incident listed the man as

"traumatized, untrusting and intimidated." He repeatedly asked the police officers not to shoot him.[59] The three perpetrators were caught and charged with a
hate crime. On July 30, 2006, sixteen-year-old Jordan Gruver was assaulted.

According to law enforcement reports, Gruver was beaten, kicked, spit on and doused
with whiskey by two Klan skinheads who mistook him for an illegal immigrant. As they
began their assault, calling him a "spic," Gruver protested that he was actually Native
American. But what his race was apparently didn't matter to his tormentors so much as
the race he wasn't—White—and they proceeded to break his jaw, ribs, wrist and teeth.[60]

The borderlands of the Navajo Nation are not the only place where violent
hate crimes against Native Americans occur. In 1999, an "Indian hunting
license," created as a poster in South Dakota, read "In the place of the big game
animals this year we will have open season on the Sioux Reservations. This will
entail the hunting of America's Worthless Siounis Pyutus, commonly known as
'Worthless Red Bastards,' 'Dog Eaters,' 'Gut Eaters,' 'Prairie Niggers' and 'F—
Indians.' "[61] In the same year, Mark Appel ran over and killed a 21-year-old
native who was passed out in the road near Sisseton, South Dakota. "Appel
admitted he made no effort to avoid the body because 'it is illegal to cross
the White line, or if it is a solid yellow line, or even if it wasn't, it is illegal to
swerve.' " Appel backed up, supposedly to see what he had hit and ran over the
man again. In Alaska in 2001, three White teenagers in Anchorage, armed with
paintball guns with frozen pellets of paint (to make the impact more significant),
went hunting for Alaskan Natives. Calling the native to their car, they pretended
to do an interview and then shot him in the face. "When one of the victims, most
of whom were inebriated, flogged down a police cruiser and told the officer he
had been shot, he was arrested for disorderly conduct and spent 10 days in jail."[62]

Perry's interviews and surveys illustrate that harassment and violence are
common occurrences for Native Americans, although the most prevalent forms
of hate incidents were name-calling and verbal harassment. She points out that
these bias "incidents" still have an impact.

We have learned from the literature on violence against women, for example, that
the daily onslaught of verbal abuse has far-reaching consequences for the victim. The
same can be said of racial harassment, to the extent that it is also an almost daily occurrence in many communities.[63]

Interviewees had the sense that hate crime was so widespread and commonplace
as to be a part of daily life, almost invisible in its penetration into their world.
A campus hate-crime survey found that 40 percent of Native Americans reported
that they had been victimized because of their race.[64] When a community is subjected to ongoing, repetitive examples of hate, both physical and nonphysical, the
impact can be pervasive and cumulative.

Hate crimes have a retaliatory effect, leading to other crimes as one group tries to "pay back" another. While some turn their anger outward at the dominant culture, others turn it on themselves; another effect is self-hatred. The Centers for Disease Control and Prevention (CDC) compile statistics on suicide rates in different demographics. From 2005 to 2009, for those 10–24 years old, Native Americans had the highest suicide rates of any group. In a study identifying suicide risk factors in Native American youth, in addition to arrest history, substance abuse, and depression, researchers found that for Native Americans living on reservations, racial discrimination was a significant factor.[65]

WAR AND THE ASIAN OTHER

"The literary and popular culture images of Asians and Asian Americans that have prevailed since the nineteenth century have become, for many Americans, real-world entities."[66] Periods of higher conflict between Americans and those of Asian descent include immigration patterns from 1848 to 1941, World War II, the Vietnam War, and the Korean War. Representations dominating the media have been limited to a narrow perspective, closing off possibilities of more positive representation and relationships. The pervasive nature of these images bolsters hegemonic perspectives now ingrained in American culture, and these images in turn create a climate in which war crimes abroad and hate crimes at home and abroad flourish.

The Japanese began immigrating to the United States in increasing numbers in the middle of the nineteenth century, settling in Hawaii and on the West Coast. As were other Asians, the Japanese were affected by the anti-immigrant movements in the early part of the twentieth century and were severely limited by the 1924 Immigration Act. The standing of the Japanese in the United States was made clear in 1922, in *Ozawa vs. US*, when the U.S. Supreme Court ruled that Japanese immigrants could not be granted citizenship because the founders of the United States were White and intended only "more of their kind to come." The court determined that the words "free White person" from the 1790 Naturalization Act, which restricted citizenship to those so described, must be adhered to. As the act stated, "The intention was to confer the privilege of citizenship upon that class of persons whom the fathers knew as White, and to deny it to all who could not be so classified."

During World War II, there was a significant difference between the mediated creations of the Japanese enemy and the German enemy. "To a much greater degree than Germans (and certainly Italians), Japanese became dehumanized in the minds of American combatants and civilians, a process facilitated by the greater cultural and physical differences between White Americans and Japanese than between the former and their European foes."[67] Throughout American media, the Japanese were likened to animals, insects, and other nonhuman undesirables. In cartoons and songs, the Japanese people were depicted as skunks, rats, monkeys, termites, and lice. Some were to be hunted, others were to be exterminated; as these images were bolstered by political and journalistic rhetoric, they became ever stronger. Much like the later "Indian Hunting License," recruiting posters actually called upon young men to join the marines for an "open season" on the Japanese.[68] "The mixture of underlying racism exacerbated by war-time propaganda in combination with hatred generated by Japanese aggression and real and imagined atrocities was a potent brew. The Japanese were loathed more intensely than any enemies of the United States before or since."[69]

Echoing Theodore Roosevelt's views on Native Americans, many believed that "The only good Jap is a dead Jap," a sentiment that was written on the trophy skulls of dead Japanese soldiers and spoken publicly by leading politicians and military commanders. At the time Japanese Americans were being removed to internment camps, the *Los Angeles Times* wrote, "A viper is nonetheless a viper wherever the egg is hatched—so a Japanese-American born of Japanese parents, grows up to be a Japanese not an American."[70] Admiral Halsey, commander of the U.S. Third Fleet during a portion of the Pacific War against Japan and notorious for making racist remarks that bordered on advocating genocide, called the Japanese "yellow bastards," "stupid animals," "yellow monkeys," and "monkeymen," and stated that "the Japanese were a product of mating between female apes and the worst Chinese criminals."[71] During the war, the motto was "Kill Japs, Kill Japs, Kill More Japs." These views were promulgated not by extremist individuals on the Internet as might be the case today but by leading commanders in our own military. The power of these figures to determine public views on the enemy was incredible.

A dehumanized enemy is a nameless and faceless "them" in contrast to "us." Cartoons depicting the Japanese as animals or insects treated the entire people as a homogenous group; cartoons depicting evil Germans singled out individuals such as Hitler as the enemy. The Japanese enemy was seen as an undifferentiated unit (common descriptors were hordes, floods) but not as individuals; this contributed to a policy of extermination that "was manifested in many ways during the war, such as not taking prisoners, killing POWs and surrendering troops, fire-bombing cities with incendiary bombs, using atomic bombs on cities, and the practices of collecting battlefield trophies from dead or near-dead Japanese soldiers."[72] Thus, ". . . a dehumanized enemy is one to whom it is easy to do terrible things while he is still living."[73] The bombing of Japanese citizens in Nagasaki and Hiroshima is proof of this. "Two days after the atomic bombing of Nagasaki, president Truman remarked: 'The only language they seem to understand is the one we have been using to bombard them. When you have to deal with a beast you have to treat him as a beast. It is most regrettable but nevertheless true.' "[74]

Popular songs during World War II were full of racist, anti-Japanese remarks such as the song entitled "We're Gonna Have to Slap the Dirty Little Jap," which included the lyrics "streak of yellow" and "sneaky little fellow." These songs began to emerge right after Pearl Harbor, and they ". . . captured the raw anger, humiliation, and feelings of betrayal that most Americans felt about Pearl Harbor. The attack also made it socially acceptable to express these emotions in ways that took on not just connotations of nationalism and patriotism, but also of race."[75] Other song titles included "When Those Little Yellow Bellies Meet the Cohens and the Kellys" and "We're Going to Find a Fellow Who is Yellow and Beat Him Red, White and Blue." The lyrics to Carson Robison's "Remember Pearl Harbor" included "we'll blow every one of them right off of the face of the Earth," "yellow scum of the sea" and "kill a hundred rats for every boy that fell." Fighting the Japanese was equated with hunting skunk. "In Robison's songs, as well as in much of American war culture, the Japanese are often dehumanized; depicted as rats and other vermin, to be 'murdered,' skinned, and have their hides nailed to the wall."[76] The Japanese were commonly depicted as monkeys in cartoons and songs. "The favorite devices of this form of propaganda included ridiculing the accent and linguistic usage of the Japanese when speaking English, rhyming 'Japs' with as many negative terms as possible, and drawing on stereotypical images."[77] While songs against Hitler and Mussolini existed, they limited their venom to the enemy leadership and not all German or Italian people. The songs about the Japanese vilified the entire race.

Hunting the Enemy

Official and popular culture comparisons with a hunt were frequent during World War I with advertisements like "Now Your Ammunition Is Getting Bigger Game." Metaphors of the hunt equated the enemy with prey animals. The hunters/soldiers collected trophies that included body parts from dead Japanese: skulls, teeth, bones, gold from the teeth, noses, and ears. "A Marine Corps veteran of the fierce fighting on Peleliu recorded in his memoirs the horrific scene of another Marine extracting gold teeth from the jaw of a wounded but still struggling Japanese, a task which he attempted to facilitate by slashing his victim's cheek from ear to ear and kneeling on his chin."[78] The collection of body parts as trophies was widely reported in the American press from the picture of a young woman gazing at the skull of a Japanese soldier sent to her by her soldier boyfriend featured in *Life* magazine to a Pennsylvania congressman who presented President Roosevelt with a letter-opener made from the arm bone of a Japanese soldier. Roosevelt later returned this as inappropriate, but the practice of trophy collecting was well known and widespread.

There was no comparable pattern of abuse of enemy dead in the battles between U.S. forces and troops of the European Axis, but the constructed images of the Japanese, on which rested these practices, were far different than those of the Germans or Italians.

Skulls left in the United States from previous wars remain, primarily those collected from Japanese soldiers during World War II, though some are from the Vietnam War as well. Many are marked with graffiti (e.g., "This is a good Jap") and the names of American soldiers. Associating the Japanese (and later the Vietnamese) with game animals made it easy for American soldiers to view their enemy as an acceptable site for collecting body parts as war trophies. According to Harrison, two conditions must hold true to enable the collecting of human body parts as trophies of war: first, hunting of animals fulfills an important part of the male identity in a particular culture and second, the enemy has been dehumanized through propaganda and historically constructed negative images.[79] "Clearly, not all hunting societies have engaged in taking human war trophies, and the problem is therefore to identify the conditions under which such societies may employ metaphors of hunting, or rather live these metaphors, in warfare. In the case of the Euro-American armed forces, the answer has much to do with racism."[80]

Harrison points out that collection of Japanese trophy skulls and other body parts represented the far end of a continuum while the common and generally accepted military practice of taking possessions from prisoners and enemy dead was at the other, making Japanese bodies the site for retribution, degradation, and a display of power. "Although trophy-taking seemed to vanish from public memory after the Pacific War, the same schemata of predation suddenly re-emerged intact a generation later in Vietnam, and the same transgressive practices resurfaced, in relation to another people. The idea of racialized trophy-hunting seems to have proved enduring, though different peoples might be made to enter and exit the role of victims as political circumstances changed."[81] U.S. soldiers in Iraq and Afghanistan still used hunting metaphors and collected body parts from their victims during the most recent wars in those areas.

Entries in Charles Lindbergh's diary chronicle his fellow soldiers taking enemy body parts as trophies of war. "They often bring back the thigh bones from the Japs they kill and make pen holders and paper knives and such things out of them." And another entry, "The officer said he had seen a number of Japanese bodies from which an ear or a nose had been cut off. 'Our boys cut them off to show their friends in fun, or to dry and take back to the States when they go. We found one marine with a Japanese head. He was trying to get the ants to clean the flesh off the skull, but the odor got so bad we had to take it away from him.' It is the same story everywhere I go." As he watches these occurrences, Lindbergh notes, "It seemed impossible that men—civilized men—could degenerate to such a level. Yet they had. [I]t was we, Americans, who had done such things, we who claimed to stand for something different. We, who claimed that the German was defiling humanity in his treatment of the Jew, were doing the same thing in our treatment of the Jap."[82]

In postwar years, collected skulls presented a perplexing problem, as the Japanese (and later the Vietnamese) have refused to take back a skull unless it can be proven to be one of their citizens. "A small subfield of forensic anthropology concerns the identification and analysis of human skulls collected by military personnel as war souvenirs and trophies. Most of these relics originate in two twentieth-century conflicts: the Pacific War and the Vietnam War."[83] Native American bones as well are slowly finding their way home, having been collected not just through physical war, but taken by anthropologists and archaeologists in a war of cultural genocide.

The treatment of this particular enemy as less than human widened what was acceptable to collect from the dead. "Trophy-taking during the Pacific War needs to be interpreted in a similar way: not merely as an effect of the powerfully racialized wartime imagery of the Japanese as subhuman, but as one of the symbolic practices by which these conceptualizations were reproduced and sustained—in opposition to a contrasting default recognition of the Japanese as human."[84] With the media full of metaphors of the hunt and the depiction of the Japanese as any number of subhuman species, it is hardly surprising that these carried over into actions during the war.

The Japanese accused the Allies of mutilating Japanese war dead for souvenirs, attacking and sinking hospital ships, shooting sailors who had abandoned ship and pilots who had bailed out, killing wounded soldiers on the battlefield, and torturing and executing prisoners—all of which did take place.[85]

At Home

Roosevelt issued Executive Order 9066 on February 19, 1942, giving the U.S. Army the authority to remove Japanese Americans from their homes in the western United States and hold them in relocation centers. "Roosevelt's action was implemented by Congress without a dissenting vote, in the name of military necessity, and it was applauded by the vast majority of Americans."[86] In 1983, a congressional report determined that racism, war hysteria and the failure of the political leadership all contributed to this action, and finally on August 10, 1988, the United States officially apologized to the survivors for this incarceration, awarding them each $20,000.

Approximately 120,000 Japanese Americans were incarcerated in camps, some for years. Those evicted could bring only what could be carried, losing most of their possessions and property. Over two-thirds of the West Coast Japanese were American born and citizens of the United States, but this was no protection from Executive Order 9066. "The escalating demands of the press, politicians, some army and navy officers, and the general public for harsher treatment of Japanese Americans, whether they were aliens or citizens, helped to change public policy."[87] Prior to the war, Japanese immigrants were barred from citizenship as well as from some trades and professions and could not own agricultural land in many states. Those of Japanese descent born here were citizens but were legally segregated by employment opportunities and in some public places. For all of the fear, there were no cases of sabotage, espionage, or other acts of treason against the United States by any Japanese person here during the war.

The 10 relocation centers were administered by the War Relocation Authority. On three occasions, armed soldiers killed unarmed incarcerated Japanese American citizens. By January 1943, young men were allowed in and out of the camps to volunteer for military service, and in January 1944, the draft was reinstated for Japanese Americans. While families were locked up as a potential threat to U.S. security, their sons were required to fight and die for the country that considered them as lesser citizens and often as less than human.

Following World War II, anti-Japanese sentiment increased again in the 1980s when Japan was framed as an economic threat. As the U.S. auto industry declined, blame was placed on Japan's auto industry. "These conditions led to an increase in anti-Asian violence, including the 1982 beating death of Vincent Chin, a Chinese American, killed by two auto workers who had expressed hostility against the Japanese."[88] Although Chin was a Chinese American, he was killed by Chrysler plant superintendent Ronald Ebens as Ebens declared, "It's because of you little motherfuckers that we're out of work."[89] Ebens was helped by his stepson, Michael Nitz. Although convicted of manslaughter, neither served any jail time; they each received three years of probation and a fine of $3,000. This lack of serious consequence made a clear statement to Asian Americans about their worth and the fact that no differentiation is made among different Asian groups; any "Asian-looking" person can stand in for hatred against a specific group.

Vietnam

The same types of dehumanization of the enemy occurred during the Vietnam War, though this war brought hostility toward U.S. allies as well. Norman Nakamura, a Japanese American GI who served in Vietnam, provided a firsthand account of the systematic racism he witnessed during the war. According to those around him, Vietnam was populated by "gooks," inferior or nonhuman beings. "Relieved in his mind of human responsibility by this grotesque stereotype, numerous barbarities have been committed against these Asian peoples, since 'they're only 'Gooks.' "[90] These barbarities included throwing empty cans at children along the road, shooting tear gas into groups of Vietnamese, making obscene gestures and verbal remarks, and petty thefts. Some GIs considered all Vietnamese women to be whores and treated them accordingly. "The regard for these people is so low that in Lai Khe Base Camp you may hear a driver say to a new driver that it is better to run over a 'Gook' than a chicken, because when you kill a chicken, you have to also pay for the number of eggs that this chicken would have laid in a year."[91] Nakamura described many acts of random violence against civilians—including women, children, and the elderly—a result of the "severely negative stereotype." GIs were told to respect the enemy but not to trust their allies, the South Vietnamese soldiers who were considered cowardly and lacking gratitude. "When there is an act of theft by a Vietnamese from a G.I., the G.I. does not treat it as an act by an individual but as an act by the whole Vietnamese population."[92] As is typical with ethnocentrism, the Other culture is described as lacking in what our own "right" culture has. "Rather than see a non-technological culture, many G.I.'s see the Vietnamese people who are too dumb to ever be technological."[93]

The testimony of Vietnam veteran Jamie Henry in 1971 described the execution of a 10-year-old boy by Henry's company. "We shot him in the back with a full magazine M-16." This occurred on August 8. On August 16, a man was used for target practice by the same lieutenant who had ordered the boy killed. Another man was killed right after a firefight in which the company lost eight men. "He was held down under an APC [armored personnel carrier] and he was run over twice—the first time didn't kill him."[94] An hour later, the company went into a small hamlet and rounded up 19 women and children. The lieutenant called the captain to ask what to do with them. "The captain simply repeated the order that came down from the colonel that morning. The order that came down from the colonel that morning was to kill anything that moves, which you can take anyway you want to take it." Five men opened fire and killed all 19 civilians. "The executions are secondary because the executions are created by the policy that is, I believe, a conscious policy within the military."[95] With war successes during the Vietnam War measured in body counts and derogatory terms used to describe the Vietnamese such as "slope," "slant," "dink," and "zip," the Vietnamese were considered expendable at best and worthy of extermination at worst. These attitudes still linger for some. During the 2000 presidential campaign, John McCain remarked to the press, "I hated the gooks. I will hate them as long as I live." Although McCain claimed that he was referring only to his captors, the term has historically been a derogatory name for Asians.

Recently released declassified army documents verify Jamie Henry's testimony. Examples of abuse were widespread and not confined to a few "rogue" units. "They were uncovered in every Army division that operated there."[96] Cases included seven massacres from 1967 through 1971 with at least 137 civilian deaths; 78 additional attacks on noncombatants with at least 57 deaths, and "One hundred forty-one instances in which U.S. soldiers tortured civilian detainees or prisoners of war with fists, sticks, bats, water or electric shock."[97] Of the 22 soldiers eventually convicted in these cases, sentences ranged from six months to 20 years, but most were significantly reduced; the soldier who received the 20-year sentence served only seven months.

By 1983, the United States had received more than 678,000 refugees from Southeast Asia, creating conflicts with some U.S. citizens during the 1970s and 1980s. In 1981 in Galveston Bay, Texas, local American fishermen turned to the KKK to terrorize Vietnamese fishermen, claiming unfair economic competition. The Southern Poverty Law Center advocated for the Vietnamese and won protection for them from the U.S. Marshals.

In 1992, University of Miami student Luyen Phan Nguyen, 19, was chased down and beaten to death by a mob of 15 young White men. Nguyen had protested an insulting reference to his Vietnamese origins earlier at a party at an apartment complex near his home. When he then left the party, a group of young men surrounded him and beat and kicked him into unconsciousness. He died as a result of a broken neck. The men screamed "chink," "gook" and "Viet Cong" at him. " 'It was just like Wrestlemania 12,' Mr. Mills, a maintenance worker at a country club, said on the [police] tape. 'All you saw was hands, no face. I mean, we were all drinking anyway but all you saw was just hands.' " Bradley Mills, who was 20 at the time, was convicted of second-degree murder and sentenced to 50 years.[98] Dat Nguyen, the father of Luyen Nguyen, has had to put up with racial slurs in the years he and his family have been in the United States, including a boy on a bicycle who threw a cup of coffee in his face while he waited in his car for the light to change. The boy also yelled a racial slur. Thang Nguyen, speaking several months after her son's death, said, "Even now, I don't accept it. If he had died in a car accident, it would have been easier to accept. If my son were a dog, I think maybe he'd still be alive. People would have said, 'Don't hurt the dog.' " Her husband agreed. "People watched this, watched him trying to get up, and no one tried to help him. No one said, 'Stop.' If he were a dog, maybe yes."[99]

AT WAR WITH ARABS

Racism in the contemporary press is never more evident than in accounts of war, when patriotism (or rather, nationalism) is most rife. Most recently the "enemy" has been Arab.[100]

Since long before any of the recent wars with Arab countries, the image of the Arab in the American media and culture has been negative. The formation of Israel in 1948 and its strong alliance with the United States has contributed to the creation of the Arab as enemy. Negative images of Arabs come from many sources, including our entertainment media, political rhetoric, military, journalists, and now the widely expanding Internet culture.

... [T]he key industries of American mass culture, Hollywood and television, for decades have been bastions of anti-Arab stereotyping, and have consistently resisted positive or realistic representations of Arabs and Arab Americans. Negative representations in popular culture reinforce, and are reinforced by, biased and at times hostile journalism in the mainstream news media, academic polemics that urge a confrontational and aggressive approach to the U.S. role in the Middle East, and government programs and policies which are informed by anti-Arab bias.[101]

The resulting negativity toward Arabs and Arab Americans permeates American culture and "provides the basis for much of the hate crime and discrimination Arab Americans are enduring."[102]

Steven Salaita tells us that "Anti-Arab racism ... is fundamental to American race relations. Seven years before 9/11, Ronald Stockton surveyed archetypes of the Arab image in cartoons and other examples of popular culture and concluded that 'an exceptional proportion of all hostile or derogatory images targeted at Arabs are derived from or are parallel to classical images of Blacks and Jews, modified to fit contemporary circumstances ...' "[103] Anti-Arab racism wasn't born on September 11, it was merely validated once again and follow imbedded racist discourse prevalent throughout America's history.

Long held and unquestioned negative images of Arab peoples; a lack of condemnation of racism toward them in mainstream American culture and media; a lack of courage on the part of politicians, particularly those typically responsible for standing up for those on the margins; and the strength and sources of the negativity have all led to the current anti-Arab racism. Salaita points out that "Anti-Arab racists—including, one could argue, a great many elected politicians—have access to vital forums in the public sphere, where they frequently air derogatory opinions about Arabs with little, if any, public outcry. In fact, I would argue that airing derogatory opinions about Arabs has actually enhanced the appeal of numerous public figures, among them George W. Bush, John Ashcroft, Daniel Pipes, Ann Coulter, Steve Emerson, Stanley Kurtz, and Bill O'Reilly."[104] He categorizes the 2004 U.S. presidential election in many ways as a referendum on anti-Arab racism, a referendum that imbedded anti-Arab racism as a mainstream sensibility—or worse, a patriotic duty. Salaita illustrates this with a television ad for Wisconsin's Republican senatorial candidate, Tim Michels.

The commercial depicted a generic Arab, with the requisite snarl topped by a mustache, standing on a hill in a wooded area, fishing a rocket propeller from a duffel bag and aiming it at some sort of nuclear plant. Meanwhile, the ominous voiceover warns viewers about the dangers of terrorism and the threat "they" will pose if we do not strengthen the provisions of the PATRIOT Act that allow for unwarranted searches, intensive surveillance, and indefinite detention.[105]

The media are a crucial source of information, misinformation, and created image, particularly when it comes to illuminating groups outside the mainstream of American culture both through the various news media as well as in the entertainment media. "Film and television function as both art and entertainment; screen images both provide information and help shape values. Motion pictures and television programs present powerful messages that serve to educate and help to convince viewers of a particular world view."[106] Unfortunately, the created version of a people is often shorthand for culturally held assumptions and negative stereotypes, and the screen Arab is one of the strongest examples of this.

Ever since the camera began to crank, the unkempt Arab has appeared as an uncivilized character, the cultural Other, someone who appears and acts differently than the White Western protagonist, someone of a different race, class, gender or national origin. The diverse Islamic world is populated solely with bearded mullahs, shady sheikhs in their harems, bombers, backward bedouin, belly dancers, harem maidens and obsequious domestics.[107]

Jack Shaheen tracked St. Louis, Missouri, cable and network channels between 1986 and 1995. He found an average of 15–20 movies each week that gratuitously denigrated or mocked Arab Muslims. "Producers have regularly inserted unsightly Arab Muslims and prejudicial dialogue into more than 150 movies that otherwise have nothing at all to do with Arabs or the Middle East."[108] Disney's portrayal of Arabs in *The Father of the Bride (Part II)* and *Aladdin* resulted in a request from the American-Arab Anti-Discrimination Committee (ADC) that Disney edit out offensive scenes, but Disney did not respond to the request.

Shaheen also reviewed television cartoons and found that here too, the negative image of the Arab prevails. "Since 1975, more than 60 comparable [to early negative depictions of Arabs in cartoons such as Bugs Bunny, Popeye and Superman] cartoons have surfaced on television, depicting Arabs as swine, rats, dogs, magpies, vultures and monkeys."[109] Like all groups depicted as Other, film Arabs are a faceless mass lacking individuality. This lack of real/reel examples of difference affects the lives of many. "Consider the aftermath of the April 19, 1995 bombing of the federal building in Oklahoma City. Though no American of Arab descent was involved, they were instantly targeted as suspects. Speculative reporting, combined with decades of harmful stereotyping, resulted in more than 300 hate crimes against them."[110]

With the technology we have today, the whole history of film is available to the viewer. Any advances in thinking are always mitigated by the available echoes of the past. In addition to the outright depiction of Arab aggression (what Shaheen describes as propaganda disguised as entertainment), regular Arabs living normal lives are notably absent from film. "Not only do the reel Arab women never speak, but they are never in the work place, functioning as doctors, computer specialists, school teachers, print and broadcast journalists, or as successful, well-rounded electric or domestic engineers." Shaheen points out that far from presenting an increasingly balanced portrait of Arabs, "Over the last three decades stereotypical portraits have actually increased in number and virulence."[111]

With popular culture and media images forming an historical backdrop, American involvement in Arab countries in the past decades is testimony to the strength of the negative images of Arab peoples and their far-reaching consequences. American behavior toward Arab peoples in the first Gulf War, following the bombing of the federal building in Oklahoma, following the devastation of 9/11, and our subsequent involvement in Afghanistan and Iraq presents a clear indictment of culturally created stereotypes and a dehumanized Other. War crimes abroad and hate crimes at home are the result of our creations.

Persian Gulf War

Writing on the Persian Gulf War, Douglas Kellner points out that more than ever before, people related to this war through a televised commentary. The media framed the war to create a good versus evil polarization featuring Saddam Hussein as the chief villain. "According to a study by the Gannett Foundation, there were 1,170 examples in the print media and television of linking Saddam Hussein with Hitler."[112] In addition to its pro-military rhetoric, television provided racist imagery and discourses to position the public against the Iraqis, including the pervasive association of Arabs with terrorism. "During the Gulf war, the characterization of the barbaric, irrational, and immoral Iraqis was used to legitimate and conceal the arguably barbaric saturation bombing of Iraq by the United States and its coalition allies, who were driving Iraq back to a preindustrial era through their systematic destruction of its economic base."[113] Pilots bombing Iraqis likened them to insects. "Worse still, racist epithets such as 'cockroaches,' 'sand niggers,' 'camel jockeys,' and other dehumanizing terms were used to describe the Iraqis, while their slaughter was described in hunting terms as 'a turkey shoot,' 'shooting fish in a barrel,' or 'clubbing seals.' "[114] Again, the motif of the hunt with humans as prey has strong roots throughout our history of war, particularly when the enemy is created as a subhuman Other based on perceived racial differences.

The creation of Arabs as the ultimate enemy during the war had ramifications on U.S. soil that included a rising number of hate crimes against them or those perceived to be them. "Even before the war began, businesses owned by Arab-Americans were bombed, an Arab-American businessman was beaten by a White supremacist mob in Toledo, a Palestinian family riding in a car was shot at in Kansas City, and an Arab-American who appeared on a Pennsylvania television program received seven death threats."[115] Hate and violence spilled over against many people who were mistakenly perceived to be Arab or Arab-American.

The media contributed greatly to the legitimation of hate and the images of the enemy. "A radio show in Georgia proclaimed 'towelhead weekend,' telling callers to phone in when they heard the traditional Islamic call to prayer; a disk jockey in Toledo, Ohio, solicited funds from listeners to buy a ticket to Iraq for an Iraqi-American professor who was critical of the war."[116] While U.S. television and other media demonized the Iraqis and castigated them for their violence, U.S. troops were participating in the slaughter of Iraqis fleeing from Kuwait. Reporters travelling the highway leading from Kuwait City to Iraq found evidence of a massive slaughter of Iraqis who were fleeing from Kuwait. Kellner points out, "The segment [on the flight from Kuwait] was generally framed by stories of Iraqi atrocities, which presented the Iraqis as subhuman monsters and thus seemingly excused the slaughter as just punishment."[117]

September 11, 2001

Media response to the events of September 11, 2001, provided little context for the attacks. Few dared question the dominant rhetoric about demonic enemies, stockpiles of "weapons of mass destruction," and the United States as innocent victim. The ability of the media to provide continuous and narrowly focused coverage resulted in a limited perspective on 9/11 and following events. Like the Persian Gulf War, 9/11 and its aftermath played out in the media. Those who tuned in to television after the buildings were hit watched them fall in real time. The mediated view of these events was in the hands of reporters, politicians, and broadcasters who had little to fall back on except ingrained assumptions. "The war on terror, indeed, is a media war like no other before it, in which 'images of the enemy' have again emerged as a highly visible and often contentious feature of our journalistic culture, amplified by the rise of 24-hour 'real time' news and the internet."[118]

As McNair points out, the unspoken backdrop to 9/11—and the subsequent wars on terror, Iraq, and Afghanistan—included the pro-Israel stance of the United States, our policies toward and perspectives on the Palestinians, and our continuing support for a corrupt Saudi government. "The single overwhelming reason for antipathy toward the United States was not cultural license, or products, or freedom, or even people—but US policy in the Middle East, and specifically toward the Palestinians."[119] The United States' relationship with various countries and peoples of the Middle East is ongoing and complex, but as a world power, we must be aware that we have created both allies and enemies by our actions over time.

In *Media Representations of September 11*, various authors looked at the role and function of the media after 9/11 to determine the result of the images that were produced and the frames that were created to assist the public in understanding the event. They found that complicated issues with multiple meanings (such as the concept of jihad) were often simplified and summarized, thus providing a limited perspective while creating and strengthening stereotypes.[120] The media choose particular depictions of traumatic events in terms of portrayals of victims and perpetrators. After 9/11, the focus on the innocence of the victims left out past history of the harm caused by the United States in the Middle East and elsewhere. Within this discourse, it was frowned upon to have any empathy with the attackers' point of view. "By placing a taboo on empathizing with the attackers, their mission, and the background of their acts, they are placed 'outside' of 'our' world."[121] With the 9/11 attackers named as representatives of broad groups ("Arab," "Muslim"), any persons fitting these groups were potential targets of the super patriots, and the rise of hate crimes against Arabs, which increased in 2002 by 1,600 percent, indicates the very real effects of these creations. "These hate crimes are not some form of scapegoating but rather an attack on the enemy one cannot have empathy for."[122]

Since the day of the 9-11 attacks, Americans have emerged in numbers sporting red, white, and blue flag T-shirts, baseball caps, designer purses, and jewelry, and claiming a newfound patriotism and spirit of unity. These public avowals, however, have celebrated a narrowly defined and hegemonic "super-patriotism," and have been accompanied by a series of vicious and violent attacks on "Arab-looking" people, as well as incidents of vengeful retribution against visible "others" perceived by untrained eyes to be suspect in the attack.[123]

Actions against those perceived as enemies after 9/11 included verbal assaults, vandalism, workplace harassment, boycotts of Arab-owned shops and businesses, and numerous acts of violence. Super patriotism allows for more openly racist behavior than the more covert racism typical of other times. "Claims to a newfound American unity since the 9-11 attacks, thus, turn on racist standards of 'otherness,' ensuring an uneasy tolerance and solidarity among those within the hegemonic circle, but various forms of violent retribution, ridicule, and suspicion against those outside it."[124] The case of Balbir Singh Sodhi illustrates this violent retribution. Sodhi was murdered September 15, 2001, by a "super patriot," who shot him five times. Born in Punjab, India, and a member of the Sikh religion, Sodhi's turban and beard, common features of Sikhs (a religion, ironically, that preaches the equality of humankind regardless of race, religion, or gender) were his death warrant. Two years later, Frank Roque was convicted of first-degree murder in the hate crime. Roque had boasted days before the shooting that "he was going to 'kill the ragheads responsible for September 11.' " In 2003, truck driver Avtar Singh, also a Sikh, was shot and seriously wounded by someone who told him, to go back where he belonged. "The fact that so many perpetrators of hate crimes targeted Sikhs, apparently believing them to be Arabs, draws a clear connection between representations of Arabs in American popular culture and the thinking that informed some of the worst incidents in the hate crime backlash."[125]

Mark Stroman was executed in Texas in 2011 for the hate crime killing of Vasudev Patel. Stroman also killed Waqar Hasan and injured Rais Bhuiyan. While Stroman himself stated the shootings were motivated by revenge for the events of 9/11 (they took place in the weeks that followed), he mistakenly identified the three victims as Arabs. In fact, Patel was from India, Hasan from Pakistan, and Bhuiyan from Bangladesh. In his early years in prison, Stroman reiterated his stance as a "proud American" on the Internet, justifying his actions as patriotism. "In closing, this was not a crime of hate but an act of Passion and Patriotism, an act of country and commitment, an act of retribution and recompenses."[126]

By January 2002, just four months after the attacks of September 11, the Council on American-Islamic Relations had already received 1,658 reports of discrimination, profiling, harassment, and physical assaults against persons appearing Arab or Muslim, a three-fold increase over the prior year. The report included beatings, death threats, abusive police practices, and employment and airline-related discrimination.[127]

There were also murders; assaults; vandalism of homes, businesses, and places of worship; and verbal harassment.

As America moved quickly following 9/11 to setting up the rationale for the 2003 Iraq War, the media and military complex vigorously promoted a pro-war agenda, presenting information that should have been rigorously questioned but was not. Throughout the twentieth century, the news media have been an essential element in stirring and shaping public opinion, whether for a particular war or against it. While the news media have long had a role in influencing the public, what is of significance about the Iraq War is the depth and scope of duplicity prior to and during the early stages of the war.[128] "The case for war on Iraq ... consisted of at least two key arguments: that Iraq was in some way connected with the events of 9/11, and that the Iraqis possess weapons of mass destruction (WMDs), had used them in the past, and were willing to use them against the US."[129] However, neither of these proved true. The strength of the Arab enemy stereotype and the fears engendered by the enemy Other after 9/11 were enough to send us into another lengthy war.

An analysis of five speeches by President Bush after 9/11 illustrates how quickly the enemy was created and solidified. On September 11, 2001, he used the word "evil" four times, juxtaposing good/evil with us/them. On September 12, 2001, he spoke of a monumental struggle of good versus evil. On September 14, 2001, he described the enemy as dark, faceless, soulless, and a source of an evil "crusade." On September 16, 2001, his famous "evildoers" appeared, along with "evil folks," and "barbarism" in opposition to Christianity. Animal metaphors, common in creating an enemy Other, appeared in his speech of September 20, 2001, as he spoke of the enemy as animalistic, brutal, and prone to "burrow deeper into caves." He also created black and white options: "Either you are with us or you are with the terrorists." On January 29, 2002, Bush labeled North Korea, Iran, and Iraq as the axis of evil with weapons of mass destruction, and he equated Arabs and Muslims with terrorists. "In reality, 'axis of evil' is a term chosen to selectively stigmatize countries for the purpose of justifying military actions against them."[130]

"No one has been voted out of office for targeting foreign nationals in times of crisis; to the contrary, crises often inspire the demonization of 'aliens' as the nation seeks unity by emphasizing differences between 'us' and 'them.'"[131] In the reactionary atmosphere immediately following 9/11, the government started abrogating the rights of Arab Americans and alien Arabs through practices such as ethnic targeting, picking up Arabs and Arab Americans for questioning and detention, and removing those from airplanes who were visibly different. Using immigration law as a pretext and targeting primarily noncitizens, Attorney General John Ashcroft allowed people to be arrested, then looked for reasons to detain them; however, the majority charged since 9/11 have been American citizens. "In the wake of September 11, Ashcroft targeted the Arab and Muslim immigrant community, and stretched, twisted, exploited, altered and in many instances, violated immigration law to achieve his preventive detention goal."[132] Before September 11, eighty percent of Americans were against ethnic or racial profiling. After September 11, sixty percent were in favor, provided it was directed at Arabs and/or Muslims.[133] The same ethnicity-based rationale is being used against Arabs as was used to detain, deport, and hold Japanese Americans during World War II, even though we have subsequently admitted the errors of our ways and apologized for our actions.

By May 2003, five thousand such people had been detained, while not one had been charged with any crime. Immigrants were detained as material witnesses when no other options were available. Of the 44 locked up under this pretext in the 14 months after 9/11, only seven were U.S. citizens. Probable cause is not required to detain a material witness, and at least half of those locked up as such have never testified. Documentation from the Metropolitan Detention Center in New York shows physical and verbal abuse of those detained after September 11, even though there was no proof that they were guilty of anything.[134]

An "enemy combatant" can be held for an indefinite period of time without charges, hearing, trial, lawyer, or communication. By March 2003, more than 650 foreign nationals were being held at Guantanamo Bay in Cuba. Although the Geneva Convention requires prisoners of war (POWs) to be treated in a humane fashion and to be held as privileged, the Bush administration considered all as "unprivileged combatants" even though it was not known if those held were ever combatants at all. Some are as young as 13. The Enemy Alien Act authorizes the president during a declared war to detain, expel, and restrict the freedom of any citizen 14 or older of the country with which the United States is at war, thus creating a population as dangerous based solely on their national identity and not on any active behavior. During World War II, Roosevelt used the act against those of Japanese descent and then expanded it to include Italians and Germans.[135]

Muneer Ahmad points out that while most disapproved of the form that post-9/11 anger took when it led to hate crimes, they sympathized with the emotions behind the anger. "The physical violence exercised upon the bodies of Arabs, Muslims, and South Asians has been accompanied by a legal and political violence toward these communities." The laws developed in the areas of immigration law and law enforcement following September 11 "operate in tandem" with the individual hate crimes, "thereby aiding and abetting hate violence."[136]

Ahmad contrasts the hate killings of James Byrd Jr. and Matthew Shepard, viewed as "incomprehensible acts of violence," with the hate crimes following September 11, which were understood as the result of an anger felt by many even while the outlets of the anger were disapproved. He associates the post-9/11 hate crimes with crimes of passion rather than crimes of individual moral depravity (as the typical hate crime is presented) and argues that governmental policies instituted following 9/11 along with the hate crimes "mutually reinforce a shared racist ideology."[137]

The result of these mutually supportive forms of hate violence has been the creation of a new racial group, the "Muslim-looking" person. Included are not only Arabs and Muslims, but Arab Christians, non-Muslims from many countries such as Pakistan and Indonesia, South Asian Sikhs and Hindus, and "even Latinos and African Americans, depending on how closely they approach the phenotypic stereotype of the terrorist."[138] Muslim-looking people became stand-ins for the terrorists just as "Asian" people were stand-ins for the Japanese during World War II and the Vietnamese during the Vietnam War. Ahmad discusses the notion of fungibility, the fact that any person fulfilling the Muslim-looking requirement can stand in for someone who is actually an Arab Muslim. He equates the post-9/11 hate crimes with lynchings that "received the imprimatur of rationality and normalcy offered in the form of mainstream, White southern approval of the practice."[139] In a prototypical hate crime killing (such as Byrd's or Shepard's), the defect of the individual perpetrator allows society to ignore "the role that less extreme practices of racism and homophobia that permeate society may have played in reinforcing the perpetrator's prejudices."[140] While Byrd and Shepard's deaths were used to change hate crime laws and allowed the public to condemn the killings as horrendous acts of depraved individuals, the deaths following 9/11 have not served the same functions, as the bias and anger of the perpetrators resonated with too much of the country to allow the safe distancing from the typical hate crime that usually occurs.

The effects of terror extend beyond immediate victims and physical destruction to a much broader target population.[141] Terrorism aims to instill anxiety in this population, and anxiety leads to an overestimation of risk, while an externally perceived threat increases support for outwardly focused retaliatory action. "One of the most pervasive and powerful effects of threat is to increase intolerance, prejudice, ethnocentrism, and xenophobia, regardless of whether threat is defined as a widely acknowledged external force or a subjective, perceived state."[142] Whether real or perceived, threat to status or resources leads to increased prejudice against and rejection of the threatening out-group and support for punitive action. Both external and perceived threats lead to vilification of the source of the threat and promote aggressive solutions while heightening in-group solidarity. "Even more impressive, when threat is manipulated experimentally we find it to be not just a correlate but a clear *cause* of ethnocentrism, intolerance, and a desire for retaliation."[143]

The Threat and National Security Survey, a national phone survey assessing reactions to 9/11, found that perceived threat was more widespread than feelings of anxiety, and perceived threat led to greater support for U.S. military intervention. Eighty-five percent of those surveyed supported toughening restrictions on visas for foreign students and other visitors, 48 percent believed that Arabs applying for entry should undergo more intensive security checks than those from other countries, and 29 percent would put Arabs and Arab Americans in the United States under special surveillance. Those who perceived a high future threat of terrorism supported aggressive action against the enemy and were more likely to negatively stereotype Arabs and support restrictive immigration policies for Arabs.[144]

Hate crimes too have an impact beyond the victims, as they create an atmosphere of fear and apprehension. All members of the targeted group are vulnerable to attack, as are those misidentified as group members. The American-Arab Discrimination Committee (ADC) published a report on hate crimes and discrimination against Arab Americans occurring between September 2001 and September 2002. Over 700 violent incidents targeting Arab Americans or those perceived to be Arab Americans, Arabs, and Muslims took place in the first nine weeks after 9/11, including several murders. There were 165 violent incidents between January 1 and October 11, 2002, which was a significant increase over most years in the previous decade. There were more than 80 cases of illegal and discriminatory removal of passengers from airplanes after they had boarded and more than 800 cases of employment discrimination against Arab Americans. Other discrimination included service denials, housing discrimination, and a "campaign of vilification against Islam and the Prophet Mohammed by leaders of the evangelical Christian right, including Jerry Falwell, Pat Robertson and Franklin Graham."[145]

The mainstream media and publications included hostile commentary, and members of Congress made openly racist remarks. The ADC recommended that "The media should not present hate speech as a legitimate contribution to the national conversation, or rely on commentators who routinely resort to racial stereotypes and smearing entire communities."[146] They also laid blame for an atmosphere of fear on "a campaign in American popular culture and media of vicious defamation and vilification against Arabs and Islam, including defamation by well-known public figures."[147]

Abu Ghraib, Haditha, and Trophy-Taking

Many undeniably atrocious events took place after 9/11 that may well be tied to the overriding media perspective of the time. The events at Abu Ghraib prison—which included the humiliation, torture, and complete dehumanization of prisoners—happened in a culture intent on creating an ultimate enemy and justifying the need for war. Prisoners were stripped of clothing and dignity, sexually humiliated, and brutalized while smiling soldiers posed with them for pictures. "There is a crucial correlation between mainstream news media's readiness to repeatedly characterize opponents as insects or animals and what happened at Abu Ghraib, in which the metaphor of the animal is made horrifyingly literal."[148] War trophies included personal belongings and mementoes such as videos recorded on phones or photos like those taken at Abu Ghraib. "In one of the most disturbingly literal versions of the hunt metaphor, there have been eyewitness accounts of American soldiers in Fallujah tying the dead bodies of resistance fighters to their tanks and driving around with their trophies like hunters with an animal carcass tied to their hood."[149]

"Just as animal metaphors tend to become more extreme when they enter less regulated spheres such as internet blog sites, so negative stereotyping appears in some of its most vicious forms in popular culture."[150] The images, both visual and metaphorical, are seen in so many places they begin to seem natural: movies, games, political cartoons, t-shirts, the "Deck of Weasels" playing cards, and many jokes about Iraq and Afghanistan.[151]

"Haditha became a defining moment of the war, helping cement an enduring Iraqi distrust of the United States and resentment that not one Marine has been convicted."[152] On November 19, 2005, in the city of Haditha in the western Iraqi province of Al Anbar, a group of U.S. marines killed 24 unarmed Iraqi men, women, and children. The details of these murders came to light after 400 pages of interrogations were discovered by a *New York Times* reporter in a junkyard outside of Baghdad. While much of the documentation had been burned, the remaining 400 pages detailed the brutal murder of Iraqi citizens. Only one soldier was ever sentenced for the incident, marine staff sergeant Frank Wuterich, who received a suspended sentence of three months even though he was the squad leader of the group that killed the Iraqi citizens. Geoffrey S. Corn, a retired lieutenant colonel in the U.S. Army as well as a former special assistant to the judge advocate general for Law of War Matters and a professor at the South Texas College of Law, writes about the Haditha incident, pointing out that "even in war there are limits on when it is permissible to kill." He goes on to say,

"The law of war lies as the very core of military discipline, for it provides the barrier between killing required on behalf of the strategic interests of the state and the instinct of revenge and retribution so routinely aroused in the hearts and minds of young warriors."[153] While Corn makes some important points about the limits to killing during war and the need for the discipline that enforces these laws, he is wrong in stating that as with My Lai during the Vietnam War, it was only the "deplorable conduct of one platoon of soldiers and their substandard leader." In fact, in both the Vietnam War and in the recent war in the Middle East, it continually surfaces that these illegal killings occur much more frequently than earlier surmised. In *Kill Anything That Moves: The Real American War in Vietnam*, Nick Turse documents incident after incident of violence against noncombatant Vietnamese during the war, demonstrating that My Lai was part of a pervasive and systematic disregard for Vietnamese life. He also details how these killings were not just the random behaviors of individual soldiers reacting to the stress of the war, but the result of official policies and direct orders.

The troops serving in Iraq had no real understanding of the culture and history of the country. Almost none spoke or read Arabic, and "Stereotypes about Islam and Arabs solidify quickly into a crude racism, especially in the confines of the military and on the dangerous streets of Iraq."[154] Many just referred to Iraqis as "hajis," a slur, just as the Vietnamese were "gooks." Civilians were considered potential terrorists and often treated badly—stripped naked, left to stand for hours in the sun while their houses were destroyed; others were run over by convoys.

Gul Mudin

He grins at the camera, holding up the head of his dead prey like any proud hunter after a kill. But in this photograph, the prey is a 15-year-old unarmed Afghan boy named Gul Mudin, and he has been killed for sport. He is also missing a finger, a souvenir already collected from his newly dead body. Simply because they wanted to "bag a savage," two young American soldiers (Corporal Jeremy Morlock, 21, and Private First Class Andrew Holmes, 19) called Gul Mudin over, told him to stand still, threw a grenade at him, and then shot him repeatedly at close range. Even in death, Mudin continued to be treated as less than human. Staff Sargent Calvin Gibbs moved the boy's arms around and made as if the corpse were talking. Gibbs is the one who removed the finger, which he carried proudly as a souvenir. "After the killing, the soldiers involved in Mudin's death were not disciplined or punished in any way. Emboldened, the platoon went on a shooting spree over the next four months that claimed the lives of at least three more innocent civilians."[155] Morlock eventually pled guilty to killing three Iraqi citizens and was sentenced to 24 years in prison. Gibbs, who had in his possession finger and leg bones as well as a tooth taken from Afghan corpses, received life in prison. Ten other men in his squad, which called itself the Kill Team, were also convicted on a variety of charges. In news reports, the squad is often described as "rogue," asserting that this type of incident is unusual and random. However, given the treatment of Afghans and Iraqis throughout the wars in the Middle East, it is unlikely that history will prove this true.

There are many similarities in the creation of the enemy Other in the wars discussed in this chapter. Metaphors likening an entire population to animals, insects, or disease surface time after time. Ideas about "lesser" peoples who do not value human life the way "we" do, who do not feel pain the way "we" do, who do not share "our" (Western) values also appear when we are at war with those considered Other. Body parts collected as trophies, brutal killings of noncombatants, and mistreatment of prisoners and civilians are features of these wars. Native Americans were slaughtered, moved, confined, and the victims of attempted cultural and possibly actual genocide. Japanese in the United States were taken from their homes and confined during World War II while Japanese noncombatants in Japan died by the hundreds of thousands through relentless bombings of Japanese cities. Although President Roosevelt condemned the bombing of China by Japan prior to World War II, by the end of the war, 66 cities—including Hiroshima and Nagasaki—had been bombed by precision raids and general urban area attacks. An estimated 400,000 Japanese civilians were killed.[156] The history of the Vietnam War now includes incident after incident of brutality visited on Vietnamese civilians by troops who considered them less than human. Similar incidents from the Middle East wars continue to surface.

It is not just how we create an enemy Other and conduct ourselves in war. These creations spill over onto American soil as fellow citizens are created as Other, as representatives of a hated group, and are the victims of hate crimes. Hate crimes provide one of the most powerful methods of containment and extermination, whether the daily insidious and accumulative effects of verbal harassment and abuse or the less frequent but powerful assaults and murders. In many cases, the person who is the victim does not even belong to the hated group: Vincent Chin, a young Chinese man, was killed because of hatred for the Japanese. Balbir Singh Sodhi, a Sikh, was killed because his murderer assumed he was an Arab. With a wealth of cultural sources contributing to our creations (news and entertainment media, political rhetoric, information and conversations on the Internet, and images in our texts from our earliest years) as well as laws, official policies, and the inequalities structured into our society, the roots of hatred allowed to flourish during a war remain with us for a long time and take a serious toll on American citizens. We are creating fear and rage in those we abuse at home and abroad, and if the results are further acts of terrorism against us, we must shoulder that responsibility.

NOTES

1. Debra Merskin, "The construction of Arabs as enemies: Post–September 11 discourse of George W. Bush," *Mass Communication and Society* 7, no. 2 (2004): 159.

2. Ibid., 161.

3. John Dower, *War without Mercy* (New York: Pantheon, 1986).

4. Erin Steuter and Deborah Wills, *At War with Metaphor: Media, Propaganda, and Racism in the War on Terror,* (Lanham, MD: Lexington Books, 2008), 4.

5. Sam Keen, *Faces of the Enemy: Reflections of the Hostile Imagination* (San Francisco: Harper & Row, 1991), 10.

6. David E. Stannard, *American Holocaust: The Conquest of the New World* (New York: Oxford University Press, 1992), 126.

7. Barbara Perry, *Silent Victims: Hate Crimes against Native Americans,* (Tucson: University of Arizona Press, 2008), 30–31.

8. Fergus M. Bordewich, *Killing the White Man's Indian: Reinventing Native Americans at the End of the Twentieth Century* (New York: Doubleday, 1996), 35.

9. Doris Seale and Beverly Slapin (ed.), *A Broken Flute: The Native Experience in Books for Children* (Washington DC: Altamira, 2005), 2–3.

10. Stannard, *American Holocaust*, 66.

11. Christopher Columbus, Diary, October 11, 1492, http://www.historyisaweapon.com/defcon1/diarioofchristophercolumbus.html

12. Bordewich, *Killing the White Man's Indian*, 36.

13. Allen W. Trelease, *Indian Affairs in Colonial New York: The Seventeenth Century* (Lincoln: University of Nebraska Press, 1997), 72.

14. Bordewich, *Killing the White Man's Indian*, 31.

15. Ibid., 32

16. Ralph K. Andrist, *The Long Death: The Last Days of the Plains Indians* (New York: Collier, 1964), 87.

17. Ibid., 89.

18. Ibid., 91.

19. Ibid., 351.

20. Thomas Jefferson's Indian Addresses, http://libertyonline.hypermall.com/Jefferson/Indian.html.

21. Ibid.

22. Stannard, *American Holocaust*, 121.

23. Andrew Jackson, Fifth Annual Message to Congress, December 3, 1833, http://www.presidency.ucsb.edu/ws/?pid=29475.

24. Roosevelt, *The Winning of the West, Homeward Bound Edition*, vol. 1, 1910, Appendix A to Chapter 4(online at www.britannica.com/presidents/article-9116965).

25. Theodore Roosevelt, "The expansion of the White races," January 18, 1909, http://www.theodore-roosevelt.com/images/research/speeches/trWhiteraces.pdf.

26. Ibid.

27. See Laurence M. Hauptman, "Governor Theodore Roosevelt and the Indians of New York State," *Proceedings of the American Philosophical Society* 119, no. 1 (1975): 1–7.

28. Hermann Hagedorn, *Roosevelt in the Bad Lands* (Whitefish, MT: Kessinger, 2003), 355.

29. Peter C. Rollins and John E. O'Connor (ed.), *Hollywood's Indian: The Portrayal of the Native American in Film* (Lexington: University of Kentucky Press, 1998), foreword.

30. Perry, *Silent Victims*, 137.

31. See, for example, "The Emergence of the Plains Indian as the Symbol of the North American Indian," *Annual Report of the Smithsonian Institution*, 1964, 531–544.

32. Arlene B. Hirschfelder, *American Indian Stereotypes in the World of Children: A Reader and Bibliography* (Metuchen, NJ: Scarecrow, 1982), 50.

33. Seale and Slapin, *A Broken Flute*, 50.

34. Hirschfelder, *American Indian Stereotypes*, 35.

35. Ibid., 43.

36. Rollins and O'Connor, *Hollywood's Indian*, 12.

37. Ibid., 81.

38. Perry, *Silent Victims*, 5.

39. Barbara Perry, "From ethnocide to ethnoviolence: Layers of Native American victimization," *Contemporary Justice Review* 5, no. 3 (2002): 233.

40. Perry, *Silent Victims*, 53.

41. Ibid., 54.

42. Ibid., 77–78.

43. Gabriel Chrisman, "The fish-in protests at Franks Landing," http://depts.washington.edu/civilr/fish-ins.htm, accessed February 10, 2011.

44. Dean Chavers, *Racism in Indian Country* (New York: Peter Lang, 2009), 65.

45. Chrisman, "Fish-In Protests."

46. Donald Lee Parman, *Indians and the American West in the Twentieth Century* (Bloomington: Indiana University Press, 1994), 179–180.

47. http://cnie.org/NAE/docs/chippewa.html#trwvd.

48. Daniel J. Perkins, "Institutionalized vilification: A case study of the reinforcement of hegemony through norms of 'news values,' " *Viewpoints on War, Peace and Global Cooperation.* Annual Journal of the Wisconsin Institute, 1996–1997, 60.

49. Chavers, *Racism in Indian Country*, 66.

50. Rodney Barker, *The Broken Circle: A True Story of Murder and Magic in Indian Country* (New York: Simon and Schuster, 1992), 173.

51. Perry, "From ethnocide to ethnoviolence," 231–247.

52. Nathan Wheeler and Emily Ronald, "Navajo Community and Farmington, New Mexico," *Pluralism Project at Harvard University*, http://pluralism.org/reports/view/68, accessed November 5, 2010.

53. Susy Buchanan, "Indian Blood," *Intelligence Report* 124 (Winter 2006), www.splcenter.org/get-informed/intelligence-report, accessed November 5, 2010.

54. Ibid.

55. Barker, *Broken* Circle, 170–171.

56. Ibid., 171.

57. "Indians: Now, Navajo power," *Time*, June 24, 1974.

58. See, for example, Emilie Karrick Surrusco, "Under the New Mexico sky," *Carte Blanche* 10 (Fall 2009), http://www.carte-blanche.org, accessed November 5, 2010.

59. Buchanan, "Indian blood," 2006.

60. Ibid.

61. Chavers, *Racism in Indian Country*, 69.

62. Susy Buchanan, "Malign neglect," *Intelligence Report* 124 (Winter 2006).

63. Perry, *Silent Victims*, 77.

64. Ibid., 109.

65. Eve Bender, "Study identifies suicide risk factors in Native-American youth," *Psychiatric News* 38, no. 11 (2003): 28.

66. Renny Christopher, *The Viet Nam War/The American War: Images and Representations in Euro-American and Vietnamese Exile Narratives* (Amherst: University of Massachusetts Press, 1995), 112.

67. James J. Weingartner, "Trophies of war: U.S. troops and the mutilation of Japanese war dead, 1941–1945," *Pacific Historical Review* 61, no. 1 (February 1992): 53.

68. Dower, *War without Mercy,* 90.

69. Weingartner, "Trophies of War," 54.

70. Dower, *War without Mercy,* 80.

71. Carl K. Savich, "War, journalism, and propaganda: An analysis of media coverage of Bosnian and Kosovo conflicts," http://www.rastko.rs/kosovo/istorija/ccsavich-propaganda .html, accessed December 31, 2009.

72. Ibid.

73. Weingartner, "Trophies of War," 67.

74. Ibid., 67.

75. Authentic History Center, http://www.authentichistory.com/1939-1945/3-music/ 04-PH-Reaction/index.html.

76. Ibid.

77. W. Anthony Sheppard, "An exotic enemy: Anti-Japanese musical propaganda in World War II Hollywood," *Journal of the American Musilogical Society,* June 22, 2001, 306.

78. Weingartner, "Trophies of War," 56.

79. Simon Harrison, "Skull rrophies of the Pacific War: Transgressive objects of remembrance," *Journal of the Royal Anthropological Institute* 12, no. 4 (2006): 818.

80. Ibid., 819.

81. Ibid., 832.

82. Charles Lindbergh, *The Wartime Journals of Charles A. Lindbergh*, (Boston: Harcourt Brace Jovanovich, Inc., 1970), 919.

83. Harrison, "Skull Trophies of the Pacific War," 818.

84. Ibid., 831–832.

85. Dower, *War without Mercy,* 61–62.

86. Roger Daniels, "Incarcerating Japanese Americans," *OAH Magazine of History* 16, no. 3 (Spring 2002): 19.

87. Ibid., 21.

88. Japanese American Citizens League, "When hate hits you: An Asian Pacific American hate crime response guide," http://www.jacl.org/public_policy/documents/WhenHateHits.pdf.

89. Yip, Andrea. "Remembering Vincent Chin," *Asian Week*, June 5–13, 1997.

90. Norman Nakamura, "The nature of G.I. racism," *Modelminority,* June/July 1970, http://www.modelminority.com/printout74.html, accessed March 17, 2009.

91. Ibid.

92. Ibid.

93. Ibid.

94. Ibid.

95. Ibid.

96. Nick Turse and Deborah Nelson, "Formerly secret files show coverup of Vietnam atrocities," *Seattle Times*, August 8, 2006.

97. Ibid.

98. "Man found guilty in bias beating in Florida," *New York Times*, October 22, 1992.

99. Mike Clary, "Dream turns to tragedy: Haunted by a son's brutal death, a Vietnamese immigrant family struggles to understand racial hatred in a 'great country' like America," *Los Angeles Times*, February 2, 1993.

100. Steven Chermak, Frankie Y. Bailey, and Michelle Brown (eds.), *Media Representations of September 11* (Westport, CT: Praeger, 2003), 119.

101. Hussein Ibish (ed.), "Report on hate crimes and discrimination against Arab Americans: The post–September 11 backlash, September 11, 2001 to October 11, 2002," *ADC Research Institute*, 2003, 120.

102. Ibid.

103. Steven Salaita, "Beyond Orientalism and Islamophobia," *New Centennial Review* 6, no. 2 (Fall 2006): 250–251.

104. Ibid., 254.

105. Ibid., 259.

106. Jack Shaheen, *Arab and Muslim Stereotyping in American Popular Culture* (Georgetown, VA: Center for Muslim-Christian Understanding, Georgetown University, 1997), 11. Available at http://www12.georgetown.edu/sfs/docs/Jack_J_Shaheen_Arab_and_Muslim _Stereotyping_in_American_Popular_Culture_1997.pdf

107. Ibid., 12.

108. Ibid., 13.

109. Ibid., 26.

110. Jack G. Shaheen, "Reel bad Arabs: How Hollywood vilifies a people," *Annals of the American Academy of Political and Social Science* 588 (July 2003): 172.

111. Ibid., 188.

112. Douglas Kellner, *The Persian Gulf TV War* (Boulder, CO: Westview, 1992), 63.

113. Ibid., 187.

114. Ibid., 247.

115. Ibid., 249.

116. Ibid.

117. Ibid., 405.

118. Brian McNair, *Images of the Enemy* (New York: Routledge, 1988), 2.

119. Gregory Orfalea, *The Arab Americans: A History* (Northampton, MA: Olive Branch, 2006), 331.

120. Chermak et al., *Media Representations of September 11*, 28.

121. Ibid., 80.

122. Ibid., 80.

123. Ibid., 31.

124. Ibid., 32.

125. Hussein Ibish, *Report on Hate Crimes*, 120.

126. Bill Mears, "Texas inmate set to die for hate crimes in 9/11's wake," CNN Justice, July 16, 2011, http://www.cnn.com/2011/CRIME/07/15/texas.death.row.hate.crime/.

127. David Cole, *Enemy Aliens: Double Standards and Constitutional Freedoms in the War on Terrorism* (New York: New Press, 2003), 47.

128. Deepa Kumar, "Media, war, and propaganda: Strategies of information management during the 2003 Iraq War," *Communication and Critical/Cultural Studies* 3, no. 1 (March 2006): 49.

129. Ibid., 54.

130. Sheldon Rampton and John Stauber, *Weapons of Mass Deception* (New York: Tarcher, 2003), 115.

131. Cole, *Enemy Aliens*, 5.

132. Ibid., 25.

133. Ibid., 48.

134. U.S. Department of Justice, "Supplemental Report on September 11 Detainees' Allegations of Abuse at the Metropolitan Detention Center in Brooklyn, New York," December 2003.

135. Cole, *Enemy Aliens*, 92–93.

136. Muneer I. Ahmad, "A rage shared by law: Post–September 11 racial violence as crimes of passion," *California Law Review* 92, no. 5 (2004): 1262.

137. Ibid., 1264.

138. Ibid., 1279.

139. Ibid., 1289.

140. Ibid., 1290.

141. Leonie Huddy, Stanley Feldman, Charles Taber, and Gallya Lahav, "Threat, anxiety, and support of antiterrorism policies," *American Journal of Political Science* 49, no. 3 (July 2005): 593.

142. Ibid., 594.

143. Ibid., 594.

144. Ibid., 596.

145. Hussein Ibish, *Report on Hate Crimes and Discrimination against Arab Americans*, 8.

146. Ibid., 9.

147. Ibid., 17–18.

148. Steuter and Wills, *At War with Metaphor*, x.

149. Ibid., 88.

150. Ibid., 99.

151. Ibid., 105.

152. Michael Schmidt, "Junkyard gives up secret accounts of massacre in Iraq," *New York Times*, December 14, 2011, http://www.nytimes.com/2011/12/15/world/middleeast/united-states-marines-haditha-interviews-found-in-iraq-junkyard.html?_r=0, accessed November 6, 2013.

153. Geoffrey S. Corn, "Haditha and My Lai: Lessons from the law of war," *Jurist*, June 2, 2006, http://jurist.org/forum/2006/06/.

154. Chris Hedges and Laila Al-Arian, *Collateral Damage: America's War against Iraqi Civilians*, (New York: Nation Books, 2009), 88.

155. Mark Boal, "The Kill Team," *Rolling Stone* 1128 (April 14, 2011): 60.

156. Dower, *War without Mercy*, 41.

3

Unwelcome Hordes:
Immigrants and Hate

The history of U.S. immigration policy and law provides a partial history of nativist, racist, ethnocentric, and xenophobic tendencies in America. From the beginning, American citizenship was reserved for those possessing desirable racial or cultural attributes. Congress passed the Naturalization Act in 1790 stating that citizenship could be granted only to "a free White person." In 1882, the Chinese Exclusion Act denied citizenship to Chinese immigrants living in the United States and prohibited all Chinese laborers from entering the United States for the next 10 years. The Immigration Act of 1917 (Barred Zone Act) created an "Asiatic Barred Zone" restricting immigrants from Asian countries along with idiots, imbeciles, alcoholics, criminals, the insane, and those with dangerous contagious diseases. The 1924 Immigration Act (Johnson-Reed Act) set national origin quotas for immigrants to the United States. This act not only excluded all Asian immigrants, it limited immigration visas to 2 percent of a particular nationality's total in the United States at the time of the 1890 census. This increased the percentage of visas available to immigrants from the British Isles and the countries of western Europe while restricting immigrants from southern and eastern Europe.

John Higham's work on nativism in America, which he describes as "intense opposition to an internal minority on the grounds of its foreign ('un-American') connections,"[1] is useful for an understanding of the treatment of many immigrant groups in American history. Higham traces three main nativistic themes in the period from 1860 to 1925 that began with anti-Catholicism, moved to include a fear of foreign radicals, and finally evolved into a racial nativism that defined the Other in racial or biological terms, a movement from what one did to who one was. Early concerns with religion and radicalism moved to include a concern with biological race at precisely the time when new groups of immigrants from southern and eastern Europe, as well as Asia, were coming to America in increasing numbers. Physical and cultural differences attributed to the new groups fueled American fears that without restrictions on immigration, the American national character (whatever that was) would be "bred out."[2]

Many journalists writing in the early part of the twentieth century believed that the future of America depended on the ability of immigrants to assimilate, to throw off each nation's "peculiarities," and to meld into the dominant (European) American culture. The melting pot would work only as long as foreign races could be melted into the American amalgam and become "good" American citizens. As ideas of racial superiority came to the fore, along with the belief that traits and character were dependent on hereditary transmission rather than environment, calls to restrict immigration from particular countries became more prevalent. "Until unrest and class cleavage upset the reign of confidence in the 1880's, the assimilationist concept of a mixed nationality had tempered and offset pride in Anglo-Saxon superiority. But when Anglo-Saxon enthusiasts felt their society and their own status deeply threatened, they put aside their boasts about the assimilative powers of their race."[3] The early part of the twentieth century saw a variety of movements that pushed for and achieved regulations on immigration that were race and ethnic group specific.

Today, the struggle with immigration continues in full force, particularly during election years, as it has become a highly politicized issue with widely differing opinions on what the issues are and what the solutions should be. Numerous immigration acts have been passed in the past few decades as various presidents have tried to come to terms with their own ideas on immigration reform as well as the views of their constituents. These include the Immigration Reform and Control Act of 1986, which provided a path to citizenship for undocumented immigrants who had been in the United States since before 1982 (this act also made it a crime to hire an undocumented immigrant); the Immigration Act of 1990, which increased the total number of immigrants allowed each year; and the Illegal Immigration Reform and Immigrant Responsibility Act of 1996, a complicated piece of legislation that dealt with issues such as the enforcement of immigration law (including border patrol issues), potential sanctions for employers who hire undocumented immigrants, and regulations regarding services and assistance for "aliens."

In this chapter, I look at three different groups who met opposition and hate as they arrived in this country in significant numbers: the Chinese and Italians in the late nineteenth and early twentieth centuries, and Mexicans in the latter part of the twentieth century into the present. There are many similarities in the way each of these groups was imagined and depicted by the dominant culture in the media, in political rhetoric, in law, and in pseudo-scientific explanations for difference.

CHINESE

As California developed during the nineteenth century, particularly with the mid-century discovery of gold, Chinese immigrants were welcomed for the labor they could provide as miners, railroad workers, cooks, launderers, and later farmers. However, as gold mines petered out and a succession of difficulties hit the newly formed state (drought, completion of the railway, many fewer mining jobs—all of which led to increased unemployment), blame for economic woes combined with racial prejudice led to strong anti-Chinese sentiments that eventually spread throughout the country. The end results included both hate crimes and legislation aimed at excluding the Chinese from the United States. "During all of this period they were seldom if ever considered purely on their merits, but always from the viewpoint of their effect upon the numerous problems confronting the people of [California]."[4] The Chinese were castigated for their willingness to work for lower wages, for their presumed inability to assimilate, for their acceptance of crowded and poor (but cheap) living conditions, and for assumptions made about their moral and social beliefs.

In *The Unwelcome Immigrant*, Stuart Miller looks at the dominant images of the Chinese in American culture and their origins, particularly during the period from 1785 to the Chinese Exclusion Act of 1882. The United States had been trading with China since the end of the eighteenth century, missionaries were traveling to China in increasing numbers, and events in China brought news stories to the attention of the American public. Miller points to images provided by those with "inside" information from China—traders, diplomats, and Protestant missionaries—each of whom had a different purpose in going to China and thus constructed their images of the Chinese from a variety of perspectives. The majority of traders traveling to China considered the Chinese to be "ridiculously clad, superstitious ridden, dishonest, crafty, cruel and marginal members of the human race who lacked the courage, intelligence, skill, and will" to work toward improving their lot in life.[5] Diplomats travelling to China between 1785 and 1840 were, for the most part, European, aristocratic, educated, and of high social status. Their strong ethnocentric biases were clear, and the Chinese suffered by comparison with Western notions of proper dress, technological advancement, and progress. Two recurring themes were the use or purpose Americans saw in a particular immigrant group and the differences they noticed between the newcomers and themselves.

Of the three groups providing inside views of China, the Protestant missionaries had the widest audience in America through their books and journals, the
religious press, and their sermons. New York City itself had 52 religious publications in 1850, and a religious revival in the United States in the mid-1800s
brought great support for missions in China.[6] The missionaries arrived with preconceived images of the Chinese and then fit what they saw into these creations.[7]
Faced with the sheer numbers of Chinese "heathens" arriving in America, many
Americans, through ignorance and long held stereotypes, responded with fear,
animosity, and even violence. Failure to convert to Christianity was taken as a
sign of a mass character defect of a degenerated people and the work of the devil,
and the Protestant missionaries played a significant role in creating the negative
images of the Chinese in the western United States in the nineteenth century.
"Thus China served the missionary and minister as a useful illustration of
the evils of paganism and the benefits of Christianity. The worst pictures of
Chinese society also helped to enlist greater support for the missionary cause."[8]
All three of these groups were responsible for the negative images of the Chinese:
to the traders, the Chinese were dishonest and crafty; to the diplomats, they were
backward and ignorant; and to the missionaries, they were heathen and
degenerate.

The development of the mass media created a conduit for images of China
and the Chinese to be disseminated widely and quickly. The advent of the penny
press, a cheaply made, mass produced and distributed tabloid, made it possible to
reach large numbers of people quickly. Miller looked at magazines, newspapers,
and textbooks from 1785 to 1840 to determine trends in the treatment of the
Chinese. "A sample of forty-nine such texts reveals a highly unflattering picture
of the Chinese by 1820, one that dominated this genre over the next two
decades ..."[9] The U.S. Civil War colored perceptions of Chinese immigration
with beliefs that Chinese coolie labor was too close to slavery for comfort. The
pseudo-scientific development of theories of race during the century contributed
ideas as to the innate superiority of the Caucasian race and perceptions that the
Chinese Other was too dissimilar to successfully assimilate into American society.
Concerns with disease and germs contributed to fear of the Chinese. "The com-
mentaries of traders and missionaries were replete with references to Chinese
stagnation, slavishness, inferiority, and dirt; but it was the interaction of these
conceptions with popular considerations and anxieties dealing with industrializa-
tion, slavery and civil war, racial assimilation, and disease that proved to be
crucial."[10]

Sandmeyer grouped anti-Chinese ideologies under three main headings: economic, moral and religious, and social and political. "What many considered
the most fundamental objection to the Chinese was their difference from Americans in racial characteristics and their unwillingness to adopt American customs
and ideals."[11] Fear of difference coupled with concern for economic competition

led to waves of violence against the Chinese during the second half of the nineteenth century. Organized labor was one of the main groups to work toward restricting and eventually excluding Chinese immigrants, and American labor groups grew in strength partially due to their strong opposition to Chinese labor. With a balance of power distributed evenly between the two main political parties, labor unions developed a strong enough influence during elections to be able to force politicians to support an anti-Chinese immigration stance not only in local California elections, but in national elections as well.[12]

Anti-Chinese sentiment led to laws aimed at curbing immigration and reducing Chinese ability to work in the United States. Taxes on foreign miners (the Chinese paid $58 million in taxes to the state of California between 1852 and 1870),[13] taxes on those ineligible to become American citizens (the Chinese were excluded from citizenship, *In re Ah Yup*, 1878, which determined that the Chinese were of the Mongolian race and therefore not White, referring to the 1790 Immigration Act, which excluded all but Whites from citizenship), taxes on crowded housing conditions (the Cubic Air Ordinance), a law requiring any person put in jail to have hair cut to one inch of the head (the Queue Ordinance), and the Sidewalk Ordinance (which banned Chinese from carrying vegetables or laundry in baskets hanging from shoulder poles) were all designed to put pressure on the Chinese immigrants that would force them out of the country. In 1872, California added the Chinese to the prohibition against marriages between Whites and Blacks. Chinese immigrants could not work for federal, state, or local governments or educate their children in public schools. While some of these measures were overturned due to unconstitutionality (and a practical inability to enforce them), they illustrate the ill will felt throughout the state of California toward the Chinese. Laws forbidding the Chinese to testify in California courts against any White person (*People vs. Hall*, 1854) "opened the way for almost every sort of discrimination against the Chinese. Assault, robbery, and murder, to say nothing of lesser crimes, could be perpetrated against them with impunity, so long as no White person was available to witness in their behalf."[14] Beyond the popular images of the Chinese, these structural inequities created the Chinese as a lesser group in American society and provided validation to those who acted against the Chinese.

Many laws and treaties restricting Chinese immigration were passed on the eve of national elections, showing the strength of Chinese immigration as a political question in addition to a strong racial prejudice.[15] Denis Kearney of the California Workingman's Party became well known for his opposition to Chinese immigrant labor. In an 1878 speech, he described the Chinese worker as "a cheap working slave" and went on to say, "These cheap slaves fill every place. Their dress is scant and cheap. Their food is rice from China. They hedge twenty in a room, ten by ten. They are whipped curs, abject in docility, mean, contemptible and obedient in all things. They have no wives, children or dependents."[16]

This demeaning description comparing the Chinese to animals and denigrating their character was common rhetoric.

Invective against the Chinese included the belief that the American way of life and the future of the White race were doomed without restrictions on Chinese immigration. California's Governor William Irwin (1875–1880) stated, "The subversion of our civilization is involved in this Chinese emigration, because, if the influx of this race continues, they become the laborers of our country . . ."[17] The racial basis for anti-Chinese sentiment was strong. A memo sent to Congress in 1886 by a state anti-Chinese convention named the struggle in the west with the Chinese a matter of life and death, "of the very existence of the White race."[18]

California's second Constitution as written included discriminatory measures against the Chinese, including equating them with idiots, criminals, and the insane. It denied them the vote and made it a misdemeanor to employ a Chinese worker. The circuit court declared most of this Constitution to be illegal; however, it demonstrates the depth of feelings against the Chinese in California at the time.

Eventually, agitation in California and other western states spread anti-Chinese sentiment nationally, and in 1882, the Chinese Exclusion Act was passed, restricting immigration specifically from China for a period of 10 years and again denying U.S. citizenship to Chinese residents who were born in China. Ten years later, the Geary Act extended the period of no immigration an additional 10 years and added a requirement that all Chinese residents of the United States carry permits. It was not until 1943 and the passage of the Magnuson Act that the Chinese Exclusion Act of 1882 was repealed. However, this act limited Chinese immigrants to 105 per year.

Denis Kearney asked that his audience "not believe those who call us savages, rioters, incendiaries, and outlaws. We seek our ends calmly, rationally, at the ballot box. . . . But, we know how false, how inhuman, our adversaries are. . . . We shall arm. We shall meet fraud and falsehood with defiance, and force with force, if need be."[19] The kinds of actions taken as a result of hatred for the Chinese were not calm and rational, but violent and harsh.

Hate Crimes

In her work on the violence used throughout the second half of the nineteenth century to drive the Chinese out of California and other western states, Jean Pfaelzer puts to the lie Kearney's assertions regarding calm rational behavior at the ballot box as the chosen method for change. In case after case, she describes whole towns, even whole counties, that determined they would drive the Chinese out by whatever means handy—and the means were often violence against person and property. These hate crimes took place against a backdrop of media portrayals, popular culture sources such as songs and cartoons, political rhetoric, and angry public outbursts that made it clear in what low esteem the Chinese were held. "Photographs, advertisements, placards, local newspapers, court records and testimony, campaign documents, songs, business cards, and diaries fabricate a history of docile but wily Chinese invaders—dirty, diseased, and exotically enticing—even as they record the expulsions and reveal how Chinese immigrants fought back."[20]

On October 24, 1871, two Chinese were knifed to death and 17 more were lynched in Los Angeles. "Their mangled bodies were found hanging from a wooden awning over a carriage shop, from the sides of two prairie schooners parked around the corner, from a gutter spout, and from a beam across the wide gate of a lumberyard. One of the victims wore no trousers, and a finger had been severed from his left hand."[21] The long queues were cut off some corpses as souvenirs, and even women and children took part in the lynching. Victims' bodies, like those in wartime, were again the site of retribution and trophy collection, illustrating the dehumanization of the Chinese in America. In 1880, Chinese laundrymen were lynched in Denver, Colorado. "Victims of lynching were poked, prodded, jeered at, beaten, tortured, hanged, shot and dismembered. Sometimes they were castrated, sometimes decapitated."[22] On November 3, 1885, the Chinese in Tacoma, Washington, were given a mere four hours to pack their belongings and leave town. Helped by the mayor himself, townspeople dragged those who did not immediately comply out of their houses.

In Eureka, California, in 1885, a city councilman was accidently killed in the crossfire between two Chinese men. A mob of more than 600 White men looted Chinese stores and told the Chinese they were to be on the docks by the next morning to be shipped out of town. They put up a gallows with the sign "Any Chinese Seen on the Street After Three O'clock Today Will Be Hung to This Gallows."[23] More than 500 Chinese were loaded onto ships the next morning with some of their hastily gathered belongings and shipped to San Francisco. "In only two days the Chinese community in Eureka was gone, and the policy banning its return endured until the 1950s."[24] The purge in Eureka led to purges elsewhere in the state, and hundreds of Chinese had to flee, leaving behind their livelihoods and their possessions while their belongings were looted by those who had forced them out. By the end of the 1880s, approximately 200 towns in the Northwest had driven out the Chinese. "The physical, cultural, and national differences between Chinese and White—exposed and shaped by advertisements and political campaigns, by cruel cartoons and popular songs—split a global working class residing in California."[25] The anti-Chinese faction, however, continually gained ground during this time.

Focus on the overt, violent racism against the Chinese in the nineteenth century drew attention away from the more insidious and paternalistic racism of politicians, missionaries, and social reformers. After the U.S. Civil War, notions of race and racial hierarchies were becoming solidified. Focusing on the racism of the working class made it easy for the upper classes to be ignored, but without the racism of the leaders in American society, racist attitudes would not have become codified into laws restricting the basic rights and privileges of racial Others such as the Chinese.[26] Murphy points to the juncture between anti-Chinese Whites, pro-Chinese Whites, and the Chinese themselves as the place where racialization of Whites and Chinese occurred. "Through using cartoons, the racialized-border role the Irish played in the imagination of working-class uncivilized Whiteness is also repeatedly highlighted alongside the racialized representations of Chinese workers as unequivocally non-White."[27]

Pro-Chinese Whites were in many instances more anti–working class than intrinsically supportive of Chinese immigrants. They could, on one hand, disapprove of calls for restricting Chinese immigration and speak against the violence perpetrated against the Chinese while on the other hand retain their own ideas of racial superiority over the Chinese. This unquestioning assumption of racial hierarchy solidified it even more strongly in American culture than the violent acts against the Chinese did; individual violence could be condemned, while the racism that permeated American culture could be ignored. Immigration and citizenship have always been connected to notions of race. The 1790 Naturalization Act restricted citizenship to Whites, and court cases and official documents such as the U.S. Census also helped define the Chinese as non-White. Anti-Chinese rhetoric included fears of race mixing and contributed to antimiscegenation laws such as the one that caused White women to lose their citizenship if they married a noncitizen.

Murphy points to the two sides of the Chinese stereotype: celestial (wily and sly, untrustworthy, devious, immoral) and coolie (hardworking, lower class, degenerate), and how these combined to provide a basis for the enduring modern stereotype of the model minority. "Depending on their social position, different groups of Whites had competing views of the Chinese and their abilities. What these contradictions show are the ways racist discourse became transposed from racialized group to racialized group depending on the needs of the particular Whites."[28]

The nineteenth-century Black press used the anti-Chinese movement to try to improve Black position in the racial hierarchies of the times. The Black press, in focusing on the purported depravities of the Chinese (opium use and addiction, disease, prostitution, sexual predation of young White girls, violence), "constructed these ... persons as embodiments of premodern, alien difference."[29] The stories of Chinese difference served as a counterpoint to the Black press's narrative of the racial uplift of Black Americans, highlighting the capabilities of Blacks and their incorporation into modern American society. One difference was the Christianity of Black Americans in contrast to the "heathen" Chinese. The supposed lack of ability to assimilate on the part of the Chinese was strongly contrasted with stories of Black belonging and growth.[30]

As Murphy points out, the profession by pro-Chinese Whites of a more positive or sympathetic view of the Chinese functioned more as a statement of disapproval of the working class than real sympathy for the Chinese; Jun points to the Black press's formation of the Chinese immigrant as alien more as a device for negotiating Black exclusion than as a racist statement about the Chinese. Anti-Chinese legislation could easily turn into anti-Black legislation, and the Black press worked to increase Black space from the Chinese. "Although Black Orientalism was a means of narrating the development of Black subjects into American modernity, the passage of the Chinese Exclusion Act in 1882 did not consolidate Black national identity, but rather exposed the tenuous status of Black citizenship itself." The result in the Black press was "almost unanimous opposition to this unprecedented form of race-based immigration exclusion."[31] However, this press, while speaking against legislating racially exclusive policies, continued to distance itself from the Chinese as a group in terms of customs, morals, and religion that the press labeled as inferior. These attacks even intensified after the 1882 Chinese Exclusion Act was passed. "Black press concerns that the Chinese Exclusion Act would be followed by more race-based legislation were dramatically substantiated less than a decade later by the Supreme Court's decision that racial segregation was an entitlement of White citizenship."[32]

"For decades American traders, diplomats, and Protestant missionaries had developed and spread conceptions of Chinese deceit, cunning, idolatry, despotism, xenophobia, cruelty, infanticide, and intellectual and sexual perversity. This negative image was already reflected in American magazines and geography textbooks before 1840 . . ."[33] Once the Chinese were banned, newspapers and politicians provided justifications for the continued need for exclusion. The Chinese already here were subjected to rampant discrimination and a variety of actions that would be labeled hate crimes today, from vandalism to assault to murder.

ITALIANS

Italian immigrants from the southern part of Italy began arriving in America in increasingly large numbers in the 1880s. Between 1900 and 1910, southern Italian immigrants represented the largest of the many groups coming to the United States. While the majority of early Italian immigrants came from northern Italy, those in the latter part of the nineteenth century were primarily from southern Italy, an area of poverty and harsh physical conditions. Of the over 4 million southern Italians who eventually came to America, 96 to 97 percent were farmers or laborers.

Many of the new immigrants landed and stayed in American cities, forming Little Italies in part as a reflection of ethnic solidarity, in part because of the obvious language barrier, and in part as a reaction to the increasingly negative attitudes of mainstream Americans toward the new immigrants from southern and eastern Europe. Italians fit all three of Higham's main nativistic themes as the majority were Catholics, a number of Italian radicals became nationally known, and the overwhelming majority were from the south of Italy, an area that appeared to cause great concern for Americans in terms of racial categorization.

Wealthy young Englishmen and Americans were in the habit of doing the "grand tour" of Europe to study painting, architecture, and agriculture in the 1800s. Thomas Jefferson, Washington Irving, James Fennimore Cooper, and many others travelled to see the grandeur of Italy. Traveling with preconceived notions of the culture and peoples, they viewed Italy and its people through a distorted image of ideas. Encountering the realities of the current (at the time) Italian people and culture, the seeds of the northern/southern split were planted and brought back to the United States in travel writings, fiction, and magazine articles.[34]

A common device in articles on Italian Americans in the early part of the century was to create a split between immigrants from northern and southern Italy. This geographical split was the result of a model of a cultural/racial split that carried with it serious implications. Immigrants from the north of Italy were considered to be similar in appearance and culture to the earlier northern European immigrants, and these immigrants were accepted as enough "like us" as to present no real threat to American society. Those from the south of Italy, however, were felt to be very different both culturally and racially, and were even categorized by some writers as belonging to a different (non-White or at least non–pure White) race. The geographical split was held to be responsible for numerous physical, character, and cultural deficiencies of the southern Italians. What lay behind the use of geography and climate as an explanation for cultural differences was a concern with the racial purity (i.e., "Whiteness") of the southern Italians.

Descriptions of southern Italians included terms like "swarthy" and a "brunette nationality." Speculation as to the ancestry of this group led to a linking of southern Italians with the Iberians of Spain and the Berbers of northern Africa. Physical types varied along a line created by journalists. "The region north of this line . . . is inhabited by a very broad-headed and tallish race, the North Italian. All of Italy south of the Apennines and all of the adjacent islands are occupied by a long-headed, dark, 'Mediterranean' race of short stature."[35] The small size of the southern Italian was equated with numerous physical problems, such as a high infant mortality rate, believed to indicate a lack of physical stability. There was a clear indication of the type of labor that was fitting for the southern Italian as, much like an animal, "they are wiry and muscular and capable of prolonged physical exertion."[36] The complexions and physical makeup of the southern Italians were taken as an indication of a lack of moral and emotional strength as well.

According to sociologist Edward Alsworth Ross, a proponent of eugenics as well as a prominent early criminologist, "That the Mediterranean peoples are morally below the races of northern Europe is as certain as any social fact. Even when they were dirty, ferocious barbarians, these blonds [northern Europeans] were truth-tellers."[37] Ross categorizes the Italians from southern Italy as physically inferior, ignorant, superstitious, unreliable, lacking in mechanical aptitude, and having a hatred of school.

Arthur Sweeney, writing on "mental tests for immigrants" in 1922, graded immigrants' mental abilities with A, B, C, and D. He categorized those receiving a D/D–grade as having the mental age of less than 11 and stated that 45.6 percent of immigrants coming to the United States were in this group. For Italians, 63.4 percent were in this group. "He is a reflex arc, rather than a reasoning being." Sweeney was not opposed to immigrants, as he saw the need for their labor; he was opposed to immigrants from certain areas of the world. "It is time to awaken to the necessity of protecting this country from the influx of the worthless. Unless we do so we shall degenerate to the level of the Slav and Latin races, with their illiteracy, ignorance and consequent degradation."[38] The headlines of articles written in the early part of the twentieth century point to a concern with the purported criminal activities of the Italian immigrant. While today, Italian Americans are linked with organized crime in the public imagination, early concern was not only with the beginnings of organized crime (the Camorra or Black Hand movement, which was an early organized crime movement from Italy), but with more typical street crime. Some examples of such headlines are "Italy Tries to Keep Grip on Criminals," "Could Keep Out Italian Criminals," "President Taft and New York's Italian Criminals," "Italian Crimes Baffle Police," and "Italian Outlaws." Using animal metaphors, writers spoke of "predatory crime" and described Italian criminals as "preying upon their honest and industrious compatriots."[39] Other descriptive terms included "criminal invasion," "exotic desperadoes," and "medieval savages of the Mafia and the Camorra." Cartoons illustrated concern with an increase in Black Hand activity; one illustrated an inattentive United States as the system of law is overrun; another showed Italy kicking out its criminals who are grasping, again with the Black Hand, for America.

The involvement of Italian-Americans in crime filled many pages of the public print. Each incident reported became the occasion for a call for the enactment of restrictions on immigration and for laws enforcing deportation of criminals. Ironically, even though these newspapers acknowledged that accounts of criminal activity were magnified, they nevertheless persisted in featuring stories about the topic.[40]

What is useful in the example of the Italian American is the use of metaphoric language to create a particular image, the importance of the metaphors in providing an understanding of the underlying assumptions and beliefs about this group, and the fact that actual figures on Italian crime, which were not disproportionate to their percentage of the population at the time, were not in any way crucial to the discussion. The metaphoric construction of the Italian criminal was sufficient.

An 1883 *New York Times* article titled "The Importation of Italian Fleas: An Infernal Plot" equated the Italian immigrant with the flea. "Unless the importation of this infamous insect is checked the whole country will swarm with Italian fleas. Our own native flea will disappear before its formidable competitor. The Chinese invasion of which the Pacific States complain is as nothing in comparison with this Italian pest. We must have at once stringent rules against the importation of the pauper fleas of Europe." The article goes on to suggest a treaty like the one with China prohibiting the entrance of further immigrants from Italy or a duty that "no Italian immigrant can afford to pay."[41]

Many of the prevalent social movements and the dominant models for structuring American society showed up in the metaphorical language applied to Italian Americans in the early part of the twentieth century. The move to a racial nativism and the new "scientific" groupings of the world's peoples into hierarchically structured racial groups were evident in discussions of the attributes of "warm-blooded" southern Italians. The Italian Americans were created by the media as a criminal class as a means of dealing with deeper rooted, less articulated fears about racial and cultural difference. Metaphors explicate truth relative to a particular conceptual system, and those who have the power to impose their metaphors on the culture have the ability to define what is considered to be true. "The Italians were represented and constructed in scientific treatises, government reports, political oratory, journalistic accounts, literature, the visual arts, caricature, and myriad other venues of popular culture."[42] These sources, fictional as well as those that were presumed (often erroneously) to be factual, contributed to the national discourse and the creation of the Italian immigrant Other. The sources fed on one another and became part of an overwhelming mix of racist and nativist ideologies.

Immigration Restriction

According to the 1880 census, there were 44,000 Italians in the United States at the time. By the 1890 census, the population had grown to 480,000 and during the decade from 1900 to 1910, over 2 million more arrived. In 1894, the Immigration Restriction League was founded in Boston by those who opposed the large numbers of "undesirable" immigrants coming from southern and eastern Europe. One of its founders, Prescott Hall, served as the general secretary for the league from its beginning until 1921. Hall wrote about the "Future of American Ideals," asking if there was "a danger that the race that has made our country great will pass away." He spoke of the definite American type that existed in the country at the time of the Civil War—a race from northern Europe that "has always been distinguished for energy, initiative, and self-reliance." The immigrants that had been coming since that time were people of "entirely different races," that is, from Mediterranean, Asiatic, and African stocks. "The South Italian, which constitutes the largest element in our present immigration, is one of the most mixed races in Europe and is partly African, owing to the negroid migration from Carthage to Italy."[43] Hall supported the idea that "half-breeds of any races are inferior to their parents, just as alloys of metals are not as valuable as the metals themselves."[44] He worried, "What would happen if a large Mediterranean population should be colonized in our Southern States and should interbreed with the negro population it finds there?"[45] He already has categorized the southern Italians as a mixed breed. His concern with southern Italians is echoed, he points out, by Westerners' concern with "Asiatics."

Whiteness

"Whiteness was contingent on a number of factors, including occupation, residence, and the presence of other immigrant or non-White groups."[46] Although by today's classifications of race, which seem immutable, this may seem impossible, it serves as a good reminder of the created nature of race and the fluid nature of racial categories. Some immigrants, like the southern Italians, had to become "White." Like Black Americans (though to a much lesser degree), Italians were targeted for lynching based in part on their racial Otherness. "In both cases, the victims were depicted as subhuman, animal-like. However, while Blacks were often represented as a sexual threat to American womanhood, the Italians were usually seen as a threat to the American working man, American society, and American national character."[47] Biologically, southern Italians were considered to be somewhere between the Black and White races and were excluded from some "White-only" schools.[48]

Many Italian immigrants remained in poor working-class neighborhoods longer than most other European immigrants, often living among people of color, and this created "a particular anxiety to assert a White identity in order to effectively distance themselves from their Brown and Black neighbors, and receive the ample rewards that come from being White."[49]

Italians also learned that they were racially "other" in the United States in ways that went beyond language: lynchings; the refusal of some native-born Americans to ride streetcars with or live alongside "lousy dagoes"; the exclusion of Italian children from certain schools and movie theaters, and their parents from social groups and labor unions; segregated seating in some churches; and the barrage of popular magazines, books, movies, and newspapers that bombarded Americans with images of Italians as racially suspect.[50]

Due to concern with the rising number of immigrants from southern and eastern Europe, in 1907, President Theodore Roosevelt appointed a commission of senators, representatives, and economic experts to study immigration and its consequences. It was headed by Senator William P. Dillingham of Vermont, who was a restrictionist, as were many of the other members of the commission. Three years and 41 volumes later, the commission decreed that the new immigrants, representing inferior races, brought with them crime, disease, ignorance, and an inability to assimilate to the United States.[51] According to the Dillingham Commission's Dictionary of Races, there were 36 discernible races in the United States. This categorization distinguished northern and southern Italians as separate races, and in agreement with social scientists of the nineteenth century, attributed Black roots to southern Italians. "Southern Italians were especially dangerous because they might carry African blood."[52]

George Cunningham argues that Italians were considered a hindrance to White solidarity in Louisiana. Brought to the state in part to supplement the decreasing supply of Black labor after the Civil War and in part because Democrats believed they might lose control of the Black parishes unless the White population could be increased, Italians from southern Italy worked and lived alongside Black Americans and at least initially, failed to maintain the same distance between the groups that White Americans stuck to so rigidly. "In sugar cane fields, Italians performed tasks which native Whites considered as suitable only for Negroes."[53] The Whites of Louisiana considered the Italians to be non-White. "Regarded by the native White society as racially different and socially inferior, Sicilians interacted freely with their Black coworkers while retaining their separate ethnic identity apart from both White Americans and African Americans."[54] In 1898, Louisiana held a constitutional convention to discuss, among other things, eligibility for the vote. Of concern were both the Black vote and the vote of lower-class White groups considered by many not to be true Whites at all. "In the quarrel over foreigners' voting, it became obvious that the Italian and not the Negro was the real problem which the convention faced."[55] Newspapers reporting on the situation included the *Homer Clipper*, which stated that "according to the spirit of our meaning when we speak of White man's government, they [Italians] are as Black as the Blackest Negro in existence."[56] As Cunningham points out, "The wrangle over disfranchising Negroes in Louisiana left a lesson for the Italians. They had better adopt the customs, prejudices, and way of life of White Louisianans as soon as possible. They must look with loathing upon everything that the native White loathed. Once they did so, the Italians could gain acceptance among the native Whites, though not at first on a basis of complete equality."[57]

"Whether they like it or not, Italian Americans cannot escape the fact that they weren't always White. They were lynched, burned out of homes, chased, captured and killed by vigilantes and the Ku Klux Klan."[58] As new immigrants, those from southern Italy faced discrimination from social, religious, economic, and political sources. As Connell tells us, they became "Whites on a leash"— considered to be White as long as they behaved and "acted White."[59] The price of becoming White for Italian immigrants was accepting the dominant culture of racism in America.

Toni Morrison points out that each new immigrant group achieves the transition into American culture "on the backs of Blacks" as they learn to distance themselves from Black Americans in order to make their way up the racial hierarchy. "In race talk the move into mainstream America always means buying into the notion of American Blacks as the real aliens. Whatever the ethnicity or nationality of the immigrant, his nemesis is understood to be African American."[60] In the early days of southern Italian immigration to the United States, this group identified more closely with their Black neighbors than with the dominant White society. It took painful years to learn the reality that Morrison articulates.

Hate Crimes

In common with Jews, Poles, Mexicans, and others, Italians were pilloried by insulting nicknames—such as wop, Dago, and guinea—abused in public, isolated socially, cheated of their wages, pelted in the streets, cuffed at work, fined and jailed on the smallest pretenses, lynched by nativist mobs, and crowded into slums and reeking tenements.[61]

Sicilians were encouraged to come to Louisiana at the end of the nineteenth century to supplement the decreasing Black labor force and to increase the percentage of Whites in the area. However, they soon met with hostility from local Whites due to their Roman Catholicism, their clannishness, and their purported criminal proclivities. More importantly, "The perceived racial characteristics of Southern Italian immigrants would play the primary role in the sort of racial violence they would experience in the American South at the hands of White mobs."[62] The willingness of Italian immigrants to work side by side with Black Americans, including serving them in their stores, was a factor behind the use of lynchings to "insure White supremacy" in the South. Nativist and racist feelings against the Italian immigrants led to lynchings such as the 1890 New Orleans incident where 11 Italians were killed. New Orleans police chief David Hennessey was shot and killed on October 15, 1890. Before dying, he claimed that he was shot by "dagoes," but that was the only description he gave. Many immigrants in the vicinity were rounded up and "within twenty-four hours, the police had arrested forty-five people, mainly Sicilians . . ."[63] The first trial of nine defendants began on February 16, 1891, and it required vetting 780 prospective jurors "before twelve people were found who were free of prejudice against

Italians or capital punishment."[64] Six of the defendants were found not guilty; three were given a mistrial, and two were never tried.

A group of approximately 150 prominent citizens formed the Committee on Safety and posted a notice inviting people to a mass meeting the day after the trial concluded. Organizers included prominent attorney William Parkerson, newspaper editor John Wycliffe, and attorney Walter Denegre. The notice in the New Orleans *Times-Democrat*, which included the names of leading citizens, read: "All good citizens are invited to attend a mass meeting . . . at Clay's Statue, to take steps to remedy the failure of justice in the Hennessey case. Come prepared for action." Thousands appeared the next day. Urging the crowd to follow him to the parish prison where the Italians were still being held (even though they had been found not guilty), Parkerson led the way. The end result was the shooting and/or hanging of 11 Italians, including a 14-year-old boy. "Despite the enormous bloodshed, New Orleans newspapers praised the mob action."[65] The 11 Italians who were lynched were not the only ones in the city to suffer. "Some of the lynchers also hurled threats at the Italian consulate and molested other Italians in the city."[66] Numerous newspapers in Louisiana and other areas of the South condoned the lynching, as did Theodore Roosevelt, who at a party with (in his words) "dago diplomats," described the lynching as "a rather good thing."[67]

In March, a grand jury convened to look at the lynching. Their report was released in May. "While the grand jury condemned mob violence in general, it condoned its use in New Orleans."[68] The grand jury refused to indict anyone for the murders, even though it was clear that the names of many who were involved were known. A newspaper description of the lynching in New Orleans stated, "The little jail was crowded with Sicilians, whose low, repulsive countenances, and slavery attire, proclaimed their brutal natures."[69] *Leslies Weekly* determined, "Probably no reasonable, intelligent, and honest person in the United States regrets the death of the eleven Sicilian prisoners in the New Orleans jail, Saturday, March 14th. Whether they were members of the law-defying Mafia or not, they belonged apparently to the lowest criminal classes, and *on general principles deserved*, and no doubt expected, *to meet a violent death*."[70]

The film *Linciati: Lynchings of Italians in America* documents the treatment of Italian immigrants in America at the end of the nineteenth and beginning of the twentieth centuries. While the film focuses on the New Orleans case, it also provides information and statistics on many other lynchings. Heather Hartley, the film's creator, defines lynching as an act carried out by a mob of three or more who attempt by injury or death to prevent legal arrest, detention, trial, or punishment of someone accused of a crime. Lynching is thus a circumvention of due process. The mob that attacked the parish prison in New Orleans and eventually killed 11 Italians went there with the purpose of killing only the six believed to be involved in the case. The 14-year-old boy was to be spared, as were several others, but in the heat of the moment, all 11 were shot or hanged. The two Italians who were dragged outside and hanged were then shot at while they were hanging. One of the dead had 41 gunshot wounds. Once the Italians were dead, the crowd came forward to take souvenirs from the bodies. On the day following the incident, the public was allowed to see the bodies on display.

Following the murders in New Orleans, Henry Cabot Lodge wrote an article entitled "Lynch Law and Unrestricted Immigration." Lodge stated that while Americans are basically law-abiding people, and though on the face of it should deplore the actions of the mob in New Orleans, in this case there was a need to consider the matter more fully. "Such acts as the killing of these eleven Italians do not spring from nothing without reason or provocation."[71] He goes on to say that however terrible lynchings are, not being able to trust a jury or the legal system is infinitely worse. In a statement of egregious falsehood, Lodge said, "The killing of the eleven prisoners had in it no race feeling whatever. There has been no hostility to the Italians in America, as such." He blamed the underlying cause of the incident on "the utter carelessness with which we treat immigration to this country."[72] It is not race based, according to Lodge, but the fault of the classes of immigrants that are allowed into the country. However, he goes on to speak of "races totally alien" to the makeup of the United States that are causing problems: Poles, Bohemians, Hungarians, Russians, and Italians exemplify a deterioration of race. His solution is for "an intelligent and effective restriction of immigration" based on a discriminating selection of those we would allow in, a selection based on country of origin and ability to read and write.

An Italian was lynched in Gunnison, Colorado, in 1890. "In West Virginia, in 1891, rumors that drunken immigrants had slit the throats of an American family led to the lynching of a number of Italians. Two years later, lynchers killed Italians in Denver. In March 1895, a time of labor strife in Walsenberg, a town near the coal fields in southern Colorado, a group of miners slaughtered six Italian laborers who had been implicated in the murder of a saloonkeeper. In the following year, in the small Louisiana town of Hahnville, a mob dragged six Italians from a jail and hanged three of them." In Mississippi, nativists beat up Italian agricultural workers and launched a movement to keep their children out of White schools.[73]

Louis Carrari, 40, was murdered at his home in front of his five children in August 1920 in West Frankfort, Illinois. Pointing to the then current view that Italians were a different race, an article in the *New York Times* about the incident started out, "Race warfare between English and Italian speaking residents broke out afresh today . . ." Carrari was shot three times, and his skull was crushed with a meat cleaver. "The exodus of foreigners started shortly after midnight, following the burning of homes in an Italian suburb." The school, pool hall and clubhouse were also burned in an Italian area. "When the mob invaded the residence district foreigners were dragged out of their homes, beaten with clubs and stoned. Some were taken into the woods, beaten and left on the ground. In some cases shots were fired."[74]

Five Italians, three of whom were brothers, were lynched in Tallulah, Louisiana, in 1899 following a disagreement over a goat. These were the only five Italians living in the town at the time. The dead included not only those directly involved in the confrontation, but friends of theirs as well, and an attempt was made to lynch the brother-in-law who lived in another town altogether. However, he was warned in time to make his escape. While several Black Americans were willing to testify as to those responsible, the court would not take their testimony, and one was murdered. A Black newspaper, describing the many lynchings that took place in 1899, listed "colored," "White," and "Italian" as the three groups lynched.

Dr. Richard Gambino, former director of Italian-American Studies at Queens College, points out that "Hollywood has given an image over the years that Italian-Americans are inferior, physical, anti-intellectual. . . . There is the criminal image of the Italian-American. This is not a healthy basis for a self-image to succeed in life or education."[75] The four Hollywood images he points out—inferiority, physicality, ignorance, and criminality—were all models underlying the descriptive treatment of Italians by early newspaper journalists and others. These same models are still showing up in newspaper articles as well as in popular culture sources such as novels and Hollywood movies.

MEXICANS

What contributed to the management and control of immigrants "making sense" was, I would argue, the way immigrants where characterized in the media's national discourse. Since 1965, the magazines increasingly represented—imagined—immigrants as different, not-assimilated, outside, and morally questionable Others to the community of the nation. Moreover, immigrants also were represented as threats to the nation in a variety of ways: by transgressing the nation's borders and making claims on the nation's sovereign territory, by reproducing and forming communities in the United States, by changing the racial composition of the nation and undermining the political unity of the nation, and by adding to environmental/population pressures.[76]

Leo Chavez, in *Covering Immigration*, looked at how the highly debated issue of immigration was presented in the American print media (specifically in national magazines) between 1965 and 1999, and the relationship between this national coverage and subsequent political decisions. Chavez documented a recurring split between our traditional view of ourselves as a proud nation of immigrants and the divisive nature of trends to limit immigration throughout the past decades. His interest was the "prevailing climate" surrounding the issue of immigration and what this meant for immigration policy. Magazine covers present a particular representation of the immigration debate, and the images chosen frame a particular American identity, culture, and nation.[77]

Chavez began with magazine covers from 1965, when the United States passed immigration reform that finally abolished national quotas. The change in law led to greater numbers of Asian and Latin American immigrants, with fewer arriving from European countries. Chavez examined 76 magazine covers published by 10 different popular magazines between 1965 and 1999. In addition to coding each one as "alarmist" (66 percent), "affirmative" (25 percent) or "neutral" (9 percent), he did an in-depth analysis of the images contained on the covers and their use of symbols to tell a particular story about immigration and immigrants to the American public. "The covers rely on metaphors, tropes, and allusions to grand narratives of the nation to draw on shared, but often taken-for-granted understandings of American identity, history, and characteristics of various immigrant groups."[78] The mid-1970s was the start of a discourse that labeled Mexican immigrants as an external threat to the nation as well as a threat from within.

The magazine covers provide a discourse on who is considered "us" and who is Other; this changes over time as the Others of the past blend in and become part of the accepted fabric of American inclusion. Common images included the Statue of Liberty (either to represent our idea of ourselves as a nation of immigrants or to show the statue in peril due to invading Others), the use of an "infinityline" (an infinite line of immigrants coming from somewhere off the page and made up of a mass of indistinguishable people lacking any individuality), water or flood imagery common to immigration discourse, the U.S. flag (often in peril), borders (again delineating "us" and "them"), and metaphors of war and invasion.

In the 1970s, there was growing concern about the increasing number of immigrants, the decreasing number of European immigrants, language differences, and undocumented or illegal immigration. The 1980s saw increasingly alarmist coverage of immigration, with a growing focus on Latin American immigrants. "Through image and text, immigration from Latin America is associated with destructive tendencies such as ripping, tearing, invading, flooding, displacing, and exploding, which far outweigh its association with any positive productive contributions."[79] In 1986, the Immigration Reform and Control Act was passed in an attempt to decrease undocumented immigration. As Chavez points out, "alarmist covers increased in intensity in the years preceding passage of the 1986 immigration reform law."[80] Following passage of the act, there was a decrease in magazine covers dealing with immigration until the early 1990s, when immigration became a political issue once again. "As the nation entered the 1990s, two issues—multiculturalism and race—dominated public discourse about the implications of immigration for the nation."[81] Association of race with nation and the assumption that White Europeans were and should continue to be the majority appeared in magazines such as the *National Review* (whose cover depicted the Statue of Liberty holding out her hand to stop immigrants with the accompanying words "Try Australia"). "Thus, race, in the guise of the 'face of America,' has emerged as a central issue in the anti-immigration discourse." Race talk is couched in terms of assimilation, acculturation, and concerns with language acquisition rather than biological discourse, but race is still the basis for the discussion.[82]

The 1990s saw concerns with assimilation and ethnic warfare, particularly between Black Americans and incoming immigrants. "Central to the discourse was the way demographic trends were changing America. Images of Whites being squeezed out of the nation by growing numbers of Latinos and Asians were featured prominently on magazine covers."[83] Increasingly alarmist covers appeared in the early 1990s, and in 1994, California tried to pass Proposition 187 to deny health care, education, and other publicly funded assistance to undocumented immigrants.

For Mexican immigration in particular, "the imagery has been overwhelmingly alarmist."[84] Out of 16 covers on the subject, 15 were alarmist and one was neutral. "Alarm is conveyed through images and text that directly or metaphorically invoke crisis, time bomb, loss of control, invasions, danger, floods, and war."[85] The magazines played upon fears of the dilution of "American" culture, the "takeover" of the American southwest by Mexicans, the threat contained in reproduction as Mexican immigrants have children, and fears of job loss to immigrants. The use of maps on magazine covers "articulate a particular view of the world," often creating Mexico as the source of problems for the United States.[86]

Chavez argues that while the covers do not cause policy changes, "... the discourse on invasions, loss of U.S. sovereignty, and Mexican immigrants as the 'enemy,' surely contributed to an atmosphere that helped to justify increased militarization of the border as a way of 'doing something' about these threats to the American way of life."[87] While the national discourse on immigration in general is somewhat balanced, the story of Mexican immigration is one of conflict, disaster, and a corruption of American culture and racial stock by invaders.

"Discourse, as this analysis underscores, does not exist apart from practice. Discourse is a practice that helps produce the common-sense view of the world that legitimizes, affirms, and even rationalizes other practices."[88] Magazines, as Chavez points out, are in the practice of "constructing subjects as citizens," and so the discourse contained on their covers is of importance politically, historically, and socially. We must be more aware of the "commonsense" view of issues such as immigration that are constructed for us by the media and the role of images in forming particular world views. How a particular topic is framed by the media determines to an extent the reality of that topic; defining immigration as a "problem" with a limited range of "solutions" narrows the immigration debate in ways that we must clarify.

Framing

"Framing is at the center of the . . . immigration debate," and the "immigrant as illegal" is the most commonly used frame. Language has an essential role in framing an issue and determining what appropriate solutions might be. Defining immigrants as criminals dehumanizes those thus labeled and points to a legal/punitive solution such as deportation and increased security along the U.S.-Mexico border. Lakoff and Ferguson argue against the seemingly logical progression from illegal immigrant to the need for border security to the war on terror, stating the illogic of equating immigrants who come to America to fulfill the American dream with those who come to destroy it. "It is this understanding of the issue that also prompted the House to pass the punitive HR 4437, which includes a provision to make assisting illegal immigrants while they are here a felony. It is seen as aiding and abetting a criminal." These authors propose an alternative frame for the immigrant issue of "economic refugee," which might then result in compassion as a response.[89]

Knoll and Redlawsk surveyed Iowa votes during the 2008 Iowa caucus campaign to see what effect, if any, different framing had on immigration policy preferences. This election featured candidacies by Tom Tancredo and Fred Thompson, both of whom centered their campaigns on the immigration issue and ". . . tried to out-do each other with their focus on border security and taking a hard line with the illegal immigrants already in the country."[90] Voters' perceptions are conditioned by issue framing in the media and by politicians. The authors found a decrease in support for conditional citizenship for immigrants when the label "Mexican" was inserted in the survey. They also found that "[w]hen we classify immigrants as 'Mexican,' voters are more punitive in their policy preferences than when ethnicity is unspecified."[91]

Brader, Valentino, and Suhay looked at how and whether elite discourse on immigration shapes public opinion and action on immigration policy. "Public debates about immigration, like those in other domains, often suggest the interests, values, or lifestyles of citizens are in harm's way. Elite discourse tends to emphasize adverse consequences for jobs, taxes, crime, schools, cultural norms, or social harmony."[92] They found that news about the purported costs of immigration increased White opposition to immigration far more when Latino immigrants were featured as opposed to European immigrants; ". . . group cues and the emotions they triggered proved critical to changing attitudes and behavior. Citizens *felt* more threatened by Latino immigration, not European immigration, and this feeling triggered opposition to immigration and multilingual laws, prompted requests for information, and led people to send anti-immigration messages to Congress."[93] The researchers demonstrated the impact of anxiety on actual behavior, which has implications for public debates over important policy issues; if rhetoric containing religious, racial and/or ethnic cues can trigger negative emotional responses, elite discourse needs to be carefully examined and decoded.

Citrin and colleagues looked at the effects of economic factors on public opinion toward immigration policy and discovered that while personal economic circumstances play only a small role in forming opinions, beliefs about the state of the national economy, concerns over taxes, and general feelings about Hispanics and Asians are "significant determinants of restrictionist sentiment." [94] Negative assessments about the economic and social costs of immigration are consistently related to opinions favoring restrictions on immigration. "Whatever their conceptual status, beliefs about the economic consequences of immigration have political ramifications when they serve as legitimating arguments for restrictionist policies in a culture that discourages open expressions of nativism or xenophobia."[95]

The Luntz Research and Strategic Services, a public opinion company, provides language for politicians to use when talking about immigration. The company recognizes the importance of linguistic choices when presenting this issue to voters. "Linguistically, as you enter the debate, there are four key themes that must represent the core of your message: prevention, protection, accountability and compassion."[96] Geared toward Republicans and moderate Democrats, Luntz focuses on "the problems created by illegal immigrants already here" while preventing others from coming. Rhetoric suggested includes the issue of English as *the* first language. For example, "We resent the fact that we have to pay to educate illegal immigrants, but what makes us angrier is to educate them in a foreign language."[97] Stress is placed on the word "illegal," on chaos, on "playing by the rules," and the "flood" of "illegal immigrants" coming to the country. Another focus point is immigrants' overuse of "our" systems: schools, hospitals, streets, and highways so that "we" don't have access. "Right now, hundreds of illegal immigrants are crossing the border almost every day. Some of them are part of drug cartels. Some are career criminals. Some may even be terrorists."[98] Luntz thus is providing politicians with unfounded statements that tie immigration to terrorism.

Metaphors and Stereotypes

Using two significant events in immigration news as their focus dates, researchers analyzed mainstream U.S. print news articles for their metaphors regarding immigrants. The two events, the May Day marches (a series of public protests against proposed changes in immigration policy in 2006) and the signing of the Secure Fence Act by President Bush in October 2006, both resulted in numerous articles on immigrants and immigration. These authors compared what they found in 2006 to the metaphors from the 1990s when the dominant metaphor was the "immigrant as animal," including descriptions of hunting, catching, attacking, and eating.[99] "In the 1990's, depictions of immigrants were not limited solely to animals, but as soldiers or invaders of the land, as *weeds* that infest the land, as *burdens* on society, and as *diseases* infecting the body politic. Indeed, all predominant and secondary metaphors of 1990 mass media language disparaged immigrants."[100] The authors point out that the metaphors of the 1990s were used both by opponents and supporters of Proposition 187, leaving no other discourse available to the public through which to create the immigrant. Proposition 187 included a section prohibiting undocumented immigrants from using public health care and education as well as other social services in California.

In the first group of newspapers reviewed (May 2006), these authors found the "immigrant as criminal" to have replaced the "immigrant as animal" as the predominant metaphor. "Illegal immigrant" is the term most often found both in the print media and in many government documents. The press often blurs the distinction between the misdemeanor offense of entering the country without proper paperwork and more serious felonies.[101] Other common metaphors from the May 2006 analysis included the typical use of water terms ("flood," "pouring," "flow"), the "immigrant as object" to be imported or thrown out, the "immigrant as burden," and the "immigrant as alien." In contrast, more humanizing metaphors were also found with the use of the frames of "undocumented," "human," "worker," and "contributor." By October 2006, however, the print media was again moving away from a "rough balance of human and traditional representations of immigrant issues," to the former primarily pejorative view.

Immigrants are portrayed as stubborn weeds or mounting levels of trash that must be cleaned up, or as a costly illness that damages the economic health and cultural dominance of the nation. Immigrants are described as forces that can wipe out entire communities and the traditional American lifestyle, or as potential terrorists and criminals seeking only to harm the nation. Given these descriptions, the only solution appears to be to build a fence, hire more border patrol agents, and build more detention centers.[102]

The use of these embedded stereotypes continues to marginalize Mexican immigrants as foreigners on American soil, as Other. Both the external (non–group member perceptions) and internal (how immigrants understand themselves and their place in American society) effects are negative. Differences are often seen to denote inferiority, and these include accent, language spoken, language abilities, and appearance. "Recent manifestations of the foreigner label is [*sic*] evidenced by the English only movement. This movement is championed by an organization called U.S. English, whose goal is to establish English as this nation's official language."[103] Speaking English is equated with assimilation and loyalty to the United States. "Other characterizations of the outsider or foreigner have also had the external effect of justifying individual and institutionalized violence."[104]

Nativism

Racism and nativism, while distinct phenomenon, often go hand in hand. Updating the three major antiforeign traditions that John Higham delineated in *Strangers in the Land*, George Sanchez points to "an extreme antipathy towards non-English languages and a fear that linguistic difference will undermine the American nation" as one of these three newer traditions. The second fear is that racialized immigrants are now privileged above Whites due to affirmative action programs and support for multiculturalism. This fear is tied to the belief that immigrants who do not assimilate into American culture remain a separate and threatening Other while using resources that "should" belong to native born Americans. Sanchez's third antiforeign sentiment is the belief that immigrants come here to feed off of the American welfare, education, and health care systems while contributing nothing to American society, the "drain on public resources" argument put forth by many nativists who ignore evidence that many immigrant groups actually underutilize government assistance.[105]

Alvarez and Butterfield argue that support for Proposition 187 in California was an example of cyclical nativism fueled by California's economic depression in the early 1990s. They also cite the role played by the politicization of the issue of illegal immigration in the gubernatorial and senatorial elections. The authors delineate three previous periods of increased nativism against both legal and illegal Mexican immigrants that "have coincided with economic downturns brought about by wars and stagflation and have resulted in stricter immigration laws." In the 1994 California election, candidates such as Pete Wilson "blamed California's poor economic conditions on the presence of illegal immigrants, particularly illegal Mexican immigrants, thereby framing the issue of immigration in nativist terms."[106] The authors found that rather than party identification in the election, it was each voter's choice of governor that was significant in determining his or her support for Proposition 187, demonstrating that the campaign rhetoric of the chosen candidate played an important role in views on immigration. "Governor Wilson was reelected during bad economic times by focusing his campaign on illegal immigrants and blaming them for the state's precarious financial situation, shifting the election from a referendum on the incumbent to immigration."[107]

Sanchez points to Wilson's political career as he went from supporting the easing of immigration restrictions to an adamantly anti-immigrant position that helped propel him to a political comeback. "Pete Wilson's ill-fated presidential campaign in 1995–96 cannot obscure the fact that his career remains the epitome of opportunistic politics, taking full advantage of America's long-standing fears of immigrants and foreigners when such a strategy can bring success at the polls."[108]

Anti-Immigrant Groups and Rhetoric

There has been an increase in the past three decades of nativistic, anti-immigrant groups that have played significant roles during elections, and many of these anti-immigrant groups have clear ties to racist organizations. "In the eyes of most of these groups, immigrants (typically, non-White immigrants) are responsible for nearly all the country's ills, from poverty and inner city decay to crime, urban sprawl and environmental degradation."[109] Among these groups are the American Immigration Control Foundation (founded in 1983 and headed by John Vinson, a founding member of the White supremacist League of the South); the California Coalition for Immigration Reform (founded in 1994 and headed by Barbara Coe, who refers to Mexican immigrants as "savages" and was a co-sponsor of Proposition 187); the Federation for American Immigration Reform, or FAIR (founded in 1978 by John Tanton, who is a leading voice in anti-immigrant rhetoric as well as the English-only movement); the National Organization for European American Rights (founded in 2000 by David Duke, formerly of the KKK); and NumbersUSA, which is categorized by the Southern Poverty Law Center as the most reasoned of the anti-immigrant groups.

Anti-immigrant commentary from high-profile national media personalities such as Lou Dobbs also contribute to the national discourse on immigration. Dobbs has linked undocumented immigrants to diseases such as tuberculosis, malaria, and leprosy; calls them an invasion; and states categorically that "illegal aliens are criminals."[110] He hosted a debate on immigration in Hazleton, Pennsylvania, in April 2007. Hazleton had passed the Illegal Immigrant Relief Act, which suspended business licenses of employers who hired or landlords who rented to undocumented people. Three months later, Luis Ramirez was murdered in nearby Shenandoah because he was Mexican. His murderers were teenagers who punched him, knocked him down, and kicked him repeatedly in the head while telling him and his "fucking Mexican friends" to move out of Shenandoah and go back to Mexico. In an article written for the *New York Times*, Sean Hamill notes, "Many people believe the debate fueled by Hazleton's actions helped create the environment that led to Mr. Ramirez's death."[111] Derrick Donchak and Brandon Piekarsky, two of those accused of Ramirez's death, were found not guilty at their trial in state court. However, they were subsequently charged with federal hate crimes under the Federal Housing Act, and in 2010, the federal jury found them guilty and sentenced them to nine years in prison.

"After the beating, Mr. Walsh [Colin Walsh, a co-defendant] said Mr. Piekarsky joked with his friends about getting a Hispanic name tattooed on their bodies, and they hatched a story they would tell police, one that would exclude any references to racial slurs being uttered that night or kicking [Ramirez]."[112] Donchak and three police officers from Shenandoah were charged with covering up the crime. One of the three officers was acquitted, but the other two were convicted of filing a false police report (Matthew Nestor) and lying to the FBI (William Moyer).

Policies

In August 2011, the Department of Homeland Security, under Secretary Janet Napolitano, announced that it would review the 300,000 pending deportation cases in federal immigration courts to give priority only to those cases in which undocumented immigrants had committed serious crimes or posed a danger to the public. Those not posing a risk would be allowed to apply for a work permit. This attempt to spend limited resources on the most serious cases met with applause by some and concern by others (e.g., politicians who see it as a means of moving toward amnesty for undocumented immigrants). President Obama, in June 2012, also called for an immediate end to deportation for undocumented immigrants under 30 who were brought to the United States before they were 16. These immigrants, provided they are in school or have a high school or equivalent degree and are law abiding, can apply for a two-year work permit. A report from the Immigration Policy Center in August 2011 states that while fewer Mexicans are entering the United States, fewer are also leaving. Three-fifths of unauthorized immigrants in the United States have been here for more than a decade. "In other words, Mexican immigrants are staying and they are becoming more and more integrated into U.S. society."[113]

Mary Romero looked at the use of racial profiling in immigrant law enforcement and the function that immigration raids serve to maintain a subordinate status for working-class Latino citizens and immigrants. Latinos are targeted by their skin color, accents, and choice of language in addition to geographic areas where large populations live and shop. Romero found that Latinos were "demeaned, humiliated and embarrassed" during immigration raids and enforcement, creating an atmosphere of tension, fear, and distrust of law enforcement agents. Additionally, the timing of these raids coincided with the needs of the employers. ". . . [T]he INS rarely raided the fields during harvest time and scheduled massive immigration roundups during periods of economic recession and union activity."[114] She cites the 1975 Supreme Court decision that "Mexican appearance" was a legitimate consideration under the Fourth Amendment for making an immigration-related stop.[115]

The Chandler Roundup was an immigration raid that took place in 1997 in Chandler, Arizona (the use of the term "roundup" reinforces old cowboy images and the notion that Mexicans are strays in need of rounding up and moving on). During a five-day period, 432 Mexicans suspected of having undocumented status were arrested. Areas where arrests took place included public shopping places, street corners, and trailer parks. There were public encounters as well as raids on private homes. Romero identified five patterns of immigration law enforcement that created harm for Mexican Americans: discretionary stops based on ethnicity and class; use of intimidation to subordinate and demean those stopped; the reinforcing of Mexicans as "alien," "inferior," and "criminal"; restriction of movement only for Mexicans; and "limited access to fair and impartial treatment before the law."[116]

Two investigations occurred after the Chandler raids, one by the state attorney general's office and the other by an independent investigation paid for by the city of Chandler, which produced a three-volume report. The independent report "privileges the INS and police's documentation of a growing immigration problem and presents the 'roundup' as the official response," while the state attorney general's report, with supporting documents, presents the issue of immigration from the community's perspective.[117] The independent report minimized civil rights violations and included only violations that were corroborated by police officers. It contained terms such as "hordes" and "streams" to categorize immigrant movement into the area, and rather than including the history of the area (which once belonged to Mexico), restricted Mexican presence to "immigrants," "laborers," and "criminals," thereby "making American citizens of Mexican ancestry invisible."[118]

In 2010, Arizona's governor, Jan Brewer, signed a strict immigration bill (SB 1070) into law. The new law made it a crime to be in the country illegally, made failure to carry immigration documents a crime, and allowed police broad power to detain and question anyone they believed might be here illegally. In addition, it provided penalties for those hiring, sheltering, or transporting unregistered immigrants. An injunction was placed on the law due to concerns with its constitutionality. In 2012, the U.S. Supreme Court, in *Arizona vs. United States*, upheld the provision that required police to do status checks during law enforcement stops but struck down three other provisions.

Maricopa County

In May 2012, the U.S. Department of Justice filed a civil lawsuit against Sheriff Joseph Arpaio, the Maricopa County Sheriff's Office (MCSO), and Maricopa County, Arizona. The suit followed several years of complaints, investigation, and a failure on the part of the MCSO to resolve blatant and continuing discrimination against Latinos. The MCSO and Arpaio have fostered a "culture of disregard for Latinos that starts at the top and pervades the organization."[119] This culture includes use of derogatory terms, unconstitutional law enforcement practices, discriminatory practices in jail settings targeting those who do not speak English, and illegal retaliation against critics that subjects "them to baseless criminal actions, unfounded civil lawsuits, or meritless administrative actions."[120] The MCSO refused to cooperate voluntarily, and the civil suit was the Department of Justice's response. Arpaio has played a significant role in immigration politics as Republican candidates sought his backing; he was courted by Bachmann, Perry (whom he endorsed), Romney, and Cain in their 2012 bids for the presidency. Arpaio has become "a potent symbol of the antipathy many Americans feel about illegal immigration."[121]

The sheriff's office targets Latino drivers with blatant racial profiling and fails to investigate sexual abuse cases in the Latino community. "The Sheriff's office has acknowledged that 432 cases of sexual assault and child molestation were not properly investigated over a three-year period ending in 2007."[122] The U.S. Department of Justice, Civil Rights Division, sent a letter to the MCSO on December 15, 2011. Its findings included unlawful stops and arrests of Latinos; punishment of Latino inmates who do not understand commands in English, often resulting in a denial of critical services (such as serving as trustees and having access to early release programs); "a chronic culture of disregard for basic legal and constitutional obligations"; the use of excessive force against Latinos; and the use of racial slurs both in English and Spanish.[123] "Our investigation also found that MCSO detention officers call Latinos 'wetbacks,' 'Mexican bitches,' 'fucking Mexicans,' and 'stupid Mexicans' when either talking among themselves or addressing Latino inmates."[124]

Latino drivers were found to be four to nine times more likely to be stopped than non-Latinos and the victims of Fourth Amendment violations against unreasonable seizures. Stops were routinely based on appearance, including skin color, and Spanish language use rather than any evidence of illegal behavior. "Overall, the [legal] expert [hired to review the situation] concluded that this case involves the most egregious racial profiling in the United States that he has ever personally seen in the course of his work, observed in litigation, or reviewed in professional literature."[125] The MCSO correlates all Latino, Spanish-speaking people with undocumented people. The Department of Justice noted that the MCSO's focus on immigration enforcement has compromised the safety and security of county residents, as violent crime rates have increased significantly; in a three-year period, there was a 166 percent increase in homicides.[126] "Sheriff Arpaio's own actions have helped nurture MCSO's culture of bias." He has frequently distributed racially charged constituent letters that include "crude, ethnically derogatory language about Latinos."[127]

In February 2009, a Latino citizen was stopped, allegedly for a failed brake light. When the man exited his car, "the MCSO deputy purposefully struck [him] with his patrol car, pinning [him] under the vehicle and dragging him for more than ten feet." The deputy did not remove the man and instructed other deputies arriving at the scene to leave him there. He was eventually extracted by the fire department. "The deputy's actions caused serious injury, including broken bones, burns, and other injuries."[128] A lawsuit against the deputy and the MCSO was eventually settled for $600,000. The deputy was charged with aggravated assault. In May of the same year, another Latino citizen was pulled over, allegedly for speeding. Several deputies pulled him from his car, "twisting his arm, head, and neck and causing [him] to fall and hit his face on the pavement." He ended up at a medical facility, where he was treated for face, neck, shoulder, and back injuries. The man "was never charged with any offense that might explain the officers' use of force." While he was initially charged with speeding and failure to produce identification, both charges were dropped.[129] The Department of Justice required the MCSO to correct the issues within 60 days. The MCSO refused to accept an outside independent monitor, and therefore, the Department of Justice filed a civil suit. While we do not classify these police actions as hate crimes, they would be marked as such if committed by a regular citizen, as the victims were targeted on the basis of their ethnicity.

Lynching

"For decades lynch mobs terrorized persons of Mexican origin or descent without reprisal from the wider community."[130] Mexicans have typically been left out of discussions of lynch mob violence in U.S. history, but a significant number of Mexicans (at least 597) were lynched during the nineteenth and early twentieth centuries. Carrigan and Webb provide the first systematic analysis of Mexican lynching victims. They focus on lynching as a "retributive act of murder for which those responsible claim to be serving the interests of justice, tradition, or community good." They believe that the statistics put forth in their article are a conservative estimate of the actual number of Mexican lynch mob victims. The total number of Mexicans lynched was fewer than Black Americans lynched, but due to the smaller Mexican population, "the chance of being murdered by a mob was comparable for both Mexicans and African Americans."[131] The four states with the greatest number of lynchings of Mexicans were Texas, California, Arizona, and New Mexico.

While vigilantes were believed to serve a purpose in many frontier areas that lacked formal legal structures, the majority of Mexicans put to death by lynch mobs were killed in areas with already existing systems. "The lynching of Mexicans not only occurred in areas where there was a fully operating legal system but often involved the active collusion of law officers themselves." In fact, most were executed by mobs that denied them even the semblance of a trial, as these mobs acted less out of a real interest in legal justice than "an irrational prejudice towards racial minorities."[132] Mexicans were taken from jails and courtrooms, and hanged or shot. The Texas Rangers were guilty of the most systematic abuse of legal authority. "Their brutal repression of the Mexican population was tantamount to state-sanctioned terrorism."[133]

Lower-class Mexicans, who were the primary targets of White vigilantes, were considered racially inferior as well as innately criminal. These stereotypes provided the "pretext for acts of repressive violence." Carrigan and Webb go on to state that "[t]he primacy of racial prejudice is underlined by the acts of ritualized torture and sadism that accompanied the lynching of Mexicans."[134] A significant number of victims suffered some type of physical mutilation, including burning and shooting bodies after hanging. There were many multiple lynchings as well. "Accusations of criminal misconduct by an individual Mexican resulted in indiscriminate acts of retribution. The identity of the victim was therefore of less consequence than the symbolic message contained in the mob's violent reassertion of Anglo sovereignty."[135] In July 1877, as many as 40 Mexicans were randomly killed as the result of the murder of one Anglo. The authors point out that the alleged crimes of Mexican lynching victims ranged from murder, theft, and robbery to categories such as being of Mexican descent (10 victims), witchcraft (3 victims), courting a White woman (2 victims), being a successful cartman (1 victim), and refusing to play the fiddle (1 victim).

Historical events also contributed to increased mob violence against Mexicans. The decades of unrest and conflict along the U.S.-Mexico border were periods of increased violence on both sides. Lynching was also tacitly and sometimes openly supported by the mainstream press and by politicians. "In 1881, the Mexican Ambassador reported to Secretary of State James Blaine the lynching of an alleged horse thief in Willcox, Arizona. Although Blaine conceded that the man was hanged illegally, he also observed that he and his accomplice 'were probably outlaws' and that he therefore deserved his fate."[136]

Removal of Those of Mexican Ancestry

Approximately 1 million people of Mexican ancestry, close to 60 percent of whom were U.S. citizens, were forcibly removed from the United States during the Great Depression in the 1930s. These families were removed from California, Michigan, Colorado, Texas, Illinois, Ohio, and New York. "The people rounded up were often herded onto trains and buses or driven by social workers to the border. This was true for citizens by birth and those who had lawfully naturalized to become citizens."[137] Citing the "bedrock principle" of U.S. immigration law that supposedly protects U.S. citizens from deportation, Johnson goes on to say that this "ethnic cleansing" destroyed lives, as families were torn apart and Mexican American and Mexican communities in the United States were terrorized. In addition to the immediate consequences for many, the long-range effects included strong pressure on the Latino community to assimilate into American culture as quickly as possible, leaving behind native language and traditions. "The California legislature passed a bill that would have created a commission to historically document the events of the repatriation; Governor Schwarzenegger, however, vetoed the law."[138]

Zoot Suit Riots

In 1943, during World War II, riots broke out in Los Angeles between White navy and marine corps members and Latino youth over the wearing of zoot suits. The zoot suit "uniform" consisted of "a flamboyant long coat, with baggy pegged pants, a pork pie hat, a long key chain, and shoes with thick soles."[139] The Los Angeles riots led to riots in other cities such as Chicago, San Diego, Philadelphia, and New York. The Los Angeles press ran numerous articles on Mexican American youths and the "Pachuco" subculture, characterizing them as baby gangsters and hoodlums. The Pachuco subculture was made up of Mexican American youth rebelling against their parents' values through music, language, and dress. Although Mexican Americans were overrepresented in the military, and many of those attacked in the riots were too young to serve, White military men resented the dress and attitude of the young Latinos and took it upon themselves over the course of several weeks to beat and strip any Latinos they found wearing zoot suits. This expanded to include those who were not wearing them but were identifiable as Mexican American. The press was at least partially responsible for fostering the negative atmosphere that led to the riots and during the riots placed the blame on the Latinos. An article in the *Los Angeles Times* stated, "Juvenile files repeatedly show that a language variance in the home—where the parents speak no English and cling to past culture—is a serious factor of delinquency. Parents in such homes lack control over their offspring."[140]

Young men were dragged out of movie theaters and other public places, stripped of their suits (which were then burned), beaten, and in some cases urinated on. The Los Angeles Police Department turned a blind eye to the perpetrators and primarily arrested the young Latinos for disturbing the peace, vagrancy, and rioting. The newspapers supported the attacks, seeing them as a "cleanup" of gangs in Los Angeles, and included one-sided reporting of the events, listing only the injuries to the sailors and marines. Police rounded up Latino youths on suspicion of inciting to riot, but not the servicemen or the civilians who actually started the trouble. The summary in *La Opinion*, a Spanish language newspaper, painted a completely different picture of events. "Since last Thursday evening various groups of marines and soldiers have attacked Mexican zoot suiters throughout the city of Los Angeles. Although the youth did nothing to provoke the attack or for that matter to resist the attack, many were severely wounded."[141]

The mayor of Los Angeles insisted that there was no racial discrimination involved in the attacks. "Navy men emphasize, and police agree, that in most instances the sailors, aided in a few cases by soldiers, and sometime by taxicab drivers, showed a spirit as of a college fraternity initiation."[142] It was hardly an initiation into a sought-after fraternity since the victims were scorned, considered inherently inferior, and never invited to become "one of us." The police practice was to accompany the caravans in their cars, watch the beatings, and then jail the victims. "At one point, the servicemen hired taxicabs and drove through the Mexican barrio stripping and beating youths at random. They were followed by the police who arrested the Pachucos for public disturbance. The riots lasted more than ten days and resulted in beatings of hundreds of Mexican youth."[143]

The riots were "motivated by wartime frustrations and racial stereotyping against Mexican-American youth. Soon after the event, analysts recognized that systematic discrimination in education, employment, housing, and social services were the root causes of this violence and that the news media, police, and local, state, and federal government officials were responsible for fueling an anti-Mexican atmosphere."[144]

Recent Hate Crime Trends and Incidents

In 2003, Latinos were targeted in 45 percent of hate crimes based on ethnic bias or nationality. By 2012, this number had risen to 59.4 percent. The Leadership Conference on Civil Rights, in a 2009 report, linked a significant rise in hate crimes against Latinos with the pervasive anti-immigrant rhetoric in the media. Coupled with political rhetoric and the increased presence of anti-immigrant hate groups on the Internet, the climate surrounding the immigration debate has been increasingly negative.[145] The surge includes the death of Juan Varela in Arizona in May 2010 while Arizona's immigration law, SB 1070, was being hotly debated in the media. This second-generation American was shot to death in Phoenix by his White neighbor, Gary Thomas Kelly, who shouted: "Hurry up and go back to Mexico, or you're going to die." Kelly then shot Varela in the neck, killing him. Many believe that tensions over the immigration bill helped fuel the incident. "Varela was killed during a week marked by protests and announcements that U.S. cities would boycott Arizona as a result of its new immigration law, Senate Bill 1070."[146] Kelly was convicted of second-degree murder and sentenced to 27.5 years in prison.

Stacey and colleagues looked at the relationship between recent trends in Hispanic immigration and an increase in hate crimes targeting Hispanics. In their background discussion, they point out that these trends have coincided with increased public and political debate over immigration policies in general. Policies such as Senate Bill 1070 in Arizona, coupled with increasingly virulent anti-immigration rhetoric from politicians, talk show hosts, and others "perpetuate an immigrant-as-threat narrative" that depicts recent immigrants as economic, cultural, and national security threats.[147] Since immigrants as a group are not protected under hate crime law, Stacey and colleagues' research focused specifically on hate crimes against Hispanics. One goal of this research was to separate beliefs about immigrants and crime from realities. "The public perception, often sustained by the media, is that immigrants, particularly those who are undocumented, are in large part responsible for crime rate increases."[148] According to these authors, research for the most part suggests just the opposite.

"Importantly, anti-immigrant sentiment fueled by changing patterns of immigration also may put non-immigrant Hispanics at risk of being victimized by hate crime. The fear surrounding immigration and its impact on communities is not necessarily focused solely on foreignness but also contains a strong racial and ethnic component."[149] Just as "Asian" or "Arab/Muslim-looking" labels suffice to broaden hate crimes against a particular group, the notion that any Hispanic can stand in for an "illegal immigrant" as the focus of hate regardless of actual status expands the group to include American citizens of Hispanic background or those perceived as such.

Echoing earlier studies that found a relationship between demographic change and hate crime rates (an influx of minority group members is related to increases in racially motivated hate crime), these authors found that there are "higher levels of anti-Hispanic hate crime in periods and places with higher levels of Hispanic immigration."[150] They did not find evidence that anti-Hispanic hate crime was triggered by economic reasons. "Taken together, these results suggest that anti-Hispanic hate crime is a consequence of Hispanic immigration, and arguably the fear and anger it produces in segments of the majority population . . ."[151] In addition, "Prior research has shown that public views of immigration are shaped more by perceived cultural threats, especially to English language dominance, than by economic position or outlook, political ideology, or even fear of crime."[152] While there are numerous factors involved in the rise of hate crime, this research demonstrates that perceptions about cultural differences of and perceived threats from newcomers are important factors to consider in an attempt to reduce hate-based offenses. The sources of these perceptions include the media, politicians, and hate groups.

Since immigration is often coupled with crime in public rhetoric, Lee and fellow researchers looked at homicide rates in three border cities to determine whether immigration increases homicide rates. In the three cities studied (Miami, El Paso, and San Diego), they found that "immigration generally does not increase levels of homicide among Latinos and African Americans."[153] Even though studies of immigrants from Europe in the early part of the twentieth century tended to show less involvement in crime than by those born in America, "the stereotype of the criminal immigrant has persisted."[154] Updating those early studies to include the large numbers of Latino immigrants after 1965, these authors argue that while statistics show lesser degrees of involvement in crime, stereotypes rampant in political rhetoric and the media "provide ideological support for restrictive immigrant legislation" such as California's Proposition 187.

There exists a schism between beliefs and sociological theories regarding immigrants and crime, and the reality that immigration can actually lead to more stable cities is not part of the national dialogue. While many push the notion that immigrants will bring high levels of crime to the United States, a growing body of research suggests just the opposite.

CONCLUSION

There are many similarities in the public discourse surrounding immigration by the three groups discussed in this chapter. The Chinese, Italians, and Mexicans have all been created as Other as they have arrived in America. This Otherness has been coupled with racism. Economic fears, such as displacement in the workforce, have contributed to the reception these groups found when they arrived in the United States, but underlying that has always been a strain of racist nativism. This is found today with other groups, such as the Hmong and Somalis, who have faced similar prejudice when they arrived in the United States.

The metaphors we have used historically to describe immigration have been consistent. Water metaphors such as "flooding" or "waves" remain common, and the idea of new immigrants "drowning out" an "American" way of life continues today. Other common metaphors have likened immigrants to animals, insects, and diseases. All these constitute the immigrant as a problem and an uncontrollable threat to America. Concerns with the ability of new immigrants to assimilate into American society continue today as well, although past concerns regarding assimilation have proven wrong time and again. Immigrant Others are repeatedly constructed in such as way as to be "too different" in terms of culture, language, and customs to fit within the mainstream of America. This has given rise to both legal and extralegal responses. We have passed laws limiting some groups, excluding others, and welcoming only those we consider "like us." Violent responses have contained and terrorized those who made it to our shores. As with wartime enemies, immigrants have been framed as a threat to an American way of life and have been created in the same dehumanized way as external enemies. Violence and hate show each group the spaces available to it and where it may not go both figuratively and literally. The idea that those at the bottom deserve to meet a violent death due to their imagined character appears throughout American history.

Creating immigrant groups as criminals is not new, although in the past, this may not have been on the scale we see today. Italians were created as criminals when they arrived during the nineteenth and early twentieth centuries. Today, Mexican immigrants are labeled "illegal" in the popular discourse. These frames serve to problematize immigrants and create them as a threat, and this threat is often the basis for hate crimes committed against them. This creation ignores the hate imbedded in the system in places like Maricopa County, where complete disregard for the law and constitutional rights results in great harms to immigrants and American citizens alike.

NOTES

1. John Higham, *Strangers in the Land: Patterns of American Nativism, 1860–1925* (New York: Atheneum, 1978), 4.

2. Ibid., 142.

3. Ibid., 137.

4. Elmer Clarence Sandmeyer, *The Anti-Chinese Movement in California* (Chicago: University of Illinois Press, 1991), *11*.

5. Stuart Miller, *The Unwelcome Immigrant: The American Image of the Chinese, 1785–1882* (Berkeley: University of California Press, 1969), 36.

6. Ibid., 60.

7. Ibid., 53.

8. Ibid., 77.

9. Miller, *Unwelcome Immigrant*, 93.

10. Ibid., 166.

11. Sandmeyer, *Anti-Chinese Movement in California*, 38.

12. Ibid., 41.

13. Jean Pfaelzer, *Driven Out: The Forgotten War against Chinese Americans* (New York: Random House, 2007), 31.

14. Sandmeyer, *Anti-Chinese Movement in California*, 45.

15. Ibid., 58.

16. John Soennichsen, *The Chinese Exclusion Act of 1882* (Santa Barbara, CA: Greenwood, 2011), 127.

17. Sandmeyer, *Anti-Chinese Movement in California*, 59.

18. Ibid., 98.

19. Soennichsen, *Chinese Exclusion Act of 1882*, 128.

20. Pfaelzer, *Driven Out*, xxvii.

21. Ibid., 47.

22. Ibid., 54.

23. Ibid., 125.

24. Ibid., 133.

25. Ibid., 165.

26. Erin L. Murphy, " 'Prelude to imperialism': Whiteness and Chinese exclusion in the reimagining of the United States," *Journal of Historical Sociology* 18, no. 4 (December 2005): 462.

27. Ibid., 460.

28. Ibid., 483.

29. Helen H. Jun, "Black Orientalism: Nineteenth-century narratives of race and U.S. citizenship," *American Quarterly*, 2006, 1052.

30. Ibid., 1054.

31. Ibid., 1059.

32. Ibid., 1061.

33. Miller, *Unwelcome Immigrant*, 201.

34. Alexander DeConde, *Half Bitter, Half Sweet: An Excursion into Italian American History* (New York: Scribner, 1971), 22, 33.

35. "The races that go into the American melting pot," *New York Times*, May 21, 1911, 2.

36. Salvatore J. LaGumina, *WOP! A Documentary History of Anti-Italian Discrimination* (Toronto: Guernica, 1999), 341.

37. Ibid., 135.

38. Ibid., 189–196.

39. Frank Marshall White, "Fostering foreign criminals," *Harper's Weekly*, May 8, 1909, 7.

40. LaGumina, *WOP*, 87.

41. Ibid., 67-8.

42. Joseph P. Cosco, *Imagining Italians: The Clash of Romance and Race in American Perceptions, 1880–1910* (Albany: State University of New York Press, 2003), 17.

43. Prescott Hall, "The Future of American Ideals," *North American Review*, January 1912, 95. http://www.unz.org/Pub/NorthAmericanRev-1912jan-00094.

44. Ibid., 98.

45. Ibid., 99.

46. Cosco, *Imagining Italians*, 16.

47. Ibid., 155.

48. Higham, *Strangers in the Land*, 169.

49. Jennifer Guglielmo and Salvatore Salerno (eds.), *Are Italians White? How Race Is Made in America* (New York: Routledge, 2003), 4.

50. Ibid., 11.

51. William J. Connell and Fred Gardaphe (eds.), *Anti-Italianism: Essays on a Prejudice* (New York: Palgrave Macmillan, 2010), 27.

52. Guglielmo and Salerno, *Are Italians White?*, 56.

53. George Cunningham, "The Italian: A hindrance to White solidarity in Louisiana, 1890–98," *Journal of Negro History* 50 (January 1965): 24.

54. Guglielmo and Salerno, *Are Italians White?*, 61.

55. Cunningham, "The Italian," 34.

56. Ibid.

57. Ibid., 36.

58. Connell and Gardaphe, *Anti-Italianism*, 1.

59. Ibid., 4.

60. Toni Morrison, "On the backs of Blacks," *Time*, Fall 1993, 57–58.

61. DeConde, 102.

62. Connell and Gardaphe, 25.

63. Barbara Botein, "The Hennessy case: An episode in American ,nativism, 1890," *Louisiana History: The Journal of the Louisiana Historical Association* 20, no. 3 (Summer 1979): 265.

64. Ibid., 269.

65. Ibid., 272.

66. DeConde, 122.

67. Cristogianni Borsella, *On Persecution, Identity & Action: Aspects of the Italian-American Experience from the Late 19th Century to Today* (Boston: Dante University Press, 2005), 239.

68. Botein, "Hennessy case," 275.

69. LaGumina, 73.

70. Ibid., 84. Emphasis added.

71. Henry Cabot Lodge, "Lynch law and unrestricted immigration," *North American Review* 152, no. 414 (May 1891): 602. http://www.jstor.org/stable/25102181.

72. Ibid., 604.

73. DeConde, 125.

74. LaGumina, 201.

75. Felicia Lee, "At youth's wake, grief, anger and talk of racism," *New York Times*, September 30, 1989, B4.

76. Leo R. Chavez, *Covering Immigration: Popular Images and the Politics of the Nation* (Berkeley: University of California Press, 2001), 301.

77. Ibid., 4.

78. Ibid., 16.

79. Ibid., 103.

80. Ibid., 127.

81. Ibid., 136.

82. Ibid., 214.

83. Ibid., 173.

84. Ibid., 215.

85. Ibid., 216.

86. Ibid., 245.

87. Ibid, 253.

88. Ibid, 302.

89. George Lakoff and Sam Ferguson, "The framing of immigration," Rockridge Institute, 2006. http://academic.evergreen.edu/curricular/ppandp/PDFs/Lakoff%20Framing%20of%20Immigration.doc.pdf.

90. Benjamin R. Knoll and David P. Redlawsk, "Framing labels and immigration policy attitudes in the Iowa caucuses: 'Trying to out-Tancredo Tancredo,'" *Political Behavior* 10 (2010): 2. http://www.rci.rutgers.edu/~redlawsk/papers/Framing%20Lables%20and%20Immigration%20Policy%20Attitudes.pdf.

91. Ibid., 12.

92. Ted Brader, Nicholas A. Valentino and Elizabeth Suhay, "What triggers opposition to immigration? Anxiety, group cues, and immigration threat," *Journal of Political Science* 52, no. 4 (October 2008): 959.

93. Ibid., 975.

94. Jack Citrin, Donald P. Green, Christopher Muste, and Cara Wong, "Public opinion toward immigration reform: The role of economic motivation," *Journal of Politics* 59, no. 3 (August 1997): 858.

95. Ibid., 877.

96. Luntz Research and Strategic Services, "Respect for the Law & Economic Fairness: Illegal Immigration Prevention," October 2005 http://images.dailykos.com/images/user/3/Luntz_frames_immigration.pdf (accessed February 6, 2014).

97. Ibid., 2.

98. Ibid., 9.

99. Otto Santa Ana, Sandra L. Trevino, Michael J. Bailey, Kristen Bodossian, and Antonio de Necoches, "A May to remember," *Du Bois Review: Social Science and Research on Race* 4, no. 1 (March 2007): 212.

100. Ibid., 213.

101. Ibid., 219.

102. Ibid., 227.

103. Ediberto Roman, "Who exactly is living *la vida loca?* The legal and political consequences of Latino-Latina Ethnic and racial stereotypes in film and other media," *Journal of Gender, Race & Justice* 4, no. 1 (Fall 2000): 54.

104. Ibid., 55.

105. George J. Sanchez, "Face the nation: Race, immigration, and the rise of nativism in late twentieth century America," *International Migration Review* 31, no. 4 (Winter 1997): 1011, 1021.

106. R. Michael Alvarez and Tara L. Butterfield, "The resurgence of nativism in California? The case of Proposition 187 and illegal immigration," *Social Science Quarterly* 81, no. 1 (March 2000): 169.

107. Ibid., 177.

108. Sanchez, "Face the nation," 1013.

109. Southern Poverty Law Center, "Anti-immigration groups," *Intelligence Report* 101 (Spring 2001), http://www.splcenter.org/get-informed/intelligence-report/browse-all-issues/2001/spring/blood-on-the-border/anti-immigration-.

110. Ibid.

111. Sean D. Hamill, "Mexican's death bares a town's ethnic tension," *New York Times*, August 5, 2008.

112. Joe McDonald, "Jury in Shenandoah hate crime case hears racist music," *Times Tribune*, October 9, 2010, http:/thetimes-tribune.com/news/jury-in-shenandoah-hate-crime-case

113. Immigration Policy Center, "Mexican migration patterns signal a new immigration reality," IPC, August 2011. http://www.immigrationpolicy.org/just-facts/mexican-migration-patterns-signal-new-immigration-reality (accessed February 6, 2014).

114. Mary Romero, "Racial profiling and immigration law enforcement: Rounding up of usual suspects in the Latino community," *Critical Sociology* 32 (2006): 449. http://crs.sagepub.com/content/32/2-3/447.refs.html.

115. Ibid., 453.

116. Ibid., 463.

117. Ibid., 456.

118. Ibid., 460.

119. U.S. Department of Justice, "Department of Justice files lawsuit in Arizona against Maricopa County, Maricopa County Sheriff's Office, and Sheriff Joseph Arpaio," May 10, 2012, http://www.justice.gov/opa/pr/2012/May/12-crt-602.html (accessed October 16, 2012).

120. Ibid.

121. Marc Lacey, "U.S. finds pervasive bias against Latinos by Arizona sheriff," *New York Times*, December 15, 2011, 2. http://www.nytimes.com/2011/12/16/us/arizona-sheriffs-office-unfairly-targeted-latinos-justice-department-says.html?pagewanted=all&_r=0.

122. Thomas E. Perez, Department of Justice, Civil Rights Division, Letter to Bill Montgomery, Re: United States' Investigation of the Maricopa County Sheriff's Office, December 15, 2011, 16. http://www.justice.gov/crt/about/spl/documents/mcso_findletter_12-15-11.pdf (accessed October 16, 2012)

123. Ibid., 2.

124. Ibid., 11.

125. Ibid., 6.

126. Ibid., 8.

127. Ibid., 11.

128. Ibid., 15.

129. Ibid., 15.

130. William D. Carrigan and Clive Webb, "The lynching of persons of Mexican origin or descent in the United States, 1848–1928,"*Journal of Social History* 37, no. 2 (Winter 2003): 411.

131. Ibid., 414.

132. Ibid., 416.

133. Ibid., 416–417.

134. Ibid., 419.

135. Ibid.

136. Ibid., 427.

137. Kevin R. Johnson, "The forgotten 'repatriation' of persons of Mexican ancestry and lessons for the 'war on terror,' " *Pace Law Review,*. Paper 39, 5–8, http://digitalcommons. pace.edu/lawrev/39.

138. Ibid., 13.

139. Richard Griswold del Castillo, "The Los Angeles 'zoot suit riots' revisited: Mexican and Latin American perspectives," *Mexican Studies* 16, no. 2 (Summer 2000): 369. http:// www.jstor.org/stable/1052202.

140. Gene Sherman, "Youth gangs leading cause of delinquencies," *Los Angeles Times*, June 2, 1943, http://web.viu.ca/davies/h324war/zootsuit.riots.media.1943.htm.

141. Edward J. Escobar, *Race, Police and the Making of a Political Identity: Mexican Americans and the Los Angeles Police Department, 1900-1945*, (Berkeley: University of California Press, 1999), 200, 221.. http://web.viu.ca/davies/h324war/zootsuit.riots.media.1943.htm.

142. "28 zoot suiters seized on coast after clashes with service men," *New York Times*, June 11, 1943, http://web.viu.ca/davies/h324war/zootsuit.riots.media.1943.htm.

143. Griswold del Castillo, "Los Angeles 'zoot suit riots' revisited," 370.

144. Ibid., 368.

145. Leadership Conference on Civil Rights, "Confronting the new faces of hate: Hate crimes in America, 2009," June 2009, http://www.civilrights.org/publications/hatecrimes/.

146. Brittany Smith, "Phoenix man gets 27 years in neighbor's death," July 5, 2011. http:// www.azcentral.com/news/articles/

147. Michele Stacey, Kristin Carbone-Lopez, and Richard Rosenfeld, "Demographic change and ethnically motivated crime: The impact of immigration on anti-Hispanic hate crime in the United States," *Journal of Contemporary Criminal Justice* 27 (2011): 279. http:// ccj.sagepub.com/content/27/3/278.refs.html.

148. Ibid., 281.

149. Ibid.

150. Ibid., 292.

151. Ibid., 293.

152. Ibid., 294.

153. Matthew T. Lee, Ramiro Martinez, Jr. and Richard Rosenfeld, "Does Immigration Increase Homicide? Negative Evidence from Three Border Cities," *The Sociological Quarterly*, Vol. 42, No. 4 (Autumn, 2001), 559.

154. Ibid., 560.

4

The Color of Hate:
Race, Space, and Place

As the unmarked category against which difference is constructed, Whiteness never has to speak its name, never has to acknowledge its role as an organizing principle in social and cultural relations.[1]

Starting with the court case *Hudgins vs. Wright* (1806), Ian F. Haney Lopez describes how three generations of women were declared free, rather than slaves, due to the racial connotations associated with long straight hair and how "... law serves not only to reflect but to solidify social prejudice, making law a prime instrument in the construction and reinforcement of racial subordination."[2] He proposes a theory of race "as a social complex of meanings we continually replicate in our daily lives" as he repudiates any biological basis for race. I start this chapter with the same understanding. Race is not a biological construct, but rather one that has been created; it is the meaning given to perceived physical and cultural differences that defines race in America today. Racial categories change with time and place, and are configured by chance (birth), context, and—to some extent—choice. However, American history is rife with beliefs and actions based on the biological notion of race, that each race has at the least its own physical characteristics and at the worst, its own mental and behavioral limitations based on innate determinants. As Haney Lopez states, "Genetic differences correlate to geography, not to notions of race."[3]

Ethnicity theorists focus on the importance of ethnicity, based on culture and descent, and meld the experiences of racial minorities with those of European ethnic groups in what Haney Lopez describes as an "embarrassingly ahistorical comparison." This melding is at least the partial basis for comparisons between ethnic groups and Black Americans in terms of progress, disregarding how differently these groups have been treated in American history. While European ethnics are divided into specific nationalities, ethnicity theorists consume similarly distinct groups into "Asian," "Latino," and "Native American." My concern with these theorists is the second flaw that Haney Lopez articulates, that by their thinking, "racism permeates U.S. society through individual antipathies and psychoses, and not because the institutions central to American life, such as the federal and state governments, the judiciary, the marketplace, and the media systematically create and perpetuate racist norms."[4] In considering Black Americans as victims of hate crimes, it is clear that while the media focuses on individual perpetrators of hate, the structural supports for hate are deeply imbedded in our societal institutions and are far more responsible for maintaining racial imbalance and inequalities than the actions of individual haters. Unfortunately, for many Americans, the belief that racism has either mostly vanished or is housed only in aberrant individuals while American society is "fully committed to social justice for minorities" blinds them to the realities of race and hate today.

In this chapter on race and space, I focus solely on Black Americans as the group that historically and today has been the most impacted by racist hate. Negative stereotypes abound for many groups within American culture. Those related to Black Americans have existed since before the days of slavery and enabled White Americans to enslave Blacks in the first place and then confine them with rules and cultural norms of segregation, biased law enforcement practices, limited access to economic and social advancements, and violence.

As Omi and Winant point out in their classic work on race, concepts of race and racial categories have always been politically contested and used for political gain, and these categories have changed over time, both reflecting and shaping our racial understandings.[5] They point to the social nature of race rather than an essential racial characteristic of a particular group. Membership in racial groups changes over time as ideas of who belongs where change. One need only look at Italians coming to America in the nineteenth century to compare how they were originally categorized (non-White) to where they fit today. Each era contains "commonsense" ideas and beliefs as to what constitutes racial groups at that particular time. Some linger beyond their "use by" date, such as notions of biological superiority/inferiority. It is in looking backward that we can see how created these definitions were, how based on the biases and contexts of different time frames and spaces. We need to push ourselves to see what the current creations are, to recognize so that we do not unwittingly contribute to structural inequities that foster hate.

Historian Barbara Fields, too, points out that race is an ideological construct rather than an objective, observable physical thing. She argues that relationships between Europeans and Africans had much more to do with the development of racial categories than the mere color difference between the two groups. "Ideas about color, like ideas about anything else, derive their importance, indeed their very definition, from their context. They can no more be the unmediated reflex of psychic impressions than can any other ideas. It is ideological context that tells people which details to notice, which to ignore, and which to take for granted in translating the world around them into ideas about that world."[6] The idea that a White woman can give birth to a Black child while a Black woman cannot give birth to a White one demonstrates the ideology behind the misconception of race as a biological fact. Physical characteristics may be noticeable, but their meaning is given by context and ideology. Race is a product of history, not of nature, an ideological construct used to create the structure of society in a way that benefits one particular group of people. Racism in the hands of different groups may function through different means (structural through laws, personal through racial epithets or violence) and with different intents; however, the end result is maintenance of the social structure in such a way that those with power retain that power.

Sam Torres looked at the extent of hate crimes against Blacks and found that between 1992 and 1996, reported hate crimes against Black Americans increased 52 percent. "Of all the hate crimes reported in 1996, approximately 61% were motivated by racial prejudice, and in these incidents, African Americans were the victims in 66% of the cases reported to police."[7] He identifies the three most common types of hate offenders: "young thrill seekers" who may act to earn respect from their friends, the reactive offender who feels attacked or insulted in some way by the victim (seeing an interracial couple, having Blacks move into "his" neighborhood), and the least common type, the "hardcore fanatic." Torres points to social and political factors that create a climate in which hate crimes are more likely to occur. These include rates of unemployment; racial stereotypes in the media, including race-biased advertisements and radio talk show commentary; and the use of "race-baiting" language.[8] He identifies "trigger incidents," single high-profile incidents that due to this climate of hate may "set off a cycle of retaliatory incidents or even a large scale racial disorder." The Rodney King beating in March 1991, the murders in Howard Beach and Bensonhurst in New York City in the 1980s, and more general factors such as an increase in production from Japanese auto and electronics manufacturers are examples of trigger incidents. The conservative backlash of the 1980s against such developments as affirmative action, bilingual education, and the debates over immigration are elements that have contributed to this climate.

Psychologists writing about multicultural competence in their field argue the need to explore the dynamics of contemporary forms of racism insidiously "buried deep within the worldviews and everyday narratives of well-intentioned people."[9] They describe *aversive racism* whereby Whites who consciously support equality also "harbor negative beliefs about Blacks that are expressed only subtly and in situations in which discrimination will not be obvious to others or themselves" and *color-blind racism*, which can be identified through basic frames that include cultural racism (culturally based explanations for difference), naturalization (naturalizing such phenomena as housing segregation as normal), and minimization "or the suggestion that race has no relevance."[10] White interviewees described race in their own lives as a "nonissue," the negative impact of racism on people of color as "exaggerated," and the racist attitudes of their friends and family as "a matter of opinion rather than as manifestations of racism itself."[11] Avoidance of their own racism includes minimizing racism as a problem in society or locating it in individuals or geographies distant from themselves. These authors warn that if this denial of racism is not dealt with in their clients, the "trauma, physical harm, and psychological exhaustion sustained by people of color as they withstand the effects of racism every day of their lives" will continue to be an ongoing and significant problem.[12]

Color-blind racism, according to Bonilla-Silva, Lewis, and Embrick, is the central racial ideology of the post–civil rights era. They describe components of this ideology as avoidance of direct racial language, projection (projecting racist attitudes and behavior onto Blacks as the reason for housing and educational segregation), the use of diminutives ("a little," "a bit") to mitigate racist opinions, and an incoherence of speech when some Whites talk about sensitive racial issues. The ideology of color-blind racism is based on cultural, rather than biological, explanations for difference in social standing and opportunities, and beliefs that discrimination and the need for affirmative action programs are things of the past. Based on the 1997 Survey of College Students' Social Attitudes and the 1998 Detroit Area Study, they documented the ways in which Whites expressed racist beliefs about Blacks while purporting not to be racist themselves, including the racial stories that typically accompany color-blind racism. "To have salience and currency, ideologies must produce narratives that explain the world in ways that make sense to people, that convey its major frames; these stories are then the conveyor belts that transport the new racial frames."[13] The commonalities in the responses from subjects provide a view into the dominant racial ideology of the present. These include "the past is in the past" (racism is over, the harm done is past, we need to move on), "I didn't own any slaves" (don't blame me for past wrongs, I'm not responsible and things are fine now), "If other groups have made it, how come Blacks haven't" (it's lack of motivation and hard work that keeps Blacks from success), and "I didn't get the job because a less qualified Black person did" (usually signifying the purported negative impact of affirmative action on Whites). "The fact that old and young alike, working class and middle class, and male and female respondents all told these stories and told them so similarly is evidence that they are *collective* narratives."[14] These narratives, illustrating the current ideology of race, "help most Whites maintain a color-blind sense of self and, at the same time, to reinforce views that help reproduce the current racial order."[15]

CULTURAL CONSTRUCTIONS OF SPACE

My concern is with both literal and figurative space. Many individual hate crimes take place around notions of space and to whom certain spaces belong (or more importantly, do not belong). Ideas as to "our" space and transgressions of space by racial Others have been created historically and continue today. Grace Elizabeth Hale looked at the culture of segregation in the South in the years 1890 to 1940 and how segregation really became the foundation of southern society during this time. Many elements contributed to this culture, not the least of which was advertising. "Advertising created an increasingly national market in part through the circulation of Black imagery that figured the implied consumer as White."[16] The whole South was riddled with reminders of the separation of Black and White space, from public toilets labeled "Colored" and "White," to separate waiting rooms for transportation, to restaurants, schools, churches, hotels, and houses. Space itself was publicly racialized and labeled, created in separated but unequal segments, as the places allowed Black Americans were inferior and marginalized. Advertisements made use of Black images to sell products to White people with stock characters such as "Uncle Tom" (e.g., Uncle Ben's rice) and "Mammy" (e.g., Aunt Jemima) to sell products, effectively placing the Black image back in the days of slavery and under the control of Whites. The development of trade cards in the late 1870s gave advertisers an easily distributed way to use visual imagery to sell their products. Using nonthreatening images of Blacks, "[a]dvertisers hoped this sentimental racism would attract the attention of middle-class White women who increasingly controlled household spending."[17] However, the most popular Black images were those depicting Black adults "absurdly trying to mimic their White 'superiors.'"[18] These images contained Blacks in their "proper place" while reassuring Whites that the races would never be equal.

Trade cards gave way to nationally circulated magazines in which advertisements used Black-figured embodiments of products such as Black thread that would not lose its color when wet or soap so strong it could change Black children into White. "Most companies played upon the older and much less transgressive trade card themes of colorfastness and associations of Blackness and dirt, Whiteness and cleanliness."[19]

While Black images could be used to advertise products for White consumers, Black bodies were separated in actual space. Segregated areas included movie theaters (Blacks in the balcony, Whites below) and restaurants that refused to serve any but White people. Deference was expected in public encounters: while shopping, Blacks were supposed to step back and wait until all Whites had been served just as on the sidewalk a Black person should step back and yield the space to a passing White. "Blacks often could not try on clothing, hats, gloves, or even shoes. At best, some establishments permitted African Americans to try on hats only with a cloth over their heads and dresses, skirts, shirts, and pants only over other clothing."[20] Even death had to be segregated. "State health codes often demanded that White undertakers handle only White bodies, creating a secure and often profitable business for African American morticians."[21] In Alabama, a law prevented White nurses from touching Black patients.

COLORISM

Judgment on skin color takes place in the public eye, but what is not as obvious is the judgment of skin tones within racially or ethnically defined groups. Both from outside Black America as well as within, colorism, a judgment of a person's worth based on lightness or darkness of skin tone, exists and plays out in harmful and destructive ways.

Humphrey and Schuman studied the portrayal of Blacks in magazine advertisements between 1950 and 1982, since depictions of Blacks in the mass media can have significant influence on White attitudes, particularly for those who have little to no face-to-face contact with Black people. In turn, White attitudes toward Blacks heavily influence how Blacks are depicted in magazine advertisements, as the mainstream media is dominated by Whites. Since "... survey data indicate that Whites are most willing to accept integration and equal treatment in the area of employment, less so in the area of close social contact and residential integration, and least so in the area of interracial marriage," they predicted that magazine advertisements would reflect these beliefs. They found a steady increase in the number of advertisements using Black models (decreasing somewhat after the election of Ronald Reagan), although Blacks were overrepresented as sports figures. In the 1950 ads, Blacks were presented in subordinate positions to Whites 62 percent of the time and never presented in dominant roles. By 1980, eighty-nine percent of the ads showed Blacks and Whites in equal status roles. "In 1950, then, ads present a picture of a largely segregated world in which Blacks come into contact with Whites only through their work-related roles as porters, cooks, and servants. By 1980, this picture had changed dramatically in that Blacks are no longer presented as servants." The world according to the advertisements in the 1980s was, however, still segregated.[22] As these authors demonstrate, "advertisements usually portray Whites as Whites like to think of themselves and Blacks as Whites like to think of Blacks."[23]

Kevin Keenan looked at mass media advertisements featuring Black Americans to determine if there were biases related to skin tones and physical features. In mainstream magazines between 1989 and 1994, he found that Blacks in ads typically had lighter skin tones and more Caucasian features than those depicted in editorial photographs. When both males and females were featured, Black females typically had lighter skin than Black males. Since slavery, when Blacks with lighter skin tones often ended up with the more prestigious jobs inside while those with darker skin worked outside, discrimination against darker skins both from outside Black America and from within have persisted. Keenan coded for physical characteristics such as complexion, eye color, width of nose, and prominence of lips and found statistically significant differences in complexion and eye color between Blacks in advertisements and those in editorial photographs.[24]

Keith and Herring looked at the effects of skin-tone variations on Black education, occupation, and income and found that "not only does complexion have significant net effects on stratification outcomes, but it is also a more consequential predictor of occupation and income than such background characteristics as parents' socioeconomic status."[25] The relationship between skin tone and position is traceable back to the days of slavery. The mixed (mulatto) population began to become differentiated from the pure Black population in terms of labor privileges, opportunities for education, and advancement. Darker skin and Black physical characteristics were considered negative attributes and signs of inferiority. Following the Civil War and Emancipation, the mulatto population emerged as the elite group within the larger Black population. Keith and Herring found that very light skinned Blacks were "substantially more likely to be employed as professional and technical workers," while those with darker complexions were "more likely than all others to be laborers."[26] Skin tone was found to have a statistically significant effect on educational level achieved, with lighter skinned Blacks reaching higher levels than darker skinned Blacks. Family income also increased as skin tones lightened. "Also, darker-skinned respondents in the NSBA were about twice as likely to report that they had been the victims of discrimination within the last month than were those with light skin complexions."[27]

Audrey Elisa Kerr has written about the national folk culture of Black communities in regard to rumors and legends surrounding complexion-related lore and what the meaning attached to this lore might be. Folklore surrounding a topic, particularly when there is a lack of written record, can help determine anxieties and concerns, and what a community believes its history to be. The folklore surrounding complexion anxieties includes the numerous tests that were purported to have been used in the twentieth century to determine who was acceptable (those whose skin was lighter than a paper bag or whose skin was light enough for veins to be visible, for example) and who was too dark and therefore unacceptable for entrance into a number of institutions such as churches, social clubs, and even colleges. As Kerr points out, complexion discrimination within the Black community is the implosion of racism—an internalization of the White mainstream's views on acceptability and standards of beauty and appearance. Complexion tests started as Whites tried to ensure that Blacks could not "pass" as White and gain entrance to White institutions, and they continued within the Black community as well as mainstream attitudes took root.

Within the Black community, the color complex works from two perspectives—those who are considered too dark and therefore inferior or those considered too light and therefore not Black enough to be genuine. Children considered too light can be the subject of name-calling and taunts from their peers. "While the parents of Black children often prepare them for the possibility that White children may call them 'nigger,' few parents seem to warn them about hateful name-calling from their 'own people.' "[28] Blacks have been inundated with products to lighten their skin, change their eye color (contact lenses), and straighten their hair. There are more skin lighteners on the market than ever before, including many used in Latin America, India, and some Asian countries.

"American Negro women of the nineteenth century sometimes rubbed lye directly on their skin, and others applied harsh acidic products made for removing dirt and grime from floors and walls."[29] In addition to bleaches, there are chemical peels that burn off a layer of skin or dermabrasion, which strips the skin's layers off with a wire. But a double standard exists in terms of judgment for altering appearance. While Blacks are judged for altering their appearance and often assumed to hate their physical selves, White women who darken their skin through tanning, straighten and dye their hair, and submit to plastic surgery to alter facial features are not. These changes are acceptable within the dominant standard of beauty and are not assumed to mean a denial of (racial) self. This creates yet another boundary between what is acceptable for White women and what is allowed to Blacks, and shows the hypocrisy of skin tone categories, as darker tones for White women may be darker than the lightest Black skin but remain in a separate and privileged category. Rather than actual physical difference, it is the ideology behind the differences that determines the meaning.

In the United States, by the 1880s and 1890s, skin bleachers were widely advertised and used. These products today are not advertised to change non-White skin into White, but instead purport to lighten skin tones several shades. Advertisements for these products have always far outnumbered articles reporting on their harmful effects and tell women that success in the job market and romantic success depend on lighter skin. "For all products, dark skin is associated with pain, rejection, and limited options; achieving light skin is seen as necessary to being youthful, attractive, modern, and affluent—in short, to being 'all that you can be.' "[30] Skin-lightening products are a multibillion dollar global industry. With the Internet to provide advertisements, research, comparisons, discussions, and the products themselves, it is easier than ever before to acquire them. Beauty may be in the eye of the beholder, but that eye is trained and constrained by what is presented by the media and popular culture within the context of a long history of racism and dominance.

"Racial formation theory argues that racial projects construct the meaning of race via images and explanations about racial categories that are manipulated to maintain White dominance."[31] Eurocentric features are valued by the general population over Afrocentric features, and this standard affects the Black population as well. Black women, more so than Black men, continue to be pressured to live up to ideals of White beauty, with the result that products for lightening skin, straightening hair, and changing features are widespread. Fair and Lovely skin lightener has over 38 million users worldwide. Body images are given meaning by "systems of representation"—the media tell us what to value and what to devalue. This causes conflict within the Black community as the competing values of authenticity (darker skin) come up against those of privilege (lighter skin).[32]

Discussing the attraction many Black men seem to have for lighter skinned Black women, Spike Lee points to years of "being inundated with media from the time you're born that constantly fed you the White woman as the image of beauty."[33] As one who has dealt openly with colorism, Lee's films *School Daze* and *Jungle Fever* center on this issue. First in literature and then in minstrel shows, plays, and film, judgments based on determinations of beauty have been publicly imagined and stated. Color has been a significant piece of this creation. "In nineteenth-century literature, color was crucial to the characterization of Blacks, especially women. When portrayed as the love interest of either a Black or a White man, the Black heroine was typically light skinned, beautiful, and passive."[34] Many mulattoes in fiction met tragic ends. On stage, Blacks were allowed limited roles that included the same tragic mulatta and for men, the "brute." The role of the brute was primarily given to darker skinned Black men. "As they traditionally had in literature, the mulatta and brute characterizations of Negroes in theater and later in film functioned to alleviate Whites' anxieties about rampant race mixing while maintaining the myth of White superiority."[35] As Daniel Leab points out, "The stage mulatto served to reinforce popular notions about White superiority. The merest drop of Negro blood was a taint from which there was no redemption . . ."[36]

Early films contained Blacks in five basic roles: the *Tom* (childlike, submissive, friendly to Whites), the *coon* (lazy, ignorant), the *Black buck* (violent, lecherous, criminal), the *mammy* (happy in slavery, maternal, devoted to "her" White family), and the pervasive and tragic *mulatta*. Lighter skinned women were given the sexual roles while darker skinned women played the "mammy." "Passing" was a popular theme in films from the 1940s and 1950s. Warnings in these films, along with the tragic mulatta figure, were "none too subtle: if you do not mix races, you will be generously rewarded; if you try to pass as White, tragedy awaits."[37] The only way for a mulatto character to avoid a tragic end was to discover that he or she was actually White. The Code of the Motion Picture Industry prohibited any on-screen romantic contact between a White and a Black actor and actress. In the 1950s and 1960s, Black actors and actresses began to have more varied roles, "but dark skinned Black men continued to be cast as brutes . . ."[38] The 1970s brought a slew of "blaxploitation" films where Black men were portrayed as pimps and drug dealers in the inner city. Between 1970 and 1992, fifty-two movies in this genre were made. While these films often perpetuated a stereotypical version of what Whites expected Blacks to be, they also provided starring roles for Black actors and actresses, and characters who embodied an anti–status quo heroism that could be read by the Black community as a challenge to mainstream portrayals.

BLACK AS CRIMINAL

In April 1986, while serving a sentence for first-degree murder in Massachusetts, Willie Horton entered a Maryland home, raped a woman, and assaulted her companion. Horton had been released on a weekend pass by the state's furlough program. Although Horton's crime was certainly reprehensible, he would have slipped fairly quietly into the annals of criminal justice history had not George Bush's campaign manager, Lee Atwater, decided to use Horton as a tool against Democratic candidate Michael Dukakis. By the time the 1988 election was over, Willie Horton had become a household word and a symbol to the American public of the heart of the nation's crime problem, a young Black male guilty of repeated violent crimes against White people.

Although Bush denied the racial overtones of the images his campaign created, Horton too clearly symbolized ingrained and long-held fears about Black males entrenched in American culture. Willie Horton was the perfect example of what many Americans had long believed to be a threat—a Black male who raped White women and killed White children. The roots of "Hortonism" go back centuries and are found in American history and popular culture. In recent decades, politicians and the news and entertainment media have used the image of the Black criminal as support for a variety of purposes. Horton as a symbol resonates with notions of Black sexuality and criminality that play on emotional responses, continuing the inherently racist nature of the criminal justice system in American society which is bolstered by dominant media images based on race and bias.

From earliest contact between the European/White world and the African/Black world, the physical features of the African peoples connected with cultural beliefs of the Europeans to form the basis of stereotypes that continue to this day. "Perceiving their own Whiteness as 'normal,' Whites attempted to account for the 'abnormal' color of the Africans."[39] Beginning with a skin color that connoted evil, sin, death, and impurity, in a world where the ideal woman was "White and red,"[40] Europeans were predisposed to consider Black Africans as abnormal or subhuman. Before the sixteenth century, the Oxford English

Dictionary used synonyms such as "soiled," "dirty," "foul," "deadly," and "wicked" to define the color Black. "Long-held, unconscious cultural meanings associated with their color has helped insure that Blacks are stereotyped as base and inferior."[41]

Of the earliest and most enduring stereotypes were the ones that had to do with Black sexuality. The comparison of Africans to apes included a belief in both an exaggerated sexuality in the two groups as well as an exaggeration as to genital size. By forging this link between apes and Africans, the European belief in Africans as lewd, lascivious, and wanton was given an outlet.

Far more common and persistent was the notion that there sometimes occurred "a beastly copulation or conjuncture" between apes and Negroes, and especially that apes were inclined wantonly to attack Negro women.[42]

The fictional relationship between Blacks and apes continues to be reflected today in stories of HIV being passed from apes to man through sexual contact in Africa, and in White supremacist group ideologies that create "mud" races (Blacks, Asians, Latinos) as the product of this kind of contact. The presumption of heightened sexuality in Black men particularly was not an insignificant part of the creation of stereotypes and beliefs regarding Blacks by Europeans. As American society developed in the New World and as Blacks were brought to this continent as slaves, the assumptions and tensions surrounding Black sexuality became ingrained in American law and popular culture. Concerns with miscegenation led to laws forbidding interracial sex and marriage.

Although neither a widespread nor long-lived practice, several states in the 1700s enacted laws allowing the use of castration as a punishment for Black males guilty of particular crimes. Until 1722, South Carolina legally required masters of slaves who escaped four times to castrate the slave. Pennsylvania and New Jersey enacted short-lived laws that prescribed the castration of Blacks for the attempted rape of a White woman. The use of castration again was an element in the struggle for dominance over Black men and points to the animalistic metaphors used to describe Blacks. Just as a bull or a stallion could be subdued by emasculation, so could the Black man. "In some colonies, moreover, the specifically sexual aspect of castration was so obvious as to underline how much of the White man's insecurity vis-a-vis the Negro was fundamentally sexual."[43] Virginia's castration law was repealed in 1769 for supposedly humanitarian reasons, "but the repealing statute specifically declared that it might still be inflicted for one particular offense—rape or attempted rape of a White woman."[44]

The power given White women, particularly in the South, who had only to point a finger at a Black man and cry rape (where merely "leering" at a White woman could bring a two-year stint on a chain gang) was incredible. In Springfield, Illinois, in 1908, a three-day anti-Black riot occurred in which six were killed. The cause of the riot was a White woman's charge of being raped by a Black man.[45] The case of the nine Black youths charged with raping two White women in 1931, the Scottsboro case, became a well-known example of the power of White womanhood. The two women originally charged that the nine Blacks (who were between the ages of 13 and 20) had raped them. One woman later took back her testimony and testified for the defendants. The other presented conflicting testimony and lied on the stand. In his instructions to the jury, Judge William Callahan stated, "Where the woman charged to have been raped, as in this case, is a White woman, there is a very strong presumption under the law that she would not and did not yield voluntarily to intercourse with the defendant, a Negro; and this is true, whatever the station in life the prosecutrix may occupy, whether she be the most despised, ignorant and abandoned woman of the community, or the spotless virgin and daughter of a prominent home of luxury and learning."[46] By 1950, all of the defendants were freed, having served a collective total of 104 years of imprisonment for what was, in all probability, a racial hoax. False accusations of rape were the basis of many lynchings in the past century.

POPULAR CULTURE AND BLACK SEXUALITY

Popular versions of southern history and Black character have been around for centuries. The minstrel shows of the 1800s presented a particular version of people and events to the American public. With the advent of film, particularly longer films like *The Birth of a Nation*, the ability to reach a mass audience with a carefully created image of Black people was monumentally increased. The popular culture resonated with the same stereotypes of Black character, behavior, and sexuality that drove the legal system during this time.

At the beginning of the twentieth century, concern with racial purity and with Black sexuality appeared as a common theme in "miscegenation plays." These plays dealt with the problems rising from sexual relationships between Whites and Blacks, and were based on a firm belief in White superiority and the need to keep the White race pure of any supposedly inferior blood. Plays like *The Real Widow Brown* in which devious Black women passed as White to trick White men into marriage resonated with the cultural tensions over Black sexuality and the problematic desire of White men for Black women. With the advent of film, the same themes and stereotypes were transferred to the new medium, with the potential of reaching much larger audiences.

In Humanity's Cause (1911) depicts a Confederate soldier who is saved on the battlefield by a blood transfusion from a Black man but becomes a changed man, "a brute who disgusts even his long suffering sweetheart," and death of both the soldier and the Black man whose blood corrupted him is offered as the only solution. In *The Nigger* (1915), a newly elected anti-Black southern governor learns that he has Black blood. He must then give up his job and his White girlfriend.[47] Film catalogues listed numerous examples of these cautionary films about the dangers of miscegenation, and they also included films that continued to depict other Black stereotypes such as "the catching, tarring and feathering and burning of a Negro for the assault of a White woman."[48]

The 1915 film *The Birth of a Nation*, produced by David Wark Griffith and based on a 1905 Thomas Dixon novel/play entitled *The Clansman*, is the logical descendant of the stereotypes and fears of Black sexuality and violence that permeated the minstrel shows, stage productions, and early short films. "In the Dixon and Griffith products, Black men were portrayed as violent sexual savages who derived particular satisfaction in raping White women."[49] The Black characters in *The Birth of a Nation* included Gus, who pursues the young Flora Cameron to her death (since death is preferable to rape) and the mulatto Silas Lynch, who portrays not only the horrors of mixed blood, but also the Black rapist as he tries to force Elsie Stoneman into marriage. *The Birth of a Nation* was not the only film to use the long-lived stereotypes of Black sexuality, but according to one author, "no movie has played quite such an unfortunate role in the history of the Black in America."[50] Precisely because the film attempted to teach a history lesson, the scenes and roles assigned Blacks had a real impact on audience perceptions of the Black race. In addition, the previous century's creation and solidification of stereotypes and popular ideas concerning the history of the Civil War era made the film believable since it meshed so completely with long-established beliefs about Black sexuality and the inferiority of those with any Black blood.

David O. Selznick's 1939 movie *Gone with the Wind* continues with an only slightly more subtle version of *The Birth of a Nation*. *Gone with the Wind* emphasizes southern Blacks as faithful, ignorant, and servile. Scarlett is attacked by both a Black and a White renegade as she drives through the deteriorating Atlanta after the war. She is rescued by a loyal Black, Big Sam, who kills the Black attacker (while the other falls to his death, thus removing the necessity for a Black man to kill a White one). "As with the Griffith film, many movie goers accepted David O. Selznick's 1939 movie as historical and social truth."[51]

The frequency and endurance of images of aggressive Black male sexuality toward White women in American culture speaks to the strength of these images and their potency for the American public. It is small wonder then that Willie Horton was so readily accepted as the epitome of American criminality during the 1988 election. He had been constructed and refined during several centuries of Black-White contact.

In more recent times, drug laws have been used to imprison large numbers of Blacks. The debate over the harms done by crack versus powder cocaine and the differences in sentences for offenses involving these two drugs point to racial discrimination. For possession of 500 grams of powder cocaine, the sentence required under federal law is five years. For crack cocaine, it takes only 28 grams to earn this same sentence. In 1991, of 479,000 crack users, 49.9 percent were White (238,000), 14.2 percent Hispanic (68,000), and 35.9 percent Black (172,000). The majority of users of crack, not powder cocaine, were thus White, although the images of Black crack users were by far the more prevalent. However, in 1992, 92.6 percent of defendants convicted for crack cocaine use nationally were Black, and only 4.7 percent were White. The U.S. Sentencing Commission recommended that Congress equalize the sentences for crack and powder cocaine, concluding that the distinction between crack and powder are primarily social, not physiological; Congress voted 332–82 to overrule the recommendation. In the *U.S. vs. Clary* (1995), the court concluded that the racial disparities in the federal crack laws were driven primarily by White fear of Black crime.

POLITICIZATION OF CRIME

While historiography and popular culture genres have supplied vivid images of Black sexuality and criminality, the politicization of street crime in twentieth-century America did much to lock these images firmly into place in American psyches and in the policy decisions of the criminal justice system.

Ideas on personal risk of victimization are based, in part, on the issues raised by politicians in conjunction with the media. The fear of victimization, which fuels a push for tougher political stances, is often disproportionate to the actual risk, and those depicted as the typical perpetrators of crime (young, male, Black) are, in reality, those most likely to be the victims of violent crime. Politicians use incidents of crime such as the Willie Horton case for campaign material and the media uses these incidents for entertainment purposes. The result is a particular focus and prescribed reaction to the crime problem in American society.

The media depict crime as the product of predatory strangers who are not only evil, but also Black or young, and therefore to many doubly menacing. These presentations allow us to evade the reality that violence and larceny take place in our midst, often perpetrated by those close to us.[52]

The creation of the Black male as the shorthand symbol of the American crime problem was built by pieces through a variety of presidential campaigns. In the 1964 presidential race, Republican Barry Goldwater converted Black demands for racial equality into "hooliganism," stressing the growing menace to personal safety by "bullies and marauders" and the need for public officials to keep the streets safe. Goldwater voted against the Civil Rights Act and implied that violent Blacks would take over if Johnson were to be elected, repeatedly making the point that "our wives, all women, feel unsafe on our streets."[53]

In 1968, George Wallace's allusions to the need for law and order were couched in thinly (if that) veiled racial terms. Wallace and others carried on what Goldwater had started in turning demands for equality into acts of simple criminality. "The fusion in the public mind of damage done in demonstrations and riots with individual acts of predatory robbery and assault became a vision of criminality in which Blacks figured very prominently." Of Wallace's supporters, 90.5 percent agreed that most actions taken by Blacks to get what they wanted were violent. Louise Day Hicks, in her 1967 campaign for mayor of Boston, "made great political capital out of protestations that, as a White woman, she could not walk safely in the streets of Boston."[54] Wallace appealed to the middle class, whose fears about the increasing economic and political power of Black Americans made them particularly susceptible to his inflammatory rhetoric.

In 1968, Nixon, too, campaigned on the issue of law and order. In addition to his concerns with the Vietnam War, and often linked to public reaction against the war, the issue of crime in the streets (with accompanying racial overtones) was central to his campaign. Eugene McCarthy was the only presidential candidate who, during the 1968 campaign, would not participate in the law and order debate, "maintaining that the phrase had become code for the suppression of Blacks."[55] The 1968 election transformed many conflicts into a symbolic expression of fear, equating dissent with deviance, protest with criminality, and demands for equality with overthrow of the government. These equations worked to strengthen the image of Black criminality and the fear and distrust of Black political power long held by paranoid Whites.

In 1988, Lee Atwater engineered one of the most successful media campaigns based on race and crime for George Bush's bid for the presidency. Although Atwater and Bush may not have known the specifics behind the fears and anxieties aroused by the image of the Black rapist, and the centuries of stereotypes and racial interactions that were contained in the particular symbol represented by Horton, they clearly knew and sought the type of public reaction this image would engender. As a violent criminal, but particularly as a Black criminal who perpetrated a sexual offense against a White woman, Horton's use in the presidential campaign strengthened the already dominant voices in American society that marginalized Blacks and defined the crime problem in terms of Black males. "Hortonism taps into a particularly thick vein of racial paranoia that is a quarter-inch below the surface of White American consciousness."[56] The result of the politicization of street crime has been to create the Black male as the typical criminal; the particular result of the war on drugs has been to criminalize a whole generation of Black men, incarcerating a high percentage in state and federal prisons. More Black inmates were sentenced for drug offenses in 2011 than inmates of other races or of Hispanic origin.[57]

HATE CRIMES, RACIAL PROFILING, AND SPACE

Albert Meehan and Michael Ponder found that Black Americans were the subjects of significant racial profiling, including both surveillance and stops, when driving through predominantly White areas. Profiling is sensitive to the combination of race and location and "... significantly increases as African Americans move farther from stereotypically 'Black' communities and into wealthier, Whiter areas: a phenomenon we call the *race-and-place* effect."[58] The police patrol neighborhoods with preformed ideas about these places. "These include assumptions and expectations about the criminality of African Americans."[59] Meehan and Ponder collected data from a medium-sized suburban police department with over 100 officers in a predominantly White (98 percent) city of close to 75,000 residents. They were particularly interested in the use of squad cars with mobile data terminals (MDT), which provide immediate access to the FBI's National Crime Information Computer as well as state and local databases. "Our goal was to answer two questions: (1) Do police officers proactively surveil African American drivers at a rate that is significantly higher than their proportion of the actual population of drivers on the road? And (2) Does police behavior vary by place?"[60] They found that Black drivers were twice as likely as White drivers to be queried on the MDTs. As Black drivers moved from predominantly Black areas of the city to the farthest sectors of the White community, their chance of being the subject of a query increased significantly. The high "rate" of Black criminality or contact with the law then becomes a self-fulfilling prophecy as Blacks are stopped at disproportionate rates compared to White drivers.[61] "Because racial profiling is a product of pervasive and institutionalized patterns of racial segregation in American society, it is not helpful to treat racial profiling as an effect of individual officers, consciously or unconsciously taking advantage of their occupational positions to act on their individual prejudices."[62] The authors found racial profiling to be department wide and not limited to a few individual officers.

The American Civil Liberties Union (ACLU), discussing a Department of Justice report on racial profiling in 2007, stated that the report "shows an alarming racial disparity in the rate at which motorists are searched by local law enforcement."[63] Blacks were approximately three times as likely to be searched during a traffic stop, twice as likely to be arrested, and nearly four times as likely "to experience the threat or use of force during interactions with the police." While previous reports had detailed similar disparities in these categories, they also reported that the "hit rate" of illegal activity or contraband was less likely for Blacks than for Whites. Racial profiling is unconstitutional and affects the ability of the Department of Justice and other law enforcement bodies to carry out their mission successfully. It also sends a clear message to minority groups in the United States that the police see them as a problem based on their race rather than as a constituent to protect and support. In addition, it perpetuates stereotypes and provides an atmosphere in which Black people are defined by their skin color as criminal regardless of evidence to the contrary. This stereotype contributes to an atmosphere that breeds hate crimes against Black Americans as police action marks Black Americans as appropriate targets for race-based behavior.

Reports on racial profiling around the United States include a Minnesota study (2002) that found Blacks, Hispanics, and Native Americans to be stopped more often than Whites, although contraband was found more frequently in searches of Whites' cars; an Arizona study (2006–2007) showing the highway patrol was significantly more likely to stop Blacks and Hispanics than Whites and more likely to search their cars, while Whites who were searched were more likely to be carrying drugs, guns, and/or other contraband; and a Texas study (2005) that again showed greater stops of Blacks while more contraband was found on Whites. "In Newark, New Jersey, on the night of June 14, 2008, two youths aged 15 and 13 were riding in a car driven by their coach, Kelvin Lamar James. All were African American. Newark police officers stopped their car in the rain, pulled the three out, and held them at gunpoint while the car was searched. James stated that the search violated his rights. One officer replied in abusive language that the three African Americans didn't have rights and that the police 'had no rules.' The search of the car found no contraband, only football equipment."[64] In Washington DC, a class action suit was filed (2013) alleging that District of Columbia police "have inappropriately targeted young, Black motorcyclists by hitting them with their squad cars to confiscate illegal bikes . . ."[65]

Minority pedestrians are also subject to racial profiling. In the information collected for the lawsuit *Floyd vs. City of New York* (2008), the court found that between 2005 and 2008, approximately 84 percent of stops were of Blacks and Latinos, though they made up 25 and 28 percent of the population, respectively, in New York City. While Whites made up 44 percent of the population, only about 10 percent of the stops were of Whites. Blacks made up 85 percent of those frisked during this time period, while only 8 percent were White. On August 12, 2013, a federal judge found the New York City Police Department liable for "a pattern and practice of racial profiling and unconstitutional stop-and-frisks."[66] The judge ordered a court-appointed monitor to oversee needed reforms to the department's policing practices.

The End Racial Profiling Act (ERPA) was introduced in the U.S. Senate and House in 2011 but has yet to pass. The act would prohibit profiling by race, religion, ethnicity, or national origin at all levels of law enforcement. "Despite overwhelming evidence of its existence, often supported by official data, racial profiling continues to be a prevalent and egregious form of discrimination in the United States."[67]

INTERNET HATE GROUPS

With new technology come new ways of spreading hate. Within the United States, hateful speech on the Internet is protected by the First Amendment, and White supremacists and other hate groups have increased their presence on the web. The Internet provides easy access to and fast dissemination of hate material. Recent research looks at the motivations, membership, and ideology of these groups.

To ascertain the motivations behind the actions of neo-Nazi groups and youthful Ku Klux Klan (KKK) members, Raphael Ezekiel interviewed leaders and other members of these groups in Detroit. He articulated the groups' basic ideology of race as an absolute biological category that determines each race's attributes. Whites were considered children of God and civilization builders, while people of color were either "mud" races (the result of mating between Whites and animals) or the children of Satan (Jews) who were out to destroy the White race. For many in these groups, there was an overriding fear that White people were losing ground in some apocalyptic struggle.[68] At the leadership level, Jews were considered the primary source of evil and in control of the mud races, while at the membership level, most "exhibited intense prejudice against African Americans that tended to reflect the general prejudice of their families and neighborhoods."[69] Members typically joined already hating Blacks but had to be taught group ideologies regarding the evils of Jews.

Common factors influencing membership include the local presence of a racist group, publicity for that group, and the ease of accessing White racist propaganda on the web. Ezekiel points to a connection between economics and racist activity. It is not so much that Whites turn to racist behavior in poor economic conditions but that the historical periods in which "propagandists from the political, business, or labor communities mobilized racial hostility by identifying a racial group as the cause of economic problems" were the periods of increased racist activity.[70] In other words, what we are told to believe about economic conditions and inequities and who is responsible for them has a great impact regardless of the validity of these mediated messages. While White racism continues to be a "major strand in American culture," politically it is more likely to be expressed as covert messages through code words and assumptions than as outright racism. "Probably the greatest effect of White racism today is its capacity to slow institutional change. Policies that help institutional racism to continue to flourish do much more to hurt minority people than do hate crimes."[71]

While Ezekiel points out that most hate crimes are not committed by members of groups like those he studied, "the leaders and lieutenants of those groups are morally responsible to a nontrivial degree for racial violence in the United States"[72] due to their impact on the climate of race and the visibility of their racism in American culture. However, he warns that a focus on hate crimes as individual actions may all too often recuse the general population from actually thinking about racism and the imbedded nature of racial injustice in American society. Proposing actions against the few, highly visible perpetrators helps preclude action against the many more hidden and structural elements of racism and hate.

Ku Klux Klan groups are still the most common type of hate group in the United States, though many assume they have basically disappeared. In addition to fears of non-White minorities encouraged by a Jewish conspiracy, the Klan is also extremely anti-immigration and anti-immigrant. The KKK has been involved in many hate activities, including lynching, bombings, and move-in violence. "In the early 1990s, when officials attempted to integrate a public housing project in Vidor, Texas, various Klan factions used intimidation tactics designed to keep Blacks from moving in and encourage those residing in the project to move out."[73]

A report on skinheads in America published by the Southern Poverty Law Center details their origins and their role in hate crimes in America today. While skinheads are not native to the United States, they have come here from Europe and other White-majority areas, and they became a growing movement here in the last decades of the twentieth century. Groups such as the Chicago Area Skin Heads (CASH), the Skinheads of Chicago (SHOC), and the Dallas Hammerskins have raised the skinhead profile in the United States with vicious attacks on immigrants and Blacks. While there are skinhead groups who are not racist, publicity has centered on the actions of those who are.

Music has always been an important element in attracting members to the racist skinhead subculture. Hate rock music includes lyrics that are anti-immigrant, anti-Black, and anti-Semitic. Due to First Amendment protections, the United States "has become a main provider of music to skinheads internationally."[74] Hate music is used to recruit new members and to bring in needed revenue for a variety of hate organizations. Two music companies that deal in hate music are Resistance Records and Panzerfaust Records; for some record labels, this music is a multimillion-dollar business. "Most importantly the music brings like-minded individuals together in terms of smaller music shows at bars and larger music festivals held on private property. The music helps members feel like they are part of something bigger and there are others out there who feel the same way they do."[75] Wade Page was shot to death by the police after killing six people at a Sikh temple in Oak Creek, Wisconsin, in 2012. He had previously led a hate rock band in North Carolina called End Apathy. In 1999, drive-by shootings by Benjamin Nathaniel Smith targeted Blacks, Jews, and Asians in Illinois and Indiana. He killed two and wounded 10 before he crashed and died during a police chase. He was recruited through the White power music scene.

The Boston based website Hatewatch (started in 1995 by David Goldman), which indexed and linked hate groups on the Internet to expose them, shut down in 2001, declaring the battle against hate groups had been won. However, the Southern Poverty Law Center (SPLC) states that since 2000, the number of hate groups in the United States has increased by 67 percent. According to the SPLC, which monitors hate groups and other extremists and now hosts its own Hate-watch site, there are currently over 1,000 hate groups across the country. "This growth in extremism has been aided by mainstream media figures and politicians who have used their platforms to legitimize false propaganda about immigrants and other minorities and spread the kind of paranoid conspiracy theories on which militia groups thrive."[76] The web provides easy access to hate messages and groups, and social media also contribute to the hate discussion. "The anti-hate community overestimated the impact of the Web and underestimated the importance of chat rooms, newsgroups and e-mail."[77]

The Hammerskin Nation, founded in Dallas in the late 1980s, is a hate group with ties to the hate rock music scene. It also has an online presence. Its ideology of White supremacy is espoused by primarily young White men inclined to violence. "The Hammerskin Nation is the most violent and best-organized neo-Nazi skinhead group in the United States."[78] The group regularly sponsors concerts showcasing hate rock groups. In Texas, Black American Donald Thomas was murdered by three members of the Confederate Hammerskins in 1991. They were 16 years old and after downing two cases of beer while listening to skinhead fight songs, they decided they wanted to do a "drive-by." In Alabama, two Hammerskin members killed a homeless Black man, hitting him with a baseball bat and kicking him. In California's Riverside County in March 1999, Randy Bowen, a Black man, was assaulted by a group of White supremacists. Two were convicted of assault and a hate crime three years later. The two were members of the Western Hammerskins.

MULUGETA SERAW

Ethiopian immigrant Mulugeta Seraw was killed by a skinhead wielding a baseball bat in a confrontation between three Ethiopians and a group of skin-heads on November 13, 1988. Three of the skinheads were convicted in his death: Kenneth Mieske for first-degree murder (included in his plea was his state-ment that he killed Seraw because of his race), Kyle Brewster for first-degree manslaughter and second-degree assault, and Steve Strasser for first-degree man-slaughter and second-degree assault. Mieske, Brewster, and Strasser were all members of the skinhead gang East Side White Pride in Portland, Oregon. The case was important for a number of reasons, not the least of which were the guilty pleas to a hate crime in an area known to members of the Black community as the most prejudiced city in the west. Other reasons included the publicity the case and the skinhead movement in general received nationally and the civil suit brought by Morris Dees and the Southern Poverty Law Center against Mieske,

Brewster, Tom Metzger, his son John, and the White Aryan Resistance (WAR) for liability in the death of Seraw. Tom Metzger, one of the best-known White supremacists, produced a cable television show entitled *Race and Reason.*

Even before the publicity surrounding both the criminal and civil cases, the rise of the skinhead movement, their ties to the Internet, and their connection to hate rock groups had been featured in the press, including an episode of the *Oprah Winfrey Show*, Geraldo Rivera's show, *Larry King Live*, and *Donohue.* The publicity resulted in a twofold response—condemnation from the general public and increased interest in WAR and other hate groups.[79] This raises the question of publicity in conjunction with hate that ultimately might be seen as a boon to the hate groups because it provides them with a national audience and great public access even when the publicity itself condemns them.

The Oprah Winfrey episode on skinheads was set up following other national publicity that included an article in *Time* magazine. "Immediately after the appearance of the *Time* article, the WAR skinhead contingent received the magic call that marks the division between obscurity and fame in America: a summons from Oprah Winfrey's producers. The importance of the February 4, 1988, *Oprah Winfrey Show* to the skinheads around Tom Metzger can probably not be overstated."[80] The panel on the show included John Metzger, Brad Robarge (who eventually married one of Tom's daughters), Dave Mazzella, and Mike Barrett, while Tom Metzger was in the audience along with his follower Marty Cox (who called Winfrey a monkey). Other skinheads were flown in to be members of the audience. It was clear the group was not there to have a dialogue but to spew hate on national television and after doing so, they walked off the program. This group also appeared on the *Morton Downey Jr. Show.* "What is important to grasp about *Oprah*, *Downey*, and all the skinhead shows that preceded and followed is that they did not happen only once. Rebroadcast, videoed, sold, spliced into other videos, such as a six-hour history of WAR, they became a vital organizing tool, proof of the kind America trusts most that the neo-Nazi skinhead movement was already big-time. It was as if WAR had hired a high-priced public relations firm."[81]

Rolling Stone ran an article called "Skinhead Nation" in the fall of 1988. Geraldo's show, "Young Hate Mongers" ran on November 3, 1988. During the taping, "John Metzger of the Aryan Youth Movement called Roy Innis of the Congress of Racial Equality an Uncle Tom; Innis, with Geraldo's encouragement, rose, went over to John, and began to choke him, Wyatt Kaldenberg, from the audience, threw a chair which hit Geraldo's face and broke his nose, and the rest is television history."[82] Kaldenberg, a White supremacist, was the editor for the WAR newspaper. Reaction to and discussion of the show was international, and Geraldo graced the cover of *Newsweek* the day before the 1988 presidential election. This was the context of publicity occurring just before the murder of Seraw in Portland.

Oregon has a long history of White supremacy, including exclusion of Blacks from the state (written in their constitution) and a refusal to ratify the Fifteenth Amendment endorsing Black voting rights until 1959. "In the early 1920s the state was more or less taken over by the Ku Klux Klan, whose platform of opposition to 'Koons, Kikes and Katholics' reflected the postwar mood."[83] Prejudice against Blacks occurred in the police and courts, in housing (a 1957 City Club report found that over 90 percent of the city's brokers would not sell or rent to Black people outside a very limited area), in the schools, and in public areas.[84] The police department in the early 1980s was 94 percent White. In 1981, a group of officers threw dead opossums on the stoop of a Black-owned restaurant. In 1985, a Black security guard was killed by police responding to a report of shoplifting; he turned out to be merely a bystander, yet police put him in a choke hold that killed him. "When the police chief promptly banned the controversial hold, two officers produced and sold T-shirts bearing the slogan 'Don't Choke 'Em, Smoke 'Em' in their precinct parking lot and the Police Athletic Club— on the day of [the security guard's] funeral."[85] Both sets of officers were ultimately reinstated in the department, sending a clear message to Portland's Blacks about their worth and the fact that the police department was not there to "protect and serve" them.

Publicity following the death of Mulugeta Seraw was intense not only in Portland, but nationally. The rise of skinheads had already been a hot topic, and the death of a Black man at the hands of a group of skinheads was news. "Contrary to the pattern in most communities, where, after a widely publicized racial crime culminating in arrests, racial violence tends to go down, in Portland it went up."[86] As with many hate crimes, the focus on a particular person or group ignores the role the larger society plays in fostering these crimes. Portland had a long history of mistreatment of Blacks, from individual crimes to inequities built into societal structures and institutions. The skinheads were merely the visible tip of the iceberg.

The civil lawsuit against the Metzgers and WAR, which accused them of civil responsibility for the murder, was settled in favor of Seraw's uncle and the Southern Poverty Law Center. The SPLC argued that through Dave Mazzella, who was sent by Tom Metzger to the Portland area as an "agent," there was a direct line of responsibility to those found criminally guilty for Seraw's death. A $12.5 million judgment was found against the Metzgers and WAR. On one hand, the issue of First Amendment rights could and probably should have been central to the case. According to Elinor Langer, the "story" told in court of what happened to Seraw made a compelling argument for the plaintiffs, who kept First Amendment rights to free speech out of the trial. On the other hand, the truth of what happened may well have had more to do with unplanned circumstances than deliberate actions taken to attack Black people as the result of a direct line from the Metzgers to Dave Mazzella to Ken Mieske to Mulugeta

Seraw. As Langer points out, the agency argument may well have been false, but it became true in court as the SPLC lawyers presented it against a defense that was incompetent and ill prepared. She also points out, however, that almost no one introduced as many skinheads to WAR as Dave Mazzella did,[87] and he did have direct contact with those who were found criminally responsible for Seraw's death.

Hate crimes are often seen as the fault of White supremacists due to the publicity surrounding cases such as Seraw's murder, but the United States has a long history of much larger involvement in hate violence directed against Black Americans, including participation by large groups of those considered average Americans. Lynching is the classic example of this.

LYNCHING

... the doomed victim was burned at the stake—a process that was prolonged for several hours, often as the Black male was subjected to the excruciating pain of torture and mutilation ... climaxed, ordinarily, by the hideous act euphemistically described as "surgery below the belt." "Souvenirs" taken from the mutilated body were passed out, picture postcards of the proceedings were sold by enterprising photographers, and the leading participants were written up in the local newspapers. Yet the coroner's report inevitably concluded with a finding that the death of the victim was caused by "persons unknown."[88]

In the 1800s and into the twentieth century, lynching was an all too common way of dealing with purported Black transgressions, particularly those of a sexual nature, though that was often merely the excuse when no such transgression had occurred. "The stated rationale for lynching was to protect the sanctity of the White female from the Black man."[89] Lack of trust in the criminal justice system was another reason given by Whites for taking the law into their own hands. The background context of Black Americans' status after Emancipation, the continuing need for manual labor in the South, and the fear of Black men attacking White women that rested on centuries of stereotypes and fictions all contributed to the rise of lynching. "The claim that a Negro has murdered a White person constituted the single most widely used excuse for racially motivated lynchings. The claim that a Negro had raped a White woman, however, represented the most emotionally potent excuse."[90] In 1922, the Dyer bill, an antilynching measure, was defeated. Opponents of the bill stated that lynching was the appropriate response to "the diabolical crime of rape upon the White women" and that the need to "protect our girls and womenfolk from these Black brutes" marked lynching as necessary. These were the words of Representative Thomas Upton Sisson of Mississippi.[91] Between 1882 when reliable data was first collected and 1968, of the more than 4,740 people lynched in the United States, 72.7 percent were Black.

Between 1889 and 1918, only 19 percent of the roughly 3,000 lynched were accused of rape. However, it was public perception of the crimes (often described in graphic and incorrect detail by the local newspapers) that mattered more than what actually happened. "The public's perception of lynching, fed by the media and improved means of communication, was invariably that a sexual crime by Black men had precipitated it."[92] While the protection of southern womanhood served as the excuse for lynching, White men continued to molest and rape Black women with impunity. No White man was ever lynched for raping a Black woman.

Racial violence and terrorism were used to control the Black population in the South and were "an integral part of the southern society and economy . . ."[93] While the economy was at least partially responsible for the eventual decline in lynching, it was also one basis for lynching in the first place. "The intersection of race and economics created the potential for violence, and . . . analysis yields strong support for the conclusion that economic factors were important in motivating lynchings." The number of lynchings increased as the need for workers increased; violent control was used to maintain dominance over a necessary labor force.[94] Other reasons for the practice of lynching included the success of some Blacks in terms of jobs and land ownership (hence the need to keep them in their place), the need to punish or contain Blacks who became too active politically, and the policing of petty offenses or social behavior boundaries through violence.

Lynching was an act of terrorism whose purpose was to maintain White hegemony over Black bodies, labor, and behavior. It was a constant reminder of how cheaply Black lives were held by the dominant population. The causes of death were always listed as "by persons unknown"—no one was ever charged, although photographic evidence existed as to who many of the perpetrators were. In one case, 110 Whites were questioned to determine fitness for a jury to judge the members of a lynch mob. Of the 110, seventy-six responded that they would not convict even if the accused were found to be guilty.[95] Lynching was supported by law officials (lawyers, police, sheriffs, judges), churches, politicians, and the media.

Behind many lynchings was the desire to punish Blacks who had gained any measure of power or those who refused to bow to local Whites (a Black man could be lynched for failing to take off his hat, for an improper demeanor, for failing to step aside to let a White person pass). Jeff Brown was lynched for "attempted rape" when he accidentally brushed against a White girl as he ran to catch a train. Killing Blacks became a sport and a clear reminder of place, position, and power.

The terrorism meted out by Whites rested on the racism of genteel society. If mobs lynched Blacks with calculated sadistic cruelty, historians and the academic sciences were no less resourceful in providing the intellectual underpinnings of racist thought and behavior, validating theories of Black degeneracy and cultural and intellectual inferiority, helping to justify on "*scientific*" and historical grounds a complex of laws, practices, and beliefs.[96]

Even greater numbers of Blacks were lynched legally through a southern criminal justice system that included rushed trials, no defense support, a disregard for evidence, and summary executions with no chance for appeal. The legal system itself maintained White power as Blacks had few rights in court, and many trials were merely a token show of legality before the accused was executed. In addition, many Blacks were killed through private (nonmob) murders and "nigger hunts." "The cheapness of Black life reflected in turn the degree to which so many Whites by the early twentieth century had come to think of Black men and women as inherently and permanently inferior, as less than human, as little more than animals."[97]

Many government officials supported lynching, and some even participated in it. Governor Ben Tillman (1892) of South Carolina stated that he would lead a lynch mob against a "Negro" who ravished a White woman. U.S. senator Theodore Bilbo of Mississippi believed lynching was the only "immediate and proper and suitable punishment" for Blacks who "dishonored White womanhood."[98] When John Parker Hale attempted to get an antilynching law passed in the U.S. Senate in 1848, Henry Foote, a Mississippi senator, ended his attack on Hale's law by inviting Hale to come to Mississippi. "I invite him there, and will tell him beforehand, in all honesty, that he could not go ten miles into the interior, before he would grace one of the tallest trees of the forest, with a rope around his neck, with the approbation of every virtuous and patriotic citizen; and that, if necessary, I should myself assist in the operation."[99]

Francis McIntosh was accused of murdering a deputy sheriff in Missouri. He was consequently chained to a tree and slowly burned to death. "The fire was so low that his legs and feet were burnt almost to a cinder before his other parts were to any degree affected." After the lynching, the appropriately named Judge Luke Lawless instructed the St. Louis grand jury that in considering guilt in this murder, they should indict only if they could determine that the act had been the work of a few, but if it was the work of many, "it is beyond the reach of human law." Lawless highlighted the crimes of the lynched man and the understandable reaction of the mob when confronting the death of the deputy, clearly presenting his view that no one should be held responsible for McIntosh's brutal death except for abolitionists whose influence he considered responsible for inciting the passions of the people in the mob.[100] The tendency to place blame anywhere but on the lynch mob was a common practice in the press as well.

Newspapers and Lynching

In 1938, Jessie Daniel Ames wrote an article on the editorial treatment of lynching in the 13 southern states. She found that while editors on the whole were personally opposed to lynching, their editorials were often favorable because they were "caught in the general atmosphere of a given trade territory" and could not print their own views.[101] In the press, however, most editors condoned lynchings and made excuses for the lynchers. "Newspapers and Southern society accept lynching as justifiable homicide in defense of society."[102] In their attempt to blame lynching events on all but the mob itself, newspapers blamed outside agitators for inflaming people through their support of Black citizens. Northern groups such as the International Labor Defense came south to fight against lynching. "Placing the focus on Northern invaders rather than on their own racial biases allowed the citizens to ignore the issue that would continue to haunt them throughout the Civil Rights movement."[103] One editor pointed out that "Negroes must learn—and most of them do know—that they occupy a peculiar place in this land and must keep it," thus blaming Blacks for overstepping their boundaries. Another editor blamed White people for being too "prone to be familiar with negroes and socialize with them, allowing them reasons to suppose their presence among White people is acceptable" and thus they were responsible for the deaths of the Blacks who had to be taught "their place."[104]

Journalist Ray Stannard Baker, considered a "muckraker" in the early part of the twentieth century, wrote for *McClure's* magazine. In his investigation of a lynching in Georgia (the burning of Will Cato and Paul Reed), he found the town of Statesboro, where the lynching took place, to be like any other American town. Trying to understand what could drive a typical upstanding White southerner to participate in such a horrendous act, Baker concluded that the fault lay with the "worthless" or "floating" Black rather than inherently in the racism of the White population. "In all the towns I visited, South as well as North, I found that this floating, worthless negro caused most of the trouble. He prowls the roads by day and by night; he steals; he makes it unsafe for women to travel alone."[105]

"The news media are important in the history of lynching because they helped to uphold the social order and molded public opinion on this issue."[106] Public opinion was in favor of lynching, and this was reflected in the news media as newspapers provided "abundant, even graphic coverage of vigilante violence."[107] Readers were regaled with details of torture, horrendous deaths, and the taking of body parts (both from still living victims and those already dead) as souvenirs. Blacks were assumed to be guilty, and the press justified the actions of the mobs. Economic factors (selling newspapers as well as control by business owners) contributed to the graphic way in which lynchings were described. In small towns, editors themselves could face repercussions if they spoke out against lynching, particularly when the victim was a "female member of a good family."[108]

Major newspapers such as the *Chicago Tribune* and the *New York Times* spoke against lynching but even so, their stories still contained bias such as assumptions of Black guilt and stereotypes about Black Americans being prone to murder and violence. Coverage and condemnation of lynching slowly changed over time; by the second decade of the twentieth century, even some southern newspapers were beginning to question the practice, not just because of the barbaric inhumanity of it, but also because of the reflection on Southern communities and the effect this might have on developing businesses in the area. Still, "many papers persisted in running sensational stories about lynching parties that whipped up racial hatred."[109]

Newspapers carried stories that justified the lynch mob's actions, dehumanized victims, and "assumed the Black person's race predisposed him to commit violent crimes, particularly rape . . ."[110] Perloff argues that even with these many faults, the fact that the press kept news of lynchings on the public agenda, with all their horrific details, undoubtedly contributed to the change in public opinion in the twentieth century; by 1937, seventy percent of the nation was in favor of anti-lynching legislation.[111] However, even within the framework of the constraints of historical time, place, and economic reality, newspapers could have done much more to combat lynching. "It seems abundantly clear that while the mainstream media fiddled and equivocated, thousands of people, mostly Black, lost their lives."[112]

William Cowper Brann produced a magazine in Texas called the *Iconoclast* in the 1890s, which eventually reached close to 100,000 readers both nationally and internationally. The magazine consisted of Brann's views on a variety of social, political, and economic topics and was the only magazine of its type published west of the Mississippi at that time. Brann had decided views on Blacks, describing them as "negro rape-fiends," "Black monsters," "beasts," and more. "We have hunted the Black rape-fiend to death with hounds, bored him with buckshot; fricasseed him over slow fires and flayed him alive; but the despoilment of White women by these brutal imps of darkness and the devil is still of daily occurrence."[113] Brann stated that all Blacks should be driven out, even the "good negro," as it was better to kill or banish a thousand "good negroes" than to have one White woman "be debauched." "During the slavery regime the negro kept his place like any other beast of the field . . . but when his shackles were stricken off and he was accorded political equality with his old-time master he became presumptuous, insolent—actually imagine that the foolish attempt of fanatics to humanize him had been successful—that a law of nature had been repealed by act of Congress!"[114] These were the kinds of stories in the popular press that provided the context for lynching and illustrate the creation of Black Americans as animals and criminals.

Spectacle and Souvenirs

Photographs taken at lynchings were used to spread the event beyond its physical boundaries, which served to teach other Whites a standard formula for lynching and controlled a much wider group of Blacks. Members of lynch mobs posed with the corpses of their victims just as hunters pose with the game they have killed. "In some cases, these macabre photographs were hawked from home to home and town to town, a way for the photographers to make money and for Whites who could not be present to participate vicariously in the expression of power the pictures represented."[115] Photographs were made into postcards that could be spread even farther. "Furthermore, the lynching photographs were often circulated along with photographs of the White victims of the Black alleged criminals, constructing and reinforcing a narrative of White innocence and Black guilt."[116]

While lynching as a general response had occurred for decades in the nineteenth century, by the end of the century, the victims were primarily Black, and the lynchings themselves had become more sadistic and exhibitionist.[117]

To kill the victim was not enough; the execution became public theater, a participatory ritual of torture and death, a voyeuristic spectacle prolonged as long as possible (once for seven hours) for the benefit of the crowd. Newspapers on a number of occasions announced in advance the times and place of a lynching, special "excursion" trains transported spectators to the scene, employers sometimes released their workers to attend, parents sent notes to school asking teachers to excuse their children for the event. . . .[118]

Body parts and pieces of the execution apparatus (bits of the tree from which someone was hanged, pieces of burnt wood, chain, or rope) became souvenirs. "Such human trophies might reappear as watch fobs or be displayed conspicuously for public viewing. The severed knuckles of Sam Hose, for example, would be prominently displayed in the window of a grocery store in Atlanta."[119]

The "amusement" of lynching included official photographs with proud White lynchers posed beside the remains of their victim, specially chartered trains that brought crowds to participate and watch the event, and newspaper accounts that included all the horrific details of the torture and murder. Men, women, and even children attended and participated in these large spectacle lynchings. "And by continuing and expanding the circulation of the stories, even anti-lynching activists' use of lynchings as spectacle helped maintain the power of the practice as a cultural form and aided in the cultural work these narratives performed."[120]

". . . [W]hite violence against southern Blacks was not limited only to lynchings—White men continued in more private settings to rape Black women and assault African Americans for 'reasons' ranging from Black resistance and economic success to White hatred, jealousy, and fear."[121] While more Blacks were killed by small groups of White men who hunted them down and shot or hanged them, far more publicity was given to the publicly attended tortures and killings. Hale describes how lynching developed into a spectacle for amusement that included certain rituals and structures, particularly as the growing media could spread details of each lynching far and wide. "The main event then began with a period of mutilation—often including emasculation—and torture to exact confessions and entertain the crowd, and built to a climax of slow burning, hanging, and/or shooting to complete the killing. The finale consisted of frenzied souvenir gathering and display of the body and the collected parts."[122] While alive, Luther Holbert and his wife were beaten and had their fingers and ears cut off, and then the crowd used a large corkscrew to bore holes into their flesh, removing large chunks as it was pulled out.[123]

Sam Hose was lynched in Georgia in 1899. "Before the torch was applied to the pyre the negro was deprived of his ears, fingers and other portions of his anatomy." These were handed out to the crowd. "The body was not cut down. It was cut to pieces. The crowd fought for places about the smouldering tree, and with knives, secured such pieces of his carcass as did not fall to pieces." His heart and liver were cut into pieces for souvenirs. The *Charleston News and Courier* reported on April 24, 1899, "One special and two regular trains carried nearly 4,000 persons to Newnan to witness the burning of Sam Hose, or to visit the scene of the horrible affair. The excursionists returning to-night were loaded down with ghastly reminders of the affair in the shape of bones, pieces of flesh and parts of the wood, which was placed at the negro's feet."[124]

Newspapers, which had received prior word that the lynching would take place, made sure they had representatives there, "and in the Monday edition reporters as eyewitnesses detailed the cutting off of Hose's ears, his castration, and his very slow burning."[125] While the papers spoke of orderly crowds, and a "calm, avenging White civilization," the realities of these events were far different. "The barbarism of the trophy-gathering in particular exploded any claim of White deliberateness and calm. Mob members had collected some body parts, the choice ears and penis and fingers cut off before the fire, and many spectators afterward turned 'souvenir seekers,' rushing in to push back the still-hot coals and hack up the body, cutting out the heart and other internal organs, fighting rival onlookers for the most cherished prizes."[126] Newspapers, trains, and the press were well informed before a lynching took place as was the law, yet no attempt was made to stop lynchings or to hold those in the mob responsible, pointing to the complicity of the legal system in maintaining White hegemony and relegating Black Americans to a lesser, disposable status.

Jesse Washington was lynched in May 1916 in Waco, Texas. He was accused of raping a White woman. A caption of one of the photographs taken of the lynching explains that "the mayor of Waco, who watched the entire episode from an excellent vantage point on the second floor of City Hall, was concerned that the lynchers might damage the tree but expressed no concern for the human being who was stabbed, beaten, mutilated, hanged, and burned to death before his eyes."[127] Jesse was only 17 years old at the time and thought to be retarded. A crowd estimated to be between 10,000 and 15,000 watched him die.

Before the lynching, six defense attorneys had been appointed for Washington's trial. They did nothing to represent Washington, and it took the jury a mere four minutes to determine his guilt. Sheriff Sam Fleming was running for reelection in a close race at the time of the lynching. Had he opposed the lynch mob, it is very likely he would have lost the election. Fleming left the courtroom after telling his men to let the crowd get Jesse Washington, who was then dragged down the street. The mob took off his clothes, cut him with knives, and beat him with shovels, bricks, and clubs. A chain was put around his neck and thrown over a tree. When he grabbed it, members of the mob cut his fingers off as well as his ears and genitals. Coal oil was poured over him, and he was set on fire. The chain was used to raise and lower him in and out of the fire, thus prolonging his agony.

Photographer Fred Gildersleeve took photographs during the lynching that were later sold. Afterward, pieces of bone were sold, as were teeth ($5.00 each) and some of the chain's links ($0.25). Washington's body was dragged until his head fell off. The rest of his body was then dragged to another town, where it was put in a sack and hung up for all to see. In echoes from this event down the century, James Byrd Jr.'s killing in 1998 included Byrd being dragged behind a pickup truck (though he was still alive) until he struck a culvert that decapitated him, thus mimicking the events of Washington's death. Byrd's remains were left in front of a church for public viewing.

The *Waco Morning News* reported that while a few were opposed to the lynching (or at least the extremely brutal way in which it was carried out), most people seemed satisfied with the events of the day of the lynching. "For many of Waco's Whites, the elaborately interwoven and often wholly illogical lies about Black men and the danger they posed to White women formed a thick veil that distorted the spectacle of a retarded seventeen-year-old boy chained to a tree, bleeding from dozens of wounds, without fingers, ears, toes, or genitals, writhing in a fire."[128] Elizabeth Freeman, sent by the NAACP to investigate the murder, spoke to many townspeople, both Black and White, and concluded that "the rape was either automatically assumed or, worse, made up by the authorities to facilitate Jesse Washington's conviction."[129]

"As the . . . Hose, and Washington lynchings demonstrated, then, innovations like trains and cars, telegraphs and telephones, and cheaper newspapers and photographs could expand and strengthen the power of each incident as easily as they increased White condemnation."[130] Coupled with the newly released *Birth of a Nation* with its lynching scene, the entire nation could participate in these events. Hale identifies the lynching of Claude Neal in 1934 as the end of the practice of spectacle lynching due in part to growing public condemnation of these events, the South's realization that an image of brutality did nothing to further its economic interests, and the NAACP's pamphlet about the Neal lynching that was used to push for antilynching legislation. The NAACP sent Howard Kester from the Committee on Economic and Racial Justice to report on the lynching within a week or so of its occurrence. Kester's description, based on interviews with local

Whites, Blacks, and newspaper staff, of all the awful details of Neal's torture and killing, was included in the pamphlet. The events included cutting off Neal's penis and testicles then making him eat them, cutting off his fingers and slicing his sides, burning him with red hot irons, and choking him almost to the point of death. Then the torture would start again. Finally dead, his body was tied to a car and dragged around. At one point, a woman drove a butcher knife through his body, and members of the crowd drove their cars over it.[131]

Images of the "Black beast rapist" worked to unite southern Whites in a culture of segregation and to remind Blacks of their place and what happened when they transgressed (or were thought to have transgressed) the contained spaces allotted them, as the "culture of segregation made race dependent on space."[132] Hales goes on to point out that ". . . lynchings denied that any space was Black space, even the very bodies of African Americans were subject to invasion by Whites."[133] Black bodies themselves became commodities as body parts were collected and sold as souvenirs after a lynching. "This much, these lynchings said, could never be changed: Blacks were humans who could be treated as nonhuman, and no amount of care on their part to follow the 'rules' could in the end ensure their safety."[134]

Those we rely on to encourage us to be our best possible selves by showing us injustices and how we might remedy them were all involved in supporting lynching. For decades the mainstream news media, if not outright condoning the practice, did little to provide the kind of coverage that would strengthen those who condemned the practice or support those who were too timid themselves to speak out. Instead, they blamed the victims and outside agitators while forgiving the mobs as justified. Even on the floor of the House and Senate, politicians supported the practice and refused to vote in an antilynching law, sending a clear message to Black Americans that they were not equal citizens under protection of the Constitution and the law. Law enforcement itself was often in collusion with the lynch mobs, standing back as Blacks were dragged out of courtrooms and jail cells, and slaughtered brutally outside in the streets.

MOVE-IN VIOLENCE

One of the biggest surprises about anti-integrationist violence is its universal nature.[135]

New York City in the late 1980s and early 1990s was the scene of a rising number of bias crimes, primarily perpetrated by youth under the age of 21. Incidents in New York City included the murders in Bensonhurst and Howard Beach. Hate crimes went up from a reported 235 in 1986 to 463 in 1987 and 550 in 1988. In 1982, half the confirmed hate crimes were anti-Semitic and primarily directed against property. After 1985, Blacks became the primary target of bias crimes, "and the percentage of physical assaults increased significantly."[136] Pinderhughes argues that the rising racial violence in

New York was the result of factors impacting the city's youth, which included structural conditions, ethnic and racial attitudes, peer group pressures, and community sentiment. "White youths who live in close-knit ethnic communities which fear Blacks and other minorities are supported in keeping unwanted minorities out of their neighborhoods." He points to a pattern of racially motivated violence rather than the incidental/aberration model that most news sources favor. Structural changes included "White flight" from the city as the foreign-born population increased by about 1 million. Lower-class families were finding it increasingly difficult to find affordable housing. As Italian and Jewish Americans moved within the city due to the entry of Blacks, Puerto Ricans, Asians, and West Indians, they settled in neighborhoods like Bensonhurst, Canarsie, Gravesend, and Sheepshead Bay. "All minority groups, but particularly African Americans, were perceived as a direct threat to the quality of neighborhood life, as intruders who had the potential to ruin the stable, safe, close-knit ethnic niche the White community had taken years to establish."[137] Pinderhughes found that young Whites saw themselves as victims of reverse discrimination, as they believed policies put in place to help Blacks created favoritism that disadvantaged Whites. However, these youths blamed crime and violence in the city on Blacks. "Many of the young people described crimes committed by Blacks as the main reason for racial tension in the city. There was a widespread feeling that Blacks were violent troublemakers who were especially dangerous and bold in large groups." Their assumption was that any Blacks who came into their neighborhoods were looking for trouble and to commit crimes. "Consequently, they felt that they had the right and obligation to defend their territory against Blacks; that is was up to them to 'stop the Blacks'; that if they attacked these outsiders, they would send a message to all Blacks from outside the neighborhood to stay out of their communities."[138]

Peer group pressure resulted in the need to prove one was "down with the program," and this often led to "missions" in which groups of young Whites went looking for people to harass and beat up. "You go out and you're lookin' for people. The best is if you catch a couple of Black guys. Or if you can't find no Blacks, maybe you find an Indian or an Arab or a Dominican."[139] Going on these missions provided a sense of belonging (us versus them) and a sense of power. The neighborhoods were complicit in many ways either by directly supporting activities that maintained the ethnic purity of the neighborhood or by turning a blind eye. "These kids even get rewards from some of the shopowners for taking care of Blacks who look suspicious. A fellah up the street gives away free pizza, if you can believe it."[140] After the murder of Yusuf Hawkins, members of the Bensonhurst neighborhood insisted it was not a racially motivated killing, and many refused to talk about what they knew or to help the police in any way.

Pinderhughes points to the neoconservative climate as exemplified by the rhetoric from the 1988 Bush campaign, the public positions on affirmative action and racial inequality taken by the Reagan and Bush administrations, as well as by politicians such as Jesse Helms and David Dukes, as underlying factors in the opinion formation of these young Whites. The sense of victimization espoused by the youths echoed those in the dominant conservative climate at the time. After Hawkins's murder, the press provided much commentary on the Benson-hurst neighborhood and the conditions there that were factors in the incident. As Pinderhughes rightly points out, this individual aberration explanation ignores the larger problem.

In fact, labeling Bensonhurst as a "racist community" shifts the analysis from wider con-ditions and factors to an analysis of the people of Bensonhurst—from a systemic and gen-eralizable examination of the problem to a more microscopic, individual analysis. What sets Bensonhurst apart is simply that Yusuf Hawkins died there. The statements of youths elsewhere in southern Brooklyn reveal that racially motivated attacks occur regularly in other White ethnic communities.[141]

The youths' behavior in New York was an extension of the neighborhoods' and societal attitudes prevalent at the time, translated into action on the street and often with tacit and sometimes open approval from neighbors and family. "Messages from parents, community residents, and political representatives at many different levels have been incorporated into a street ideology which pro-vides justifications for racial violence."[142]

Christopher Lyons talked about similar events in Chicago, exploring how racial composition, in-migration, and community identity all influenced racially motivated hate crimes. He found that anti-Black hate crimes were most common in homogenous White communities with a strong community identity and a recent history of Black in-migration. The defended community model describes hate crimes as expressions of power, particularly in areas where the demographics are changing long-standing racial homogeneity. A strong sense of identity in a particular community makes hate crimes against those seen as intruders more likely than in mixed communities or those that do not have such a strong sense of one identity. "The defended community perspective conceives of racial hate crimes as strategies, albeit extreme, for defending against threats posed to valued identities and ways of life."[143] Lyons agrees with Pinderhughes that defensive hate crimes (defending territory from supposed intruders) may receive at least the perception of support from the community during times when the commun-ity's demographics are first changing. He found that anti-Black hate crimes peaked in communities that were about 70 percent White. As the percentage of Whites goes down and communities become more mixed, the rate of anti-Black hate crime decreases. Lyons also found no evidence that White economic strain or changes in White employment patterns affected anti-Black hate crimes. Clearly, spatial proximity is an important factor in the shifting rates of hate crime as non-Whites move into formerly predominantly White neighborhoods and immediate contact between groups increases. Most violence against those moving in takes place in the neighborhood; perpetrators do not usually go looking for victims far from their own spaces.

Throughout the end of the twentieth century and into the twenty-first, violence and hate crimes have occurred in numerous neighborhoods as Black people move to traditionally predominantly or completely White areas. While most Americans may consider this type of anti-integration a thing of the past, it continues today. "Over the past thirty years, the overall level of racial segregation in housing has changed little. Many communities are nearly as segregated today as they were in the 1980s."[144] Blacks and other non-Whites have experienced hatred expressed through cross burning, assault, vandalism, and arson when they move into some entrenched White neighborhoods. These hate crimes take a toll on them financially and emotionally as they threaten not only parents, but children and occur in and around the place that is imagined as a safe haven, the home.

Targeting minorities who are moving into certain neighborhoods reinforces racial hierarchies and segregation. Racial zoning ordinances began to appear at the beginning of the twentieth century, particularly in the South, with the purpose of segregating housing and restricting Black people to particular areas of the city. Although the U.S. Supreme Court struck down many of these zoning ordinances as unconstitutional (*Buchanan vs. Warley* in 1917, for example), in practical terms, the actions of White landlords, real estate agents, and banks who controlled mortgage loans served to maintain segregation in many areas.[145] As the Black population in the North grew during the twentieth century, move-in violence there also increased. "In Chicago, between July 1917 and March 1921, fifty-eight homes of Black families who moved into White neighborhoods were bombed."[146]

As part of Roosevelt's New Deal, the Federal Housing Administration (FHA) was created in 1934. The FHA's program to double the number of American home owners by 1960 include a rating map of different neighborhoods based on "the quality of housing stock and racial composition" in 140 cities. Neighborhoods were rated A (best) through D (worst) based on an assessment of risk to the lender's money. Those looking for homes in D neighborhoods would have little or no chance of getting an FHA loan. While property values were an important consideration, the issue of race was paramount. The manual used by the FHA suggested that neighborhood stability hinged on maintaining the same social and racial classes within the neighborhood. "A grade of D was awarded to neighborhoods with even a few Black families. If the neighborhood had a D rating, it was redlined, and lenders were strongly cautioned against lending to those who wanted to buy properties in those areas."[147] The FHA's determination that property values go down in the presence of a Black family has created a self-fulfilling prophecy simply by defining values based on race. White fear of losing home value supports this determination and contributes to maintaining segregated neighborhoods.

Between May 1944 and July 1946, forty-six Black homes were the site of vandalism, arson, or bombing in Chicago. In a 15-month period at the end of the 1930s, there were nearly 20 bombings in Dallas. In Oregon, the Portland Realty Board forbade its members to sell houses in White neighborhoods to either Blacks or Asians. Portland residents put up "Whites Only" signs in the downtown area and at businesses close to the bus station.[148] In Detroit, "[b]etween 1943 and 1965 approximately two hundred neighborhood organizations—'civic associations,' 'homeowners associations,' and 'improvement associations'—were created to defend their neighborhoods against Black entry."[149] Attacks on Blacks moving into White neighborhoods around the country included many varieties of harassment, vandalism, destruction, and violence. Some of the incidents included putting snakes in the basement, arson bombings, shootings, stonings, dumping trash on the lawn, threats (verbal and written), destroying landscaping, beatings and other assaults, vandalizing and destroying cars, burning crosses in the yard, burning houses down completely, and setting off dynamite under houses. Some of these incidents maimed, some killed. All were designed to terrorize Black people into retreating from entrenched White neighborhoods. "Though many move-in attacks are physically violent, frequently acts of neighborhood terrorism begin with incidents of harassment—vandalism or the use of slurs and epithets—that have a low offense level but are nevertheless terrifying to those targeted."[150]

In the 1970s, Blacks began moving in to the middle-class Canarsie neighborhood in Brooklyn, New York, which was predominantly Jewish and Italian at the time. Residents formed block associations to encourage home owners to sell only to other Whites. Some took to violence to prevent Blacks from moving in, including firebombing. "National investigations of attacks on minorities in the mid-1980s identified violence directed at minority families moving to White neighborhoods as the most common form of violent racism in the country."[151] During this same time, larger organizations aimed at maintaining White-only neighborhoods started to give way to violence and harassment by smaller groups or individuals. This followed the same pattern as had happened with lynching which changed from large group events and public spectacles to more private smaller-group murders. Tensions in New York increased after three White on Black murders (Yusuf Hawkins, Michael Griffin, and Willie Turks). The attacks were well publicized, as was the aftermath of racial slurs and neighborhood protests. While newspapers and television news programs showed counterprotests against such openly racist behavior, they also provided widespread information regarding the neighborhoods' antipathy toward Black neighbors, making it clearer than ever that these areas were not welcoming for Blacks.

The label of hate crime for anti-integrationist violence provides a context and the ability to push these incidents beyond regular vandalism to something that is treated by the media and the police as important enough for a response. The targets of this violence suffer significant harm mentally, sometimes physically, to their property and to their sense of safety and well-being, leaving an increased sense of vulnerability. Publicity spreads the message of hate far more widely than just the neighborhood where the violence occurs. Extremist-perpetrated hate crimes are not the norm but have taken on a more mythological nature. Jeannine Bell's study on anti-integrationist violence works to dispel this idea. She points out that the majority of hate crimes are not committed by people in organized hate groups but by "regular" people.[152]

Census data reveal that Black-White segregation in this country has changed little in the past 20 years, and ". . . there is significant evidence throughout the 1990s and continuing until the present day that minorities who move to White neighborhoods experience violence on a nearly daily basis." In surveys that included a question about support for laws allowing home owners to decide themselves whether or not to discriminate in housing, 63.8 percent in 1973 and 27 percent in 2006 felt that the owner should have this option. While the change is significant, close to a third of those surveyed still felt that discrimination should be a choice in 2006.[153] Survey results also point to White discomfort with neighborhoods containing Black Americans (more so than those with Asian Americans and Hispanics). And as Bell so rightly points out, "Theoretical support for integration is distinctly different from the neighborhoods that Whites choose in actuality."[154] Whites with the most negative stereotypes of racial and ethnic minorities were, unsurprisingly, the group most likely to prefer neighbors who are also White.[155] Other minority groups agree in many ways with the dominant perspective as ". . . even among other people of color, such as Asian Americans and Latinos, African Americans are the least preferred neighbors."[156]

On March 21, 1997, thirteen-year-old Lenard Clark, a Black American, rode his bike with a friend into the predominantly White neighborhood of Bridgeport in Chicago. He was knocked off his bike and beaten into a coma by three White men just for being in "their" neighborhood. "The men later bragged to their friends about keeping Bridgeport White."[157] The publicity after the attack served to underscore the fact that Blacks were not welcome in Bridgeport. "When just being Black is a violation of territorial boundaries, there is nothing African Americans can do to avoid being targeted besides move to another area. Because it is impossible for individuals to change their race, if they remain in the area they are always vulnerable to attack."[158] The General Social Survey in 1990 found that more than 50 percent of Whites rated Blacks and Hispanics as less intelligent than Whites. About the same percentage of White Americans also rated them as prone to violence. An even higher percentage of Whites, over 66 percent, rated

Blacks and Hispanics as preferring to live off welfare rather than to work.[159] Dominant attitudes such as these create the context for the move-in violence that continues to take place in too many neighborhoods across the country.

Anti-integrationist violence is, unfortunately, largely unreported, and when it is reported, there is often a failure to investigate and to prosecute. Many neighbors are unwilling to help police investigate, and victims may decide to leave because prosecution may not make them comfortable with the neighborhood. This provides those who perpetrate this type of hate crime the advantage of fulfilling their desires while not being punished for their actions.

Ami Lynch looked at the role of hate crimes, particularly race-based violence, in contributing to and maintaining residential segregation in the United States. "Blacks and Whites live separately from one another, experience little contact, and do not have the opportunity to get to know each other, so they rely on salient characteristics and stereotypes to assess one another."[160] The most common hate crime offender, in contrast to public opinion, is what Lynch and others call "reactionary offenders" who respond to what they see as an intrusion into physical space (a neighborhood, for example), social circles, jobs, or the country as a whole. Like Bell, she found that the more hate crimes in a city, the higher the levels of neighborhood segregation in that city.[161] Hate crimes thus influence where people live, which in turn determines the resources available to them. Lynch states, "What becomes evident from this study is that Blacks continue to be a highly disfavored group in America. Blacks are disproportionately targeted for hate crimes . . ." A history of racism directed against Blacks has resulted in their marking as acceptable victims to hate crime perpetrators. "Blacks are the most dehumanized of racial minority groups and, although nowadays vocal vehement racism may be frowned upon in society, this does not stop the actions related to such racism from happening."[162] Beliefs about Black behavior and criminality give Whites incentive and motivation to "protect" their neighborhoods from Blacks moving in. "Hate crime is strongly tied to location and intrinsically linked to the social forces of the neighborhood."[163]

It is not random acts but the overall pattern and structure of discrimination in American society that makes hate crimes such a strong tool of hegemonic control. Anti-integrationist violence, while perpetrated by individuals, also highlights the structural inequities as the police fail to protect residents in their own neighborhoods and as the system of home ownership from neighborhood rankings to real estate practices to bank lending practices all contribute to maintaining segregation. Media publicity of hate events is a two-edged sword as it brings condemnation but also serves to spread the word more widely regarding neighborhood antipathies. Media explanations for events, particularly those focused on individual or limited models of responsibility, also contribute to maintaining the status quo and perpetuating old stereotypes.

EXAMPLES OF HATE CRIMES

On June 22, 1982, Black New York City transit worker Willie Turks decided to stop after work to get a snack with two of his co-workers, Dennis Dixon and Donald Cooper. The three drove into the Brooklyn neighborhood of Gravesend. As they left a bagel shop and got back into their car, a White youth yelled racial epithets at them. The car was soon surrounded by a group of 15 to 20 young White men who rocked the car and broke its windows. As Dixon and Cooper fled, 34-year-old Willie Turks, his arm in a cast, was pulled out of the car and beaten to death by the mob of predominantly Italian American men. Eventually, four of the men were convicted of the crime. Paul Mormando, age 19, was sentenced to two consecutive one-year terms for misdemeanor assault, second-degree riot, and discrimination. Although it is likely he was responsible not only for pulling Turks from the car, but throwing a bottle that severely injured Dixon, he served a total of seven months. While the incident was recognized as a racially motivated killing, an unprovoked attack that had everything to do with race, there was little mention of bias crime or hate crime in the press.

Howard Beach

Late on the night of December 19, 1986, four Black men were driving back to Brooklyn when their car broke down near the Howard Beach section of Queens. While Curtis Sylvester stayed with his car, the other three headed off to find a subway back to Brooklyn. These three were 23-year-old Michael Griffith (Sylvester's cousin), 36-year-old Cedric Sandiford (married to Griffith's mother), and 18-year-old Timothy Grimes. After a verbal encounter with some White teenagers, the three went to the New Park Pizzeria. While they were there, someone called the police because they were considered "suspicious looking," although they merely ordered and ate pizza. The police came, and finding that nothing untoward was happening, left. When the three left the pizzeria, they again encountered a group of White teenagers (the original few had gone back to a party and recruited others; they also collected metal baseball bats and tree limbs). The three men ran in different directions to escape the mob. Grimes escaped unscathed. Sandiford was attacked by one group while another chased Griffith, who ran out onto the Belt Parkway and was hit and killed by a car. Even after witnessing Griffith's death (his body flew 125 feet along the parkway and his head was split open), the group chasing him then returned to Sandiford and continued to beat him. Sandiford eventually got away and met up with the police on the parkway. The police treated Sandiford as a suspect, keeping him in the squad car for close to three hours just feet away from the body of his stepson and without treatment for his injuries.

Three defendants—Jon Lester, Jason Ladone, and Scott Kern—were originally charged with murder, second-degree murder, second-degree manslaughter, and assault in addition to reckless endangerment. All three were found guilty of manslaughter in the second degree and assault. The three victims in what came to be known as the Howard Beach incident were blamed by the press and the defense for being in the wrong place on the night of the attack. Both the police and the press immediately questioned their presence in Howard Beach, thus pulling some of the focus away from the crime and the perpetrators. The police, upon finding Cedric Sandiford wandering around dazed after the beating he had received, treated him as a suspect rather than a victim; the papers did the same, repeatedly questioning the statements made by Sandiford as to why he and his friends were even in Howard Beach and pointing out the fact that one of them carried a beeper (immediately creating him as a suspected drug dealer) and one carried a toy gun (thus creating a suspected robber). The use of drugs by the four Black men and the criminal histories of at least two of them gave the press plenty of fodder for assigning to the victims some measure of guilt in their own beatings and the death of one. Even though the story of the broken-down car was verified by several sources, the question of why the Blacks had ventured into this particular neighborhood kept being raised. The implication was that they had no right to be there.

The incident at Howard Beach clearly was racial in nature, and this was discussed at length in the press. The trial brought out the words spoken by Jon Lester to bring the White mob together: "There's niggers on the boulevard, let's go fucking kill them!" Many pointed to the high rate of robbery in the area, rising housing costs, fears of unemployment, fear of outsiders—particularly Blacks—and the strong Italian roots of the neighborhood as explanations for the incident. Numerous articles pointed to the fear of Black crime that existed in Howard Beach, where assumptions were that to be Black was equivalent to being criminal. The fact that the police were called simply because three Black men were eating in a pizza place demonstrates the insular nature of the neighborhood and the assumptions about dark skinned outsiders that were made.

Other writers pointed out that fear of Black crime was legitimate (though the usual victims were Black as well), and it was the Black community's responsibility to change. In many articles, the focus was pulled away from the facts (that White youths beat Black men and caused the death of one) to justifications of the Whites' behavior and a questioning of the victim status of the beaten Blacks. One writer stated, "The most fundamental unanswered question is what four Black men from Brooklyn ... were doing in Queens on that pre-Christmas Saturday evening."[164] Just as the earlier press rationalized White mob participation in lynching by blaming the Black victims, the press in the Howard Beach case attempted to mitigate the responsibility of the perpetrators.

On June 29, 2005, a group of White men once again attacked three Black men in Howard Beach, beating one with a baseball bat and fracturing his skull. The three Blacks fled into nearby swampland and through the neighborhood in an attempt to escape. One, Glenn Moore, 22, tripped over a lawn sign, and the attackers beat him with a metal bat, stole his shoes and other belongings, and ripped an earring from his ear. He was sent to the hospital with head, back, and leg injuries. Police arrested 19-year-old Nicholas Minucci and charged him with assault in the first degree as a hate crime. Two others were arrested, Anthony Ench, who pled guilty to lesser charges, and Frankie Agostini, who was given immunity in exchange for testifying against Minucci. This incident took place just blocks from the 1986 Howard Beach killing. "What do you think you're doing in this neighborhood?" In an eerie echo from 1986, the question of what three Black men were doing in Howard Beach was raised again. According to the 2000 census, of the 8,734 residents of Howard Beach, only eight were Black. Residents expressed some sympathy for Moore, "But what was he doing here at three in the morning, robbing?" Less sympathy was expressed for the White perpetrators than in the past. New York mayor Bloomberg immediately contacted Al Sharpton for advice and to assure him that racial attacks would not be tolerated. Minucci was found guilty of first- and second-degree robbery as a hate crime and was given a sentence of 15 years.

The racially created Other in America has existed since the beginning of contact with physical difference on this continent. Those created as Black have been the recipients of centuries of violence and subjugation, first through slavery and then by years of segregation and a slow movement toward integration and equality. Contestations over space have occurred and continue to occur as Black Americans move from lives as property to a freedom bound by laws and cultural practices containing them as a lesser people. These contestations have often been violent. The long history of negative images contained in the media, the law, and popular entertainment accompanies an equally long history of lynching, individual murders, and hate crimes even today. The same dehumanization that exists in war has been attached to racial Others in America and has allowed Black Americans to be tortured and killed, their bodies the site of trophy-taking and dehumanization. While individual perpetrators of hate crimes have been the focus of media attention, societal institutions too have a long history of complicity in creating Black Americans as Other and containing them, often through violence, in limited spaces. Focus on aberrant individuals such as White supremacists ignores the long history of violence perpetrated by "ordinary" White Americans on Black Americans.

NOTES

1. George Lipsitz, *The Possessive Investment in Whiteness: How White People Profit from Identity Politics* (Philadelphia: Temple University Press, 2006), 1.

2. Ian F. Haney Lopez, "The social construction of race: Some observations on illusion, fabrication, and choice," *Harvard Civil Rights–Civil Liberties Law Review* 29, no. 1 (1994): 3.

3. Ibid., 12.

4. Ibid., 24.

5. Michael Omi and Howard Winant, *Racial Formation in the United States* (New York: Routledge, 1994).

6. Barbara Fields, "Ideology and race in American history," in *Region, Race, and Reconstruction: Essays in Honor of C. Vann Woodward*, edited by J. Morgan Kousser and James M. McPherson (New York and Oxford: Oxford University Press, 1982), 147.

7. Sam Torres, "Hate crimes against African Americans: The extent of the problem," *Journal of Contemporary Criminal Justice* 15, no. 1 (1999): 48.

8. Ibid., 56.

9. Laura Smith, Madonna G. Constantine, Sheila V. Graham, and Chelsea B. Dize, "The territory ahead for multicultural competence: The 'spinning' of racism," *Professional Psychology: Research and Practice* 39, no. 3, (2008): 337.

10. Ibid., 338.

11. Ibid., 342.

12. Ibid., 343.

13. Eduardo Bonilla Silva, Amanda Lewis, and David G. Embrick, "'I did not get that job because of a Black man . . .': The story lines and testimonies of color-blind racism," *Sociological Forum* 19, no. 4 (December 2004): 560.

14. Ibid., 575.

15. Ibid., 576.

16. Grace Elizabeth Hale, *Making Whiteness: The Culture of Segregation in the South, 1890–1940* (New York: Vintage, 1998), 125.

17. Ibid., 155.

18. Ibid., 156.

19. Ibid., 163.

20. Ibid., 191.

21. Ibid., 194.

22. Ronald Humphrey and Howard Schuman, "The portrayal of Blacks in magazine advertisements, 1950–1982," *Public Opinion Quarterly* 48, no. 3 (Autumn 1984): 562.

23. Ibid., 563.

24. Kevin Keenan, "Skin tones and physical features of Blacks in magazine advertisements," *Journalism and Mass Communication Quarterly* 73, no. 4 (Winter 1996): 905–912.

25. Verna M. Keith and Cedric Herring, "Skin tones and stratification in the Black community," *American Journal of Sociology* 97, no. 3 (November 1991): 760.

26. Ibid., 768.

27. Ibid., 775.

28. Kathy Russell-Cole, Midge Wilson, and Ronald Hall, *The Color Complex: The Politics of Skin Color among African Americans* (New York: Harcourt Brace Jovanovich, 1992), 101.

29. Ibid., 49–50.

30. Ibid., 187.

31. Evelyn Nakano Glenn (ed.), *Shades of Difference: Why Skin Color Matters* (Stanford, CA: Stanford University Press, 2009), 27.

32. Ibid., Chapter 5.

33. Russell-Cole, Wilson, and Hall, *Color Complex*, 109.

34. Ibid., 134.

35. Ibid., 143.

36. Daniel Leab, *From Sambo to Superspade: The Black Experience in Motion Pictures* (Boston: Houghton Mifflin Company, 1975), 10.

37. Russell-Cole, Wilson, and Hall, *Color Complex*, 147.

38. Ibid., 149.

39. Christopher Geist and Jack Nachbar, *The Popular Culture Reader* (Bowling Green, OH: Bowling Green University Popular Press, 1983), 159.

40. Winthrop Jordan, *White Over Black: American Attitudes toward the Negro, 1550–1812* (Chapel Hill: University of North Carolina Press, 1968), 8.

41. Geist and Nachbar, *Popular Culture Reader*, 161.

42. Jordan, *White Over Black*, 31–32.

43. Ibid., 156.

44. Ibid., 157.

45. Michael LeMay, *The Struggle for Influence: The Impact of Minority Groups on Politics and Public Policy in the United States* (New York: University Press of American, 1985), 212.

46. Randall Kennedy, *Race, Crime, and the Law* (New York: Vintage, 1997), 101.

47. Leab, 17–18.

48. Thomas Cripps, *Slow Fade to Black: The Negro in American Film, 1900-1942* (New York: Oxford University Press, 1977), 13.

49. Geist and Nachbar, *Popular Culture Reader*, 167.

50. Leab, *From Sambo to Superspade*, 25.

51. Ibid., 99.

52. Diana Gordon, *The Justice Juggernaut: Fighting Street Crime, Controlling Citizens* (New Brunswick, NJ: Rutgers University Press, 1991), 161.

53. Jerome G. Miller, *Search and Destroy: African-American Males in the Criminal Justice System* (Cambridge: Cambridge University Press, 1996), 153.

54. Ibid., 174.

55. Ibid.

56. "TRB from Washington: Pandora's Box," *New Republic*, November 14, 1988, 4.

57. "U.S. prison population declined for third consecutive year during 2012," Bureau of Justice Statistics, July 25, 2013, www.bjs.gov/content/pub/press/p12acpr.cfm (accessed October 31, 13).

58. Albert J. Meehan and Michael C. Ponder, "Race and place: The ecology of racial profiling African American Motorists," *Justice Quarterly* 19, no. 3 (September 2002): 401.

59. Ibid., 401.

60. Ibid., 418.

61. Ibid., 417.

62. Ibid., 423.

63. American Civil Liberties Union, "Racial Profiling," https://www.aclu.org/racial-justice/racial-profiling (accessed February 6, 2014).

64. Leadership Conference, "The reality of racial profiling," http://www.civilrights.org/publications/reports/racial-profiling2011/the-reality-of-racial.html (accessed November 8, 2013).

65. Elizabeth Flock, "Federal suit claims D.C. cops target Black motorcyclists," *U.S. News and World Report*, http://www.usnews.com/news/articles/2013/07/23/federal-suit-claims-dc-cops-target-Black-motorcyclists (accessed November 8, 2013).

66. Dorothee Benz and David Lerner, "Landmark decision: Judge rules NYPD stop and frisk practices unconstitutional, racially discriminatory," *Center for Constitutional Rights*,

http://ccrjustice.org/newsroom/press-releases/judge-rules-floyd-case (accessed November 8, 2013).

67. Rachel Garver, "Racial profiling: 'That's just a fact,' " *ACLU*, July 23, 2009, https://www.aclu.org/blog/human-rights-racial-justice/racial-profiling-thats-just-fact (accessed November 8, 2013).

68. Raphael S. Ezekiel, "An ethnographer looks at neo-Nazi and Klan groups: The racist mind revisited," *American Behavioral Scientist* 46, no. 1 (2002): 54.

69. Ibid., 55.

70. Ibid., 61.

71. Ibid., 68.

72. Ibid., 68.

73. J. Keith Akins, "The Ku Klux Klan: America's forgotten terrorists," *Law Enforcement Executive Forum* 5, no. 7 (2006): 135. http://www.uhv.edu/asa/articles/kkkamericasforgotten terrorists.pdf (accessed November 8, 2013).

74. "Racist skinheads: Understanding the threat," Southern Poverty Law Center, http://www.splcenter.org/get-informed/publications/skinheads-in-america-racists-on-the-rampage (accessed November 8, 2013).

75. Pete Simi, "Exclusive: Interview with professor who extensively studied alleged Wisconsin mass killer," *Huffington Post*, August 7, 2012, http://www.huffingtonpost.com/brian-levin-jd/exclusive-interview-with_b_1751181.html (accessed November 8, 2013).

76. Southern Poverty Law Center, "Racist Skinheads: Understanding the Threat," http://www.splcenter.org/get-informed/publications/skinheads-in-america-racists-on-the-rampage.

77. Jay Dixit, "A banner day for neo-Nazis," *Salon*, May 9, 2001, http://www.salon.com/2001/05/09/hatewatch/ (accessed November 8, 2013).

78. "The Hammerskin Nation," Anti-Defamation League, http://archive.adl.org/Learn/Ext_US/Hammerskin.asp (accessed November 8, 2013).

79. Elinor Langer, *A Hundred Little Hitlers* (New York: Henry Holt and Company, 2003), 180.

80. Ibid., 188–189.

81. Ibid., 191.

82. Ibid., 201–202.

83. Ibid., 211.

84. Ibid., 215–216.

85. Ibid., 218.

86. Ibid., 247.

87. Ibid., 187.

88. Jerome G. Miller, *Search and Destroy: African-American Males in the Criminal Justice System*, (Cambridge: Cambridge University Press, 1996), 53.

89. Kathryn Russell, *The Color of Crime: Racial Hoaxes, White Fear, Black Protectionism, Police Harassment, and Other Macroaggressions*, (New York: New York University Press, 1998), 21.

90. Kennedy, 45.

91. Ibid., 55.

92. James Allen, *Without Sanctuary: Lynching Photography in America* (Santa Fe: Twin Palms, 2000), 24.

93. Stewart E. Tolnay and E. M. Beck, *A Festival of Violence: An Analysis of Southern Lynchings, 1882–1930* (Urbana: University of Illinois Press, 1995), 244.

94. Ibid., 250–251.

95. Allen, *Without Sanctuary*, 20.

96. Ibid., 30–31 (italics in original).

97. Ibid., 12–13.

98. Kennedy, 45–46.

99. Christopher Waldrep, *African Americans Confront Lynching* (Lanham, MD: Rowman & Littlefield, 2009), 72–73.

100. Ibid., 54–56.

101. Jessie Daniel Ames, "Editorial treatment of lynchings," *Public Opinion Quarterly* 2, no. 1 (January 1938): 77.

102. Ibid., 78.

103. Hollars, 40.

104. Ames, "Editorial treatment of lynchings," 82.

105. Waldrep, *African Americans Confront Lynching*, 186.

106. Richard M. Perloff, "The press and lynchings of African Americans," *Journal of Black Studies* 30, no. 3 (January 2000): 316–317.

107. Ibid., 318.

108. Ibid., 322.

109. Ibid., 325–326.

110. Ibid., 327.

111. Ibid., 327.

112. Ibid., 328.

113. William Cowper Brann, "The buck negro," *Iconoclast*, 1919, 16. https://archive.org/details/completeworksbr09brangoog (accessed November 8, 2013).

114. Ibid., 17.

115. Peter Rachleff, "Lynching and racial violence," *Z Magazine*, December 2002, http://www.zcommunications.org/lynching-and-racial-violence-by-peter-rachleff (accessed June 6, 2013).

116. Ibid.

117. Allen, *Without Sanctuary*, 13.

118. Ibid., 13–14.

119. Ibid., 14.

120. Hale, 226.

121. Ibid., 201.

122. Ibid., 204.

123. Allen, *Without Sanctuary*, 15.

124. Waldrep, *African Americans Confront Lynching*, 149–151.

125. Hale, 213.

126. Ibid., 213.

127. Patricia Bernstein, *The First Waco Horror: The Lynching of Jesse Washington and the Rise of the NAACP* (College Station: Texas A&M Press, 2005), 4.

128. Ibid., 126.

129. Ibid., 166.

130. Hale, 221.

131. Waldrep, *African Americans Confront Lynching*, 231.

132. Hale, 228.

133. Ibid., 229.

134. Ibid., 230.

135. Jeannine Bell, *Hate Thy Neighbor: Move-In Violence and the Persistence of Racial Segregation in American Housing* (New York: New York University Press, 2013), 194.

136. Howard Pinderhughes, "The anatomy of racially motivated violence in New York City: A case study of youth in southern Brooklyn," *Social Problems* 40, no. 4 (November 1993): 479.

137. Ibid., 483.

138. Ibid., 485.

139. Ibid., 487.

140. Ibid., 488.

141. Ibid., 490.

142. Ibid., 491.

143. Christopher Lyons, "Defending turf: Racial demographics and hate crime against Blacks and Whites," *Social Forces* 87, no. 1 (September 2008): 360.

144. Bell, *Hate Thy Neighbor*, 2.

145. Ibid., 18.

146. Ibid., 21.

147. Ibid., 25.

148. Ibid., 28.

149. Ibid., 36.

150. Ibid., 174.

151. Ibid., 56.

152. Ibid., 86–116.

153. Ibid., 97.

154. Ibid., 101.

155. Ibid., 103.

156. Ibid., 195.

157. Ibid., 114.

158. Ibid., 130.

159. Ibid., 128.

160. Ami M. Lynch, "Hating the neighbors: The Role of hate crime in the perpetuation of Black residential segregation," *International Journal of Conflict and Violence* 2, no. 1 (2008): 9.

161. Ibid., 19.

162. Ibid., 22–23.

163. Ibid., 24.

164. E. Breindel, "The legal circus," *New Republic*, February 9, 1987, 20.

5

Sinners, Fanatics, and Terrorists: The Religious Other

"From the earliest arrival of Europeans on America's shores, religion has often been a cudgel, used to discriminate, suppress and even kill the foreign, the 'heretic' and the 'unbeliever'—including the 'heathen' natives already here."[1] The prevailing notion about American history is that the nation was founded on the idea of religious tolerance and freedom; in actuality, the country's early history was filled with religious intolerance. In Florida, Spanish Catholics wiped out a French Lutheran colony in 1565. Puritans arriving in Massachusetts "did not countenance tolerance of opposing religious views,"[2] banned Catholics, and hanged Quakers. Native American religions were framed as nonexistent or heathen, and many Native Americans were killed as representatives of evil or were forced to convert to Christianity. Some Native American religions were banned.

Founding fathers Washington, Jefferson, Madison, and John Adams worked to create an American government separate from any religion and free from ties to any church. Article VI of the Constitution, ratified in 1787, states that "no religious Test shall ever be required as a Qualification to any Office or public Trust under the United States." However, some states today still have constitutional articles requiring a belief in "Almighty God" for public office. For example, South Carolina's constitution (Article 17, section 4) states: "No person who denies the existence of a Supreme Being shall hold any office under this Constitution." When New York was drafting its first state constitution in 1777, John Jay, first chief justice of the United States, "led an effort to exclude Catholics from citizenship, unless they forswore belief in transubstantiation and allegiance to the pope."[3]

Belief in a supreme being constitutes very personal ideological space, and contestations over this space have occurred for centuries. Some of the bloodiest battles and colonizations have religious ideology at their base. There is a long continuum even within particular religions between those whose belief is minimal to those who adhere to strict interpretations of doctrine. Those who doubt the existence of a supreme being or have no belief in any such entity whatsoever have also been persecuted for their lack of religious ideology. Religious antipathy can also be a contributing factor to other concerns such as race or immigration. Faith-based ideologies can provide an individual with a strong sense of what is right or wrong; they can also define who is designated Other and considered lesser by that designation.

Some groups, such as Catholics, Jews, and Muslims, have been singled out and created as religious Others during our history. The United States, for all the purported belief in religious tolerance, defines itself primarily as a Christian nation even when arguing for acceptance of other religions. School calendars in many places still reflect Christian beliefs, as do many rituals in some public meetings and events, such as opening with a Christian prayer. The hegemony of Protestantism as America's predominant religion forms the backdrop by which all other religions have been measured. Although America's history of religious disagreement and persecution has been much less contentious than in many places around the world, there were and still are groups here who have been the focus of discriminatory practices and the victims of hate crimes.

In 2012, the last year for which complete statistics are currently available, approximately 17 percent of reported hate crimes recorded by the FBI were due to religious bias. Sixty percent of those were against Jews or Jewish institutions. The majority of hate crimes against Catholics, Jews, and Muslims fall in the category of destruction of or damage to property. But crimes against persons also occur; for both Jews and Muslims, these included simple assaults (83 anti-Jewish and 55 anti-Islamic) and intimidation (87 anti-Jewish and 43 anti-Islamic). In 2013, the FBI agreed to begin tracking crimes against a number of religious groups that have not previously been tracked, including Buddhists, Hindus, Sikhs, Mormons, Jehovah's Witnesses, and Orthodox Christians. This data collection will begin in 2015.

CATHOLICS

"Since last fall [1999] nine Catholic churches in Brooklyn, N.Y., have been vandalized; statues have been decapitated and defaced. In some instances hate mail was sent as well."[4] James Martin asks whether anti-Catholicism is a real problem in the United States today. Looking back historically, he points to the enduring negativity toward Catholics that started in Britain with the English Reformation; the rise and fall of anti-Catholicism in American culture in the past centuries, with for example, the Know-Nothing movement in the middle of the 1800s; and the anti-Catholicism that was rampant during the candidacies of Al Smith (1928) and John Kennedy (1960).

FBI statistics on hate crimes based on religion showed a 9 percent increase in all crimes against religious groups in 2008 and a nearly 25 percent increase in reported hate crimes against Catholics from the previous year. Bill Donohue relates anti-Latino sentiment (as Latinos are largely a Catholic population) and attention to national issues such as abortion and same-sex marriage to an increase in anti-Catholic feeling.[5] Anti-Catholicism has long been coupled with other concerns, including immigration, race, labor disputes, and politics. Irish Catholics faced discrimination on several levels, including both religion and race, as they arrived here in increasing numbers in the nineteenth century. The Irish were not the only immigrant group held in low esteem as Catholic, but they are representative of the mixture of anxieties that surrounded religious Others, including not only religion but class, criminality, and racial ambiguity.

Due to extreme poverty in Ireland, in part caused by the potato blight during the early 1800s, Irish immigrants began arriving in the United States in increasing numbers. From 1820 to 1860, approximately one third of the immigrants arriving in America were from Ireland. By the 1840s, this rose to almost 50 percent.[6] Between 1840 and 1860, close to 1.7 million Irish arrived in the United States. As with the Italians, the question of where the Irish fit into the racial categories of the time was different than today. Concerns with Irish race, class, and behavior were tied to enduring stereotypes of the Irish that included the drunkard, the criminal, lazy, and stupid. Thomas Nast's cartoons depicted the Irish as ape-like and primitive. Nast was a mid-nineteenth-century editorial cartoonist who worked primarily for the popular magazine *Harper's Weekly*. Through his cartoons, he expressed concern with Irish ignorance, comparing them to southern Blacks as a threat to the nation. His cartoons also expressed concern with the Catholic Church. In one cartoon, Catholic bishops are depicted as alligators crawling from the water and threatening American public school children. In an 1870 cartoon, Nash showed Europe separating church and state while in America, an Irish woman sewed them back together as Catholic bishops gave their blessing.

"*Low-browed* and *savage*, *groveling* and *bestial*, *lazy* and *wild*, *simian* and *sensual*—such were the adjectives used by many native-born Americans to describe the Catholic Irish 'race' in the years before the Civil War."[7] The Irish were likened to Blacks, a comparison that drew attention to doubts about the Irish race. The Census Bureau made a distinction between the Irish and America's "native" and "foreign" populations while "[p]olitical cartoonists played on the racial ambiguity of the Irish by making their stock 'Paddy' character resemble nothing so much as an ape."[8] A cartoon in *Puck* in 1889, entitled "The Mortar of Assimilation: And the One Element That Won't Mix," shows a variety of Americans being stirred together except for the Irish man, who lingers at the top of the bowl, a dagger in his hand.[9] Irish immigrants were leaders of anti-Chinese forces in California, and many opposed freeing the slaves. Both stances may be seen as concern over economic competition and the struggle to define themselves as White through opposition to those who clearly were not. "The success of the Irish in being recognized as White resulted largely from the political power of Irish and other immigrant voters."[10]

Irish Catholics were supported in their search for power, protection, and Whiteness by the Catholic Church and the Democratic Party.[11] At the same time, they were considered by some southerners to be of less value than Blacks or mules.[12] Prejudice in the job market did exist, including ads that specified "any country or color will answer except Irish." Although today there exists disagreement over how widespread the hiring practices were that included signs that "No Irish Need Apply," Irish immigrants felt the sting of hiring prejudice through signage and newspaper ads, and in song.

The Know-Nothing political movement, established in the middle of the nineteenth century, attempted to keep Irish Catholics out of public office. Concerns with the quality of Irish immigrants and their ties to the Catholic Church and the pope gave rise to fears that as Irish Americans became involved in politics, the Catholic Church would gain a measure of control over the country. The Know-Nothing Party was "predicated on a loathing for Catholics in general and Irish ones in particular. In the popular mind, the Irish became identified with poverty, disease and violence ..."[13] The Massachusetts state government was populated by Know-Nothings after the 1854 election. Kentucky too had a strong Know-Nothing government. The Bloody Monday riots occurred in Louisville, Kentucky, on Election Day in August 1855. Mobs of Protestants attacked Catholic neighborhoods; many were injured, property was destroyed, and somewhere between 14 and 100 people were killed. Many point to the writings of George D. Prentice in the *Louisville Journal* as contributing to the riots. Prentice, himself a Know-Nothing and editor of the newspaper, wrote increasingly anti-Irish, anti-German, and anti-Catholic editorials in the days leading up to the election. On August 1, he wrote:

Are men fit to be American voters, and especially are men fit to hold office and thus to assist in wielding the power of government, who regard themselves as owing our government no allegiance from which the Pope of Rome, an inflated Italian despot who keeps people kissing his toes all day, cannot at any moment release them?[14]

In the following days, Prentice increased his invective to exhort voters to make sure, by whatever means necessary, they could cast their vote while making equally sure that every "fraudulent voter" would be kept from the polls. "As election day approached, Prentice's rhetoric became more and more hysterical." He warned what would happen if the Know-Nothing Party were not victorious: Catholics, with revenge on their minds, would ensure that their victory "would end in our political destruction, and probably our religious ruin."[15] Prentice likened the election to a war and told his readers to "Fire." Whether he meant this literally or not, many Irish and German Catholics were attacked, injured, and killed on Bloody Monday.

In 1860, an English clergyman, Charles Kingsley, described the Irish as "human chimpanzees" and "White chimpanzees."[16] Charles Loring Brace, who wrote *Races of the Old World*, placed the Irish (due to a brain size that purportedly caused mental deficiencies) as "nine cubic inches" from the English and "only four [inches] between the average African [brain] and Irish."[17] Charles Wentworth Dilke broke the races of the world into the "dear races" and the "cheap races." In 1868, Dilke wrote, "In America we have seen the struggle of the dear races against the cheap—the endeavors of the English to hold their own against the Irish and Chinese." He went on to add, "Everywhere we have found that the difficulties which impede the progress to universal dominion of the English people lie in the conflict with the cheaper races."[18] His assumption that English domination of the world is desirable speaks to the commonsense configuring of American society and worldview at the time. Dilke looked to a gradual extinction of the cheap races as a blessing.[19]

The Ku Klux Klan

Throughout past centuries, disagreement over the nature of American identity— what it means, who is included, and who is excluded—has occurred at many different moments. The Ku Klux Klan at times has contributed strong opinions and actions to this debate, and during the 1920–1925 period, "exercised substantial influence" in many communities.[20] In the 1920s, the Klan reflected many of the "common White Protestant prejudices of the era" and were not so much dissident as an "intensified expression of widely shared civic and moral values" that included racism, religious bigotry, and nativistic antagonisms toward particular ethnic groups.[21]

Factors contributing to the growth of the new Klan in the 1920s included widespread feelings of anti-Catholicism. By 1924, the Klan claimed approximately 30,000 members, among them Protestant ministers from various denominations, as the Klan intentionally targeted Protestant churches in their attempts to gain new members. Among 39 known national lecturers for the Klan between 1922 and 1928, twenty-six were Protestant ministers. "In its firm racial and ethnic exclusivity and its overt anti-Catholicism, the 1920s Ku Klux Klan acted as a sort of superlodge for White Anglo-Saxon Protestants who sought to institutionalize their cultural practices as public policy."[22] The growth of the

Klan was aided, however unintentionally, by journalists and politicians whose articles and rhetoric, even when in opposition to the Klan, generated new members. Articles generally opposed to the Klan often contained some agreement with the assumed superiority of White Anglo-Saxon Protestants and fears about a potential loss of WASP values and hegemony. In the 1920s, many native-born Protestants felt it was patriotic, rather than a reflection of bigotry, to support rule by native-born White Protestants.[23]

The 1920s included government measures limiting immigration; the candidacy of Al Smith, which brought anti-Catholicism to the forefront; and a firm color barrier, all of which illustrated a strong core of support in mainstream American culture for Klan ideals. Anti-Semitism as well as anti-Catholicism was predicated on a belief in Protestant Anglo/Nordic superiority. Actions against Catholics included tarring and feathering, the distribution of anti-Catholic pamphlets, and calls to boycott Catholic-run businesses. "The relative scarcity or concentration of Jews and Catholics in Klan hotbeds, even in the South, did not diminish the nearly universal presence of anti-Semitic and anti-Catholic rhetoric among Klansmen."[24] As Pegram points out, the "most strikingly consistent feature of the revived Klan was its antipathy to Catholicism." Fighting Catholicism was deemed necessary to defend the Protestant foundations of what it meant to be a true American. "In politics, religion, and culture, Klansmen came to regard the Catholic Church as a shorthand representation of all the alien, un-American threats against which the revived Klan had organized."[25]

Klansmen argued that there was a Catholic conspiracy against American liberties and even, ironically, encouraged the formation of a Klan-like auxiliary for Black Protestants in order to help fight Catholicism.[26] Although Blacks were considered by common belief to be secondary citizens, Catholics were considered to pose a greater threat to Americanism due to their numbers and their growing foothold in politics and other public institutions, footholds Black Americans had yet to attain. Catholics were considered a largely immigrant population that was incapable of assimilation, one that chose separatism (through parochial school education and strong community/church ties) over blending into the larger American community. "As with the racial doctrine of the Invisible Empire [KKK], its anti-Catholicism was deeply rooted in mainstream U.S. beliefs and practices."[27]

Isolated instances of violence included floggings, beatings, and church burnings, while more common practices included political conflict, social ostracism, and economic pressure in the form of boycotts and physical intimidation.[28] The Klan put paper crosses on Catholic shops to identify them while Catholics fought back with their own boycotts. In public schools, the Klan asserted its influence by working to get Catholic teachers fired and to have Bible readings instituted. In the North, violence usually surrounded Klan marches into Catholic neighborhoods; however, the violence was often inflicted against the Klan members themselves. The final political battle of the new Klan was its work against Al Smith's candidacy in 1928.

Presidential Campaigns and Catholicism

We've never had a Catholic President and I hope we never do. Our people built this country. If they had wanted a Catholic to be President, they would have said so in the Constitution.[29]

Al Smith was the first Catholic to be nominated by the Democratic Party as a candidate for the presidency, and he ran in 1928 against Herbert Hoover. The overriding concern with his Catholicism was the belief that a Catholic president would be controlled by the pope, thus giving the pope himself control over the U.S. government. Catholicism was still considered to be foreign and un-American during the 1920s. In an address given on Klan Day at the state fair in Dallas, Texas, in 1923, H. W. Evans, imperial wizard of the Knights of the Ku Klux Klan, spoke against immigration in general and some specific groups of immigrants individually. In speaking of the elements "among our people whose assimilation is impossible without the gravest danger to our institutions," Evans pointed to Catholics and their supposed allegiance not to the United States, but to the priesthood in Rome. He was particularly concerned with the advent of parochial schools in the country, schools that would teach "supreme loyalty to a religious oligarchy that is not even of American domicile."[30]

The Klan made Al Smith the target of their anti-Catholicism, printing hate pamphlets against him and holding anti-Smith rallies. One issue of the Klan's *Fellowship Forum* had a cartoon depicting Smith as a bellboy bringing alcohol to a table of fat priests and the pope.[31] Alabama senator Thomas Heflin, in a speech to the Senate on January 18, 1928, spoke against "Al Smith's crowd" as being out of line for demanding that the Democratic Party denounce the Ku Klux Klan. "It is a Protestant order and Protestants generally think that you want it denounced because you are Catholics."[32] Heflin continued, "When as Roman Catholics—not as Americans, not as Democrats—they were demanding that a Democratic convention that had nothing on earth to do with the Ku Klux fraternity, or any other fraternity, should damn it and denounce it in convention." He categorized Smith solely as a Roman Catholic—not an American and not a Democrat.[33] Hoover won the election by a landslide, and although Smith's stance against Prohibition was an important issue in his defeat, his Catholicism was also a major factor.

John Kennedy was forced to deal with anti-Catholic sentiment head-on during his campaign for president in 1960. The United States was 16 percent Catholic in 1960 yet had never had a Catholic president. In two speeches,

Kennedy spoke eloquently about the need for the American public to consider him as an American candidate for president who just happened to be Catholic instead of categorizing him, as Al Smith had been categorized, simply as a Roman Catholic. The first speech was in April 1960 when he spoke to the American Society of Newspaper Editors; the second speech, in September 1960, was addressed to the Greater Houston Ministerial Association in Texas. Kennedy believed that American newspapers were responsible for the focus on religion as an issue in the election. In addition to making it clear that he was courting votes from Americans who agreed with him regardless of their religion and not courting "the Catholic vote," Kennedy went on to remind the editors of their responsibility in determining which issues become salient during an election. "And the press, while not creating the issue, will largely determine whether or not it does become dominant—whether it is kept in perspective—whether it is considered objectively—whether needless fears and suspicions are stilled instead of aroused." Kennedy pointed out that the focus in the news had been on the "religious issue" rather than on his stance on far more important matters such as foreign policy, civil rights, and farm legislation.

In *The Making of a Catholic President*, Casey states, "From the outset, Kennedy's Catholicism was the largest roadblock on his path to the Oval Office."[34] Casey highlights the issues and concerns that Protestants had with Kennedy's (or any Catholic's) run for the presidency. These included federal funds for parochial schools, the belief that the Catholic Church hierarchy had control of Catholic politicians, the supposed mandatory attendance by Catholics in parochial schools, the issue of birth control, the issue of whether there should be an ambassador to the Vatican, and the concern that a Catholic president would appoint fellow Catholics rather than Protestants to important public offices.[35] A May 1960 Gallup poll based on a survey of 9,000 people nationwide found that 62 percent would vote for a qualified Catholic while 28 percent said they would not. Their concerns were that a Catholic would "serve the Pope" and "would introduce a sort of Catholic spoils system." The overall conclusion reached after the poll was that Kennedy was hurt more than helped by being Catholic.[36]

"With no sense of irony, the man who had helped the Southern Baptist Convention to pass a resolution calling for elected officials to be free of pressure and coercion from religious leaders set out a grand strategy to use religious leaders to build a grassroots campaign to pressure Protestants to vote against a Catholic."[37] Missouri congressman Orland K. Armstrong coordinated Protestant groups against Kennedy, including Baptists, evangelicals, Methodists, and the group entitled Protestants and Other Americans United for Separation of Church and State (POAU). Church-state separation was, ironically, one of Protestants' biggest concerns with Kennedy's Catholicism, that and the issue of religious freedom. Many used the church-state issue to mask anti-Catholic feelings in general. POUA, with 2 million members, warned that Catholics were trying to "smash big holes in the wall between religion and government in the U.S."[38] A Billy Graham article in the *Chicago Tribune* led Southern Baptists to pass a resolution repudiating Kennedy as a presidential candidate and endorsing Nixon.[39] At the grassroots level and behind the scenes, many used the religion issue against Kennedy in support of Nixon. While Nixon could claim ignorance of these goings on, it was clear from information leaked to the Democrats that the higher-ups in the Nixon campaign were well aware of what was being done on his behalf. "Aided and abetted by the Nixon campaign, a spasm of anti-Catholic literature was soaking the country to an extent not seen before or since."[40] Of more than 360 publications (purportedly delivered to more than 20 million homes), the Democratic National Committee and the Fair Campaign Practice Committee (which received 2,000 complaints about this literature) categorized 5 percent as "vile," 25 percent as "dishonest," 35 percent as "unfair" and only 35 percent as "responsible."[41]

Since 1960, the political scene has changed in terms of the role of religion and the place of Catholicism in American politics. Currently, 24–25 percent of the U.S. population is Catholic, making it the largest single denomination in the country. Approximately 30 percent of the federal legislature and 42 percent of American governors are Catholic. Vice President Joe Biden is Catholic, as is two-thirds of the Supreme Court.[42]

John Kerry, running for president in 2004, was criticized by some Catholics for using political expediency to keep his religious beliefs out of his campaign platform (specifically his stances on abortion and same-sex marriage). They argued that if he did not strictly adhere to Catholic teachings, he was not a true Catholic. "He professes to be personally opposed to abortion as an article of faith but says it is not appropriate for a member of Congress to legislate personal religious beliefs. This position is tired and intellectually dishonest."[43] Needless to say, this argument flies in the face of constitutional dictates for the separation of church and state. Archbishop Raymond Burke (St. Louis) prohibited Kerry from receiving communion in his diocese due to Kerry's abortion stance. Other bishops also openly criticized Kerry for his views not only on abortion, but on gay rights. Criticism of Kerry from within his own religion appeared more of an issue than anti-Catholic criticism from outside.

JEWS

A group of 23 Jews arrived in New Amsterdam (now New York) in 1654, refugees from Brazil, where the Portuguese were retaking the Brazilian colony from the Dutch. Peter Stuyvesant, then colonial governor of New Amsterdam, expressed concern to the Dutch West Indian Company back in Amsterdam about Jewish immigrants and requested permission to bar them from the area. In his letter, he spoke of their "customary usury and deceitful trading with

Christians" and described them as a "deceitful race—such hateful enemies and blasphemers of the name of Christ." He received a response seven months later, allowing that while the company would like to request the territories "should no more be allowed to be infected by people of the Jewish nation," they determined it to be "somewhat unreasonable and unfair" to keep them out (due to the capital that Jews had invested in the Dutch West Indian Company). Stuyvesant did manage to rule that Jews were not entitled to "a license to exercise and carry on their religion in synagogues or gatherings." A year later he continued to deny them the right to the free and public exercise of their "abominable religion."[44] Stuyvesant was also responsible for punishing those who were or harbored Quakers.

State constitutions point to the imbedded thinking contained in predominant ideologies at the time of America's birth and which groups were considered religious Others. The state of Maryland adopted a constitution in 1776 that required any person appointed or elected to public office to swear loyalty to and declare a belief in the Christian religion. Beginning in 1797, Maryland Jews attempted to have this changed to include Jews as well. It took until 1825 for the change to pass. Other state constitutions excluded not only Jews, but often Catholics, from public office. These included New Jersey, Delaware, Pennsylvania, Massachusetts, and New Hampshire.

Stereotypes regarding Jews were around long before Jews arrived in America, and they were represented in literature at the time of Jewish arrival. "Indeed, the history of the Jewish character in American literature is also a chapter in the history of anti-Semitism in the United States."[45] Many of the stock characterizations used by American authors came from English literature. Since the Middle Ages, Jews had been banned from many occupations, and the resulting number of Jews in trade and money lending brought them under condemnation, as did their purported role in the death of Christ. Literary Jews included Shakespeare's Shylock (preoccupied with money and hating Christians) and Dickens's Fagin. "... [T]he Jew was almost invariably presented in literature in connection with money."[46] The American experience brought new stereotypes that included the Jew as a dangerous revolutionary and a wielder of political power. Even the more positive stereotypes of Jews in literature revolved around money. "In neither case is the character anything like a real human being with a full range of interests and interactions, but only an agency for the generation or distribution of money."[47] Few writing about Jews in America during the nineteenth century had little direct contact with any Jewish people. Their writings reflected older stereotypes from Europe as well as new ones circulating in American culture as more Jews immigrated to the United States. "Basically, then, the persistence of the stereotype was owing to the fact that the Jew as Jew remained as alien to most Americans, essentially unknown as a human being, and hence was identified in terms of the ingrained clichés of Western civilization."[48] Regardless of ignorance or anti-Semitism, the stereotypes contained Jews in a certain frame that limited their humanity and insisted on their relationship to the world of money, a space they had been confined to due to societal prejudices that limited their vocational options.

As with other groups, the number of Jewish immigrants to the United States increased significantly during the nineteenth and early twentieth centuries. Due in part to violent anti-Semitism in Europe, Jews from eastern Europe in particular started coming to America in increasing numbers at the turn of the century. Anti-Semitism in the United States, as well as rampant nativism in the early part of the twentieth century, led to the passage of the Emergency Quota Act (Immigration Restriction Act) of 1921 that limited immigration from Europe to 3 percent of those from each country who had been living in the United States in 1910. This severely restricted Jewish immigrants. The 1924 Immigration Act further reduced these numbers, using the 1890 Census and allowing only 2 percent of the population at that time. These quotas made it very difficult during World War II for Jews to immigrate here from Germany and other countries when their lives were in danger. In 1921, before immigration restriction took effect, approximately 120,000 Jews came to the United States. That number dropped to 10,000 by 1925 as the second Immigration Restriction Act was instituted.

Leo Frank, the ADL, and the KKK

Leo Frank, a Jewish factory superintendent, was accused of raping and murdering 13-year-old factory worker Mary Phagan in April 1913 in Georgia. He was tried, convicted, and sentenced to death. Georgia governor John Slaton commuted the sentence to life in prison, transferring him to a prison farm for his safety. A month later, another inmate at the farm attacked Frank, cutting his throat with a knife and severely wounding him. Angered by the change in sentence, a mob of approximately 25 men dragged Frank from his hospital bed at the prison farm, handcuffed him, put him in a car, and drove him to a grove of trees in Marietta, Georgia, where they tied a rope around his neck and hanged him. "Postcards of the lynched Leo Frank were sold outside the undertaking establishment where his corpse was taken, at retail stores, and by mail order for years."[49]

Frank was reviled on a number of levels that had to do with antipathy felt for rich northerners in the South (he came from New York), gender issues over the protection of White womanhood, and the fact that he was Jewish. "Popular association of Jews with the vice trade and stereotypes about the alleged lust of Jewish men for gentile women made Frank vulnerable as a suspect in the first place."[50]

Tom Watson was a newspaper editor and politician. In *Watson's Magazine*, he pushed hard for Frank's conviction. "Leo Frank was a typical young Jewish man of business who loves pleasure, *and runs after Gentile girls.* Every student of sociology knows that the Black man's lust after the White woman, *is not much fiercer than the lust of the licentious Jew for the Gentile.*"[51] Watson argued that Frank was sexually immoral and depraved, and lusted after the young women working in the factory. "Here we have the pleasure-loving Jewish business man. Here we have the Gentile girl. Here we have the typical young libertine Jew who is dreaded and detested by the city authorities of the North, for the very reason that Jews of this type have an utter contempt for law, and a ravenous appetite for the forbidden fruit . . ."[52]

The case was interesting for a number of reasons. Much of the publicity surrounded the innocence of Mary Phagan and the crime of rape; however, there was never clear evidence that a rape had actually occurred. The other suspect in the case, the Black janitor, acted as a witness against Frank, though many now believe him to be the actual murderer. In Georgia during this time period, it was all too common for a Black man to be lynched on little or no evidence in a case involving a White rape victim. In this case, the janitor was bypassed as the prosecution focused on an upper-class northern Jew. As with Black lynchings, those who took part in the lynching of Frank were prominent citizens, including a former governor of Georgia, a police officer, a superior court judge, two deputy sheriffs, a former sheriff, and the Cobb County sheriff. Although numerous photographs were taken of the lynching that included members of the lynch mob, no one was ever charged. The dean of the Atlanta Theological Seminary praised the murderers as *"a gifted band of men, sober, intelligent, of established good name and character—good American citizens."*[53] Frank was pardoned posthumously in 1985 as increasing evidence pointed to his innocence.

The Frank case led to the formation of the Anti-Defamation League (ADL) in September 1913 and the re-formation of the Ku Klux Klan in 1915. "Shortly after Frank's lynching, Watson advised that 'another Ku Klux Klan may be organized to restore HOME RULE.' It was. William J. Simmons unveiled the new order two months later at a ceremony that purportedly involved many lynchers of Leo Frank."[54] The list of lynchers has since come to light, and we know that many were indeed involved in the formation of the Klan at this time.

The Anti-Defamation League works to end the defamation of Jewish people "and to secure justice and fair treatment to all." From its roots as a guardian of Jewish rights and image, it has become one of the primary civil rights organizations in America today. Among many other things, the League now monitors hate groups and rhetoric on the Internet, provides expertise on domestic as well as international terrorism, and "probes the roots of hatred" to combat extremism and anti-Semitism.

"By the end of the First World War, anti-Jewish exclusivism was evidenced by tighter control of immigration, the recrudescence of the Ku Klux Klan, anti-Semitic outpourings from Henry Ford's Dearborn *Independent*, and unguarded racist statements by some government officials."[55] Between 1907 and 1918, the Jewish population in the United States increased by 90 percent, to a total of 3,390,301. The increasing numbers of Jews led to concerns over their participation in social and public places. Jews were excluded from some hotels and clubs, and there were concerns over the number of Jewish students in colleges and universities.

The enrollment of Jewish students at Harvard University was up to 22 percent in 1922. The president of Harvard at that time was Abbott Lawrence Lowell, whose ideas on Black and Jewish enrollment at Harvard have been likened to "undisguised White Christian supremacy."[56] Lowell's plan for Harvard included setting limits on Jewish enrollment (bringing it down to 15 percent) and excluding Black students from housing in freshman dorms altogether. Lowell argued that by reducing the Jewish population at Harvard, he would reduce anti-Semitism. "Today Jews are practically ostracized from social organizations. This prejudice is reflected in the college. If there were fewer Jews, this problem would not be so."[57] Lowell couched his plan as a benefit to the remaining Jewish students, as levels of anti-Semitism would decrease. Both Lowell's ideas (excluding Black students and decreasing Jewish enrollment) were overturned by Harvard's Board of Overseers, but the question of Jewish enrollment was sent to a faculty committee to determine if changes were needed. Due to Lowell's continued pressure, the committee developed a plan that would more closely align Harvard's enrollment with the populations of various groups in America. Jews were approximately 3 percent of the population at the time, and Jewish enrollment at Harvard dropped to 10 percent.[58]

American Icons and Anti-Semitism

Automobile manufacturer Henry Ford Sr. was a leading and vocal anti-Semite in the early part of the twentieth century. Beginning in 1920, he used his publication, the *Dearborn Independent*, to attack Jews for the next eight years, eventually reaching 700,000 readers. His series of 92 articles on Jews in America was published in a volume entitled *The International Jew: The World's Foremost Problem*. The editor of the *Dearborn Independent* was William J. Cameron, who worked with Ford to produce the anti-Semitic materials. Writings in the volume attacked Jews on many fronts and included "The Scope of Jewish Dictatorship in the U.S.," "Jewish Control of the American Theater," "Jewish Supremacy in Motion Picture World," "When Editors Were Independent of the Jews," and "Jewish Degradation of American Baseball." "Jewish jazz" also came under criticism: "The mush, the slush, the sly suggestion, the abandoned sensuousness of sliding notes, are of Jewish origin. Monkey talk, jungle squeals, grunts and squeaks and gasps suggestive of cave love are camouflaged by a few feverish notes and admitted to homes where the thing itself, unaided by the piano, would be stamped out in horror."[59] With this statement, the paper managed to reference a number of prevailing stereotypes about Jews that included their supposed licentiousness, as well as their purported primitive and animalistic nature. Ford also provided Cameron with a copy of *Protocols of the Elders of Zion*, a Russian forgery "that purportedly recorded a series of lectures by a Jewish elder outlining a conspiracy to overthrow European governments."[60] Cameron then included material from the forgery in the *Dearborn Independent*.

Ford blamed Jews for many things, including control over American institutions and international business. He also blamed them for using accusations of anti-Semitism to protect themselves from criticism and for inciting violence against themselves to claim prejudice and further their quest for power.

At the beginning a few rabid Jew-baiters made themselves known and expressed their hope that at last a regular program of pogroms was to be instituted. We never knew how far these advances were made with knowledge of the Jewish leaders, but we do know that for a year and a half in this United States the Jewish press, and Jewish thugs, and Jewish politicians, and even some of the most respectable of the Jewish organizations did their utmost, and in some of the strangest ways, to compel this Study of the Jewish Question to lead into violence and disorder. There was nothing that the Jewish leaders more desperately desired or more tirelessly worked for.[61]

Ford was sued for defamation by three Jews. Aaron Sapiro's was the first case to go to trial. Sapiro sued Ford for libel, asking for $1 million, for a story Ford had written about Sapiro's involvement in the farmer's movement. In what one author described as "America's First Hate Speech Case,"[62] Ford eventually settled out of court and agreed to cease publishing any articles reflecting on Jews, although he blamed his editor (Cameron) and his personal secretary (Ernest Liebold) for printing the materials, claiming that they alone were responsible for the content of the newspaper. Although he printed an apology in his paper, he neither wrote it nor signed it himself. Hitler, who told a *Detroit News* reporter that he regarded Henry Ford as his inspiration, kept a life-size portrait of Ford next to his desk.[63]

Father Charles Coughlin was another well-known personality during the 1920s and 1930s, as he broadcast a regular radio program, *The Hour of Power*. "Throughout the 1930s, Coughlin was one of the most influential men in the United States. A new post office was constructed in Royal Oak [Michigan] just to process the letters that he received each week—80,000 on average. Furthermore, the audience of his weekly radio broadcasts was in the tens of millions . . ."[64] In addition to crusading against communism and speaking of his growing dislike for Franklin Roosevelt, Coughlin was virulently anti-Semitic. He criticized Jews in finance and he defended the Nazi regime, including Kristallnacht,[65] which he believed was just retaliation for Jewish treatment of Christians. He too used the *Protocols of the Elders of Zion*, warning of a Jewish plot to take over the world. He was an isolationist and blamed the Jews for the troubles in Europe, even though they were the victims. "In a 1938 broadcast, Coughlin helped inspire and publicize the creation of the Christian Front, a militia-like organization that excluded Jews and promised to defend the country from communists and Jews."[66] In a speech given in the Bronx, Coughlin gave a Nazi salute and yelled, "When we get through with the Jews in America, they'll think the treatment they received in Germany was nothing."[67]

Although the Christian Front was in operation for only a couple of years, it was strongly anti-Semitic and called for boycotts of Jewish merchants, held parades, and drew many to rallies like the one in Madison Square Garden in February 1939 that included Nazi sympathizers. Christian Front activities included violent attacks on Jews in New York City. "In 1940, the FBI shut down the Christian Front, after discovering the group was arming itself and planning to murder Jews, communists, and even United States Congressmen."[68]

Like Coughlin, Charles Lindbergh was an isolationist. He argued in 1941 that the United States should not involve itself in the European war and pointed at three groups that were urging American involvement against our best interests, the British, the Roosevelt administration, and the Jews. While Lindbergh explained that it was understandable that the British (already at war with Germany) and the Jews (suffering persecution in Germany) would want the United States to become involved, he also felt strongly that it was not America's role to take part in European affairs. Speaking in Des Moines, Iowa, on September 11, 1941, he stated his concerns about the Jews: "Their greatest danger to this country lies in their large ownership and influence in our motion pictures, our press, our radio and our government."[69] In addition to the typical "too much power" argument, Lindbergh categorized Jewish wishes involving the war as "not American," stating that what was in their best interests was not in the country's best interests. He thereby framed Jewish Americans as un-American.

Using the 1990 General Social Survey, Thomas Wilson looked at those who held both malevolent and benign stereotypes of Jews to determine whether benign stereotypes are really negative ones in disguise. He found no evidence that benign stereotypes were genuinely complimentary; rather, evidence supported the fact that these were merely more subtle indicators of underlying prejudice.[70] Malevolent stereotypes included the portrayal of Jews as pushy, clannish, ill mannered, dishonest, mercenary, loud, and uncouth. Benign stereotypes included financially successful, ambitious, hardworking, intelligent, and loyal to family. While the prevalence of malevolent stereotypes has declined, benign ones have not. Wilson found that those who held benign stereotypes were no more pro-Semitic than those who held no stereotypes at all. "Moreover, there is clear evidence that holders of benign Jewish stereotypes tend more than others to subscribe to the blatantly anti-Semitic belief that Jews are excessively influential."[71]

Wilson concluded that while more blatant stereotypes have declined, underlying anti-Semitism has merely become more subtle in its expression and contained in more coded wording.

In 2000 when Al Gore selected Joseph Lieberman as his vice presidential running mate, the nomination "triggered an unprecedented stream of anti-Semitic messages on the internet."[72] The messages included disparaging religious references as well as conspiracy theories regarding Jewish power grabs. America Online deleted a number of the 28,000 postings on their website for violation of its hate speech policies, and CNN suspended approximately 10 users from its chat rooms for similar reasons.

The ADL published a report on anti-Semitic propensities in America in 2011 as measured on an 11-question survey developed 40 years ago. Of those surveyed, 15 percent were considered anti-Semitic, up from 12 percent in 2009. The survey points to concerns with Jewish power as the basis for much of the anti-Semitic feeling in the United States, including beliefs that Jews hold too much power in business, too much power in the United States in general, and too much control over Wall Street. The survey also found that since 1964, a consistent 30 percent of the American population has believed that Jews are more loyal to Israel than to the United States. Long held stereotypes about Jews include the notion that loyalty is always to Israel and Judaism before anything else, and that Jews wish to control if not the entire world, then large portions of it.

Holocaust Deniers

Ignoring the massive amounts of clear and unequivocal evidence attesting to the horrors of the Holocaust, Holocaust deniers decree that the Holocaust is a myth invented to further a Jewish conspiracy and the formation of the state of Israel. In truth, Holocaust deniers show a virulent form of anti-Semitism that purports to be a revisionist and scholarly look at historical events of the twentieth century. Using an all or nothing argument, "Holocaust deniers assert that if they can discredit one fact about the Holocaust, the whole history of the event can be discredited as well."[73] The deniers refute the idea that 6 million Jews were murdered during the Holocaust, arguing instead that many fewer died, and most died from disease, rather than in gas chambers and from other forms of mass murder. The rise of the Internet has allowed scattered deniers to build a community and a visible presence, including a fast and simple way of spreading their ideas, misinformation, and anti-Semitic writings. While some countries have made it illegal to deny the Holocaust (Germany and France, for example), the United States has no such policy. Coupled with our guaranteed right of free speech, this makes American Internet sites locations that deniers all over the world can spread their venom.

Willis Carto was an integral part in getting the Holocaust denial movement started as he founded the anti-Semitic Liberty Lobby in the 1950s and through his efforts kept an organized anti-Semitism alive in the United States. In 1978, he founded the Institute for Historical Review, a legitimate-sounding but nevertheless myth-based Holocaust denial organization. "Its mission was to erase the Holocaust by any means at its disposal—including distortion, misquotation and outright falsification."[74] In 1984, Carto helped found the Populist Party, which ran former Ku Klux Klan leader David Duke as its presidential candidate. In the 1990s, Carto started *The Barnes Review*, which is now one of the nation's leading Holocaust denial publications.

Deborah Lipstadt, in her book *Denying the Holocaust*,[75] expresses her concern that as we move farther away from the events of World War II and lose the remaining survivors, those who deny the truth of the Holocaust will have greater opportunities to make their arguments. General Dwight Eisenhower recognized the potential for the rewriting of historical truth concerning the Holocaust. As the war ended, he visited death camps in Germany, determined to document what he saw so that later no one could put the events down as propaganda rather than truth. "I visited every nook and cranny of the camp because I felt it my duty to be in a position from then on to testify at first hand about these things in case there ever grew up at home the belief or assumption that 'the stories of Nazi brutality were just propaganda.' "[76] As Holocaust deniers attempt to mimic legitimate historical study and discourse, they have convinced journalists, academics, and politicians that theirs is an alternative reading instead of the complete denial of historical evidence. In 2006, a Holocaust denier ran for attorney general in Alabama and received 44 percent of the vote. Larry Darby, the candidate, claimed that only 140,000 Jews were killed during the war and most of those by typhus.

MUSLIMS

One need look no farther than the bombing of the Federal Building in Oklahoma City in 1995 to see the assumptions and stereotypes held about Muslims in America and the harm done by these creations. The bombing was immediately assumed to have been done by Middle Easterners, and headlines from a variety of newspapers proclaimed this fact.

Two days after the bombing, on April 21, the *New York Post*'s editorial cartoon displayed the Statue of Liberty under siege. Alongside Lady Liberty in the right corner are three bearded, turbaned Muslims, smiling as they burn the American flag; on the left are flames and a giant mushroom cloud. In the center is the Statue of Liberty, inscribed with this modified version of Emma Lazarus's famous poem: "Give us your tired, your poor, your huddled masses, your terrorists, your murderers, your slime, your evil cowards, your religious fanatics . . ." [77]

On April 19, 1995—the day of the bombing—CBS's Steven Emerson stated, "The bombing was done with the intent to inflict as many casualties as possible.

That is a Middle Eastern trait." On the Bob Grant show (WABC radio) on April 20, when a caller complained about the speculation regarding Muslims and the bombing, Grant replied, "In the Oklahoma case . . . the indications are that those people who did it were some Muslim terrorists. But a skunk like you, what I'd like to do is to put you up against the wall with the rest of them, and mow you down along with them."[78]

Those who wrongly fingered Muslims did not apologize when the real perpetrators were found. Somehow their assumptions, based on rumor, speculation, and years of stereotyping, were held to have some validity since Muslims were "known" to commit terrorist acts. Irresponsible reporting based on faulty assumptions and stereotypes created an atmosphere in which blame quickly landed on Arab Muslims. "McVeigh and Nichols are U.S. Army veterans and are neither Muslim nor Arabs. Still, the initial reports wrongly targeting Arabs and Muslims had caused irrefutable harm. Some callers to talk-radio stations refused to believe that Muslims were not involved."[79] American terrorists are not depicted as Christian terrorists but are seen as individual perpetrators with individual faults. They are not considered representative of any larger group. "While mainstream Christians easily disassociate themselves from fringe groups that call themselves Christian—such as the Ku Klux Klan, David Koresh's Branch Davidians or Christian militia groups—Christians have rarely made similar distinctions among Muslim groups."[80] The media has the power to ensure that individual acts are framed as the responsibility of the individual; they also have the power to create individual acts of the Other as the rule, rather than the exception.

Anger at a created Other can touch any from the targeted group or any assumed to be members. "Following the Oklahoma City tragedy, speculative reporting combined with decades of stereotyping encouraged more than 300 hate crimes against America's Arabs and Muslims."[81] More than 300 Americans suffered real consequences from the hate poured out against Muslims and Arabs based on an incident in which no Muslims or Arabs were involved. The hate also spilled over on those who were "Muslim looking."

Joseph and D'Harlingue looked at how "representational frameworks construct Islam and 'Muslims' in leading U.S.A. print news media."[82] Focusing on the *Wall Street Journal* as America's predominant conservative daily newspaper, they studied the growing role that the media plays in producing significance and meaning in daily events and "how Muslims and Islam have, post 9/11, increasingly become produced as targeted objects of surveillance and disciplining through journalistic (and other) practices."[83] Consumers rely on media framing to understand issues; journalistic choices produce a limited version of reality that becomes the normative view. When journalists rely on already available stereotypes, they imbed them further into the American psyche as the "commonsense" view of how things are.

In Op-Ed pieces from January 1, 2000 to July 31, 2007, the authors found eight predominant themes consistent with their findings in an earlier project with the *New York Times*. These included the construction of an unbridgeable gap between Muslims and the West (Muslims were constructed as Other, as unintelligible, and as in opposition to the West); Muslim belief and culture as backward and outdated, incompatible with modernity ("Muslim states are portrayed as intolerant of religious and ethnic minorities within their states, . . . as oppressive to women, as anti-Semitic."); Islam as a fanaticism that leads inevitably to terrorism; Arab Muslims as the sources of Islamic terrorism and extremism: "jihadist, sexist, and intolerant" while non-Arab Muslims are "more modern, progressive, and democratic"; a global network of terror led by Al-Qaeda and created from Arab and Muslim groups (which includes any who are pro-Palestinian liberation or critical of Israel); a threat of a significant Muslim population increase in the United States coupled with an inability to assimilate into American culture; Islam as comparable to Nazi fascism; and finally, an "us" versus "them" polemic when considering Muslims and the United States.[84]

The authors demonstrate how the *Wall Street Journal* creates and fosters an image of Islam as irreparably different from "us" and fundamentally dangerous. ". . . [T]he argument is that the paper's structure of representation participates in and contributes toward the production of politics, policy, rights and citizenship."[85] This is not surprising, as newspapers are a commodity aimed at a particular audience and representative of a limited editorial viewpoint. Muslims are constructed as noncitizens through demonizing articles, and this particular frame dictates appropriate responses. "The essentialization of Islam and Muslims prescribes, produces, and makes the Muslim as enemy, marshaling the associational imageries, which rationalize aggressive and even preemptive actions against the constructed enemy in self-defense." These representations may well lead to "an urgency of containing Islam and Muslims—including the Muslims within—which then makes violent action toward Muslims, even Muslim U.S. citizens, more palatable."[86]

Gottschalk and Greenberg consider the historical basis for some of the common stereotypes of Muslims today, pointing out that what does not fit these stereotypes is often overlooked as nonexistent. "An historical exploration of British and American literature between 1690 and 1947 demonstrates the roots and qualities of Islamophobia that Britons and American have shared."[87] Muslims represent a far more distant Other than most religious minorities within the American Protestant majority. Stereotypes include the purported misogynistic and sensual nature of the Muslim religion, a lack of modernity, and the different racial background accorded Muslim peoples. Historical sources of these stereotypes came from missionary literature (which framed Islam only in opposition to Christianity), travel writings, and journalistic writings from times of political crisis. "Politically, socially, religiously, and theologically, Muslims and their religion were seen to threaten in varying degrees and in different ways Britain and America, secularism and Christianity."[88] Other concerns focused on fears that Muslims around the world would unite in a pan-Islamism that would threaten the Christian world, including the threat of a violent Muslim crusade. The literature included a "near universal association of fanaticism with Muslim men . . ."[89] The size of the Muslim population throughout the world, described repeatedly in terms such as "hordes," was also a recurring theme.

The relationship between Christianity and Islam has been set up as an "us" versus "them" polemic of mutual exclusion resulting in the conclusion that Islam must be destroyed; we assume Islam feels the same way about Christianity, thus projecting our own paranoia. Many publications from the late eighteenth century to the mid-twentieth century included themes of "fear and threat beyond the sentiments of disapproval and loathing . . ." These stereotypes are pertinent today, and Islamophobia is easily found on websites, blogs, tweets, and emails. "On the governmental level, the Bush administration endeavored to foster pan-Islamic anxiety by imagining al-Qaeda's ambition to establish, in the president's words (2005), 'a totalitarian Islamic empire that reaches from Indonesia to Spain.' "[90]

Obama's Presidency

During his first campaign for the presidency, Barack Obama on numerous occasions had to assert his religion and deny rumors that he was actually a Muslim and had received training in Islam. There are significant problems with this. Candidates should not have to deal with false rumors surrounding their religious choices, and Obama should not feel compelled to deny being a Muslim in order to be qualified for the presidency. Antagonism and bigotry toward those who are Muslim is strong in American culture. Rumors included that Obama had attended a Muslim school in Indonesia and that he was secretly part of a Muslim plot to gain control of the United States. "In an August poll by the Pew Research Center for the People and the Press, 45 percent of respondents said they would be less likely to vote for a candidate for any office who is Muslim, compared with 25 percent who said that about a Mormon candidate and with 16 percent who said the same for someone who is an evangelical Christian."[91] Another rumor circulated that if elected, Obama would take the oath of office on a Koran the way Representative Keith Ellison (D-MN and the only Muslim in Congress) did when he was sworn in.

During the campaign, Obama's aides disputed the stories, "and in Iowa, the campaign [kept] a letter at its offices, signed by five members of the local clergy, vouching for the candidate's Christian faith."[92] Rumors came from a variety of sources, including *Insight*, a Conservative online magazine; *Human Events*, another web-published conservative magazine; and several conservative talk show hosts such as Michael Savage and Rush Limbaugh. "A CBS news poll in August showed that a huge number of voters said they did not know Obama's faith, but among those who said they did, 7 percent thought he was a Muslim, while only 6 percent thought he was a Protestant Christian."[93] The idea that labeling Obama Muslim would have been enough to derail his candidacy speaks to the strength of anti-Muslim sentiment in the United States.

Stop Islamization of America (SIOA)

The group Stop Islamization of America was founded in 2009 and is considered by both the Southern Poverty Law Center and the Anti-Defamation League to be a hate group. The organization and its founders (Pamela Geller and Robert Spencer) use fear tactics, misinformation, and complete fabrication to push their ideas of an Islamic conspiracy threatening American values, the American way of life, and American lives (negating the notion that Muslims might actually be Americans themselves). Geller posts her views on the blog Atlas Shrugs, "a Web site that attacks Islam with a rhetoric venomous enough that PayPal at one point branded it a hate site."[94] In 2010, Geller achieved widespread publicity as she led the fight against Park51, a Muslim community center planned for an area near Ground Zero in New York. During the time of national debate over the center, SIOA paid for bus ads in San Francisco, New York, and Miami (Detroit refused the ads, and Geller sued their transit authority in federal district court; the case is still pending on appeal) urging people to leave the Muslim faith. Although she lacks credentials and credibility for any who thoughtfully consider her rhetoric, Geller has been given a measure of legitimacy as she has appeared on national television (*60 Minutes*, Sean Hannity's radio show, and Mike Huckabee's television program) and been quoted by politicians such as Newt Gingrich, Rick Lazio, and Sarah Palin. She admits to being a racist Islamophobe and an anti-Muslim bigot, although she considers these accolades rather than failings.[95] Geller is representative of one side in the continuing contestation over the public images of Islam and the Muslim faith. Although SIOA works to shut down Islam in America, it purports to have the goal of religious freedom, which apparently means the freedom to worship only in the ways that Geller deems acceptable.

In 2011, Representative Peter King, chairman of the U.S. House Homeland Security Committee, held four congressional hearings to investigate the radicalization of the American Muslim community. King has made sweeping (and unsubstantiated) statements that include categorizing 80–85 percent of the mosques in the United States as controlled by Islamic fundamentalists, the Muslim community as uncooperative with investigations into terrorism, and the Muslim community overall as "a real threat to the country." During the hearings, King called witnesses who lacked credentials and instead gave anecdotal evidence, and repeatedly refused to broaden the scope of his investigation to include a larger concern with violent extremism. He continually used the label "violent Islamic extremists," thereby creating Islam itself as enemy and claimed any other label to be "political correctness," a common tactic used to try and shut down opposing viewpoints.[96]

The Council on American-Islamic Relations (CAIR) defines Islamophobia as "close-minded prejudice against or hatred of Islam and Muslims"[97] while cautioning that questioning Islam's tenets is not Islamophobia. The Islamophobic viewpoint includes beliefs that Islam is monolithic and authoritarian; is inferior, backward, and primitive; is an aggressive enemy to be feared and defeated; and is populated by manipulative and devious Muslims. When anti-Muslim comments, stereotypes, and discourse are taken as natural and as commonsense, rather than as problematic and in need of challenging, this promotes Islamophobia.

A CAIR report on Islamophobia includes results from a number of polls that surveyed trends in American feelings toward Islam and Muslims, particularly after the election of Barack Obama in 2008. A *Time* magazine poll found 28 percent of voters felt Muslims should be banned from sitting on the Supreme Court, and close to 33 percent would bar them from running for the presidency. A CBS News poll found approximately 20 percent of Americans hold negative feelings toward Muslims. "Public Policy Polling, a Democratic Party–affiliated firm, found in October 2010 that more Republicans support the hypothetical construction of a strip club than an Islamic center near Ground Zero."[98]

Politicians provide an authoritative voice for the public and are responsible to a significant degree for public perceptions on an issue. Beyond the four Republican lawmakers who accused Muslim interns on Capitol Hill of potential spying, and Representative Peter King, whose hearings on Islam and terrorism painted an entire religion with negativity, those holding or running for office have contributed to the climate of anti-Muslim sentiment in the United States. Lynne Torgerson, who ran against Keith Ellison in Minnesota, "stated her belief that Islam encourages criminal behavior and should not be protected under the First Amendment." A Republican candidate for governor in Tennessee likened Islam to a cult. A congressional candidate in Florida stated that Islam is against everything America is for.[99] The growth of the Tea Party and its mainstreaming of anti-Muslim rhetoric also contributes to a national atmosphere and culture of Islamophobia. Unable to openly express concern over Obama's race, they have attempted to frame him as a secret Muslim. When public discourse that is intolerant goes unchallenged, it can promote "impunity for perpetrators of violent hate crimes . . ."[100]

Republican presidential candidate Tom Tancredo illustrates the creation of a climate of fear with a television campaign ad he ran during the 2004 election. In the ad, Tancredo argued for border security as a defense against terrorism. "There are consequences to open borders beyond the 20 million aliens who have come to take our jobs. Islamic terrorists now freely roam U.S. soil, jihadists who froth with hate, here to do as they have in London, Spain, Russia. The price we pay for spineless politicians who refuse to defend our borders against those who come to kill." Tancredo endorses the ad with these words, "I approve this message because someone needs to say it."[101] U.S representative John Cooksey from Alabama stated on a radio interview, "Someone who comes in that's got a diaper on his head and a fan belt wrapped around that diaper on this head, that guy needs to be pulled over."[102] These are our public voices, some of our elected politicians from whom we should expect and demand better.

The CAIR Report provides a list of some of the hate crimes against Muslims that have occurred in the past few years, including assaults, verbal abuse, and vandalism. In the workplace, Muslims have suffered from intimidation, threats, and insults, such as the Sprint employee who was terminated after hanging up on a customer who told him to go to hell after first asking if he was a Muslim, women who face discrimination for wearing the hijab, or those who are called "camel jockey" and "rag head" by fellow workers.[103] Muslim students at all levels—from grade school through college—have suffered from discrimination and harassment by fellow students, bus drivers, and school administrators.

Muslims in public spaces have been victims of discrimination, particularly when attempting to fly in the years following September 11, 2001. Nine Muslims were removed from a flight in Virginia after another passenger overheard one remark about the safest place to sit on an airplane. "The passengers were removed, denied re-boarding and barred from future AirTran flights." Another passenger was removed from a plane after he was overheard speaking a language other than English. "Four Muslim men were escorted off a Delta flight when it landed at the Minneapolis–St. Paul International Airport. A flight attendant had reported suspicious behavior after one of the men dropped a pen while filling out a customs form and bent down to pick it up."[104]

Terrorism has emerged as a singularly important security issue in the past decade and the discourse surrounding this topic—"the terms, assumptions, labels, categories and narratives used to describe and explain terrorism—has emerged as one of the most important political discourses of the modern era ..."[105] In looking at the creation of the "Islamic terrorist," Jackson adopts an interpretive logic rather than a causal one, breaking his analysis into two stages. The first is textual, and he analyzed a variety of texts between 2001 and 2006 that included books, articles, reports, speeches, and documents from policy makers, think tanks, and journalists as well as the work of academics. The second stage was a critical analysis of the metaphors, labels, and assumptions found in these texts aimed to "destabilize dominant interpretations and demonstrate the inherently contested and political nature of the discourse." He looked at the ideological effects of the creation of the "Islamic terrorist" through discourse and at the purpose the particular construction serves in maintaining a particular and hegemonic version of truth. His goal is to destabilize our current creations, opening a space for other interpretations and "potentially emancipatory forms of knowledge and practice."[106]

The current discourse of "Islamic terrorism" comes from three main traditions: terrorism studies, a long tradition of orientalist scholarship, and the similarly long tradition of "cultural stereotypes and deeply hostile media representations and depictions of Islam and Muslims."[107] Dominant frames put Muslims in direct opposition to the "West" and to "America," as savages to "our" civilization, as extremists to "our" rationality. Part of the current dominant frame is the inherent violence in Islam and its accompanying terrorism. These are represented as born from Islamic doctrine itself rather than belonging to Muslim fanatics. Islam itself is framed as backward, antidemocratic, and primarily driven to destroy the West as a function of the "ideology of wrath" that radical Islam directs westward; the overarching frame regarding Islam is that it represents a major threat to the West.[108]

"Crucially, the . . . narratives imply that because 'Islamic terrorism' is fanatical, religiously motivated, murderous and irrational, there is no possibility of negotiation, compromise or appeasement; instead eradication, deterrence and forceful counter-terrorism are the only reasonable responses."[109] Much like Truman's comments regarding the Japanese in World War II as he decided to drop the bomb on two Japanese cities ("When you have to deal with a beast, you have to treat him like a beast"), Islam has been framed in such a way as to preclude any but extreme measures in response. Jackson critiques the texts he reviews regarding Islam and terrorism as vastly over simplified and riddled with misconceptions and mistaken inferences. A more realistic reading provides a different frame: practicing Muslims number over 1 billion from a variety of 50 different countries and include large groupings as well as much smaller sects; they also represent a variety of linguistic and cultural backgrounds. Islam is not innately violent or antidemocracy, nor is it antimodern. Fanatics from all religions have the ability to carry out violent acts; this does not mean that Islamic fanatics who are violent are any more representative than extremists from any other group. The violence between Catholics and Protestants in Northern Ireland is not framed as an inherent attribute of Christianity. And as Jackson points out, "the fact that the majority of terrorists are men . . . does not mean that being male predisposes one to terrorism."[110]

A different framing of the recent texts on Islam point to a revolutionary ideology rather than "a violent religious cult." Political goals include the creation of a Palestinian state; an end to American military occupation in the Arabian Peninsula, Iraq, and Afghanistan; and basic resistance to foreign occupation. "One of the most important functions of the discourse of 'Islamic terrorism' is to construct and maintain national identity, primarily through the articulation of a contrasting negative 'other' who defines the Western 'self' through negation."[111] Thus, we have determined ourselves in opposition to our creation of the Islamic terrorist. The current discourse surrounding the creation of the Islamic terrorist serves to determine which actions are considered plausible, acceptable, and commonsense, and by contrast, which ones are unacceptable and dismissed out of hand. Creating Islam as a threat removes the possibility of dealing with difference in any rational way. Creating Muslims as irrational and violent savages "normalizes and legitimizes a restricted set of coercive and punitive counter-terrorism strategies, whilst simultaneously making non-violent alternatives such as dialogue, compromise and reform appear inconceivable and nonsensical."[112] It also serves to avoid any critical look at Western ideologies and practices, and what role these have had in creating the animosity felt toward the West today.

The current discourse on Islam is used by American politicians and our allies to push for a set of policies that work in our own best interests, including the control of resources (oil), political regime changes in Iraq and Afghanistan, increased militarization, "and more broadly, the preservation and extension of a Western-dominated liberal international order."[113] The discourse has served to create strong animosity toward Muslims in America, including a surge of hate crimes after September 11, 2001. Jackson speaks to the fact that our response to the framing of "Islamic terrorism" has been military actions and mistreatment of Muslim peoples at home and abroad that are very likely to create further hostility toward the West and increase the possibility of future acts of terrorism, the exact opposite effect that we desire.[114]

CONCLUSION

With all three of these religious groups, a common stereotypical frame creates them as controlled by their religious governing structure in opposition to the U.S. government. Concerns over Catholics in politics included the belief that with a Catholic president, the pope and bishops would then have control over the United States. Anti-Catholic ideology includes the belief that Catholics are more loyal to the pope than to the United States. The same arguments arise in anti-Semitic rhetoric. Jews are believed to be more loyal to the Jewish faith and to Israel than to the United States. Fears of a Jewish plan to control the United States through politics and business morph into a Jewish plan to take over the entire world. *Protocols of the Elders of Zion* was believable to many because of the already existing stereotypes about Jewish power and control. Similar arguments are now made about Muslims and Islam. Muslims are believed to be loyal to their religion above all else and fanatical in their zeal to spread this religion throughout the world. The ironies of these beliefs should not be lost on a Christian nation that developed from other nations that colonized far reaches of the world for economic reasons but also to spread the Christian religion. The earliest history of conquest in America included the slaughter of Native Americans in part because they were framed as heathens lacking Christianity.

Negative feelings toward a particular religious group do not in themselves constitute a hate crime. It is only when people act on those feelings and commit an offense that a religious hate crime occurs. The United States has not, historically, been home to the same magnitude of violent religious-based hate crimes as have many other countries, although it is hard to distinguish among the reasons for the many Native American deaths early in our history; certainly, religious bias was a significant factor. However, at times of war, high levels of immigration, or economic stress, there have been historical moments when religion has been the basis for hate crimes. The surge of hate crimes against those believed to be Muslim attests to the strength of framing in our country's media and the long history of stereotypes and misinformation that surround a religious Other.

NOTES

1. Kenneth C. Davis, "America's true history of religious tolerance," *Smithsonian.com*, October 2010, http://www.smithsonianmag.com/history-archaeology/Americas-True-History -of-Religious-Tolerance.html, (accessed November 8, 2013).

2. Ibid.

3. Michael W. McConnell, "Is there still a 'Catholic question' in America? Reflections on John F. Kennedy's Speech to the Houston Ministerial Association," 2011, 1638. http://www3.nd.edu/~ndlrev/archive_public/86ndlr4/McConnell.pdf (accessed March 6, 2013).

4. James Martin, "The last acceptable prejudice?" *America: The National Catholic Review*, March 25, 2000. http://americanmagazine.org/issue/281/article/last-acceptable-prejudice (accessed January 31, 2013).

5. "Reported hate crimes against U.S. Catholics up by nearly 25 percent," Catholic News Agency, November 26, 2009, http://www.catholicnewsagency.com/ (accessed March 6, 2013).

6. "Irish-Catholic immigration to America," *Immigration*, Library of Congress, www.loc .gov/teachers/classroommateirals/presentationsandactivities/presentations/immigration/irish2 .html (accessed September 16, 2013).

7. David R. Roediger, *The Wages of Whiteness: Race and the Making of the American Working Class* (New York: Verso, 2007), 133.

8. Ibid., 134.

9. C. J. Taylor, "The mortar of assimilation—and the one element that won't mix," *Puck*, June 26, 1889. www.museum.msu.edu/exhibitions/virtual/Immigrationandcaricature/7572 -126.html (accessed September 16, 2013).

10. Roediger, *Wages of Whiteness*, 137.

11. Ibid., 140.

12. Ibid., 146.

13. Peter A. Quinn, "Closets full of bones," *America* 172, no. 5 (February 18, 1995): 12.

14. Thomas P. Baldwin, "George D. Prentice, the *Louisville Anzeiger*, and the 1855 Bloody Monday Riots," *Filson Club History Quarterly* 67, no. 4 (October 1993): 486.

15. Ibid., 490.

16. Quinn, "Closets full of bones," 12.

17. Ibid., 13.

18. Charles Wentworth Dilke, *Greater Britain: A Record of Travel in English Speaking Countries*, www.gutenberg.org/ebooks/41755 (accessed September 16, 2013).

19. Quinn, "Closets full of bones," 13.

20. Thomas R. Pegram, *One Hundred Percent American: The Rebirth and Decline of the Ku Klux Klan in the 1920s* (Chicago: Ivan R. Dee, 2011), x.

21. Ibid., 6.

22. Ibid., 9.

23. Ibid., 22.

24. Ibid., 58.

25. Ibid., 69.

26. Ibid., 70.

27. Ibid., 72.

28. Ibid., 79.

29. Theodore H. White, *The Making of the President, 1960* (New York: Atheneum, 1988), 105.

30. Hiram Wesley Evans, "The Menance of modern immigration," address at State Fair, Dallas Texas, October 24, 1923, http://archive.lib.msu.edu/DMC/AmRad/menacemodernimmigration.pdf (accessed March 12, 2013).

31. "The defeat of the happy warrior," *Time* 75, no. 16 (April 18, 1960).

32. "Warning against the 'Roman Catholic Party': Catholicism and the 1928 election," *History Matters*, historymatters.gmu.edu/d/5073 (accessed March 12, 2013).

33. Ibid.

34. Shaun A. Casey, *The Making of a Catholic President: Kennedy vs. Nixon, 1960* (New York: Oxford University Press, 2009), 8.

35. Ibid., 14.

36. Ibid., 25.

37. Ibid., 104.

38. "POAU-WOW," *Time* 81, no. 7 (February 15, 1963): 127.

39. Casey, *Making of a Catholic President*, 124.

40. Ibid., 177.

41. Ibid., 178.

42. McConnell, 1636.

43. James Gannon, "Kerry's Catholicism: Checked at the door," *USA Today*, June 1, 2004, http://usatoday30.usatoday.com/news/opinion/editorials/2004-06-01-gannon_x.htm (accessed March 16, 2013).

44. "Jews permitted to stay in New Amsterdam," http://www.pbs.org/wnet/heritage/spisode7/documents (accessed September 10, 13).

45. Louis Harap, *The Image of the Jew in American Literature: From Early Republic to Mass Immigration* (Philadelphia: Jewish Publication Society of America, 1974), 4.

46. Ibid., 7.

47. Ibid., 8–9.

48. Ibid., 12.

49. James Allen, "Without sanctuary: Lynching photography in America" (Santa Fe: Twin Palm, 2000), 178.

50. Nancy MacLean, "Gender, sexuality, and the politics of lynching: The Leo Frank case revisited," in *Under Sentence of Death: Lynching in the South*, edited by W. Fitzhugh Brundage (Chapel Hill: University of North Carolina Press, 1997), 176.

51. Tom Watson, "The Leo Frank case," *Watson's Magazine*, January 1915, 143 (italics in original).

52. Ibid., 160.

53. Allen, "Without sanctuary," 178 (italics in original).

54. Nancy MacLean, "The Leo Frank case reconsidered: Gender and sexual politics in the making of reactionary populism," *Journal of American History* 78, no. 3 (December 1991): 920.

55. Oliver B. Pollak, "Antisemitism, the Harvard plan, and the roots of reverse discrimination," *Jewish Social Studies* 45, no. 2 (Spring 1983): 114.

56. Simon W. Vozick-Levinson, "Writing the wrong: A. Lawrence Lowell," *Harvard Crimson*, November 3, 2004.

57. Pollak, "Antisemitism," 118.

58. Ibid.

59. Henry Ford, "Jewish jazz becomes our national music," *International Jew*, http://www.radioislam.org/ford/TheInternationalJew.pdf (accessed March 16, 2013).

60. "Henry Ford invents a Jewish conspiracy," *Jewish Virtual Library* www.jewishvirtuallibrary.org/jsource/anti-semitism/ford1.html (accessed September 8, 2013).

61. Henry Ford, *The International Jew*, Vol. 4, p. 645. http://www.radioislam.org/ford/TheInternationalJew.pdf (accessed March 16, 2013).

62. Victoria Saker Woeste, "Suing Henry Ford: America's first hate speech case," *American Bar Foundation*, http://www.americanbarfoundation.org/research/project/19 (accessed September 12, 2013).

63. Michael Dobbs, "Ford and GM scrutinized for alleged Nazi collaboration," *Washington Post*, November 30, 1998, A1.

64. U.S. Holocaust Memorial Museum, "Charles E. Coughlin," http://www.ushmm.org/wlc/en/article.php (accessed September 12, 2013).

65. A series of planned attacks against Jews in Nazi Germany and Austria in November 1938 that resulted in nearly 100 Jewish deaths and the arrest and incarceration of thousands in concentration camps.

66. U.S. Holocaust Memorial Museum, "Charles E. Coughlin."

67. "Father Coughlin: The radio priest; political vies, old time radio, and religion," http://www.fathercoughlin.org/father-coughlin-anti-semitism.html (accessed September 12, 2013).

68. Ibid.

69. Charles Lindbergh, "Des Moines speech," www.charleslindbergh.com/americanfirst/speech.asp (accessed September 8, 2013).

70. Thomas C. Wilson, "Compliments will get you nowhere: Benign stereotypes, prejudice and anti-Semitism," *Sociological Quarterly* 37, no. 3 (1996): 456–479.

71. Ibid., 472.

72. Steve Goldstein, "Anti-Semitism rises on Internet after selection of Lieberman: Most observers said the phenomenon—blamed on extremists —was probably temporary," *Philly.com* (accessed September 8, 2013).

73. U.S. Holocaust Memorial Museum, "Holocaust deniers and public misinformation," http://www.ushmm.org/wlc/en/article (accessed September 8, 2013).

74. Southern Poverty Law Center,, "Willis Carto," Intelligence Files, http://www.splcenter.org/get-informed/intelligence-files/profiles/willis-carto (accessed March 17, 2013).

75. Deborah E. Lipstadt, *Denying the Holocaust: The Growing Assault on Truth and Memory* (New York: Penguin, 1993).

76. Dwight D. Eisenhower, *Crusade in Europe* (Baltimore: Johns Hopkins University Press, 1997), 409.

77. Jack Shaheen, *Arab and Muslim Stereotyping in American Popular Culture* (Georgetown, VA: Center for Muslim-Christian Understanding, Georgetown University, 1997), 19, http://www12.georgetown.edu/sfs/docs/Jack_J_Shaheen_Arab_and_Muslim_Stereotyping_in_American_Popular_Culture_1997.pdf

78. Jim Naureckas, "Talk radio on Oklahoma City: Don't look at us," July 1, 1995, http://fair.org/extra-online-articles/talk-radio-on-oklahoma-city/ (accessed November 8, 2013).

79. Shaheen, *Arab and Muslim Stereotyping*, 20.

80. Jane Eesley, "Creating an enemy," 2, http://gbgm-umc.org/response/articles/USMuslim.html (accessed November 8, 2013).

81. Shaheen, *Arab and Muslim Stereotyping*, 25.

82. Suad Joseph and BenjaminD'Harlingue, "The *Wall Street Journal*'s Muslims: Representing Islam in American print news media," *Islamophobia Studies Journal* 1, no. 1 (Spring 2012): 133.

83. Ibid., 134.

84. Ibid., 143.

85. Ibid., 159.

86. Ibid., 160.

87. Peter Gottschalk and Gabriel Greenberg, "Common heritage, uncommon fear: Islamophobia in the United States and British India, 1687–1947," *Islamophobia Studies Journal* 1, no. 1 (Spring 2012): 84.

88. Ibid., 88.

89. Ibid., 97.

90. Ibid., 105.

91. Perry Bacon Jr., "Foes use Obama's Muslim ties to fuel rumors about him," *Washington Post*, November 29, 2007, http://www.washingtonpost.com/wp-dyn/content/article/2007/11/28 (accessed March 7, 2013).

92. Ibid.

93. Ibid.

94. Anne Barnard and Alan Feuer, "Outraged, and outrageous," *New York Times*, October 10, 10, http://www.nytimes.com/2010/10/10/nyregion/10geller.html?pagewanted=all&_r=0 (accessed November 8, 2013).

95. Ibid.

96. See, for example, Tim Murphy, "The radicalization of Peter King," *Mother Jones*, December 20, 2010, http://www.motherjones.com/mojo/2010/12/radicalization-peter-king; Sheryl Gay Stolberg and Laurie Goostein, "Domestic terrorism hearing opens with contrasting views on dangers," *New York Times*, March 10, 2011, http://www.nytimes.com/2011/03/11/us/politics/11king.html?_r=0

97. CAIR, "Same hate, new target: Islamophobia and its impact in the United States, 2009–2010," 6, http://www.cair.com/images/islamophobia/2010IslamophobiaReport.pdf (accessed November 8, 2013).

98. Ibid., 23.

99. Ibid., 27.

100. Ibid., 24.

101. Alec MacGillis, "Tancredo's politics of fear," *Washington Post*, November 14, 2007. http://www.washingtonpost.com/wp-dyn/content/article/2007/11/13/AR2007111302212.html

102. "National briefing/south: Louisiana; Apology from congressman," *New York Times*, September 21, 2001. http://www.nytimes.com/2001/09/21/us/national-briefing-south-louisiana-apology-from-congressman.html

103. Ibid., 31–33.

104. Ibid., 35–36.

105. Richard Jackson, "Constructing enemies: 'Islamic terrorism' in political and academic discourse," *Government and Opposition* 42, no. 3 (2007): 394.

106. Ibid., 397.

107. Ibid., 400.

108. Ibid., 406.

109. Ibid., 409.

110. Ibid., 415.

111. Ibid., 420.

112. Ibid., 421.

113. Ibid., 422.

114. Ibid., 424.

6

Personal Space and Identity: Hate and the Lesbian, Gay, Bisexual, and Transgender Community

The lesbian, gay, bisexual, and transgender (LGBT) community is at the heart of a contestation of very personal space in America involving the most intimate aspects of humanity, including gender, sexual identity, self-image, social relationships, and family, with the accompanying rights to have, adopt, and raise children. This space continues to be contested on a national level with public debates on issues such as same-sex marriage, LGBT membership in the military, and hate crime protections for LGBT victims. Historically, the external definition of this group has shifted among ideologies of medical abnormality, religious sin and immorality, and a more current recognition of the community as normal. Recent public discussions have highlighted issues facing this community, not the least of which is their role as victims of hate crimes and subjects of proposed, approved, or denied hate crime legislation. Political discourse about the LGBT community continues to be prevalent and forms not a consensus, but a battleground of opinions, emotions, and changing legal rulings.

Media discussions help create a variety of public images and viewpoints that serve as a constant reminder of the space allowed the LGBT community in American society. Unfortunately, some of the most virulent and hateful words and ideas about this community find their way into the media. Even those who are supportive contribute to a limited set of images as discussions remain centered around "problems" in relationship to this group of Americans. Reiterating that LGBT people are normal, moral, and deserving of complete equality reminds the public that there are those who disagree.

Identity is formed from membership in many social institutions that include the family, marriage and other personal relationships, school, religion, the military, and the workplace. Not one of these locations has been exempt from struggle for LGBT people, and much of the struggle has played out in the media, entertainment, and the news. While progress toward equality has been made recently on a number of fronts, it has come with myriad public images of hate, denial, and condemnation.

LGBT children must find suitable role models for themselves as they mature and begin to self-identify as LGBT. Unlike many children who can look to their family and immediate relationships for these models, LGBT children usually need to look outside their immediate circle because it is not often that a LGBT child grows up with parents who are the same. This makes media representations all the more vital since they are not only a place LGBT children go for information and a better understanding of themselves, but an important source of public opinion formation. Outsiders' views of LGBT children and adults are also formed from public discourse, particularly for those who do not have personal, firsthand experiences with this community as a basis for their opinions. These sources include children's books, television and film, and the news media.

CHILDREN'S BOOKS

Children's literature on what it means to be LGBT has been problematic on two accounts: content and access. "The YA [young adult] literature available dealing with homosexuality is predominantly permeated with negativity and often ends with the demise of the homosexual protagonist, reflecting our society's homophobic mentality."[1] The portrayal of homosexuality in literature for children and young adults has been a topic of contestation; debate between those who favor limiting topics for youth and those who favor a more open presentation of issues and ideas is ongoing. The book *King and King*, in which two princes decide to marry each other, was the focal point of conflict in schools, libraries, and even state legislatures. Parents filed a federal lawsuit alleging that their children's (and their) civil rights were infringed by having a teacher read *King and King* in a Massachusetts classroom. "While it's sadly not surprising that children's books with gay themes stir this kind of controversy, what is particularly troubling about these incidents is the widespread effect they appear to have, curtailing the availability and publication of more of these kinds of books."[2] Another book, *And Tango Makes Three*, based on two male penguins in the Central Park Zoo who raised a baby penguin together, topped the American Library Association's list of the Most Challenged Books of 2006. A survey in Arkansas that same year found that approximately 21 percent of public libraries, nearly 5 percent of university libraries, and fewer than 1 percent of school libraries had books containing controversial themes and characters in their collections.[3]

The Harry Potter series, once the focus of parental condemnation for its portrayals of witchcraft, again came under attack once J. K. Rowling announced Hogwarts headmaster Albus Dumbledore was gay. Immediate condemnation rang out from those who argued that this opposed Christian values. ". . . [W]ill some continue to desert clear biblical teaching and allow their kids to maintain hero-worship of an 'out' homosexual? Will some find ways to re-cast homosexuality into something different than the 'abomination' it's called in the Scripture? . . . Will we allow our kids to believe it would be perfectly appropriate for the headmaster of any school to be homosexual?"[4]

The Oklahoma House of Representatives approved Resolution 1030 in 2005 asking Oklahoma libraries to "confine homosexually themed books and other age-inappropriate material to areas exclusively for adult access and distribution."[5] The state also attempted (unsuccessfully) to pass a bill denying state funding to libraries that did not segregate these books and requiring each library to submit a yearly report to the Oklahoma Department of Libraries outlining the actions taken to restrict this material. Apparently, much of Oklahoma agrees with the bill's author, Republican state representative Sally Kern. According to a statewide poll, 88 percent of Oklahoma voters believe books such as *King and King* should be restricted to adults who can decide if a child should have access. Forty-two percent favored banning such books all together.[6] Some use other means of keeping these books out of the hands of youth: books are deliberately left unshelved or are checked out continually by adults as a way of keeping them out of circulation.[7]

Without positive role models, LGBT children can grow up with low self-esteem and self-image. And without positive images, the non-LGBT population is left with stereotypes and misinformation on which to form its opinion. In the foreword to an annotated bibliography for children and young adults, a lesbian writer compares what is currently available to young adults and children with what she faced when she was young. "We read that we were psychopaths, perhaps paranoid, and likely to be addicted to alcohol or drugs. Religious works told us we were morally deficient."[8] In addition, gay characters were often doomed to suicide, incarceration in mental institutions, or arrest. She goes on to say that books like *Lesbian and Gay Voices* can save lives and cites the high statistics on teenage suicides among homosexual children, also pointing out that gay students are much more likely to be threatened with weapons at school and have experience with violence than is the non-LGBT population.

There are many causes of homophobia. One of them is ignorance; honest, accurate books can help counter this. Homophobia is made possible when some people believe that gays and lesbians, or people perceived as being gay or lesbian, are subhuman and/or evil, expendable, and worthy only of contempt; honest, accurate books can help counter this. One result of unrelenting homophobic harassment can be a loss of self-respect and confidence on the part of the victim; honest, accurate books can help counter this.[9]

There is still a long way to go in terms of the literature available for children and young adults. Many books fall into old stereotypes, including gay characters who represent problems and fall prey to negative outcomes. It is rare that the protagonist of the book is gay; they are far more likely to be in supporting roles. "When they do take center stage, gay characters are typically portrayed as unhappy, tortured individuals who, in a sadly predictable pattern, inevitably meet an unhappy end."[10] The author goes on to say,

. . . continually relegating gay issues and characters to the realm of the problem novel reinforces the notion that homosexuality is a viable topic only when portrayed as something to be overcome, and does little to advance understanding of gays and lesbians among straight readers or to offer lesbian and gay young people the role models they desperately need.[11]

MOVIES

"The history of the portrayal of lesbians and gay men in mainstream cinema is politically indefensible and aesthetically revolting."[12] Vito Russo traces this portrayal throughout the twentieth century. With the 1930 Motion Picture Production Code as a partial guide, film versions of homosexuals have ranged from hidden and coded characterizations to more open portrayals. The code listed "any inference of sexual perversion" as a "Don't," and homosexuality was included under this edict. Homosexuality on screen has been cast primarily in male terms, and it is the movie version of what is or is not masculine that has defined the lines between gay and straight. "The popular definition of gayness is rooted in sexism. Weakness in men rather than strength in women has consistently been seen as the connection between sex role behavior and deviant sexuality."[13] To be considered feminine or weak is an insult, and early portrayals of gayness were of men who were considered "sissies."

In the postwar years, the fear that male relationships would be seen as homosexual gave rise to certain key elements in the many "buddy" films. In these films, the strongest relationships were between two male friends. Women were often incidental to the films (rendering the films sexist as well as homophobic) but were needed to prove the masculinity (and heterosexuality) of the male leads. "The primary buddy relationships in films are those between men who despise homosexuality yet find their truest and most noble feelings are for each other."[14] With the revision of the Motion Picture Production Code in 1961, films no longer needed to code references to homosexuality in terms of sissies. However, "[w]hen gays became real, they became threatening. The new sissies departed radically from their gentle ancestors; the dykes became predatory and dangerous. Lesbians were still creatures to be conquered or defeated, but now viciously so, as though they were other men."[15]

During the 1960s, gays and lesbians were routinely killed off in films. If they were overtly gay or the women predatory, they were killed. If they were repressed or tormented by their "condition," they committed suicide. Some were "cured." In the 1964 James Bond movie *Goldfinger*, the character Pussy Galore is a lesbian. James "cures" her by sleeping with her. Russo sums it up: "In the 1960s, lesbians and gay men were pathological, predatory and dangerous, villains and fools, but never heroes."[16]

With growing awareness of the AIDS epidemic and the first public misunderstandings of it as a "gay" disease, gay men became actual monsters in film. Like vampires, they contained tainted blood that could kill innocent victims with a single drop. "The multiple social meanings of the words 'monster' and 'homosexual' are seen to overlap to varying but often high degrees."[17] Those created as monsters in films often served as an impediment to the heterosexual romance of the movies' leads, obstacles to be battled and beaten before true love could win. Homosexuals were seen as such impediments.

The role of the movie in creating a particular portrait of homosexuality is an important one. "The secret signals and hidden signs of homosexuality in Hollywood features were the only frames of reference for most gays, who learned about themselves chiefly from movies that said that the whole world was heterosexual."[18] The rest of the world learned about gays from the movies as well. Prevailing political climates and cultural beliefs have been responsible throughout the history of film for the types of shorthand readings of what constitutes homosexuality. From early feminized men through predatory monsters and psychologically damaged victims, the role models presented to gays and lesbians of all ages have been distorted and damaging.

Portrayed as straight in the film *Midnight Express* (ironic in many ways due to the eventual coming out of its lead actor Brad Davis), the real Billy Hayes did love another man. However, in the movie, the character of Billy Hayes defends himself against an advance from a man by biting out the other man's tongue, which the real Billy did not, thus illustrating the view that homosexuality was considered more disgusting to movie audiences than biting out someone's tongue.[19] Biting one's own tongue is often something that homosexuals must do to remain secure in American society.

The 1980 movie *Cruising*, which combines the story of a serial killer who targets gays with the sadism and masochism (S&M) scene, became a catalyst for massive nationwide protests of Hollywood's treatment of gays. It was also the focus of antigay protests as well. "Protest leaflets against *Cruising* said, 'People will die because of this film.' In November 1980, outside the Ramrod Bar, the site of the filming of Cruising, a minister's son emerged from a car with an Israeli submachine gun and killed two gay men."[20] The shooter, Ronald Crumpley, also wounded six others.

While there has been a push to change portrayals of homosexuality in Holly-wood, the institutionalization of the images as well as concerns for profit margins and the strength of the conservative lobby in national politics have done much to limit more realistic and sensitive portrayals. Films like *Philadelphia* (1993) and *The Birdcage* (1996) have provided increasingly sympathetic portrayals but are still bound by problems (AIDS and honesty about sexuality as well as the realities of homophobia). The 2005 film *Brokeback Mountain* depicts the relationship between two male cowboys and won critical acclaim for its portrayal of the men, their struggles with their own identities, and their relationship with each other. However, the relationship is still firmly imbedded in the view the larger society has of gay men and a reminder that many consider this relationship something to denigrate. It is never just the relationship itself; it is always imbedded in the problematized space allowed the LGBT community.

TELEVISION

GLAAD, which lists itself on line as the "communication epicenter" of the LGBT movement with the responsibility to shape media narrative in inclusive and honest ways, monitors programs for inclusion of diversity. In the 2012–2013 television season, 4.4 percent of series regulars were LGBT, up from 2.9 percent the previous season. New shows such as *Modern Family* and *Glee* have contributed to this increase. The depictions of LGBT characters on television play an important role in making viewers more comfortable with the LGBT people they encounter. According to research by Edward Schiappa and others, how television portrays gay characters makes a difference. "In five separate studies, Mr. Schiappa and his colleagues have found that the presence of gay characters on television programs decreases prejudices among viewers of the programs."[21]

Schiappa, Gregg, and Hewes found that increased exposure to gay men on *Will & Grace* influenced attitudes toward gay men in general. These researchers used a combination of psychology's contact hypothesis (under appropriate conditions, interpersonal contact is one of the most effective ways to reduce prejudice between groups) and communication's theory of parasocial interaction (the idea that contact with people through the mass media gives the illusion of face-to-face relationships) to hypothesize that with greater exposure to the gay men on *Will & Grace*, levels of prejudice toward gay men in general would decrease. They found this to be true, particularly among those who had the least reported direct contact with homosexuals.[22] This study demonstrates the importance of mediated images for creating and diminishing prejudice toward minority groups.

A recent poll found that the visibility of openly LGBT characters on shows like *Glee, Modern Family*, and *The New Normal* has contributed to an increase in positive attitudes toward gay marriage.[23]

A 2005 study looked at 22 television sitcoms to determine the incidence of homosexual characters and their demographics. Only 2 percent of the 125 central characters were homosexual, and all were male between 20 and 35 years old, highlighting the fact that gay adolescents have no peer role models on television.[24] Since this is a group that spends time watching television, it is a primary source of information for them.[25] This lack of television presence implicitly articulates the values, fears, and intolerance of program developers and producers by the exclusion of a representative sample of this population and limits viewers' understanding to a particularly narrow framing. Of the 125 characters, none were bisexual.[26]

In the 1980s, television began portraying characters with AIDS as the disease was being associated with homosexuality in the news media. Social policies are dependent on public attitudes, and the predominant media frames for an issue foster a particular viewpoint and a focal point for action and reaction. By framing AIDS as a gay problem, initial preventive measures and solutions were limited in ways that were harmful to a much larger population that considered itself immune to the epidemic. "The media perpetuated this association by framing AIDS as a gay disease, particularly during the period when the disease was being defined for the public." The implication that gays are responsible for AIDS "furnishes new reasons to discriminate against gays and gives new power to antigay movements." Gays could be considered not only a threat to the dominant culture, morality, and lifestyle, but now a threat to life as well.[27]

Gays and lesbians on television were long relegated to a sexless existence with implications of romance but never physical manifestations on screen. "Over the years, expressions of same-sex affection between women were more accepted than those between men. In November 1989, the sitcom *Thirtysomething* lost more than $1 million in ad revenue when it showed two men in bed together, even though a preceding kiss was axed."[28] Ellen DeGeneres came out on television in 1997. "But not long thereafter, her same-sex kiss on the show prompted a parental advisory warning, and the program's ratings dropped as it began to focus more on gay issues." Three episodes of *Ellen* were devoted to the public coming-out of the lead character at the same time actress Ellen DeGeneres was also coming out. Public reaction seemed to be primarily positive at first, but after a season of poor ratings, the show was canceled in May 1998. DeGeneres felt the network was not supportive, especially in terms of promoting the show, while ABC executives felt the program had turned into her soapbox to discuss lesbian issues.[29]

The mass media provides the broadest common background of assumptions about what things are, how they work, and why. The power to represent "reality" is of extreme importance, particularly to those who have little or no contact with the groups being represented. Our understanding of the world often comes from fictional representations. The important first stories on AIDS linked it with gay men and their lifestyle, and portrayed those with AIDS as either victims or villains. Television comes directly into our homes, and the recurring characters from our favorite shows share our personal space, becoming a part of our understanding and ideas as to what those they represent are "really" like. According to the theory of parasocial interaction, we form relationships (albeit one sided) with these characters, feeling a bond of intimacy even though the character is fictional. This gives a lot of power to the representations of Other that find their way into our homes on a regular basis. It can limit our understanding of the LGBT population in many ways and through limited framing and development, denies this community a full, complex humanity.

BOY SCOUTS OF AMERICA

The Boy Scouts of America (BSA) has faced numerous lawsuits since the early 1990s attacking its practice of excluding openly homosexual boys and young men from participation either as Scouts or as Scoutmasters. However, following a vote by the National Council at its annual meeting in May 2013, as of January 1, 2014, openly gay boys may now be Boy Scouts. The Membership Standards Resolution now reads, "No youth may be denied membership in the Boy Scouts of America on the basis of sexual orientation or preference alone."[30] The Scouts will continue to prohibit openly gay men from serving as Scout leaders, however.

In 2000, the U.S. Supreme Court ruled that private organizations such as the Boy Scouts have the right under the First Amendment's freedom of association to set membership standards that include banning homosexuals from participation (*Boy Scouts of America vs. Dale*). Arguments in favor of banning gays included such specious reasoning as to equate homosexuality with child molestation and pedophilia. In addition, homosexuality was considered by some as immoral and unclean. "His [Dale] presence as an assistant scoutmaster would interfere with the Scouts' choice not to propound a point of view contrary to its beliefs." While the Scouts discourage any discussion of sexuality, whether heterosexual or homosexual, they feared that including homosexuals in their ranks would be taken as a mandate to push the "homosexual agenda" to adolescent boys. Many Scout troops are sponsored by religious organizations such as the Catholic Church and the Mormon Church, which is the nation's largest sponsor of Scouting troops. The Mormon Church has stated it will continue its sponsorship, though "[c]hurches of various faith denominations in Alabama, Georgia, Kentucky, Idaho and other states have ended Scouting programs because the [new] policy goes against church teachings . . ."[31]

GENDER-NEUTRAL RESTROOMS

Restrooms have long been a contested space in America, from the racially seg-regated restrooms in the South to the many that are inaccessible to those with disabilities. Sexual identity has also created an issue for those trying to take care of a basic need. Khadijah Farmer used a women's restroom in a New York City restaurant following a Gay Pride march. While she was in the stall, a male bouncer entered the restroom, banged on her stall door, and informed her that someone had complained that a man was using the women's restroom. Although Farmer showed the bouncer her driver's license to prove that she was female, a demeaning act in itself, he did not accept her explanation and escorted her and her friends from the restaurant before they could finish their meal. "I shouldn't be harassed when I'm just trying to do something everyone in the world does. I was thrown out of the restaurant because of who I am and how I look. It was humiliating."[32]

When individuals do not fit the dominant view of what a male or female is expected to look like, conflict over the personal space of the restroom can be an issue. Riki Dennis, a transsexual, stopped to use a women's rest room at a rest stop and was assaulted by a man who, assuming she was male, believed her to be "hitting" on his girlfriend. Riki is now a member of People in Search of Safe Restrooms (PISSR), which is active primarily on college campuses where gender-neutral restrooms are appearing.[33] For students such as Rolan Gregg, who was born female but lives his life as a male, this provides a safe alternative to the regular male-female restroom choices. "The problem with not passing [as a male] is that my risk of violence is really high. So going to the bathroom becomes really scary."[34]

When an appropriate bathroom is not available, those whose gender identity does not fit the mainstream view either place themselves at the least in the posi-tion of embarrassment, in discomfort until an appropriate restroom can be found, and at the extreme in the path of violence. Problems occur due, in part, to assumptions made about what is an appropriate appearance for a man or a woman. There are those who are unwilling to share public/private space with anyone perceived as different, and this unwillingness can be strong enough to result in a violent attack.

MILITARY

The rationale behind "Don't ask, don't tell" (DADT) held that gays and les-bians serving in the military would create a risk to the morale, good order, disci-pline, and unit cohesion that are essential to military operations. The policy prohibited gays and lesbians from discussing their sexual orientation or their homosexual relationships. As long as sexual identity was hidden, this information could not be sought out by commanding officers. In passing "Don't ask, don't tell" legislation, Congress mandated three grounds for expelling homosexuals from the military. These included engaging in or attempting to engage in a homosexual act, stating that you are homosexual or bisexual, and marrying or attempting to marry someone of the same sex. The policy was instated in December 1993 in the early days of the Clinton administration as a compromise between his campaign promise to allow all citizens, regardless of sexual orientation, to serve openly in the military and those who wanted to ban homosexuals from military service altogether. Clinton received enough complaints from citizens and military personnel to agree, reluctantly, to the compromise. The policy officially ended in September 2011 following a federal appeals court ruling that barred further enforcement of it. During its tenure, opinions on the policy were split primarily along party lines, particularly during election years. In 2007, for example, in a debate in New Hampshire, all the Democratic candidates raised their hands in agreement with ending the policy, while none of the Republican candidates concurred.

For the Democratic candidates, several issues were important. One was the number of gays and lesbians serving in the military at the time and contributing to the war in Iraq. Gays and lesbians also tend to vote Democratic, and thus, this was an important constituency. Republicans, on the other hand, had gone on record as stating that wartime was no time to change a policy that seemed to be working. "Senator John McCain of Arizona declared it would be a 'terrific mistake' to 'even reopen the issue,' adding that the troops now in the field were 'the very best.' "[35] Arguments against gays in the military included a belief that they would be disruptive to morale and would create issues of trust, particularly in front-line units.

Public opinion on this issue has changed in recent years. In 1994, The Pew Research Center found that 52 percent of Americans favored allowing gay men and lesbians to serve openly in the military; by 2006, this number had risen to 60 percent. Younger adults and Democrats made up the largest groups in favor of this policy change.[36]

In May 2008, the federal appeals court in California reinstated a lawsuit that challenged the "Don't ask, don't tell" policy. The case in question was brought by flight nurse Major Margaret Witt, who was discharged from the air force after it became known that she was a lesbian. She filed a lawsuit challenging the DADT policy, and in 2006, the case was dismissed by Judge Ronald B. Leighton of the federal district court in Tacoma, Washington. The U.S. Court of Appeals reinstated much of the lawsuit and sent it back to Judge Leighton for further proceedings. "The decision was notable for the standard the appeals court instructed Judge Leighton to use in considering the case. The panel said judges considering cases claiming government intrusion into the private lives of gay men and lesbians must require the government to meet a heightened standard of scrutiny."[37]

The government must show that for every case, an important government interest is at stake and that intruding into a plaintiff's personal life would significantly advance that interest. In a settlement reached in 2011, the air force dropped its appeal of the court decision and removed Witt's discharge so that she can retire with full benefits.

To continue to serve, gays and lesbians had to hide their identity, always watching what they said and did, and how they behaved in public. They were also required to be celibate and forego any intimate relationships. The military has a double standard that goes into effect during wartime because deploying those who are gay or lesbian is a valid option during war (which one could argue is when you need to pay the strictest attention to the morale of the unit, any breaches of security, any issues of forced intimacy among those living and working together). It created hypocrisy as well as unnecessary and demeaning requirements.

Between 1980 and 1990, the Department of Defense (DOD) expelled an average of 1,500 men and women for homosexuality each year, 78 percent of whom were men. A Government Accountability Office (GAO) report points out that the major psychiatric organizations within the United States disagreed with the Department of Defense policy "and believe it to be factually unsupported, unfair, and counterproductive."[38] The GAO report goes on to discuss the costs of expelling this group since recruitment and training of their replacements represented a real cost to the military. The costs for investigating servicemen and -women to determine if they were homosexual were significant.

The 1957 Crittenden Report and the Department of Defense's Personnel Security Research and Education Center (PERSEREC) report both found that homosexuals were no more of a security risk than heterosexuals. The PERSEREC report, which was commissioned by the Department of Defense to study conditions related to trust violations—including drug abuse, credit history, and homosexuality—pointed out that the policy preventing homosexuals "was based on the same rationale used to limit the integration of Blacks."[39] The GAO report noted that "the DOD policy is based on military judgment and that scientific or sociological analyses are unlikely to affect its policy of excluding homosexuals from the military."[40] The first PERSEREC report came out in 1988 and was criticized by the Pentagon as being based on flawed research. A second report, published in 1999, looked for connections between sexual orientation and suitability for service. This report found that gay service members did better than heterosexual ones in terms of most areas of adjustment.

A report on the success of "Don't ask, don't tell," also looked at the success of the "Don't pursue" and "Don't harass" additions to the policy. "Don't pursue" was an attempt to stop witch hunts aimed at uncovering homosexuals in the military. "Don't harass" was an attempt to stop all levels of harassment of those believed to be homosexual. The report found that while "Don't pursue" was meeting its goals, the "Don't harass" portion "remains the one area of the policy still in need of significant improvement."[41] The report concluded, "When homosexual members can abstain from prohibited conduct, the policy has permitted them to serve honorably despite their sexual orientation."[42] The use of the word "despite" in this statement illustrates the stigma of abnormality attached to the LGBT community.

ALLEN SCHINDLER

On October 27, 1992, Allen Schindler Jr., a petty officer in the navy stationed in Japan, was beaten to death by two of his shipmates. Schindler, 22, was killed because he was gay. He had recently told his commander that he was gay because he wanted a discharge. Terry Helvey and Charles Vins beat Schindler so severely that every organ in his body was destroyed, and the medical examiner compared his body to victims of fatal airplane crashes. A navy investigator told the court that Helvey admitted to killing Schindler and had stated that he hated homosexuals, did not regret his actions, and would do it again because Schindler deserved it. Charles Vins, in exchange for testimony against Helvey, was given a sentence that resulted in his serving 78 days. "Mr. Vins was tried in November at a court-martial that went unnoticed because it took place before the Navy had said Mr. Schindler was homosexual. Apparently in a plea agreement he was in effect given a four-month sentence and a bad-conduct discharge."[43] Terry Helvey was sentenced to life imprisonment; although he was eligible for parole as of 2002, he has not yet been released.

The Schindler killing attracted attention for a number of reasons that included the brutality of the murder, the possibility that it was a hate crime, the proximity of the murder to President Clinton's new "Don't ask, don't tell" policy, and concerns that the navy may have attempted to cover up the significance of Schindler's homosexuality when first dealing with the crime. "Friends of Mr. Schindler have said that just before his death he had complained that as word of his sexual orientation spread among the crew of the Belleau Wood, he was being harassed by the other sailors."[44] Other shipmates of Schindler's who also are homosexual described life on the ship as "living hell" for homosexuals.[45] Harassment ranged from verbal insults to intimidation to physical attacks. "The slaying of Mr. Schindler, a 22-year-old radioman, has become a symbol of the anxieties unleashed by President Clinton's proposal to end the ban on homosexuals in the military, even though his death came before Mr. Clinton took office."[46] Although it occurred before the passage of DADT, the issue of gays and lesbians in the military was being debated publicly. "Gay-rights leaders have argued that the case underscores how the Navy condones hostile attitudes toward homosexuals. They are using Mr. Schindler's killing to battle for President Clinton's proposal to allow homosexuals in the armed services. And people who support the existing ban point to Mr. Schindler's case as an example of how dangerous it would be to try to integrate homosexuals."[47]

Terry Helvey admitted that he beat Schindler to death but in court gave no reason for the killing. He pleaded guilty to the murder but not premeditation, and by accepting the plea, the court did not require a discussion of the motives behind the murder. "At first, few people outside a tight circle in the Navy seem to have known that Mr. Schindler may have been killed because of his homosexuality, and the Navy appeared to have gone out of its way to keep the matter quiet."[48] However, friends of Schindler's wrote a letter to *Pacific Stars and Stripes* (a military newspaper) expressing their concern that the navy was covering up the murder. The paper wrote an article on the case, including the fact that Schindler had told his commander about his homosexuality and that he had been harassed on the ship. The navy originally told Schindler's mother that he had died as the result of falling on his head during a fight.

Helvey initially told navy investigators that he beat Schindler because Schindler had made a sexual advance to him in the restroom. He admitted three weeks later that this was a lie.[49] In the sentencing phase of the proceedings, the issue of Schindler's homosexuality was not raised. Helvey said he had attacked Schindler while drunk but made no mention of attacking him because he was gay. After sentencing, the navy released documents that described how Helvey had stalked Schindler "then punched and kicked him furiously, at least in part because he hated homosexuals."[50] At one point, the navy disclosed a story from another sailor that the disagreement between Helvey and Schindler was an argument between two homosexuals who were in a relationship. While this story was later debunked, many felt it was released as an argument against Clinton's proposal to end the ban on gays in the military. In the documents released concerning the case, "He [Helvey] admitted that he hated homosexuals and that he knew Mr. Schindler was homosexual. Mr. Helvey was also quoted as telling the investigator that he found homosexuality 'disgusting, sick and scary,' but denying that he would seek out homosexuals to beat them. Then he added, 'I regret that this incident happened and I feel like it could have been averted had homosexuals not been allowed in the military.' "[51] According to the testimony of Charles Vins, in following Schindler that night, "We knew he was on restriction for confessing to be a homosexual and was being kicked off the ship."[52] Charles Vins, who was given a light sentence in return for his testimony, was later found not only to have witnessed the attack, but to have taken part in it as well.

SAME-SEX MARRIAGE

In 1996, Congress passed the Defense of Marriage Act (DOMA), which was signed by President Bill Clinton. The act, whose purpose was to "define and protect the institution of marriage," defined marriage as a legal union between one

man and one woman, with the word "spouse" reserved for a person of the opposite sex. In addition, it held that no state need recognize a same-sex marriage that
is legal in another state. The Senate voted 85–14 in favor of DOMA.

In November 2003, the Massachusetts Supreme Judicial Court ruled that its
state constitution guarantees equal marriage rights for same-sex couples.
President Bush responded in his January 2004 State of the Union address by saying that "we" must "defend the sanctity of marriage" and the next month stated
his support for a federal constitutional amendment defining marriage as an
arrangement between one man and one woman. By May 2004, same-sex couples
began marrying in Massachusetts. In May 2008, the California Supreme
Court ruled that banning same-sex marriage was unconstitutional. However,
California's Proposition 8, which restored the definition of marriage as a union
between one man and one woman only, was placed on the ballot in the fall of
2008 and passed. Proposition 8 was subsequently declared unconstitutional in
Perry vs. Schwarzenegger in 2010. The U.S. Supreme Court refused to hear an
appeal in 2013, thereby upholding the *Perry* decision. On June 26, 2013, the
U.S. Supreme Court ruled that Section 3 of DOMA, which prevented the federal
government from recognizing same-sex marriages, was unconstitutional. This
followed rulings in other federal courts since 2010 that had already declared it
unconstitutional in terms of specific issues of equality in areas such as public
employee benefits, estate taxes, and bankruptcy.

States are currently divided in their stand on this question. Thirteen states
have now legalized same-sex marriage by a variety of means. Twenty-nine others
forbid it in their constitutions, while six prevent it by statute. Some states allow
civil unions between same-sex couples, which provide the same spousal rights
to the couple. Other states allow domestic partnerships that grant a range of
spousal rights.

Arguments for allowing same-sex marriage include civil rights to equal treatment, economic concerns regarding issues such as inheritance, parental rights
and child support, health care benefits as well as Medicare and disability benefits,
and hospital visiting rights. The U.S. General Accounting Office (GAO) issued a
report to the U.S. Senate in 2004 that listed "a total of 1,138 federal statutory
provisions classified to the United States Code in which marital status is a factor
in determining or receiving benefits, rights, and privileges."[53] These include
wide-ranging categories from Social Security and related programs to veteran's
benefits, employment benefits, immigration and naturalization benefits to crimes
and family violence.

Recent studies have pointed to the harm done to the LGBT community by
stigma, discrimination, and prejudice. During the 2006 election, when nine
states included constitutional amendments to limit marriage to one man and
one woman, lesbian, gay, and bisexual adults reported significantly more minority stress and higher levels of psychological distress than those surveyed in other

states. Minority stress refers to exposure to negative media messages and negative conversations.[54]

Opposition to same-sex marriage comes from a variety of sources. Religious arguments against same-sex marriage are some of the loudest and most common. James Dobson, in *Marriage under Fire*, states that legalization or tolerance for same-sex marriage would redefine the family, damage traditional family unions, and lead to a greater number of homosexual couples.[55] Dobson is an evangelical Christian and founder of the group Focus on the Family. The Roman Catholic Church opposes recognition of same-sex marriages, believing that only hetero-sexual relationships within marriage are moral. During the 2012 elections, the Catholic Church spent close to $2 million on campaigns opposing gay marriage in four states. While the Catholic Church itself takes a stance against same-sex marriage, a 2012 Pew Research Center poll found that Catholics who support same-sex marriage now outnumbered those who do not by 52 to 37 percent.[56] A 2013 poll found that 62 percent of Catholics believe that same-sex marriages should be legal.[57] Conservative Christians believe that homosexuality is in opposition to biblical teachings. Orthodox Judaism also opposes same-sex rela-tionships and marriages. The Mormon Church argues that marriage should pri-marily be an institution of family-building, that is, a mother and a father having and raising children. This church believes that redefining same-sex marriages as legitimate when the couple cannot have a biological child of its own damages the ideal family structure.

The Washington State Supreme Court ruled in *Anderson et al. vs. King County* (2006), in which a number of same-sex couples attempted to argue that Washington's Defense of Marriage Act was unconstitutional, "Under this stan-dard, DOMA is constitutional because the Legislature was entitled to believe that limiting marriage to opposite-sex couples furthers procreation, essential to the survival of the human race and furthers the well-being of children by encourag-ing families where children are reared in homes headed by the children's biologi-cal parents. Allowing same-sex couples to marry does not, in the legislature's view, further these purposes."[58] However, the law does not prohibit marriage for those who intentionally do not have children, who are unable to have chil-dren, or who choose to adopt. Many same-sex couples do have children, often biologically related to one member of the couple (and sometimes both), and studies have shown that children raised by same-sex couples flourish as well as do those in families with heterosexual parents.

In *Perry*, the American Psychological Association (in conjunction with several other groups, including the American Psychiatric Association) detailed research supporting its statement that there is no scientific basis for determining that gay and lesbian parents are any less capable than heterosexual parents when it comes to raising psychologically healthy and well-adjusted children. They cited research from more than two dozen empirical studies that "are impressively consistent in their failure to identify deficits in parenting abilities or in the development of children raised in a lesbian or gay household."[59]

Polls conducted by the Pew Research Center have found that public acceptance of homosexuality—including same-sex marriage, gay adoption, and gays serving openly in the military—has risen over past years. From a poll taken in 2001 that showed 57 percent in opposition to gay marriage, combined data from two polls in 2013 show that slightly over 50 percent of Americans are now supportive of same-sex marriage, while 43 percent oppose it. The change occurred across many lines, including age (seniors became more in favor), and religion (both Catholics and nonevangelical Protestants decreased their opposition). "A solid majority of Catholics and White mainline Protestants (56% and 55% respectively) favor allowing gay and lesbian couples to legally marry, compared to only 23% of White evangelical Protestants. Nearly 8-in-10 (77%) Americans who are not affiliated with any religion support same-sex marriage."[60]

Following the trend in public opinion toward approval of same-sex marriage, public opinion on gay adoption is also moving toward acceptance. In 1999, fifty-seven percent of Americans opposed allowing gays and lesbians to adopt children. In a 2006 poll, those who favored allowing gay adoption had risen to 46 percent, with 48 percent opposed. A poll from 2011 found that a majority of Americans, 56 percent, favored this, while those opposed had dropped to 36 percent.[61]

POLITICAL RHETORIC, 2008

The importance of LGBT issues on a national level is illustrated by the 2008 election campaigns. The websites of the presidential candidates from both main political parties included statements about marriage, employment, service in the military, and—more broadly—hate crime legislation as they relate to LGBT citizens. Republicans Mitt Romney, John McCain, and Mike Huckabee took hard lines on their websites, stating they were opposed to same-sex marriage and would not include the LGBT community under hate crime legislation. All three supported a constitutional amendment stating that marriage could only be between one man and one woman. Huckabee stated, "What's the point of keeping the terrorists at bay in the Middle East if we can't keep decline and decadence at bay here at home?" In 1992, he responded to an AP questionnaire in which he called homosexuality "an aberrant, unnatural, and sinful lifestyle."[62] Democrats Hillary Clinton, John Edwards, and Barack Obama took a different stance on hate crime legislation, as all three supported including the LGBT community as a protected group. They too, however, did not support same-sex marriage but did support civil unions with accompanying rights for same-sex couples. Clinton and Obama have since publicly given their support for same-sex marriage.

HATE CRIMES AND THE GAY PANIC DEFENSE

Karen Franklin looked at the prevalence rates and motivations for antigay harassment and violence by noncriminal young adults with a mean age of 24. "In an anonymous survey of 484 young adults, 1 in 10 admitted physical violence or threats against presumed homosexuals, and another 24% acknowledged name-calling."[63] Franklin found four motivational themes: peer dynamics, antigay ideology, thrill seeking, and perceived self-defense. Peer dynamics involves motivations based on trying to live up to friends' expectations, including proving toughness and/or heterosexuality. Antigay ideology motivated those holding negative attitudes toward homosexuality "such as disgust, hatred, religious and moral values, and the belief that homosexuals spread AIDS."[64] These individuals justify their actions as a righteous response to homosexuals' perceived moral transgressions. Thrill seekers were motivated by a desire for excitement and fun, and a wish to feel strong. As with those motivated by peer dynamics, this group has a relative lack of animosity toward homosexuals. Those motivated by self-defense feel themselves to be victims of perceived homosexual aggression or flirtation. Compared with nonassailants, those who admitted assault held more negative attitudes toward homosexuals and higher levels of masculinity ideology, and had higher levels of social drinking.

Franklin also looked at what motivated others to restrain from harassing; these included fear-avoidance, nonviolence, personal contact (gay friends and family members), and moral beliefs. "Perhaps the most startling finding is the commonplace nature of antigay behaviors among a young noncriminal population, with one third of this college sample in a politically liberal and reputedly tolerant geographic region admitting to physical violence or name-calling directed at homosexuals."[65]

Primary offenders were young men with a strong masculine ideology and peers who were against homosexuality. "Particularly intriguing is the finding that a sizable proportion of individuals who engage in physical confrontations with homosexuals perceive their actions as self-defense. Rather than inventing victimization scenarios, it is more likely that they interpret the words, actions, and demeanors of presumed homosexuals based on their belief in the sexually predatory nature of the homosexual."[66] These beliefs are based on media-driven images of the LGBT community.

The gay panic defense is a legal tactic used in cases of assault or murder. The defendant claims that due to homosexual panic (a temporary psychosis due to an unwanted homosexual advance), he or she committed the assault or murder in a state of uncontrollable violence much like temporary insanity. Some states and courts have moved toward banning the use of the gay panic defense, and the American Bar Association recently voted to curtail the use of both gay and transgender panic defense arguments during prosecutions.[67]

As the definition of homosexuality has moved from a psychiatric disorder (ending in 1973) to a politically debated question that pits biology against arguments of environment, choice, and religious beliefs, the gay panic defense has moved from its original focus on gay panic as a mental illness contributing to a reduction in the defendant's ability to formulate the necessary intent for murder to gay panic as a provocation defense that places partial blame on the victim for provoking the defendant and aims at mitigating murder to voluntary manslaughter. "The phrase 'homosexual panic' and its corresponding psychological condition were first posited in 1920 in the pages of *Psychopathology* by psychiatrist Edward J. Kempf."[68] Kempf and others described homosexual panic as stemming from an individual's reaction to events that threatened his (or her) self-image as a heterosexual due to repressed homosexual tendencies. "Typically, the defense argued that the homicide victim provided the triggering stimuli that initiated a violent, uncontrollable psychotic reaction in the latently gay defendant."[69]

Jurisdictions that allowed arguments of diminished capacity started accepting homosexual panic as an argument negating the *mens rea* necessary for first- or second-degree murder. This only occurred until the removal of homosexuality as an illness in 1973. However, the panic defense is still used in courts today as a defense for murders committed even when the victim did not use any violence to "provoke" the confrontation. The defense is officially known as the nonviolent homosexual advance (NHA) defense and is a "heat of passion" defense that puts the blame on the victim for making a homosexual advance, causing a "reasonable and ordinary person" to be provoked to the point of losing self control and killing. The "rules of provocation" include adequate provocation, a killing in the heat of passion that must be sudden with no time for the passion to cool, and a causal connection between the provocation, the passion, and the fatal act.[70]

Juries struggle with these elements, finding it difficult to define adequate provocation and the reaction of a reasonable man. "Thus, to find adequate provocation, the jury must apply the reasonable man test to the factual circumstances and conclude that the defendant's homicidal response was understandable because the victim's conduct would have caused the loss of normal self-control in any ordinary man with typical human shortcomings."[71] The presumptive fact is that the reasonable man is a heterosexual and a man.

Arguments for the use of panic defenses include those based on the constitutional right a defendant has to a complete defense in court; automatically banning a particular argument would therefore limit the defense. "As part of their testimony criminal defendants regularly explain their mental state during the commission of offenses. This testimony is invaluable to juries who must decide whether the requisite elements of criminal intent existed at the time of an offense."[72]

Those opposed to the use of this defense "argue that NHA capitalizes upon society's heterosexist and homophobic disposition . . ."[73] As Christina Chen points out, the benefits of the defense lie overwhelmingly with the heterosexual male and the burden with the homosexual male, thus making it a doctrine that is inherently both sexist and heterosexist.[74] "Viewed in the context of its legal ramifications and the reality of larger socio-cultural phenomena, the provocation doctrine's disparate impact upon historically marginalized groups is unjustifiable and can not be reconciled with the law's egalitarian aspirations or revered guiding principles of fairness and justice because the law makes these principles unattainable by definition."[75] Robert Mison argues that the defense "is a misguided application of provocation theory and a judicial institutionalization of homophobia."[76] He goes on to add that "murderous homophobia" should be considered an irrational characteristic of the individual killer rather than a defense taken as standard and acceptable behavior.

In November 2004, ABC's *20/20* did a program on the Matthew Shepard case that, through interviews with his murderers, Aaron McKinney and Russell Henderson, attempted to demonstrate that the case was not really about homophobia and a hate crime but about a drug crime. "After ignoring the terms of the sentence [McKinney was under a gag order as a part of his sentencing agreement] and interviewing both prisoners, reporter Elizabeth Vargas disclosed her finding that methamphetamine abuse and robbery were the true motivations for the 1998 beating of Shepard . . ."[77] Although the gay panic defense was attempted in the trial (until it was banned by the judge), McKinney argued in this interview that in reality, he just wanted to "beat him up and rob him"[78] The *20/20* story came at a time when keeping gays in the closet was part of the national agenda, with movements to amend the Constitution to deny any attempts at legalizing gay marriage, when the best the military had to offer gays was "Don't ask, don't tell" and when politicians were campaigning with assurances to the public that their stance on gay rights was and would remain conservative. "ABC's story is in many ways less an erasure than devaluation, a version of events that wants to downplay not so much the existence of same-sex relations as the homophobia that surrounds them. It challenges the validity of those who claim homo-hate to be an integral part of our culture and who see a deep-seated animus reflected in the continued legal use of the homosexual panic defense."[79]

GAY PANIC CASES

Scott Amedure and Jonathan Schmitz agreed to be on the *Jenny Jones Show* in 1995. Schmitz believed the show to be about "secret admirers" when in fact the true topic was "same-sex secret crushes." During the taping, Amedure admitted to having a crush on Schmitz, his neighbor. When Schmitz found out during the taping that his secret admirer was a man, he proclaimed himself to be hetero-sexual. Three days later after finding a possibly suggestive note from Amedure on his front door, Schmitz bought a shotgun, went to Amedure's home, and killed him. Schmitz called 911 and admitted to the killing, stating that the *Jenny Jones Show* was the cause. He was found guilty of second-degree murder and sentenced to 25 to 50 years in prison. Schmitz's defense argued that Amedure was unrelent-ing in his pursuit of Schmitz, that he was violent and controlling, and that Schmitz had been deliberately misled in terms of what the show was actually about. The defense also argued that Schmitz lacked the mental state necessary to have committed premeditated murder due to factors including emotional stress from the events of the show that led to his "snapping." "Schmitz told police that he killed Amedure because he was humiliated and feared other people would think he was gay."[80]

Ahmed Dabarran, an assistant district attorney in Fulton County, Georgia, who was openly gay, was found beaten to death on the couch in his apartment in Cobb County, Georgia, in 2001. Roderiqus Reed was arrested for his murder. During the trial, Reed argued that although he struck Dabarran on the head and left the apartment with the victim's cell phone, wallet, and car, he was acting in self-defense. Reed was tried on charges of murder and robbery but was acquitted in 2003. "According to experienced trial attorneys present in the courtroom, the Cobb prosecutor totally blew the case. He was indifferent and inept, and his dis-dain for this gay crime victim was obvious despite the fact that Ahmed was an as-sistant district attorney in neighboring Fulton County."[81] The defense argued that Reed killed Dabarran to protect himself from unwanted sexual advances and that he was forced to have sex with Dabarran at gunpoint by a third man. Although the medical examiner testified that Dabarran was killed in his sleep, the jury found Reed not guilty of felony murder, malice murder, and armed rob-bery. "Controversy is not new to Cobb County over its treatment of gays. In 1993 the Cobb County Commission passed a resolution stating that the 'gay life-style' was incompatible with community standards."[82]

Gwen Araujo was born biologically male and named Edward Araujo Jr. She was a transgender person living as a female when she became friends with Michael Magidson, Jaron Nabors, Jose Merel, and Jason Cazares. She was reported to have had sexual encounters with at least two of them. At a party on October 3, 2002, when it was discovered that she was biologically male, Magidson began to choke her while Merel and Nabors assisted. She was beaten with a frying pan, a can of tomatoes, and a barbell weight. She was then strangled with a rope, tied up, and wrapped in a blanket and dumped in a wooded area. Gwen was 17 years old. The autopsy showed that she died from strangulation in conjunction with blunt force trauma to the head. In the first trial, the defense argued that although Magidson was involved in Araujo's death, he was acting in the heat of passion and should therefore be found guilty of manslaughter and not murder. This trial ended in a mistrial with the jury unable to decide if the murder was premeditated. In the second trial, three defendants testified, blaming each other as well as Nabors, who pleaded guilty to manslaughter and testified for the prosecution. The jury found Magidson and Merel guilty of second-degree murder but not of a hate crime. They deadlocked on the verdict for Cazares, who eventually agreed to a plea of voluntary manslaughter. "Magidson's attorney, Michael Thorman, said after the verdict that he hadn't been claiming a panic defense. He defined that approach as justifying violence in response to a mere sexual overture from someone of the same sex. In this case, he said, actual sex was involved, leading to 'a surge of rage and violence' fueled by emotions, deception and alcohol."[83]

Gregory Love and Aaron Price were both undergraduates at Morehouse College in Georgia. Love glanced into a shower stall where Price was showering. His version of events was that he had left his glasses behind and without them on, thought it was his roommate. Price's version was that he felt threatened by attention from a gay man, so he went back to his room, got a baseball bat, and returned to hit Love at least seven times in the head. Love ended up with a seven-inch scar, chipped teeth, and a brain clot that required surgery. Price was arrested the following day. He was found guilty of aggravated assault and aggravated battery, and was sentenced to 10 years in prison.

Fulton County Superior Court judge Jerry Baxter reduced Price's sentence to seven years in May 2003 after expressing regret about the length of the sentence (10 years) that he had originally handed down. Baxter felt the original case should never have come to trial, but Price refused a plea bargain so that he could raise the gay panic defense during the trial. Price was the first defendant to come to trial under Georgia's hate crime law. He was found not guilty of a hate crime even though Love testified that Price's attack followed homosexual slurs.[84] Georgia no longer has a hate crime law. Its original law contained no categories and was overturned by the Georgia Supreme Court in 2004 because it was too vague. Although new legislation has been introduced each year since then (with sexual orientation included as a category), it has never passed.

Other Morehouse students expressed no surprise that the incident happened, citing repeated episodes of antigay and antilesbian behavior. The Morehouse College Task Force on Tolerance and Diversity emailed college alumni a questionnaire entitled "Survey of Attitudes and Behaviors toward Homosexuality." Some of the questions gave an alarming view into what the administration was thinking: How far should Morehouse go to separate heterosexuals and homosexuals in the residence halls? To what degree do you think homosexuality is immoral? How much does Morehouse's reputation for enrolling homosexual men affect your pride in the College? How much should Morehouse allow students to be open about their homosexuality on campus?[85]

In 2004, Estanislao Martinez repeatedly stabbed Joel Robles with a pair of scissors. While he did not deny this, he believed he should be excused due to transgender panic. The two men were out drinking together and then went back to Martinez's apartment. Martinez believed Robles to be a woman. After engaging in sexual activity, Martinez flew into a rage when he realized Robles was a man and stabbed him 20 times. The public defender argued that while Martinez's rage did not justify the crime, it should excuse it to some degree because Martinez was in shock upon realizing that he was with a man rather than a woman. Martinez pleaded guilty to voluntary manslaughter and was sentenced to only four years in prison.[86]

Transgender and gay panic defenses are similar. Both argue that due to either a mistaken belief in the gender of the victim or a sexual advance from someone of the same sex, the defendant is somewhat justified in violent action due to panic over the situation. This defense is used not to deny actions, but to deny culpability and to place blame on the victim himself or herself. While the Robles case did not go to trial, the defense lawyer was preparing a transgender panic defense. Martinez was not charged with a hate crime in this case.

As the result of the Robles case, the Gwen Araujo case, and others, the Gwen Araujo Justice for Victims Act was signed into law in 2006 in California. Through this law, California officially states that it opposes the use of societal bias against a victim in order to decrease a defendant's culpability in court and looks to provide materials for prosecutors to help prevent bias from affecting trial outcomes.

MEDIA COVERAGE AND EFFECTS

The courtroom is not the only venue in which bias comes into discussions of blame for a crime. A number of studies have been done that looked at media presentations of hate crimes related to sexual preferences to determine the media's causal attributions when talking about these types of crimes. For example, researchers looked at media reports after Matthew Shepard's murder to determine the focus of blame for the murder. "It was predicted that media sources from different political/ideological viewpoints would differ in their attributions regarding Matthew Shepard's murder, and these differences in attributions would be associated with overall attitudes toward homosexuality and hate crimes in general."[87] The media under scrutiny in that research study included perspectives that ranged from blaming the two perpetrators for Shepard's death to blaming the political climate created by the conservative right.

An integral factor in determining media perspective is where the cause of homosexuality itself is seen to rest. Those who see it as a choice as opposed to those who see it as innate in origin frame discussions of blame very differently: ". . . stigmas perceived as controllable were more likely to elicit anger and less likely to elicit liking or pity."[88] Even for those who believe homosexuality to be innate, there is still the implication that a stigma exists, that it would be wrong to have chosen to be homosexual if one had the choice, rather than an understanding of homosexuality as a normal development, such as being left handed, that simply manifests itself in a certain portion of the population.

Research has found that conservatives are more likely to place the blame for poverty on personal and controllable causes, while liberals are more likely to attribute it to situational influences. Research has also shown that while individuals favor situational explanations for their own negative experiences, they tend to attribute personal responsibility when negative things happen to others. "This research indicates that negative events experienced by a member of the in-group are more likely to be attributed to situational causes, and negative events happening to an out-group member are more likely to be attributed to personal causes."[89]

Following Matthew Shepard's death, researchers looked at "spontaneous" attributions and predicted that conservatives would favor personal responsibility only when this explanation supported their political viewpoints, and both liberals and conservatives would emphasize situational factors when they reinforced their existing ideological beliefs. "As predicted, articles coded as more conservative downplayed the situational causes of the crime (e.g., political climate) ... and emphasized situational causes of homosexuality (e.g., homosexuality can be healed or converted). .... Conversely, articles coded as more liberal emphasized the situational causes of the crime and downplayed the situational causes of homosexuality."[90]

Liberal articles emphasized situational attributions when blaming conservatives for their role in creating the political climate that led up to Shepard's murder but avoided situational attributions related to the possibility of the climate influencing homosexuality itself. Conservative articles emphasized situational attributions in terms of influencing or converting homosexuals but avoided them in terms of the Shepard murder. "Articles that were more likely to attribute homosexuality to controllable causes also were coded as less likely to have favorable attitudes toward homosexuals or antigay hate crime legislation."[91]

Another study looked at the nature and consequences of media coverage of hate crimes. Again, researchers looked at the frames and causal attributions offered for making sense of hate crimes. "Absent alternative sources of information, the media construct for many citizens an image of what hate crimes are, why hate crimes occur, and who the victims are."[92] How the media frame a particular issue determines to a large extent how the public thinks about the issue and about possible solutions. "Specifically, the media framing occurs in two principal ways. First, journalists provide their own news frames that make sense of political issues. ... Second, the media transmit the elite debates over how to frame issues."[93] For example, if homosexuality is seen as a normal part of American culture, stories dealing with homosexuals reflect that frame. If homosexuality is seen as a problem or a stigma, the focus of news stories then reflects that.

204 • Hate Crime in the Media

When homosexuality was linked with communism, gays were created as a national security risk. With the beginning of the AIDS epidemic, stories on homosexuals were framed in terms of blaming their lifestyle for the disease. The social problem frame has not entirely disappeared, but stories about gays who faced harassment and discrimination started to appear at the same time that the American Psychiatric Association declassified homosexuality as a mental illness. "The increasingly liberal environment did not last, however, as Anita Bryant's crusade to overturn first a Miami gay rights ordinance (which she did) and then every other one across the nation, injected conservatism back into press coverage."[94]

While the mainstream press was equating homosexuality with social problems, the gay press published arguments refuting the psychiatric claim that homosexuality was unnatural. "In gay publications, attention to gay rights emerged in the 1950s and quickly intensified."[95] The gay press in the 1960s included much coverage of activism and militancy with stories on marches, demonstrations, and lawsuits. The gay media provided political interpretations of these events and demanded rights for their constituencies. "When Anita Bryant took to the political stage, mainstream media coverage witnessed a decline in attention to gay rights. The gay media, by contrast, actively fought back, attacking Bryant, expanding their coverage of local gay rights issues and reporting on the activities of gay rights organization ignored by the mainstream media."[96]

Mainstream newspapers and gay newspapers frame discussions of hate crimes very differently. Researchers used antigay and progay rights frames to code articles from three papers: the *New York Times*, the *Washington Post*, and the *Washington Blade*, which is a gay newspaper. Antigay rights frames included ideas that hate crime legislation is redundant, hate crime is a myth, hate crime legislation creates crimes based on thoughts, and hate crime legislation creates special rights. The frames included the viewpoint of "traditional morality," that hate crimes are retribution for immoral behavior, and homosexuality is immoral. Pro–gay rights frames determined that hate crimes are a problem that must be addressed, hate crimes are fundamentally different from other crimes and therefore merit new legislation, criminal motives are legitimate factors in determining sentences, hate crime legislation promotes equal rights, and hate crimes target gays as groups rather than individuals and are therefore a threat to a community.[97]

The researchers found, not surprisingly, that the *Washington Blade* gave greater coverage to hate crimes than did the two mainstream papers. Both the *New York Times* and the *Washington Post* showed a spike in coverage of hate crimes after the Matthew Shepard murder.

The Uniform Crime Report data show a slow rise in hate crimes beginning in 1995, whereas the coverage shows a sharp leap with 1998 and 1999. One cannot attribute this increase in coverage to a sharp spike in hate crimes nationwide. It seems the mainstream press "discovered" the hate crime issue in 1998. This further reinforces the point that Shepard's murder served as a focusing event gaining the issue considerable coverage.[98]

Comparisons of the three newspapers also show that the *Washington Post* was far more likely to blame the victim for responsibility for the crime while the *Washington Blade* found such explanations implausible. "Fully one-fifth of the *Post* articles dealing with a specific hate crime raise the possibility that it was the fault of the victim."[99] While the researchers found the gay press to be more likely to use pro–gay rights frames, they found the mainstream press to provide considerable attention to arguments using both pro– and anti–gay rights frames.[100]

NEWS AND SEXUALITY

Former senator Larry Craig (R-ID) was arrested in the Minneapolis–St. Paul airport in August 2007 for purportedly making advances to an undercover policeman in a restroom. According to the arresting officer, Craig made gestures that are considered indications that he wanted to have sex. Craig had a strong voting record against gay rights, including opposition to same-sex marriage. After first pleading guilty to disorderly conduct, Craig attempted to withdraw his plea and when that failed, he filed an appeal. His guilty plea was upheld on appeal. Senator Craig completed his congressional term rather than resigning as he initially intended to do following his arrest, but he has not run for office again.

Since Craig's initial denial of any behavior that could be construed as homosexual, including his statement, "I am not gay, I never have been gay," spoken on national television on August 28, 2007, the *Idaho Statesman* printed articles identifying several men who say they had sexual encounters with Craig. In addition to his legal battle, Craig also faced an inquiry by the Senate Ethics Committee.[101]

Florida state representative Bob Allen (R–Merrit Island) was also arrested in 2007, for soliciting an undercover male police officer in a park bathroom. Allen offered the officer money to perform oral sex with him. According to reports, Allen's defense was that he felt intimidated by the officer, a Black man, and he felt he needed to go along with the officer because he was threatened. Allen resigned his political office late in 2007 after a jury found him guilty of soliciting sex from an undercover police officer.[102]

The arrests of Craig and Allen bring up a number of important issues in terms of the presentation of homosexuality in the news. Both were Republican lawmakers who had a history of voting against gay rights. Both vigorously denied first the incident and then the accompanying meaning of a same-sex encounter by stating they are not, nor ever have been, gay. The news media then found examples to show, in the case of Craig, that this was not one isolated incident. Allen preferred to blame purported intimidation by a Black man rather than admit to any "taint" of homosexuality, finding it more acceptable to be labeled racist than gay. While pointing out the hypocrisy in both men's actions is laudable for the news media, the fact that the stigma of homosexuality carries with it career-breaking consequences for these two men is of major importance. Craig could not simply state that he was wrong to solicit public sex; he felt the need to adamantly deny that he was a homosexual and to distance himself from a group that he has traditionally treated as second class. This speaks to the strength of the stigma attached to openness about homosexuality for public figures. Rather than adding detail after detail as to why Craig or Allen may or may not be homosexual, the media might question why it matters in the first place and why the stigma of homosexuality is such that politicians feel the need to deny it so strongly.

Fifteen-year-old Sakia Gunn was stabbed to death in Newark, New Jersey, on May 11, 2003. She was killed purportedly because she and her friends rebuffed a man's advances by stating that they were lesbians. Sakia's killer, Richard McCullough, was charged with bias murder, intimidation, and weapons offenses. He eventually pleaded guilty to aggravated manslaughter, aggravated assault, and bias intimidation in 2005 and received a sentence of 20 years in prison. While Gunn's murder led to a number of antiviolence vigils and rallies in Newark, and more than 2,500 people attended her funeral, the news coverage of her death was nowhere near the coverage after Matthew Shepard's murder. Although newspapers tell us that coverage of a particular incident is based on reader interest, studies show that coverage is often determined by the race, class, gender, and age of those involved. Shepard was a White, middle-class young man as opposed to Gunn, who was a cross-dressing poor Black young woman. In the month each murder occurred, there were 448 stories on Shepard and eight on Gunn. The highest number of stories in a month for Gunn was 28; for Shepard, it was 735. Over a period of one year, the number of stories on Shepard increased each month.[103]

The LGBT population is still created as Other in America and in the media, even as improvements in representation and policy are occurring in areas such as same-sex marriage and open participation in the military. This creation has led to some of the most violent and vicious hate crimes in the past decades as large numbers Americans have resisted fights to normalize this community. Many see the contestation over the spaces allowed sexual identification and gender identification to be particularly personal and problematic, and groups from all political ideologies have resisted giving ground even while others in the same groups have been supportive. Media discourse has continually framed this population as problematic, from categorizing homosexuality as a disease itself to the original framing of the AIDS epidemic as a homosexual problem. Each fight in the public discourse for space for the LGBT population has brought accompanying negative images and derogatory discourse. Even the discourse supportive of the LGBT population is forced to argue within the frame of "problem," thus reinforcing the Otherness of this population.

NOTES

1. Dave Webunder and Sarah Woodard, "Homosexuality in young adult fiction and non-fiction: An annotated bibliography," *Alan Review* 23, no. 2 (Winter 1996), http://scholar.lib.vt.edu/ejournals/ALAN/winter96/webunder.html (accessed November 28, 2007).

2. Josh Getlin, "Gay references touchy in children's literature," *Seattle Times*, January 5, 2004, A9.

3. Debra Lau Whelan, "Gay titles missing in most AR libraries," *School Library Journal*, January 1, 2007. http://www.schoollibraryjournal.com/index (accessed 11/28/2007.

4. Linda Harvey, "Christian parents: Stop trusting Harry Potter," *WorldNetDaily*, February 21, 2008, http://worldnetdaily.com/news/article (accessed February 21, 2008).

5. "Oklahoma bill would restrict gay books," *Library Journal*, March 13, 2006, http://www.libraryjournal.com/index (accessed February 21, 2008).

6. "Lawmakers vote to restrict access to homosexual-themed children's books," May 9, 2005, http://www.lsb.state.ok.us/house/news7551.html (accessed February 21, 2008).

7. Frances Ann Day, *Lesbian and Gay Voices: An Annotated Bibliography and Guide to Literature for Children and Young Adults* (Westport, CT: Greenwood, 2000), xi.

8. Ibid., ix.

9. Ibid., xii.

10. Michael Thomas Ford, "Gay books for young readers: When caution calls the shots," *Publishers Weekly* 241, no 8 (February 21, 1994), 24.

11. Ibid.

12. Vito Russo, *The Celluloid Closet: Homosexuality in the Movies* (New York: Harper & Row, 1987), 325.

13. Ibid., 4–5.

14. Ibid., 70.

15. Ibid., 154.

16. Ibid., 122.

17. Harry M. Benshoff, *Monsters in the Closet: Homosexuality and the Horror Film* (Manchester: Manchester University Press, 1997), 3.

18. Russo, *Celluloid Closet*, 98.

19. Ibid., 86.

20. Ibid., 238.

21. Brian Stelter, "Gay on TV: It's all in the family," *New York Times*, May 8, 2012.

22. Edward Schiappa, Peter B. Gregg, and Dean E. Hewes, "Can one TV show make a difference? *Will & Grace* and the parasocial contact hypothesis," *Journal of Homosexuality* 51, no. 4 (2006): 15–37.

23. "'Glee,' 'Modern Family' and other LGBT-themed TV shows drive gay marriage support: Poll," *Huffington Post*, November 5, 12.

24. Gregory Fouts and Rebecca Inch, "Homosexuality in TV situation comedies: Characters and verbal comments," *Journal of Homosexuality* 49, no. 1 (2005): 34–35.

25. Ibid., 36.

26. Ibid., 35.

Hate Crime in the Media

27. R. Jeffrey Ringer (ed.), *Queer Words, Queer Images: Communication and the Construction of Homosexuality* (New York: New York University Press, 1994), 92.

28. Liz Highleyman, "Milestones for queers on television," *Lesbian News* 33, no. 1 (August 2007): 20–24.

29. Bonnie Dow, "Ellen, television, and the politics of gay and lesbian visibility," *Critical Studies in Media Communication* 18, no. 2 (2001): 124.

30. Boy Scouts of America, "Membership Standards Resolution," www.scouting.org/sitecore/content/membershipstandards/resolution

31. Annie Z. Yu, "Boy Scouts' decision on gays tests loyalty of members," *Washington Times*, June 9, 2013.

32. "Woman sues restaurant for Pride-Day ejection," *Gender Public Advocacy Coalition*, December 17, 2007, http://www.gpac.org (accessed January 2, 2008).

33. Patricia Leigh Brown, "A quest for a restroom that's neither men's room nor women's room," *New York Times*, March 4, 2005.

34. Ibid.

35. Robin Toner, "For 'don't ask, don't tell,' split on party lines," *New York Times*, June 8, 2007, http://www.nytimes.com/2007/06/08/us/politics/08gays.html?_r=0 (accessed November 11, 2013).

36. Ibid.

37. Adam Liptak, "Federal court reinstates suit on gays in military," *New York Times*, May 22, 2008, http://www.nytimes.com/2008/05/22/us/22gay.html (accessed November 11, 2013).

38. U.S. General Accounting Office, "Homosexuals in the armed forces: United States GAO report," June 12, 1992, http://www.fordham.edu/halsall/pwh/gao_report.asp (accessed November 11, 2013).

39. Ibid.

40. Ibid.

41. Chad Carter and Antony Barone Kolenc, " 'Don't ask, don't tell': Has the policy met its goals?" *University of Dayton Law Review* 31, no. 1 (2005): 19.

42. Ibid., 24.

43. James Sterngold, "Navy plans murder charge in death of gay sailor," *New York Times*, February 4, 1993, http://www.nytimes.com/1993/02/04/us/navy-plans-murder-charge-in-death-of-gay-sailor.html (accessed November 11, 2013).

44. Ibid.

45. "Gay Sailor Tells of a 'Living Hell,' " *New York Times*, March 8, 1993, http://www.nytimes.com/1993/03/08/us/gay-sailor-tells-of-a-living-hell.html (accessed November 11, 2013).

46. Ibid.

47. James Sterngold, "Gay sailor's killer allowed lesser plea, limiting trial," *New York Times*, May 24, 1993, http://www.nytimes.com/1993/05/24/us/gay-sailor-s-killer-allowed-lesser-plea-limiting-trial.html (accessed November 11, 2013).

48. James Sterngold, "Slaying of gay sailor is admitted; Shipmate says it was unplanned," *New York Times*, May 5, 1993. http://www.nytimes.com/1993/05/04/us/slaying-of-gay-sailor-is-admitted-shipmate-says-it-was-unplanned.html (accessed November 11, 2013).

49. Sterngold, "Gay sailor's killer allowed lesser plea."

50. James Sterngold, "Killer gets life as navy says he hunted down gay sailor," *New York Times*, May 28, 1993, http://www.nytimes.com/1993/05/28/world/killer-gets-life-as-navy-says-he-hunted-down-gay-sailor.html?pagewanted=all&src=pm (accessed November 11, 2013).

51. Ibid.

52. Kerry Rutz, "Allen R. Schindler," *Kerry Rutz Murder Series*, Kerryrutz.com, http://kerryrutz.com/m1.html (accessed November 11, 2013).

53. GAO-04-353R Defense of Marriage Act, http://www.gao.gov/assets/100/92442.html (accessed November 11, 2013).

54. Sharon Scales Rostosky, Ellen D. B. Riggle, Sharon G. Horne, and Angela D. Miller, "Marriage amendments and psychological distress in lesbian, gay, and bisexual (LGB) adults," *Journal of Counseling Psychology* 56, no. 1 (January 2009): 56–66.

55. James Dobson, *Marriage under Fire: Why We Must Win This Battle* (Peabody, MA: Multnomah, 2004).

56. Sara Gates, "Roman Catholic Church leadership poured $2 million into fight against marriage equality: Report," *Huffington Post*, November 15, 2012.

57. Steve Peoples, "Catholic influence wanes amid same-sex marriage fight," *MPRNews*, http://minnesota.pulbicradio.org.

58. *Anderson et al. vs. King County*, www.courts.wa.cov/newsinfo/content/pdf/759341opn.pdf (accessed August 21, 13).

59. *Perry vs. Schwarzenegger*, http://documents.nytimes.com/us-district-court-decision-perry-v-schwarzenegger (accessed November 10, 2013).

60. "Survey: Majority of Americans say they support same-sex marriage, adoption by gay and lesbian couples," *Public Religion Research Institute*, May 19, 2011, http://publicreligion.org/research/2011 (accessed August 22, 2013).

61. Ibid.

62. "Mike Huckabee defends advocating isolation of AIDS patients in 1992 Senate race," FoxNews.com, December 9, 2007, http://www.foxnews.com/story/2007/12/09/mike-huckabee-defends-advocating-isolation-aids-patients-in-12-senate-race/ (accessed November 10, 2013).

63. Karen Franklin, "Antigay behaviors among young adults: Prevalence, patterns, and motivators in a noncriminal population," *Journal of Interpersonal Violence* 15, no. 4 (April 2000): 339.

64. Ibid., 347.

65. Ibid., 354.

66. Ibid., 354.

67. James Nichols, "American Bar Association votes to curtail use of 'gay panic,' 'trans panic' defense," *Huffington Post*, www.huffingtonpost.com/ (accessed August 22, 2013).

68. Christina Pei-Lin Chen, "Provocation's privileged desire: The provocatin doctrine, 'homosexual panic,' and the non-violent unwanted sexual advance defense," *Cornell Journal of Law and Public Policy* 10, no. 1 (Fall 2000): 199.

69. Ibid., 201.

70. Ibid., 205.

71. Ibid., 208.

72. Dan Waterhouse, " 'Panic defense' ban bill gutted," *Queer Eye* in *Community Alliance*, September 2006. http://www.fresnoalliance.com/home/magazine/2006/Sept%2006%20pg%208-14.pdf

73. Christina Pei-Lin Chen, "Provocation's privileged desire," 216.

74. Ibid., 228.

75. Ibid., 235.

76. Robert B. Mison, "Homophobia in manslaughter: The homosexual advance as insufficient provocation," *California Law Review* 80, no. 1 (January 1992): 133–178.

77. Casey Charles, "Panic in *The Project*," *Law and Literature* 18, no. 2 (2006): 226.

78. Ibid.

79. Ibid., 229.

80. "Talk show murder trial begins," CNN.com, October 7, 1996, http://edition.cnn .com/US/9610/07/jones.trial (accessed January 27, 2008).

81. "Gay man murdered in Cobb, killer walks," March 14, 2003, www.cobbcandlelightvigil .com.

82. Ibid.

83. Michelle Locke, "Advocates: Murder verdicts a blow to 'gay panic' defense," Associated Press, September 16, 2005.

84. Jeff Dore, "Mixed verdict for ex-Morehouse student," *WSBTV Atlanta*, June 11, 2003, http://wsbtv.com/news (accessed January 9, 2008).

85. Chanel Lee, "Homos 101: Premier Black college is a study in anti-gay discrimination," *New York Village Voice*, August 12, 2003. http://www.villagevoice.com/2003-08-12/news/ homos-101/ (accessed February 7, 2014).

86. "Man gets four years in prison for transgender slaying," FoxNews.com, October 1, 2005, http://www.foxnews.com (accessed January 9, 2008).

87. Ryan M. Quist, "Attributions of hate: The media's causal attributions of a homophobic murder," *American Behavioral Scientist* 46, no. 1 (September 2002): 93.

88. Ibid. 94.

89. Ibid., 96.

90. Ibid., 101.

91. Ibid., 104.

92. Kimberly Gross and Seth Goldman, "Framing hate: A comparison of media coverage of anti-gay hate crimes in *Washington Post, New York Times* and *Washington Blade*," Presented at the Annual Meeting of the American Political Science Association, August 28–31, 2003, 1. http://citation.allacademic.com/meta/p_mla_apa_research_citation/0/6/2/5/1/pages62510/ p62510-1.php (accessed November 10, 2013).

93. Ibid., 5.

94. Ibid., 8.

95. Ibid., 10.

96. Ibid., 11.

97. Ibid., 16–17.

98. Ibid., 19.

99. Ibid., 22.

100. Ibid., 25-27.

101. See, for example, "Craig insists 'I am not gay,' police say he sought information for lawyer," *Idaho Statesman*, August 28, 2007; Dave Karsnia, "Lewd conduct report," Minneapolis-St. Paul International Airport Police Department, June 12, 2007, http://media .washingtonpost.com/wp-srv/politics/ssi/craig_police_report_082807.pdf

102. See, for example, "Republican Bob Allen arrested in male sex scandal," *AlaskaReport*, August 4, 2007, http://www.alaskareport.com/news/z46491_bob_allen.htm; Laurin Sellers, "Florida state rep. Bob Allen guilty in bathroom-sex case," *Orlando Sentinel*, November 10, 2007, http://articles.orlandosentinel.com/2007-11-10/news/boballen10_1_allen-florida -house-viera

103. Laura Castaneda and Shannon B. Campbell (eds.), *News and Sexuality: Media Portraits of Diversity*, (Thousand Oaks, CA: Sage, 2006), 168–169.

7

The Language of Hate: Hate Speech, Hate Talk, and the First Amendment

"Language is, and always has been, the means by which we construct and analyze what we call 'reality,' "[1] and far from being "just words," language provides us the ability to define ourselves "as individuals and as members of groups; it tells us how we are connected to one another, who has power and who doesn't."[2] A wide range of discourse related to disparagement and hate in our culture includes disparagement humor, slurs, naming, the (mis)appropriation of cultural elements from nonmainstream cultures, and the derogatory comments of public figures. This discourse is visibly disparaging in terms of race, sex, gender, sexual identity, or ethnicity. "But other kinds of talk and text that are not visible, so called covert racist discourse, may be just as important in reproducing the culturally shared ideas that underpin racism. Indeed, they may be even more important, because they do their work while passing unnoticed."[3]

Imbedded in this discourse are questions of power, hegemony, and voice. There are legal ramifications as well, as we continue to consider elements of hate crimes and the role of hate speech in our legal system. Conflicting amendment rights have come into play at the crossroads between freedom of speech and equal protection, yet little is heard about the responsibilities that come with those rights.

In determining if an incident is a hate crime, one factor has been the use of derogatory, group-specific hate language (such as calling someone a racial slur before shooting them). Symbolic language, burning a cross on someone's front lawn, or hanging a noose on a tree is a part of the discourse about hate speech.

Does the source matter—whether the language is official words from a societal institution, from a radio host, from a politician elected to represent his or her constituency, or from an individual representing only his or her own opinion? What role does humor play in our culture? Who gets to decide if it is "just a joke" or something more serious? Which carries more weight, the intent of the teller or the impact on the recipient? All these questions have to do with power and who gets to determine what the "commonsense" version of reality is in public discourse. Ultimately, the default of the discourse is to maintain the status quo in terms of power hierarchies in our culture and society.

DISPARAGEMENT HUMOR

Mark Ferguson and Thomas Ford reviewed research on the purpose(s) of disparagement humor and why it is considered funny. "Disparagement humor refers to remarks that (are intended to) elicit amusement through the denigration, derogation, or belittlement of a given target (e.g., individuals, social groups, political ideologies, material possessions)."[4] It can be difficult to challenge this type of humor since the joke teller has only to say, "It's just a joke," thereby challenging the recipient not to take it as serious communication. Ferguson and Ford reviewed a variety of theories to determine what might be gained by a teller of disparaging jokes and how these jokes function in society.

Psychoanalytic theory proposes that the purpose of hostile humor is to attack an adversary by making him or her inferior or comic, resulting in a feeling of superiority for the teller. Research based on this theory has provided both support for (exposure to hostile humor decreases aggressive responses) and challenge to (exposure actually increases expressions of aggression) this as a cathartic experience.[5] Studies reviewed by Ferguson and Ford suggest that feelings of hostility toward a particular group correlate with higher levels of enjoyment when that group is the butt of disparaging humor. With sexist humor, for example, evidence suggests that, regardless of gender, people who enjoy sexist humor typically have negative (sexist) attitudes toward women.[6]

According to social identity theory, social groups compete for positive distinctiveness. Social and personal identities are separate components of the "self." Social identity refers to the portion of self-concept that comes from membership or perceived membership in a social group; personal identity is built on perceptions of an individual's unique attributes as compared to the other members of these social groups. The use of disparagement humor can solidify a social group while helping the group achieve a positive distinctiveness at the expense of another group. "For instance, if majority groups feel threatened by the social advances of racial minorities, they might communicate ethnic jokes that portray the minorities as incompetent."[7] There is a negative social consequence to exposure to disparagement humor. "It increases tolerance of discriminatory events for people high in prejudice toward the disparaged group."[8] Thus, for those already high in prejudice, disparagement humor helps create a norm of tolerance of discrimination.

Ford conducted three experiments looking at whether exposure to sexist humor increased a tolerance of sex discrimination for those high in hostile sexism (antagonism and feelings of indignation toward women). The results demonstrated that exposure to sexist humor created greater tolerance of sex discrimination among people high in hostile sexism.[9] In conclusion, Ford found, "Disparagement of social groups through humor, then, is more than a benign expression of prejudice; it expands the bounds of socially appropriate behavior, thus creating social conditions in which discrimination can be more easily rationalized as not inappropriate."[10]

ETHNIC JOKES

Ethnic jokes are a form of disparagement that "... delineate the social, geographical and moral boundaries of a nation or ethnic group. By making fun of peripheral and ambiguous groups they reduce ambiguity and clarify boundaries or at least make ambiguity appear less threatening."[11] Ethnic jokes follow some standard patterns. Jokes told in Britain about supposed Irish stupidity are very similar to those told in America about Poles, in New Zealand about the Maori, and in Finland about the gypsies.[12] There has been a long line of ethnic outsiders who have, over the years, been the butt of jokes in the United States as different waves of immigrants arrived here: the Irish, Italians, Swedes, and Poles, for example. One hypothesis is that with the rise of industrial societies and the growing complexities of life and work, people became anxious about their abilities to fit into society. By denigrating others and confining them to the "stupid" group, your own group's place in society becomes, by contrast, stronger.

According to Davies, jokes reflect a societal mood on a particular topic, and "[t]o become angry about jokes and seek to censor them because they impinge on sensitive issues is about as sensible as smashing a thermometer because it reveals how hot it is."[13] But this reasoning is invalid, as a thermometer cannot affect the temperature, while jokes and hate speech can and do affect a climate that allows this type of behavior to occur or even flourish. At some point, we cannot just say, "It's only a joke." The research by Ford and Ferguson points to some measure of actual effect on people, and research on the effects of hate speech add to their findings.

Ethnic jokes told about your own group may help negotiate the lines between assimilation into the dominant culture and retention of your own cultural traits. "In an open society the jokes indicate the existence of a known and established cultural and economic pecking order of ethnic groups regardless of official rhetoric about equality or pluralism. The butts of the jokes may be liked or disliked, but they are not esteemed."[14]

Ethnic jokes or slurs aimed at a particular group represent dominant stereotypes, beliefs about national character, ethnocentrism, and prejudice contained in imagery and humor. Unlike Davies, folklorist Alan Dundes sees ethnic jokes as more than just a thermometer of attitude. "A proverb or a joke told by members of one national group about another may be more responsible for the first group's attitudes about the second than any other single factor."[15] Dundes believes jokes not only reflect, but also form, attitudes.

In the United States, as elsewhere, individuals acquire stereotypes from folklore. Most of our conceptions of the French or of the Jew come not from extended personal acquaintances or contact with representatives of these groups but rather from the proverbs, songs, jokes, and other forms of folklore we have heard all our lives. The stereotypes may or may not be accurate character analyses—they may or may not be in accord with actual, empirically verifiable personality traits. The point is that folk stereotypes exist, and that countless people make judgments on the basis of them. There is probably no other area of folklore where the element of belief is more critical and potentially more dangerous, not only to self but to others.[16]

When humor is taken seriously by recipients, it can have serious ramifications. A series of 12 editorial cartoons depicting the prophet Muhammad were published in a Danish newspaper in 2005. Muslims around the world complained, and protests included violent riots in some countries. Humor researchers gave their perspectives on the incident and what this type of political cartoon might (or might not) mean. Christie Davies points out that insulting sacred texts and images of all religions through humor and humorous cartoons has been commonplace in Britain and other Western societies. He concludes, "The moral of the story is not so much that humor can be conflictful and can offend but rather that a sense of offense at a humorous item can be amplified and used as a political asset and weapon."[17] It is not humor per se but the reaction to it that has power. Giselinde Kuipers looks at the dissemination of humor and the potential for spreading something like the Muhammad cartoons worldwide so quickly and easily. She discusses a normative community of humor and the rules that each group or society has in place (usually implicitly) about what can and cannot be joked about, and she wonders why there was such an outcry (and violence) in response to the cartoons when economic sanctions and war do not bring the same reaction. She describes the cartoons as motivated by a desire to ridicule rather than amuse, and ". . . ridicule is often felt to be more humiliating than other forms of interaction, including physical or verbal violence."[18]

Powell argues that humor is related to social values and "normal views" of reality, and sees humor as more than a bellwether of societal views, as humor can be used as a means of control to invalidate the demands of particular groups (gays and feminists, for example). "Formalised humour will generally fulfill an ideological function in supporting and maintaining existing social relations and dominant ways of perceiving social reality. Its great danger lies in its everyday, neutral 'non-serious' apparent character."[19] Jokes can operate to control ideas, incipient ideas, and actions. "In simple terms, humour operates to set apart and invalidate the behaviour and ideas of those 'not like us' by creating and sustaining stereotypes and often projecting the practices of others to a presumed 'logical' but of course 'absurd' conclusion."[20] If the recipients do not find a joke funny, the teller's response is often "It's only a joke," implying that the audience lacks a sense of humor and is overly sensitive. Thus, the joke teller has the opportunity to denigrate twice, once with the joke and then with the following implication that the fault of reception lies with the audience rather than the teller.

In a study of racist humor on British television, Powell focused on the program *Till Death Us Do Part*, similar to America's *All in the Family*. "In this series, Alf Garnett was intended to display the narrowness, stupidity and ignorance of the bigot and thereby serve as an attack on bigotry. However, the context in which his bigotry was displayed did nothing to reinforce the intended message."[21] Powell found that what viewers got out of programs like *Till Death Us Do Part* was usually a function of the attitudes and values they brought to the program, and the racism in the show reinforced stereotypes for those who already held them rather than challenging those beliefs.

JOKE CYCLES

Researchers of jokes and joke cycles (a series of jokes based on a particular premise that appear and then disappear at various times in a culture; for example, dead baby jokes, no arms and no legs jokes, and elephant jokes) look at the circumstances surrounding jokes' occurrence, flourishing, and transmission to ask if what is reflected in the jokes at a particular moment is an accurate reflection of people's fears and concerns.

Alan Dundes studied joke cycles to find their underlying meaning and how they function as a forum for topics that often cannot be openly discussed in public. "The higher the incidence of euphemisms that scrupulously avoid direct mention of a subject, the greater the anxiety about that subject."[22] One example is physical disability. "[The] taboo against speaking frankly about physical handicaps is probably one reason why there are jokes about the handicapped. The joke typically provides a socially sanctioned outlet for talking about what normally cannot be discussed openly."[23] The series of jokes about those with no arms and no legs (popular in the 1980s) may reflect the guilt, embarrassment, pity, or revulsion some people feel when faced with a quadriplegic.

The elephant jokes of the 1960s illustrate the cathartic potential of jokes. The highly sexual content of many of the jokes, the fact that elephants come from Africa, and the number of jokes that dealt with the color of the elephant are important features in understanding this particular cycle. "The rise of the elephant joke occurred at the same time as the rise of the Blacks in the Civil Rights movement."[24] The elephant represented the White stereotype of the Black (male) with large genitals and a heightened sexual ability reflected in larger than life size, strength, and endurance. The joke cycle served to (potentially) reduce fears by joking about the object of fear or concern. With joke cycles, as Dundes points out, it is imperative that we consider the social-historical context of the particular cycles. "These jokes, like all expressions of wit, are serious business."[25] American jokes about Blacks have depicted them as an underclass; outside of society; and characterized by crime, violence, illegitimacy, promiscuity, and an aversion to the demands of work, family, and legality.[26] When these jokes are exported to other countries, however, they remain about Blacks rather than being transposed (as many ethnic jokes are) to fit the local minority or ethnic group.[27]

"Telling and enjoying sexist and racist jokes . . . is based on having certain emotional attitudes. And when the attitude presupposed by a joke is morally objectionable, then telling the joke or laughing at it is also morally objectionable."[28] De Sousa discusses the ethics of laughter in terms of the giver and recipient of humor. He differentiates between a matter of ethics and that of etiquette (the appropriate place to tell certain types of jokes versus jokes that are inappropriate no matter what the company).[29] The aim of jokes that put down or ridicule is to alienate while bringing like-minded people more into a community with each other. Some stereotypes, like the Sambo stereotype, exist to preserve a feeling of superiority by Whites over Blacks.[30] Repetition of such symbols in American culture normalizes them and turns them into accepted aspects of our worldview.

Once implanted in popular lore, an image attached to a group, an issue, or an event pervades the deepest senses and profoundly affects behavioral actions. A standardized mental picture representing an oversimplified opinion or an uncritical judgment, a stereotype is tenacious in its hold over rational thinking. It gains its power by repetitive play, presented in different guises, so that the image it projects becomes firmly imbedded in reactive levels of thought and action.[31]

The Sambo image has connotations of subordination, childishness, comedy, and humbleness. "By emphasizing Sambo, White America hoped to relate to a figure amenable to subordination whose reaction would be one of shared laughter. The result, however, was one of shared social distance."[32] Whites used stereotypes like Sambo to maintain a sense of racial superiority through hostile humor and denigration. Laughter can create a bond within a group, but it also can create lines that distance groups from one another, and these two functions work together. "Experimental studies have consistently shown that hostile humor reflects the psychological underpinnings of the verbalizer. Hostile persons prefer caustic forms of humor."[33]

SPORTS, RACISM, AND SLURS

More visibly racist than jokes and derogatory humor, slurs, epithets, and other examples of name-calling are all too prevalent in public arenas and can stand on their own or be tied to examples of extreme violence. "They appear in assault, in moments of interpersonal anger and violence, or in gratuitous verbal muggings of people of color."[34] Hate crimes often begin with slurs and epithets, painted on public and private buildings or yelled before or during an assault or murder. The victim has no way of knowing what will end with remarks and what will escalate to something much more serious. Jordan Gruver was beaten and kicked while two men called him "spic." Luyen Phan Nguyen died as men screamed "chink," "gook," and "Viet Cong" at him. Words can have greater power when uttered by well-known figures and publicized through the media. Celebrities such as actors, well-known athletes and sports announcers, politicians, and journalists all command a certain degree of power behind the words they speak in public places, and their words reach a wide audience.

Several known sports figures and commentators have, in recent years, made remarks about athletes that have caused controversy and concern. Former Ladies Professional Golf Association (LPGA) golfer Jan Stephenson made a comment in *Golf* magazine that Asians were killing women's golf and called for quotas limiting the percentage of Asians on the LPGA Tour. Stephenson stated, "Their lack of emotion, their refusal to speak English when they can speak English. They rarely speak."[35] MSNBC.com asked in a poll if Stephenson was right in her assessment that Asian players were hurting the Tour, and of the 8,439 responses, 50 percent agreed with her. Stephenson's comments, while widely communicated, were not widely challenged.[36]

In contrast, when Fuzzy Zoeller made arguably racist remarks about Tiger Woods, it became a major news story and resulted in public condemnation. In 1997 at the Masters golf tournament, Zoeller said, "That little boy is driving well and he's putting well. He's doing everything it takes to win. So, you know what you guys do when he gets in here? You pat him on the back and say congratulations and enjoy it and tell him not to serve fried chicken next year. Got it? . . . or collard greens or whatever the hell they serve."[37] Zoeller apologized publicly and to Woods privately. Woods accepted the apology, though he was "stunned and disappointed by the racially insensitive comments."[38] As a result of his comments, Zoeller was fired by his sponsor, Kmart. Zoeller's comments included the old insult of "boy" for someone who is clearly a man and the stereotype of food associated with Black culture, clearly creating an "us" versus "them" polarization, with Tiger Woods representing "them."

Shaquille O'Neal of the Los Angeles Lakers got himself into trouble with racially insensitive remarks about Yao Ming, a professional basketball player born in China. O'Neal put it down (as did Zoeller) to a misunderstood sense of humor. "I said it jokingly, so this guy [a journalist who called him on his comments] was just trying to stir something up that's not there. He's just somebody who doesn't have a sense of humor, like I do."[39] O'Neal's comment was, "Tell Yao Ming, 'ching-cong-yang-wah-ah-soh.' " Yao Ming responded graciously, stating he believed O'Neal was joking, but he added that many Asian people would not understand that type of joke. However, this was not a one-time incident with O'Neal, as he had taunted Yao Ming on several occasions in the media.[40] Tony Bruno of Fox Sports Radio defended O'Neal and then invited listeners to further insult Asian Americans with thinly veiled comments of their own.[41] These included jokes about dry cleaning services (with Bruno commenting, "No tickee, no washee").[42] Other responses to Yao Ming have included Brent Musburger's concerns that "the hordes of China" would vote Yao as the West's All-Star starter; the Miami Heat who, for Yao's first game, passed out 8,000 fortune cookies to spectators; and ESPN's referral to a "Ming Dynasty" and the "emperor" versus the kings.[43]

The controversy that occurred when radio personality Don Imus referred to the Scarlett Knights (Rutgers) college basketball team as "nappy-headed hos" was well publicized. Imus is known for his insults, which is part of his draw for many. He is one of a group of radio hosts who uses material (jokes, opinions, stories, insults) that many find offensive as part of the "shock radio" culture.

Imus, like O'Neal, said that people needed to relax about what he said because it was only meant to be amusing. Imus has repeatedly insulted different groups on the air, calling Arabs "towelheads" and referring to a *Washington Post* writer as a "boner-nosed, beanie-wearing Jewboy."[44] He was suspended for two weeks following his remarks about the Rutgers team. Several days later, CBS fired him from the show that he had hosted for almost 30 years. "He has flourished in a culture that permits a certain level of objectionable expression that hurts and demeans a wide range of people," CBS chief executive Leslie Moonves wrote in a memo to his staff. By taking Imus off the air, CBS hoped to help change that culture. Imus apologized repeatedly (while still defending himself as using misunderstood humor), but the controversy became national with criticism from the likes of Oprah Winfrey, Hillary Clinton, and Barack Obama.[45]

Public figures like Imus, O'Neal, Zoeller, and Stephenson could criticize athletes for their lack of skills in particular sports but chose instead to turn their critical comments to derogatory remarks based on race. The fight on the field or on the court to become a winning team is also a fight in public space for the next cultural hero. There are those who feel threatened by the changing face of sports and who subsequently lash out by setting up an "us" versus "them" polarization, fighting to maintain the traditional hegemonic public "face" of a particular sport. Boundaries around ethnicity and race are fought in the media all the time, and in the world of sports where teams and players are already in contention with each other, the fight can be particularly potent.

CO-OPTATION OF TRIBAL NAMES AND MASCOTS

Although not for the first time, in the fall of 1991 (World Series) into the winter of 1992 (Super Bowl), the use of Native American names and mascots for sports teams became a national issue. Controversy has surrounded team names such as the Cleveland Indians, the Washington Redskins, and the Atlanta Braves for decades, but these nationally known teams are merely the tip of the iceberg when it comes to the use of often derogatory or stereotypical Native American names and associated words for sports teams at all levels of play.

On a national level, "[t]he National Coalition on Racism in Sports and Media exists to fight the powerful influence of major media who choose to promulgate messages of oppression. The impetus which formed NCRSM was the clear case of media coupling imagery with widely held misconceptions of American Indians in the form of sports team identities resulting in racial, cultural, and spiritual stereotyping." NCRSM was formed in October 1991 and combines demonstrations outside of sports stadiums with educational efforts aimed at making the issue of racial stereotyping part of the national dialogue.[46]

Arguments against the (mis)use of Native American mascots center on names, logos, and team paraphernalia that represent racist stereotypes of Native Americans and Native American culture, most commonly the continuing stereotype of the bloodthirsty savage. Symbols and practices that have religious significance to Native Americans are misused and degraded by sports teams. Activists point out that other ethnic and racial groups are not subjected to the same appropriation of their culture and cultural images, nor would any countenance the use of derogatory names that Native Americans have been forced to put up with such as Redskins and Braves. Behind the controversy is, of course, the question of power and who has the right to determine how a culture is represented. "Many feel that Native Americans have had little control over societal definitions of who they are, and feel that the voices of Native Americans are rarely heard."[47] The use of demeaning mascots can negatively influence the self-image and self-esteem of Native Americans, particularly children.[48]

Those who would keep the team names and mascots argue that the association of Native Americans with bravery and strength provides an appropriate use of these mascots for sports teams. Many argue that the intent is to honor Native

Americans, not to offend or disrespect them. They are "simply having fun, supporting the team, and affirming a sporting tradition."[49]

Others are clearer about their bigotry and lack of concern for Native American viewpoints. Andy Rooney told a reporter at the Super Bowl in 1992 that the whole controversy over names of mascots was "silly" and that Native Americans have more important things to worry about. His sweeping statements included "American Indians were never subjected to the same kind of racial bias that Blacks were" and that Indians do not want any part of assimilating into larger American society. He categorized the impact of native culture as slight and totally lacking in art, while native religion was out of date and full of superstitions ". . . that may have been useful to savages 500 years ago but which are meaningless in 1992."[50] Rather than worrying about names and mascots, Rooney believed Native Americans need to concentrate on solutions to unemployment and alcoholism. While there may be other serious problems facing Native Americans today, it is wrong to ignore the power of naming and the question of hegemony in terms of who has the power to categorize, name, and limit the face of a particular group in American culture. The names are visible signs pointing to the more insidious patterns of control over those deemed Other and should be given serious consideration rather than dismissed. Above all, it is the tribes who should determine the appropriate use of their symbols, not those who co-opt them to make money.

The timing of the protests against Native American mascots coincided with widespread concerns about multiculturalism. Journalists treated the issue with sarcasm, trying to make the point that if one were to be offended by the use of the names Redskins and Braves, there would be no end to the protests by those offended over something. Like the "It's just a joke" response, the use of exaggeration and sarcasm works to negate the legitimacy of the protests. "A common strategy employed by those who engage in the backlash against multiculturalism is to trivialize the concerns of the various segments of the multicultural movement."[51]

King and others try to understand why the use of Native American symbols and derogatory names for Native Americans have come to be normalized and accepted by the majority of Americans when, by comparison, the public would not allow derogatory terms for other groups to be used in such a way. We have normalized these terms for Native Americans to the point that they no longer seem offensive to the mainstream culture or are even recognizable as derogatory. Because these names and symbols have become such a part of the American cultural fabric, when their use is challenged, the challenge is often dismissed as absurd since this is the way things "are." This dismissal provides a second occasion for disrespect, compounding the original use of derogatory names and images.

Those in favor of keeping the mascots use many arguments (e.g., balancing racist use of stereotypes with the creation of scholarships for Native American students) to justify and retain "their" mascots. "What is noteworthy here is not only that compromise is defined in White terms, but also that these proposals would be unimaginable for other ethnic groups in the United States. Can one seriously imagine a proposal that simultaneously encouraged an African-American Studies program, but leaves unchanged racist practices toward Blacks?"[52] King points to the University of North Dakota, where wealthy donor Roy Englestad threatened to revoke a $100 million gift to the university if the Fighting Sioux team name and logo were discontinued. The mascot was retained.[53] Thus, regardless of their negative impact, one can buy the use of derogatory stereotypes and thereby continue their use, demonstrating once again to Native Americans that they are inferior and a commodity as well.

Jane H. Hill's book *The Everyday Language of White Racism* looks at how the use of language in White America constantly reproduces the culture of White racism. She examines in detail the controversy over renaming Squaw Peak in Arizona, a discussion that contained many of the same arguments raised when the names of sports teams and their mascots have been either criticized or defended. The word "squaw" originated in the Algonquian tribal languages and means "woman." However, it became a pejorative word used to demean Native American women in general and is considered by most to be offensive today. Arguments for retaining the name Squaw Peak included "It doesn't bother me, so it should be ok for everyone," "The one Native American I asked said it didn't bother him," "It's the historical name and shouldn't be changed," and "It's meant to be a compliment and not an insult." The debate centers around the intent of the namer as opposed to the perception(s) of the listener. Hill argues that what often appears as common sense is really ideologically based. "... [A]s we explore the possibility of political and economic ideology, we find that 'common sense' has that status because it defines a group of people whose interests are advanced by believing it, and not because it is necessarily true or even likely."[54] Common sense, or the normal, is not free of hegemony, privilege, and consequence because so much of what is "common sense" protects the status quo in American power relationships. Mainstream America accepts as "common sense" what is in its interest to retain and often lacks the ability to recognize the created nature of this perspective or any alternative perspectives.

POLITICAL CORRECTNESS

"The myth of political correctness is a powerful conspiracy theory created by conservatives and the media who have manipulated resentment against leftist radicals into a backlash against the fictional monster of political correctness."[55]

This myth is, in large part, a reaction against multiculturalism, affirmative action, and the ongoing attempt to illuminate power relationships between those with hegemonic control over societal structures and definitions and those who are attempting to show this structure as artificial rather than natural.

Political correctness, originally used as a sarcastic reference to complete adherence to the party line by American communists in the 1930s, became widely known in the early 1990s as a conservative attack on liberal support for multiculturalism. The label is used now in much the same way the first President Bush used the term "liberal" as a pejorative in the 1988 election, dismissing large potential constituencies for their cultural activism and narrowing the boundaries of permissible political debate.[56] The 1980s saw criticisms of jokes and joke cycles deemed insensitive and harmful in their treatment of racial-, ethnic-, and gender-based groups, but these criticisms brought the political correctness backlash of the 1990s as conservatives and the media referred to the "thought police" and a supposed attempt by liberals to control speech.[57] Many on the right argued that it should remain individual choice as to language used, jokes told, and labels applied, but as some language is increasingly recognized as derogatory, arguments ensue over the proper way to solve this argument.

Just as "It's just a joke" absolves the teller of derogatory humor from being taken seriously, a label of "political correctness" negates the need to take protests against offensive labels, jokes, or comments seriously. This dismissal relegates the protests to the complaints of unreasonable, overly sensitive individuals rather than a serious attempt at a discussion over appropriate linguistic boundaries. By playing on the most absurd examples of linguistic change, those who resist changes to the status quo are able to dismiss genuine concerns and avoid looking critically at their own behavior. The issues are not trivial. A growing body of research suggests that telling disparaging jokes can increase the teller's acceptance of stereotypes associated with and discrimination against targeted groups.[58]

A December 1990 story in *Newsweek* (which had "Thought Police" across the issue's cover) claimed political correctness was much like McCarthyism.

The *Newsweek* story made "PC" a derogatory adjective and used it twenty-nine times to condemn anyone with vaguely liberal views. According to *Newsweek*, anyone who wears a prochoice or anti-Bush button is PC, anyone who favors multiculturalism is PC, and anyone who wears a tie-dyed T-shirt and sandals is a "PC person." "Politically correct," once a reference to extremists who enforced their views on others, was transformed by conservatives and the media to a term describing anyone who advocates progressive ideas.[59]

During this time, the left did not defend itself just as it allowed itself to be co-opted during an election year into believing the term "liberal" was a negative one to be avoided at all costs.

Campus speech codes became an important piece of the PC debate. In 1990, a Brown student was expelled for shouting abusive remarks at another student.

Brown's policy prohibits subjecting a person, group, or class to "inappropriate abusive, threatening, or demeaning actions, based on race, religion, gender, handicap, ethnicity, national origin or sexual orientation."[60] The incident brought debates over campus codes and "political correctness" to national attention. While many campuses had had speech codes for years, during the rise of the PC debates, the worst speech codes were held up as the norm and a reason that speech codes should be abolished. The University of Connecticut's poorly written code included rules against inappropriately directed laughter, inconsiderate jokes, and conspicuous exclusion of others from conversation.[61] Smith's included a well-meaning but badly worded warning on judging people by how they look, or "lookism." The bad examples provided fodder for conservative ridicule and argument against the more reasoned and logical protections for historically underprotected groups. The right argued against speech codes as an infringement on First Amendment rights but were fine with ruling against such things as pornography, flag burning, and books about homosexuals.[62]

Much centers around who the target is of offensive behavior. When it is those deemed Other, arguments for freedom of speech abound. When it is those considered "us," there is condemnation of derogatory speech. It is a question of what "we" require others to put up with in terms of insulting, derogatory, and hateful speech in the name of First Amendment freedoms. Clearly, the arguments between freedom of speech and the freedom to live in an atmosphere free of hateful speech and actions is a work in progress.

Kors and Silverglate argue that political correctness on campuses is in direct opposition to freedom of speech rights.[63] Policies against sexual harassment, for example, mean limitations on what you can say. "One student's freedom has to be restricted in order to assure another's." They argue that having to protect "disadvantaged students" (their use of quotation marks) based on categories such as sex, race, sexual orientation, and disability from a hostile environment is an infringement on free speech. "The vulnerability of Black students and their lesser ability to 'take care of themselves in verbal rough-and-tumble'—in short, their status as a 'protected group' that is 'in need of official protection'—is a product of history."[64] Kors and Silverglate believe that the campus speech codes were a misguided attempt to redress historical wrongs against disadvantaged groups at the cost of individual liberty. They express concern about the far-reaching consequences of limiting free speech, adding, "[h]uman history teaches that those who wield power rarely see their own abuse of it." However, they ignore this very aspect of the current hegemony on campuses and in general: Those who have always had the power to determine language, labels, and inclusion continue to fail to see that the "freedom of speech" frame privileges the status quo and ignores those who are always asked to bear the burden of hateful speech or harassment. Those who are never recipients of hate speech can righteously say that our First Amendment rights trump all else.

Kors and Silverglate worry that the codes encourage students to bring harassment suits against any who get in their way while defenders of free speech get labeled as "racist," "sexist," or "homophobic." The types of speech that the codes attempt to protect against (slurs, epithets) are not reasoned debate or differences of opinion but derogatory insults meant to demean and debase.

Jon Gould points out that even though courts failed to uphold many of the college hate speech codes, these rules still exist at least on the books and are a demonstration that ideas about limiting hate speech on college campuses have endured and become a part of American culture. "Public opinion increasingly favors the informal prohibition of racist and sexist speech . . ."[65] Gould points to the penalty enhancement of hate crimes as having roots in the college speech codes. "Rather than being considered an unconstitutional pariah, hate speech restrictions are increasingly the norm among influential institutions of civil society, including higher education, the news media, and Internet service providers."[66]

The power in names is important for concepts as well as for people. Labeling certain crimes as hate crimes gives them greater attention from the media and politicians, and a stronger response from the criminal justice system. "By naming hate crime, we as a society are forced to reckon with its existence in our midst."[67]

HATE SPEECH AND HATE CRIMES

The First Amendment protection of freedom of speech is at the core of arguments over hate speech. Critical race theorists liken speech to an act, arguing that words can and do produce changes in the world rather than just describing it. The targets of racial slurs feel them as genuine pain. On the other side, proponents of absolute freedom of speech believe that any limitations on words are an infringement of our First Amendment rights.

According to Fisch, hate speech is an "incitement to hatred" based on race, ethnicity, national origin, gender, religion, and/or sexual orientation. Hate speech may provide the motive for charging a crime as a hate crime but in itself is not a crime. The government can regulate speech that incites others to commit violence or unlawful conduct ("clear and present danger") if the intent of the regulation is to bring about immediate action and if punishment is likely to be effective. It can prohibit "fighting words" that are considered likely to result in violence against the speaker. It can regulate speech that directly threatens unlawful harm to others, and it can regulate speech that creates unlawful discrimination in the workplace (the creation of a "hostile environment"). The law distinguishes between punishing an expression of a bigoted idea and punishing an act motivated by bigotry. "Only when hatred is actualized by violence or other unlawful action or an immediate threat thereof, directed toward others or reflexively from the victim toward the hater, does the latter encounter the limits of free speech."[68]

On August 31, 2006, high school students in Jena, Louisiana, hung nooses from a tree in the center of campus. The next day, Black athletes from the school staged a silent protest by sitting under the tree. Unbelievably, the school committee that investigated the incident determined that there was no racial motivation for placing the nooses, although the day before, in assembly, a Black student had asked jokingly if Black students could sit anywhere on campus. "This decision highlights one of the key tensions concerning hate speech—whether the perpetrator's intent should play a role in determining whether a particular slur or epithet constitutes hate speech. Related to this issue is whether the act of hanging a noose *per se* constitutes hate speech."[69]

The hangman's noose has long had historical roots in lynching. "The violence and terror wrought by lynching by the Klan and others achieved its intended psychological effect, inflicting terror on the entirety of the community in which the lynching took place."[70] Bell argues it is hard to believe the statements of those at Jena and elsewhere (after Jena, many copycat noose hangings cropped up around the country) who claim not to recognize the significance of the noose in the long history of racism in the United States, particularly given the location of the nooses at Jena—hanging from a tree. Those who claim that hanging a noose is "just a joke" are deluding themselves if they believe this mitigates the terrorist threat implied by the noose, particularly for Black Americans. Many of the copycat nooses were hung in workplaces, with motivations ranging from "It's just a joke" to resentment against a co-worker. "Even when a direct message of resentment or hatred is absent, noose hangings are often accompanied, preceded, or followed by racial or ethnic slurs, which sharply emphasize the noose hanger's antipathy toward the targeted Black worker."[71]

Bell evaluates the social meaning of noose hanging by looking at how incidents are constructed by the media and how they are perceived by the perpetrators and other Whites as opposed to victims' perceptions. She found that the media presents these incidents in their historical context, in other words, as racially offensive symbols that are intended to intimidate the victims. "Publicized noose hangings are likely to have the same effect as other well-publicized hate crimes. In addition to the harm that an individual experiences when a hate crime is committed against them, research reveals that members of the community who learn of the event are harmed as well . . ."[72] However, nontargeted groups may readily dismiss hate speech and noose hangings as insignificant. Bill O'Reilly expressed the opinion that the noose was not a real threat, implying that the reaction of the Black students was based on their oversensitivity. Those who are not willing to look at the depths of racism inherent in this country too easily dismiss hateful language and insults with "It's just a joke" or implications that the recipient is at fault.

The motivation of the perpetrator is an essential element in determining whether a crime falls into the category of a hate crime. However, as Bell points out, a more victim-centered approach would provide better balance when determining the overall effects of a potential hate crime incident. After the Jena incident, new antinoose laws started appearing, although the hanging of nooses was already prohibited by employment, criminal, and general civil rights laws.[73]

The U.S. Supreme Court has dealt with symbolic speech like noose hanging before in *R.A.V. vs. St. Paul* (1992). Three teenagers burned a cross on the lawn of a Black family in St. Paul, Minnesota. The teens were arrested and charged under a St. Paul law. One of the teens, Robert Victoria, objected to the law regarding symbolic elements (in this case, the burning cross) as a violation of his freedom of speech. The city of St. Paul convicted him under the city's bias motive ordinance that forbids putting certain symbolic items on public or private property. He was also convicted on the charge of assault based on race. The Supreme Court ruled the St. Paul ordinance to be unconstitutional due to its wording prohibiting speech on particular subjects, as it was content based and because it was overbroad. The defendants were then charged in federal court with federal civil rights violations for placing the burning cross: "one law prohibits conspiracies to threaten or intimidate any person in the exercise of his federally protected rights [which include the right to own and occupy a home], and another prohibits intimidation of any person because of his race, color, religion, sex, handicap, family status or national origin."[74] In *Virginia vs. Black* (2003), another cross burning case, the Supreme Court recognized that cross burning constitutes a threat, though they determined that a crime would require more than just the burning of the cross. "As long as the statute criminalizing cross burning took care to regulate only those cross burnings intended to intimidate, the Court held that state regulation of cross burning did not violate the First Amendment."[75] The intent of the symbolic speech thus becomes an important element in determining whether a crime has been committed.

Bell's victim-based approach would punish "wordless speech" only when it contains "readily identifiable extreme symbols of racial hatred like the hangman's noose" and then only when targeted at a specific, identifiable individual.[76] "At bottom, noose hanging is threatening conduct that places the minority target in the same position as a victim of a hate or bias crime who has been racially harassed. Hate crime is very destabilizing to victims."[77] Actual hate crimes often occur in the victim's neighborhood (as with anti-integrationist violence), and one of the most destabilizing elements of these incidents is the fact that threats in our homes take away from our creation of home as a sanctuary; in addition, those who are victims of repeated discrimination and hateful speech have no way of knowing when an incident is "just" symbolic and when it will escalate into something far more dangerous.

Mark Slagle defines hate speech as speech that singles out minorities for abuse and harassment, and he says one of the most obvious forms is an ethnic slur. He looks at a variety of viewpoints, from critical race theorists to those concerned with any infringements on First Amendment rights and comes to the conclusion that speech is nothing more than words, and words do not maim or kill. The conflict and psychic pain caused by words is, in his opinion, necessary for the growth and progress of society. "In fact there is no means whereby anyone can reasonably sort out hateful speech from legitimate discussion."[78] He readily dismisses the concerns over power inequality expressed by critical race theorists, believing that the marketplace of ideas will eventually weed out derogatory speech without help from the courts. Theoretically, his arguments are valid because the freedom to express oneself is considered a fundamental right of Americans, and over time, overt expressions of hate and disdain are making their way out of the public arena through public condemnation.

However, Slagle ignores the many places in American society where a power inequality makes some speech more potent than others. For example, employment regulations exist to protect workers from sexual harassment, which is often speech based rather than overt action. We recognize the need for such protections to create a nonhostile workplace, particularly within the employer-employee power differential. Bullying often involves "only speech," yet it has resulted in terrible pain and even suicide for its victims, and many if not most schools have antibullying regulations. While we need to be very careful in terms of any limits to our First Amendment rights, we also need to consider historically marginalized groups and not be naive in believing that the more visible racial imbalances of the past have gone away, let alone the covert ones.

Several reviewers took issue with Jeremy Waldron's book on hate speech laws (*The Harm in Hate Speech*).[79] Jacob Mchangama, a Danish legal expert, believes the book is based on flawed harm theory. The central premise of the book is that hate speech undermines the equal dignity of individual members of vulnerable minorities. Pitted against this harm to individuals is the potential harm in hate speech laws themselves to infringe on freedom of speech, thought, and conscience and the risk of political abuse by those determining what constitutes hate speech. Mchangama argues that the acceptance of interracial marriages and a decrease in the number of hate crimes demonstrate that we do not need laws to regulate hate (speech) and argues we cannot know if the cumulative effect results in an "environment" of harm. "Since we cannot know for sure which forms of speech are beneficial for humankind and which are not, it is suspect to restrict speech on the basis of such purely speculative assessments."[80]

David Gordon also takes issue with Waldron's book, stating that there is no right of restraint against insult. He does not believe that the opinion of "one" speaker against another individual can cause harm enough to regulate speech.

"Would not the hostile view be merely one opinion among large numbers of others? Why would it suffice to weaken your sense of assurance that you were an equal member of society?"[81] Who has to prove harm? Waldron takes a victim-centered approach, while Gordon argues that the greater harm lies in speech regulation. Gordon believes we need evidence of harm before we restrict speech. However, he does not mention the studies that have already been done showing the effects of hate speech on its recipients. Nor does he acknowledge there are many who already have no assurance they are equal members of society; on the contrary, there is much evidence that they are not considered so.

With the debate over hate speech, it is important to keep in mind the kind of speech under discussion. While some would argue that limiting any speech limits free expression and debate in our society, in reality, the kinds of slurs, epithets, and derogatory language spewed against its victims does nothing to further debate of any kind. The line may be hard to define, but there is a difference between debating uncomfortable and contentious topics and merely yelling insults at someone due to the particular group they represent. Is there harm in hate speech? Those who argue against its regulation need to at least acknowledge the research done in this area.

Laura Leets conducted a study on how people actually experience hate speech, in this case, that directed against homosexuals and Jews. She defines harmful speech as "utterances that are intended to cause damages and/or irrespective of intent, that their receivers perceive to result in damage."[82] All the examples provided to the 120 university student participants were based on actual situations. Leets found that the short-term impacts of experiencing hate speech were emotional, while the longer-term effects were more attitudinal and behavioral; response patterns were the same as with other traumatic events such as domestic violence, assault, and robbery. Participants believed the motives behind the hate speech to be the result not merely of ignorance (which could be remedied), but as symptomatic of the perpetrators and thus a pattern rather than isolated incidents. This more pervasive view of hate effects the impact hate speech has.

Robert Boeckmann conducted two studies with Asian American university student participants. "Results indicate that hate speech directed at ethnic targets deserves more severe punishment than other forms of offensive speech and petty theft. Hate speech also results in more extreme emotional responses and, in the case of an Asian target, has a depressing influence on collective self-esteem."[83] The study's aim was to understand the harm of hate speech from the victims' perspectives. He raises the question of what defines the hated characteristic as a group attribute rather than as an individual attribute. For example, does being overweight qualify as a group characteristic or an individual one? For those who represent a group, the harm can be greater. "Offensive speech with broad social consequences appears to warrant more severe punishment."[84]

"The harms thesis—the assumption that words harm people—is a defining feature of sexual harassment, hate speech, verbal abuse and obscene telephone call (OTC) offenses."[85] Jay raises the question of whether there is a positive benefit to harmful speech or if it causes serious enough harm to warrant regulation. "Similar to sexual harassment, hate speech is protected until it rises to the level of a threat."[86] He points out that it is hard to get objective evidence of harm, and it is also unethical to abuse people in order to conduct a study on the harm of particular types of speech. "Evidence of harm is present in harassment, discrimination and OTC cases, but it is indeterminate in verbal abuse research. There is no evidence of harm from fleeting expletives or from conversational or cathartic swearing."[87] For Jay, we must prove substantial harm that outweighs our freedom of speech rights, and we must prove that government action can significantly improve the situation. He argues the need to move beyond "commonsense and folk psychology views of harm," which may be inaccurate, and look at actual research done on harm. To start, we need a clear definition of harm itself.

Mullen and Smyth looked at suicide rates among ethnic immigrants to the United States to determine if a relationship exists between rates of suicide here and the use of hate speech about these particular groups. They found that "the suicide rates for ethnic immigrant groups in the United States were significantly predicted by the negativity of the ethnophaulisms [ethnic slurs] used to refer to those ethnic immigrant groups."[88] These authors point to the need for more research in this area to determine exactly what the negative effects of hate speech may be on vulnerable groups, effects that can include psychological, social, and economic harm to group members.

In a pilot study aimed at quantifying hate speech on talk radio, Noriega and Iribarren looked at three conservative talk radio programs, the *Lou Dobbs Show: Mr. Independent*, the *Savage Nation*, and the *John & Ken Show*. Using qualitative content analysis, the study team examined transcripts from these shows to determine which vulnerable groups were targeted and how they were depicted on the shows. "The research team then identified four types of statements that were made relative to these targets: unsubstantiated claims, flawed argumentation, divisive language (that is, 'us-them' constructions), and dehumanizing metaphors."[89] The study found numerous unsubstantiated claims on all three shows (37 percent were unsubstantiated, with 11 claims proven false, 18 found unverifiable, and 13 found to be distorted).[90] Unsubstantiated claims were found to magnify the sense of an immigrant threat (immigrants as criminals). The researchers looked at the use of "us versus them" constructions on the shows (such as the use of collective pronouns) and found that particular phrases "tended to posit an insurmountable sociopolitical, racial, or cultural divide between a show's audience and targeted vulnerable groups."[91] They also studied how the shows linguistically created particular groups as Other. In this case, the primary targets were undocumented immigrants. Targeting occurred through the use of code words, word repetition, and an established alignment between hosts and guests that was in opposition to the targeted groups. While this pilot study found no examples of hate speech as defined in a National Telecommunications and Information Administration (NTIA) report, they did find that "vulnerable groups were defined as antithetical to core American values, which were attributed by hosts to themselves, their audience, and the nation."[92]

The 1993 NTIA Report to Congress was entitled *The Role of Telecommunications in Hate Crimes*. NTIA undertook "an examination of the use of telecommunications, including broadcast radio and television, cable television, public access television, and computer bulletin boards, to advocate or encourage violent acts and the omission of crimes of hate against designated persons or groups."[93] In addition to messages threatening imminent unlawful action, they also considered cases in which a speaker intended to create "a climate of hate or prejudice, which in turn may foster the commission of hate crimes."[94] Although unable to link hate crime commission to telecommunications due to a lack of clear data, NTIA did find that "individuals have used telecommunications to disseminate messages of hate and bigotry to a wide audience." NTIA concluded that the best remedy to hate speech is more speech to counteract it and promote tolerance, rather than government regulation.

Jeremy Waldron defends laws that forbid "group defamation" and believes hate speech regulation contributes to the public good. In addition to our First Amendment rights, he argues that citizens have the right to be free from abuse and defamation, from humiliation, discrimination, and violence. "The aim is simply to diminish the presence of visible hatred in society and thus benefit members of vulnerable minorities by protecting the public commitment to their equal standing in society against public denigration."[95] By his definition, hate speech can include visible signs of hate such as cross burning, posters, leaflets, and Internet sites as well as more traditional speech such as racial epithets. His concern is with the visible environment that vulnerable groups must negotiate each day.

Words That Wound, written in 1993, was a response to the rise in hate speech on college campuses (which was followed by the creation of new or revised campus speech codes). The four authors advocate public regulation of racially abusive speech, believing that any First Amendment issues are outweighed by the harm done to the victims. As critical race theorists, they speak not only of blatant forms of racism, they also look closely at how racism is deeply ingrained in American society and culture and what this means for the daily, subjective lives of victims of racism. "Our work presented racism not as isolated instances of conscious bigoted decision making or prejudicial practice, but as larger, systemic, structural, and cultural, as deeply psychologically and socially ingrained." Words can be actual "weapons of oppression and subordination."[96]

Contributing author Mari Matsuda believes that an absolutist First Amendment position contributes to racism because it sends the message that American society will tolerate racist speech and behavior. "A legal response to racist speech is a statement that victims of racism are valued members of our polity." As she points out, "Tolerance of hate speech is not tolerance borne by the community at large. Rather, it is a psychic tax imposed on those least able to pay."[97] By viewing incidents of racism as isolated, by brushing them off with the idea that they are pranks or jokes or should not be taken seriously, we contribute to the endemic racism in American society. "Racist hate messages, threats, slurs, epithets, and disparagement all hit the gut of those in the target group. The spoken message of hatred and inferiority is conveyed on the street, in school yards, in popular culture, and in the propaganda of hate widely distributed in this country."[98] This argument is in opposition to those who believe that the "one word" of hate is balanced by all the other words.

Matsuda would require three characteristics for hate speech to qualify for legal action: the message must be of racial inferiority, it must be directed against an historically oppressed group, and it must be persecutory, hateful, and degrading. She includes symbolic messages as well (such as swastikas and burning crosses). "If the historical message, known to both victim and perpetrator, is racist persecution and violence, then the sign is properly treated as actionable racist speech."[99] The protection of racist speech in American society is in itself a form of state action because it supports the "commonsense" status quo and benefits those already wielding power while minimizing the concerns of targeted groups.

Charles Lawrence III, another contributing author to *Words That Wound*, is troubled by the distinction between First Amendment protections for racist speech and "fighting words" that are not protected. "The goal of White supremacy is not achieved by individual acts or even by the cumulative acts of a group, but rather it is achieved by the institutionalization of the ideas of White supremacy." Lawrence points out that those who are not victims of racist behavior often "simply do not see most racist conduct" since they experience the White-dominated world simply as "the world."[100] For example, in the case of fighting words, this exception to First Amendment protection is based on a White male point of view. "It is accepted, justifiable, and even praiseworthy when 'real men' respond to personal insult with violence." On the other hand, those who are victims of racial insult are not given the same protections.[101] Lawrence calls for us to listen to the voices of the victims of hate speech and to realize that this type of speech does indeed inflict real harm. "The Black student who is subjected to racial epithets, like the Black person on whose lawn the Klan has burned a cross, is threatened and silenced by a credible connection between racist hate speech and racist violence."[102] We must recognize that some words and symbols rest on centuries of real threat, physical violence, and death, and therefore cannot be relegated to "just words." Many violent hate crimes start with words.

Fighting words are defined as "those words which by their very utterance inflict injury or tend to incite an immediate breach of the peace."[103] They are one of the few exceptions to First Amendment rights to free speech. "The exemption of fighting words from constitutional protection is grounded in part on the potentially violent response of the individual to whom the words are directed."[104] But what exactly constitutes "fighting words," and are these not potentially very different depending on whether our "reasonable man" is White, Black, Jewish, or LGBT? Some consider the idea that a person should be free from hate speech if they are in the workplace, the privacy of their own home, or a captive audience. This was a factor in the school speech codes, as students in college, particularly since they are paying tuition and housing costs, are owed an education in a nonhostile environment.

Language plays a vital role in the creation of Other in American society, and speech can be paramount in fostering negativity and hate. Who gets to determine public representation as well as what we require groups of Americans to absorb in terms of hateful speech is a continuing debate. As we moved from the civil rights era into the conservative backlash of the 1980s and 1990s, arguments over speech took place on college campuses, in the media, and in the courts. We argued over constitutional rights in terms of whether First Amendment rights are always sacrosanct even in the face of hateful verbal and symbolic language, and what that meant for the constitutional right to equal protection under the law. We argued over hegemony and representation, and who has the right to determine whether the impact of certain language is strong enough to warrant regulation. With the conservative backlash came a rise of hate speech and symbolic acts of hate on campuses, which resulted in college speech codes, well meaning but rarely well constructed. Arguments over the validity of these codes, as well as over local hate speech ordinances, made their way into the Supreme Court while at the same time, those who did not want to recognize the harm to already marginalized Americans used the term "political correctness" to dismiss changes in speech as unnecessary. To date, the United States still allows a wide range of hateful speech spoken in person, symbolically, and through our media, although overall public sentiment provides some boundaries for what is considered acceptable from our political leaders as well as our citizens. Paula Deen's public issue with past racist speech is just the latest example of the power of public condemnation to mitigate the use of hateful speech.

NOTES

1. Robin Tolmach Lakoff, *The Language War* (Berkeley: University of California Press, 2000), 20.

2. Ibid., 41.

3. Jane H. Hill, *The Everyday Language of White Racism* (Malden, MA: Wiley-Blackwell, 2008), 41.

4. Mark A. Ferguson and Thomas E. Ford, "Disparagement humor: A theoretical and empirical review of psychoanalytic, superiority, and social identity theories," *Humor* 21, no. 3 (2008): 283–284.

5. Ibid., 285.

6. Ibid., 295.

7. Ibid., 298.

8. Thomas E. Ford and Mark A. Ferguson, "Social consequences of disparagement humor: A prejudiced norm theory," *Personality and Social Psychology Review* 8, no. 1 (2008): 79.

9. Thomas E. Ford, "Effects of sexist humor on tolerance of sexist events," *Personality and Social Psychology Bulletin* 26, no. 9 (November 2000): 1105.

10. Ibid., 1106.

11. Christie Davies, "Ethnic jokes, moral values and social boundaries," *British Journal of Sociology* 33, no. 3 (September 1982): 383.

12. Ibid., 384.

13. Christie Davies, *Ethnic Humor around the World: A Comparative Analysis* (Bloomington: Indiana University Press, 1990), 9.

14. Ibid., 322.

15. Alan Dundes, *Cracking Jokes* (Berkeley: Ten Speed, 1987), 96.

16. Ibid., 116.

17. Paul Lewis (ed.), "The Muhammad cartoons and humor research: A collection of essays," *Humor* 21, no. 1 (2008): 5–6.

18. Ibid., 10.

19. Chris Powell (ed.), *Humour in Society* (New York: St. Martin's, 1988), 100.

20. Ibid., 100.

21. Ibid., 158.

22. Dundes, *Cracking Jokes*, 3.

23. Ibid., 16.

24. Ibid., 51.

25. Ibid., 54.

26. Christie Davies, *The Mirth of Nations* (New Brunswick, NJ: Transaction, 2002), 187.

27. Ibid., 188.

28. John Morreall (ed.), *The Philosophy of Laughter and Humor* (Albany: State University of New York, 1987), 226.

29. Ibid., 229.

30. Ibid., 250.

31. Ibid., 250.

32. Ibid., 253.

33. Ibid., 255.

34. Hill, *Everyday Language of White Racism*, 49.

35. ESPN News Services, "Longtime pro critical of Commissioner Too," October 11, 2003. http://sports.espn.go.com/golf/news/story?id=1635065 (accessed November 10, 2013).

36. Eric Adelson, "Stephenson's comments grossly unchallenged," *ESPN: The Magazine*, October 14, 2003. http://sports.espn.go.com/golf/news/story?id=1637830

37. "Golfer says comments about Woods 'misconstrued,' " http://www.cnn.com/US/9704/21/fuzzy/ (accessed November 10, 2013).

38. Barry Wilner, "Woods accepts apology from Zoeller," http://www.texnews.com/tiger/accept042597.html (accessed November 10, 2013).

39. Robert Zarate, "Is Shaq a racist or just ignorant? Anti-Chinese slur sparks widespread debate," *Chicago Maroon*, January 17, 2003. http://chicagomaroon.com/2003/01/17/is-shaq-a-racist-or-just-ignorant-anti-chinese-slur-sparks-widespread-debate/ (accessed November 10, 2013).

40. Hunter Cutting (ed.), *Talking the Walk: A Communications Guide for Racial Justice* (Oakland, CA: AK Press, 2006), 98.

41. Irwin Tang, "Inside the Shaquille O'Neal taunt controversy: A day-by-day account of the NBA 'Ching-Chong' incident, from the man who started it all," *AsianWeek*, March 21, 2003, http://www.asianweek.com/2003/03/21/inside-the-shaquille-oneal-taunt-controversy-a-day-by-day-

42. Irwin Tang, "Inside the Shaquille O'Neal taunt controversy," *Asianweek*, March 26, 2004, 18. http://search.proquest.com/docview/367339470/B2EE822B5673423DPQ/1?accountid=14586

43. Irwin Tang, "Inside the Shaquille O'Neal taunt controversy: A day-by-day account of the NBA 'Ching-Chong' incident, from the man who started it all,"

44. James Poniewozik. "The Imus fallout: who can say what?," *Time*, April 12, 2007, http://content.time.com/time/magazine/article/0,9171,1609807,00.html

45. "MSNBC drops simulcast of Don Imus show," *Today*, April 13, 2007. http://www.today.com/id/17999196#.UvVNVYWa7nI

46. National Coalition on Racism in Sports & Media, www.aimovement.org/ncrsm/index.html (accessed November 10, 2013).

47. Laural R. Davis, "Protest against the use of Native American mascots: A challenge to traditional American identity," *Journal of Sport & Social Issues* 17 (April 1, 1993): 14, http://jss.sagepub.com/content/17/1/9.full.pdf (accessed November 10, 2013).

48. Ibid., 14–15.

49. Ibid., 15.

50. Andy Rooney, "Indians seek a role in modern U.S.," *Union*, March 11, 1992, http://www.bluecorncomics.com/rooney.htm (accessed November 10, 2013).

51. Davis, Protest against the use of Native American mascots," 18.

52. C. Richard King, "Defensive dialogues: Native American mascots, anti-Indianism, and educational institutions," *Studies in Media & Information Literacy Education* 2, no. 1 (February 2002): 6, http://utpjournals.metapress.com/content/h0wn53167646u075/fulltext.pdf (accessed November 10, 2013).

53. Ibid.

54. Hill, *Everyday Language of White Racism*, 34.

55. John Wilson, *The Myth of Political Correctness: The Conservative Attack on Higher Education* (Durham, NC: Duke University Press, 1995), xv.

56. Ibid., 16.

57. Lewis, 114.

58. Ibid., 122.

59. Wilson, *Myth of Political Correctness*, 14.

60. Ibid., 90.

61. Ibid., 93.

62. Ibid., 94–95.

63. Alan Charles Kors and Harvey Silverglate, "Codes of silence: Who's silencing free speech on campus—and why," Reason.com, November 1998. http://reason.com/archives/1998/11/01/codes-of-silence

64. Ibid.

65. Jon B. Gould, *Speak No Evil* (Chicago: University of Chicago Press, 2005), 6.

66. Ibid., 174–175.

67. Lisa Yun, 29.

68. William B. Fisch, "Hate speech in the constitutional law of the United States," *American Journal of Comparative Law* 50 (2002): 491.

69. Jeannine Bell, "The hangman's noose and the lynch mob: Hate speech and the Jena Six," *Harvard Civil Rights, Civil Liberties Law Review* 44 (2009): 330.

70. Ibid., 332.

71. Ibid., 344.

72. Ibid., 346.

73. Ibid., 350.

74. Fisch, "Hate speech in the constitutional law of the United States," 467.

75. Bell, The hangman's noose and the lynch mob," 342.

76. Ibid., 355.

77. Ibid., 345.

78. Mark Slagle, "An ethical exploration of free expression and the problem of hate speech," *Journal of Mass Media Ethics* 24 (2009): 248.

79. Jeremy Waldron, *The Harm in Hate Speech* (Cambridge, MA: Harvard University Press, 2012).

80. Jacob Mchangama, "The harm in hate speech laws," *Hoover Institution Stanford University Policy Review*, December 1, 2012, http://www.hoover.org/publications/policy-review/article/135466 (accessed November 9, 2013).

81. David Gordon, "The harm in hate-speech laws," May 30, 2012, http://mises.org/daily/6070/ (accessed November 9, 2013).

82. Laura Leets, "Experiencing hate speech: Perceptions and responses to anti-Semitism and antigay speech," *Journal of Social Issues* 58, no. 2 (2002): 342.

83. Robert Boeckmann and Jeffrey Liew, "Hate speech: Asian American students' justice judgments and psychological responses,"*Journal of Social Issues* 58, no. 2 (December 2002): 363.

84. Ibid., 377.

85. Timothy Jay, *Cursing in America* (Philadelphia: John Benjamins, 1992), 81.

86. Ibid., 83.

87. Ibid., 93.

88. B. Mullen and J. M. Smyth, "Immigrant suicide rates as a function of ethnophaulisms: Hate speech predicts death," *Psychosomatic Medicine* 66, no. 3 (May–June 2004): 343.

89. Chon A. Noriega and Francisco Javier Iribarren, "Quantifying hate speech on commercial talk radio," Chicano Studies Research Center, November 2011, 3, http://www.chicano.ucla.edu/files/WP1QuantifyingHateSpeech_0.pdf (accessed November 10, 2013).

90. Ibid., 6.

91. Ibid., 7.

92. Ibid., 10.

93. U.S. Department of Commerce, "The role of telecommunications in hate crimes," i, http://www.ntia.doc.gov/legacy/reports/1993/TelecomHateCrimes1993.pdf (accessed November 9, 2013).

94. Ibid.

95. Jeremy Waldron, "Dignity and defamation: The visibility of hate," *Harvard Law Review* 123 (2010): 1600, http://www.harvardlawreview.org/media/pdf/vol123_waldron.pdf (accessed November 10, 2013).

96. Mari J. Matsuda, Charles R. Lawrence III, Richard Delgado, and Kimberle Williams Crenshaw, *Words That Wound: Critical Race Theory, Assaultive Speech, and the First Amendment* (Boulder, CO: Westview, 1993), 5.

97. Ibid., 18.

98. Ibid., 23.

99. Ibid., 41.

100. Ibid., 62.

101. Ibid., 69.

102. Ibid., 79.

103. Milton Heumann and Thomas W. Church (eds.), *Hate Speech on Campus* (Dexter, MI: Northeastern University Press, 1997), 25.

104. Ibid., 25.

8

Conclusion: Reframing the Other

The metaphors and frames we use to create enemies when we are at war are the same metaphors and frames we use to create the Other within our borders. Wartime propaganda creates a dehumanized enemy Other that frames conflict in such a way that the solution requires killing a great number of people. We frame Others as lacking in what we determine to be logical and natural, positioning their dehumanization as common sense. Common depictions of the enemy include comparisons with animals or insects, and these same frames have been used to describe unwanted immigrants or those whose religion or skin color differs from "ours." These images become prevalent in our media, including popular as well as academic writings. The Other is typically created by how useful or harmful they appear to us: Native Americans were created as noble savage when we treated with them as sovereign nations, as enemy savages when we wanted their lands, and as heathens for missionaries to convert.

Those deemed Other have often been framed as prey, and the metaphor of the hunt leads to great numbers being killed. As with animal prey, the bodies of our enemies are the site of trophy-taking as parts are cut off from both the living and the dead and are retained as souvenirs. Native Americans, Japanese, Vietnamese, and Arabs all have been dehumanized as our enemies, depicted by the media as animals, insects, diseases, and other nonhuman entities. Even our allies during the Vietnam War were created thus. The wartime treatment of the enemy has been merciless, as the accounts from the Native American, Japanese, and Vietnamese wars have shown. Our recent wars in the Middle East continue this tradition. We have created the Arab/Muslim enemy and depict Islam as a culture so alien as to preclude its subsistence side by side with mainstream America.

Hate crimes against those deemed "Muslim" show the strength of these creations as those with no ties to either Arab countries or Islam have been killed because they were thought to be Muslim. The dramatic increase in hate crimes against those thought to be Muslim after the Oklahoma City bombing in 1995 and the terrorist acts of September 11, 2001, vividly illustrate the impact of these frames.

Unwanted immigrants continue to be described with common metaphors that include water (floods, deluges) and other uncontrollable entities such as plagues, germs, insects, and hordes. While those like "us" (Anglo-Saxon, White, Protestant) are accepted and acceptable as new citizens, many others have been considered too different to assimilate, and our hospitality has been lacking. Who these unwanted guests are changes over time, but we never seem to learn that each group finds its place and becomes part of the American amalgam. The Chinese were banned from many arenas and defined by law as lesser humans. Many were killed or assaulted, their homes and businesses destroyed as they were bodily thrown out of many areas in the West. They were framed in the media as innately different, as devious, as deviant, and as economic threats even as they built railroads and produced needed goods and services. Intolerance was codified in our legal system and in our laws controlling immigration, and it has been supported by those (police, judges, lawyers) who are supposed to protect all citizens. Many new immigrants, particularly at the end of the nineteenth century, were defined by race; Italians and Irish immigrants were framed as non-White when they first arrived. This frame left little space for immigrants to prove their equality and their humanity other than stepping on Blacks to prove that they were indeed "White." White supremacist groups such as the Ku Klux Klan formed to maintain barriers between the accepted "us" and the unacceptable Other, often through the commission of violent hate crimes.

We use large categories such as "Asian," "Native American," and "Hispanic" that subsume smaller but unique groups, thereby allowing anyone fitting in the larger group to stand in for members of the unique cultures. By blurring unique attributes into indistinct Other, we dehumanize and diminish many cultures. We mock the Other in our public culture through songs, cartoons, movies, books, comics, news reports, and even video games that contain stereotypes and harmful metaphors, teaching the public that the Other is something lesser to be denigrated rather than respected. Difference is framed as a fault rather than as a positive attribute. What politicians say to get themselves elected often pushes emotional buttons to get public reactions and votes, regardless of the consequences or the truth of the framing. Public discourse and framing lead to practice; they are not independent but interwoven. How we imagine and depict people contributes to how we treat them. Framing an immigrant group as sympathetic refugees in need of our help produces a very different reaction than the frames that equate new groups with plagues who will overrun our country and never become "one of us." Since the start of Operation Gatekeeper (October 1994), more than 6,000 people have died trying to cross the U.S.-Mexico border. The militarization of the border—including additional manpower, gates, and surveillance equipment—has pushed crossing areas into the most dangerous territories and has resulted in many deaths. Our zeal to ensure that Others do not become us/U.S. lets us allow this travesty.

The created notion of biological race with ideas of inherent deficits and negative group attributes has been used to maintain separation between groups of people in American culture. Those considered racially Other (other than White) have consistently been framed as lower than those framed as White as the frames are primarily provided by Whites themselves. Control through laws and hate crime violence has taken place surrounding contestations over sharing space between and among races. Many hate crimes take place in homes and neighborhoods as well as in public spaces where different groups collide. The idea that only certain types of people can live in certain neighborhoods has led to violence when others intrude. Physical space and personal space meet on sidewalks; shared public facilities such as drinking fountains, bathrooms, and swimming pools; not to mention public schools and hospitals. The believed taint of the racial Other precluded sharing these spaces for many years, and laws, unwritten codes of behavior and violent hate crimes let racial Others know on a daily basis that they were lesser human beings. Ideals of skin color and shade as well as facial features and types of hair permeate the popular culture and have resulted in products that damage the self physically and psychologically as those without the "right" attributes try to move themselves closer to the mainstream. These same ideals of beauty and womanhood created the White woman as vulnerable to advances from the Other, from Black men, Jewish men, and immigrant Others. The framing of this threat as a rampant desire in the Other was used as an excuse for lynching thousands of Blacks and from keeping racial Others out of the country or confined in limited spaces and occupations when they were allowed in as immigrants.

Politicians are responsible for much of the rhetoric used to create Others and for determining how they are then treated. Political rhetoric, as well as laws passed by our politicians, has built discrimination and unjust treatment into our systems of law, education, housing, and employment to name but a few. The creation of Blacks and others as inherently criminal has contributed to their treatment as lesser citizens and even to their deaths. In September 2013, a Black man was shot dead by a police officer who sent 12 bullets his way, 10 of which hit their target. The man had just been in a car crash and had knocked on a woman's door to obtain help in the middle of the night. She called 911 to report a potential robbery, her immediate assumption being that he was a criminal and a threat. The police arrived, and as the unarmed man ran toward them for help (the car crash was described as significant), one of the officers shot him dead.[1]

Our notions of race underlie much of the creation of Others in war, in our arguments over immigration and who may be a full citizen, and in our ideas regarding acceptable religions. Hatred toward racial Others has been strong, and the language of hate is still contained in our growing media on websites, Facebook, blogs, and Twitter. These are spaces and places where people can post anonymously and can create support communities that bolster ideas of hierarchy, inequity, resentment, and hatred.

While this country was purportedly founded on religious tolerance, religious difference has been at the root of violence and hate for centuries. Discrimination against religious Others was built into state constitutions from the beginning of the United States as a nation. We have created fears of other religions as controlled by non-American forces and created members of these faiths as more loyal to church than country. Conspiracy theories abound regarding an imminent domination of America by Catholics, Jews, and now Muslims. At the same time, we accept without question that Protestant values are imbedded in our government and other institutions while members of the religious right continue to push for even more intrusion of their religion into schools and the government. The church and state separation built into our constitution and country from the beginning needs to include all religions, not just the ones deemed "not us." While violence against those practicing nonmainstream religions has been much less here than in other countries, hate crimes continue against many religions today. Recent hate crimes against Muslims and those identified as "Muslim looking" continue and spill over onto other religions such as Sikhs and Hindus. Holocaust deniers denigrate Jewish people with their fabrications and cruel denial of fact.

"The pervasiveness of antigay bias in the United States . . . suggests that, rather than an expression of individual psychopathology, antigay behaviors may be extreme manifestations of dominant cultural values."[2] The space accorded the LGBT population was and still is hotly contested and violently defended. This group has been framed as abnormal, from definitions of mental illness, to frames of sinners damned by God, the sexually perverted, and carriers of disease. Violence against the LGBT population is often extreme when hate crimes are committed. Media preference for particular LGBT representatives maintains boundaries around what is acceptable as a public face for this population. Matthew Shepard was presented as young, innocent, and not sexually mature, and it is no accident that his particular case became the representation of anti-LGBT hate as his image quickly spread internationally. While a great deal of media and political attention surrounded his death, many other LGBT people die in hate crimes and are ignored by the media. Discrimination against the LGBT population, as with race, is built into our legal system, which still limits marriage, health and other benefits, and adoption in many states. Changes in participation in the military and the Boy Scouts have occurred only recently, and while some states now allow same-sex marriage, this is a continuing and contentious battle.

Images of the LGBT population in our popular culture provide a public view of this group, but they also contribute elements from which the LGBT population develops its own version of identity, and these images continue to deny this group full humanity. We still accept open antihomosexuality from our politicians, in the news media, and in our popular culture, repeatedly framing the group as different and lesser. As we publicly argue for or against equal rights and normality, we continue to reinforce the same negative stereotypes, as the mere act of questioning equality denies this group equal humanity. Old ideas as to choice and disease still exist in our media. Although in decreasing numbers, politicians and other public figures still argue that this group can be cured or can choose to change, bolstering the notion that they are not normal and should want to change. When Ohio senator Rob Portman discovered his son was gay, he publicly made a statement about rethinking his stance against same-sex marriage. In response to this, Andrea Lafferty of the Traditional Values Coalitions posted a statement equating acceptance of gays with acceptance of drunk drivers. Her note at the bottom of the statement, in case the reader should be confused, says, "Drunk driving is immoral. I abhor it. I also believe homosexuality is immoral and sinful."[3] Joseph Farah (editor in chief of the WorldNetDaily website) went a step farther and in his column entitled "Be Glad Portman's Son Isn't Serial Killer" equated homosexuality with being a serial killer.[4]

We have built rejection into our legal system with the gay panic defense, which postulates that it is a normal and natural reaction to invoke violence when approached by a same-gendered person. The same was true in the past when a Black man approached a White woman (or was deemed to have approached one, which might include brushing past her on a sidewalk while running to catch a train). Is death really a necessary reaction to an unwanted advance? Women face such advances from men every day and usually do not resort to violence, choosing simply to say "no" or even "no thank you."

A discourse of Otherness is imbedded in our culture. Our language choices create and frame how we think about difference. Included in our discourse are contestations over who has the power to define one's own group and its public representation. It is rarely the group itself that gets to determine the dominant images, analogies, and metaphors used by the media. Hate crime has been defined by and imbedded in our legal systems, but arguments over the clash between freedom of speech and truly hateful speech, between our right to speak our minds and our right to equal protection under the law, continue today. Who gets to decide what trumps what? It is usually not those who have been marginalized and framed as Other. The hegemony of the dominant is implicated in all creations of Other and in an environment that contributes to hate crimes that serve to police the boundaries of inclusion. These boundaries are created and maintained through violence and discrimination that lets Others know where they can and cannot go without consequences. Jokes, racial slurs, and the use of the Internet to spread hateful commentary also construct boundaries. Hurtful rhetoric is easily dismissed with "It's just a joke," and accusations of "political correctness" serve to shut down conversations about real equality. Slurs by public figures represent louder voices than those of the general public, and media reporting of these incidents ensures that they are heard and repeated widely. Each incident is invariably accompanied by an argument over how important words are and who gets to determine if what is said is significant. The contestation among production, intent, and reception remains strong. The public has become much more condemning of public figures who utter hateful language even as we determine that hateful speech is not in itself a hate crime. This public condemnation serves to expand the boundaries of inclusion over time.

PEOPLE WITH DISABILITIES

In January 2013, Linda Weston was indicted in federal court on 196 counts for holding people with disabilities hostage in her home in terrible conditions to collect their Social Security money. In addition to charges of kidnapping and murder, Weston was charged with a hate crime against those with disabilities, which is the first time the federal hate crime law that now protects people with disabilities has been used. In 2011, Weston's landlord discovered four malnourished adults living in terrible conditions in the basement of her Philadelphia apartment building. One was chained to the boiler; all were malnourished and had been held captive with only a bucket to use as a bathroom. Weston has now been charged with the deaths of two disabled women in her care over the past decade. Her victims had been drugged, starved, denied medical care, forced into prostitution, and assaulted. Weston's own niece was also abused and held captive. She was found locked in a closet with burns, open wounds, badly healed broken bones, and signs on her ankles that she had repeatedly been shot with a pellet gun.[5]

Dorothy Dixon, a pregnant woman with a mental disability, was tortured, used for target practice, and kept as a prisoner until she died so that her captors could claim her disability checks. "Evidence suggested that Dixon's body had been scalded from head to toe with boiling water and was riddled with wounds from a BB gun, some infected and others in varying stages of healing."[6] She also had missing teeth, deep cuts on her scalp that went all the way to the bone, and burns from a hot glue gun. Michelle Riley, one of those indicted in the case, pleaded guilty to first-degree murder and received a sentence of 45 years in prison. Riley took Dixon's monthly Social Security check that Dixon received because she had a developmental disability.

Jennifer Daugherty, described as having the mental abilities of a 12- to 14-year-old, was tortured and murdered by six people she believed to be her friends. She was 30 years old at the time of her death. Daugherty was tortured for 36 hours before she was killed. Her captors forced her to drink detergent and urine, punched her, cut her hair, painted her face with nail polish, and then stabbed her repeatedly before cutting her neck and wrists. Her body was wrapped in Christmas decorations and stuffed into a trashcan in a middle school parking lot. "The sadistic attack on Daugherty was anything but unique. Still, few Americans are aware of the special vulnerability of people with emotional, intellectual and physical disabilities to extraordinary violence."[7]

According to the Bureau of Justice Statistic's 2009–2011 report on crimes against those with disabilities,[8] persons with disabilities are more than twice as likely to be victims of violent crimes than those without disabilities. They are more than three times as likely to be the victims of serious violent crime (rape/ sexual assault, robbery, and aggravated assault) than those who are not disabled. The Crime Victims with Disabilities Awareness Act of 1998 mandates that the National Crime Victimization Survey include statistics on crimes against those with disabilities. The act is intended to increase awareness of the victimization of those with disabilities in order to develop strategies to combat the problem. Attacks against people with disabilities are often perpetrated by people who know them: family members, neighbors, caretakers, and those who pretend to be friends. "Victims with disabilities are often extremely reluctant to report attacks out of fear that their tormentors will retaliate. They may have psychiatric or intellectual deficits that seriously interfere with their capacity to recognize false friendships or to report crime."[9] As with violent crimes against the LGBT population, crimes against people with disabilities often include a higher level of brutality than violent crimes against the general population, as perpetrators often engage in the same type of overkill that is seen in violent crimes against LGBT people. Perpetrators of crimes against people with disabilities are often young and act in groups, which is common for perpetrators of hate crimes in general.

Hate crimes against many groups exist in America today, including those I have discussed in this book but also those I have not: people with disabilities, older adults, and women, for example. There are also hateful acts against those who may not be recognized as a protected group but nevertheless are created as Other and treated as lesser, such as those who are overweight. Our public images of these groups and the way they are framed by the media have helped create them as targets of hate.

IMPORTANCE OF IMAGE

Crayola crayons changed their "flesh"-colored crayon to "peach" in 1962 in part due to the civil rights movement. Today, they make a set of eight multicultural skin–colored crayons. However, other companies still produced "flesh"- colored nylons, tights, makeup, plastic bandages, and ace bandages. These are the kinds of "commonsense" assumptions that define our culture in a particular manner. To label one color as "flesh" while our nation contains a mix of skin tones reduces our mix of peoples and cultures to "us" against "not us." Yes, this is one small example, but our social structure, our media, our systems of justice, employment, education, and more are full of these unnoticed examples that create borders between those who publically stand for what is America and those who are marginalized.

Lest you argue that images in the American media have no real effect, consider the protest recently about the cover of *Rolling Stone* magazine that featured the face of the accused Boston marathon bomber Dzhokhar Tsarnaev. The protest was over the attention paid to him and the fact that the magazine used an attractive picture, thereby making him in a sense a "star." However, the point of the article was to show that he came from a fairly regular family background and yet developed into a "monster." While some called for boycotts of the magazine and some newsstands refused to stock it (CVS and Walgreens, for example), the sales of this issue doubled from previous ones. Clearly, the American public believes that presentation of a person or issue is of paramount importance in how we think about the issue, how we frame the "good" and the "bad," and who is deserving of attention. The public believes these images are important in determining how we frame individuals and the resulting actions taken. But we do not look at the everyday framing of groups in our society with the same critical eye. We become so familiar with certain depictions that they gain commonsense status, and we no longer look closely or question the way in which the world is framed for us by the media. While many criticized the recent cover of *Rolling Stone*, the same critical eye is not applied to the daily frames of immigrants as a dehumanized and criminalized mass, to the framing of Black Americans as inherently criminal or responsible for their own marginalized place in society, or to the frames of the LGBT population as immoral and sexually deviant.

New population estimates from July 2001 based on the 2000 Census reported that Latinos had become the most prevalent minority in the United States. After the census announcement, a group of Latinos wrote an "Open letter to African-Americans from Latinos" pledging to combat competitiveness that the new statistics might engender between their populations as well as to remind the Latino population of the unique historical experiences of African Americans. Competition between these groups has been fostered by stereotypes and misunderstandings. Duke University research points to the prevalence of old stereotypes of Blacks as lazy and untrustworthy in the newly arriving Latino population. Many of the misconceptions are based on cultural portrayals of Blacks on television such as American sitcoms "in which Blacks are portrayed as clowns, buffoons and crooks."[10] A popular comic strip in Mexico from 1963 to 1977 entitled *Memin Penguin* included a mammy-like character who lived in a rundown house in a poor neighborhood. "A popular afternoon *telenova* on Mexican TV in 2005 had a comedian in Blackface chasing after light-complexioned actresses in skimpy outfits. Ads have featured Mexicans in Afros, Black face, and distorted features. The most popular screen stars in film and on TV, and the models featured on magazines and billboards, are White or fair skinned with sandy or blond hair."[11] Mexico has a rigid hierarchy based on class, caste, and skin color; the U.S. standard of beauty has been globalized, and recent technology has made it easier and faster to disseminate images worldwide. In southern Africa, colorism is a byproduct of European colonialism. The desire for white skin and European features marks areas that are still being colonized by European standards like a persistent replicating virus. Even as the colonizers are leaving, their ideals of appearance linger to maintain white/White dominance. Many products for lightening skin contain poisonous elements like mercury, and mercury soaps used in Africa are manufactured in the European Union in countries such as Ireland and Italy. "Distribution of mercury soap has been illegal in the European Union since 1989, but its manufacture has remained legal as long as the product is exported."[12] Thus, the dominant society manufactures a harmful product to sell to those who have accepted their ideal of beauty; it will not allow its "own" citizens to use it, but it is fitting for "them." It is not only remnants of colonialism that cause the desire for lighter skin, but the global spread of Western consumer culture. Just as bodies are changed by fast-food diets that have spread internationally, skin and hair are also changed by the continued spread of limited Western ideals of beauty.

Black unemployment, education levels, and other markers of success are often measured disparagingly against newly arrived immigrant groups without taking into consideration the different circumstances surrounding each group's arrival and treatment in this country.[13] According to Hutchinson, Blacks and Latinos commit the majority of hate crimes in Los Angeles, and these are committed against each other.[14] In a 1998 poll by the National Conference, Latinos were found to be three times as likely as Whites to believe Blacks incapable of getting ahead,[15] while Blacks may see immigrants, particularly undocumented immigrants, as economic competition.

SIKHS, MUSLIMS AND THE CREATED OTHER

Confusion over who is actually Muslim in America continues today. Due to the created mediated image of Muslim, many non-Muslims have been attacked and even murdered based on this creation. Members of the Sikh religion fall into this category, and in 2015, the FBI will begin tracking hate crimes committed against Sikhs. In the days following September 11, 2001, numerous Sikhs, mistakenly identified as Muslim, were attacked as Americans took out their anger on targets they believed were representative of the terrorists. The power of created image and the assigning of certain generic traits to Muslims can be impli-cated in the hate crimes against a religion that has nothing to do with either the events of 9/11 or with Islam. Because male Sikhs typically wear turbans on their heads as well as beards, they have fallen into the generic "Muslim-looking" category.

Sikhs make up the world's fifth largest religion, and their numbers are esti-mated to be approximately half a million strong in the United States. In the days following 9/11, Balbir Singh Sodhi was shot and killed outside his gas station in Arizona. A year later, his brother Sukhpal Singh was shot while driving his cab in California. In 2009, Jasmir Singh was attacked by three men outside a grocery store in New York City and lost vision in his left eye. Two years later, his father, Jiwan Singh, was attacked in New York City and accused of being related to Osama bin Laden. All were Sikhs, and all were attacked because of the dominant frames and ideologies we have regarding Muslims.[16]

When it comes to the Other in American society, we take acts of individuals and assign blame to the whole group. If one Hmong hunter shoots at White hunters, the whole Hmong population is implicated in this action. When an individual who is Muslim commits an act of terror, hate crimes rise against any who are taken to be Muslim. In contrast, a White terrorist such as Timothy McVeigh does not stand as representative of young White men in general. Iden-tification of the Oklahoma City bomber did not lead to any hate crimes against White men. However, more than 300 "Muslim-looking" people were attacked after the first mistaken reports about Arabs/Muslims/Middle Easterners. We frame groups as Other with stereotypes and then assume all individual members possess the attributes we have created. Black Americans were framed as lesser humans, and lynch mobs murdered many Blacks merely as a reminder to the whole group of their inferior status. Various immigrant groups have been created as too different to assimilate, and laws excluding or limiting their immigration resulted, marginalizing them and thus slowing their assimilation and creating a self-fulfilling prophecy. When wrong by one group member becomes a group attribute in the media, we allow legislation against the group, discrimination against the group, and the visiting of hate crimes upon individual members of the group as a result.

Contestations over real and figurative space continue in American culture. Arguments over identity and belonging, over who represents America and who is pushed to the margins occur decade after decade, even century after century, through similar media frames and recurring metaphors even as the groups under scrutiny change. We contest large spaces through war, creating enemies to destroy. We contest who is allowed in our country and where we put immigrants in our hierarchy once they are here. We contest who is allowed in our neighbor-hoods, in our churches, in our public spaces, and—on a more personal level—who we want our children to marry. But it goes beyond that as we contest what we think Others should be allowed to have and do. Same-sex marriage does not diminish opposite-sex marriage, yet many people are unable to agree to allow the LGBT community the same rights as the heterosexual community. Practicing your own religion is not diminished by someone else's practice of a different religion, yet many people are unwilling to allow religious choice outside their own narrowly framed beliefs. Our public discourse on all these issues includes political rhetoric, the news and entertainment media, the widely expanding and far-reaching social media that instantly lets an event become a worldwide discussion, and the academic community's research and analysis. All these serve to frame our contestations in particular ways, frames that have historically created a climate in which hate crimes, war crimes, and hate speech flourish to maintain the borders between "our" space and "theirs." An historical look shows us that those at one time deemed Other are now often considered full members of the mainstream, yet we continue to create and marginalize each new group as Other as they come along, using the same metaphors of dehumanization and the same hateful acts that have been used in the past to let the Others know they are not wanted. There are some who are still fighting to be part of the mainstream, taking steps forward in increments but always having to fight dominant frames and metaphors that dehumanize and marginalize them.

Who is responsible for changing this? How can we read our cultural presentations more critically? Clearly, the American public is capable of this, as the reaction to particular media framings demonstrates. In 1994, for example, there was public condemnation of *Time* magazine's altered mug shot of O. J. Simpson on its cover. The photograph had been manipulated to make Simpson darker and more sinister looking.[17] While it would be wonderful to believe that the media itself in its many incarnations, along with politicians and others with public prominence, will apply a more critical eye to the effects of their frames on the basis of effects on humanity rather than on their bank accounts or election/reelection potential, it is unlikely that this will happen on a large scale. It lies in the hands of the American public to consider these frames more critically, to question what viewpoint is being presented, and to protest frames that dehumanize others, particularly when those others have already been created as Other. We should argue against hateful acts not just because they have been additionally criminalized in our legal system, but because they diminish us all by their spread of terror and hate.

NOTES

1. "Man seeking help after North Carolina car crash shot by police," *Reuters,* September 15, 2013. http://www.reuters.com/article/2013/09/15/us-usa-police-accident -idUSBRE98E0AT20130915.

2. Karen Franklin, "Antigay behaviors among young adults: Prevalence, patterns, and motivators in a noncriminal population," *Journal of Interpersonal Violence* 15, no. 4 (April 2000): 340.

3. Anne Rafferty, "A painful admission," Traditional Values Coalition, http://www .traditionalvalues.org/content/home/36644/ (accessed September 29, 2013).

4. Joseph Farah, "Be glad Portman's son isn't serial killer," March 18, 2013, 'http://www .wnd.com/2013/03/be-glad-portmans-son-isn't-serial-killer (accessed September 29, 2013.

5. Denise Noe, "Linda Ann Weston and the Philadelphia dungeon case," *Crime Library,* May 21, 2013, http://www.trutv.com/library/crime/blog/article/linda-ann-weston (accessed September 27, 2013; Kathy Matheson, "Linda Weston and 4 others charged for allegedly confining adults to Philadelphia basement," *Huffington Post Crime,* January 23, 2013, http:// www.huffingtonpost.com/2013/01/23/linda-weston-charged (accessed September 26, 2013).

6. Edecio Martinez, "Pregnant mom Dorothy Dixon beaten, boiled, used as target practice while captors collected her money," http://www.cbsnews.com/2102-504083_162 -6120209.html (accessed September 26, 2013).

7. Jack Levin, "The invisible hate crime," March 1, 2011, http://www.psmag.com/legal -affairs/the-invisible-hate-crime-27984 (accessed September 26, 2013).

8. Erika Harrell, *Crime against persons with disabilities, 2009–2011: Statistical tables* (Washington, DC: U.S. Department of Justice, Bureau of Justice Statistics, December 2012).

9. Levin "The invisible hate crime".

10. Earl Ofari Hutchinson, *The Latino Challenge to Black America* (Los Angeles: Middle Passage, 2007), 26.

11. Ibid., 27.

12. Evelyn Nakano Glenn (ed.), *Shades of Difference: Why Skin Color Matters* (Stanford, CA: Stanford University Press, 2009), 171.

13. Hutchinson, *Latino Challenge to Black America,* 37.

14. Ibid., 62.

15. Ibid., 64.

16. "History of hate: Crimes against Sikhs since 9/11," *Huffington Post,* August 7, 2012. http://www.huffingtonpost.com/2012/08/07/history-of-hate-crimes-against-sikhs-since-911_n _1751841.html.

17. Deirdre Carmody, "Time responds to criticism over Simpson cover," *New York Times,* June 25, 1994. http://www.nytimes.com/1994/06/25/us/time-responds-to-criticism-over -simpson-cover.html.

Index

Abu Ghraib, 57
Advertising, 109–10, 112
Amedure, Scott: murder, 199–200
Anti-Defamation League (ADL), 162, 166
Anti-immigration groups, 89
Anti-integrationist violence. *See* Move-In violence
Arabs: as enemies, 50–51, 56–57; hate crimes against, 52–53; media images of, 47–50; stereotypes of, 49; war crimes against, 57–59
Araujo, Gwen, murder, 200–1, 202
Asians: hate speech effects on, 228; stereotypes of, 217, 218
Assimilation, 66, 84

Bell, Jeannine, *Hate Thy Neighbor: Move-In Violence and the Persistence of Racial Segregation in American Housing*, 135, 138–41
Bensonhurst, 6–9, 136–37
Birth of a Nation, 117, 134
Bisexual. *See* LGBT
Black press: Chinese, 72–73
Blacks: in advertising, 109–10; colorism, 110–13; in film, 113–14, 116–17; hate crimes against, 107, 136–37, 141–44; imagery, 109–110; lynching, 127–35;

move-in violence, 135–41; racial profiling, 120–21; stereotypes of, 216–18; stereotype as criminal, 8–9, 114, 115–18;
Boy Scouts of America, 188
Burzinski, Michael: murder, 1–2
Bush, George W.: campaign, 114, 119; same-sex marriage, 194; speeches after 9/11, 53–54
Byrd, James, Jr., 12, 55

Campus speech codes, 222–24
Carto, Willis, 166–67
Catholics: anti-Catholicism, 153, 155, 157–59; hate crimes against, 152–53, 156; immigrants, 153
Chavez, Leo, *Covering Immigration,* 82–85
Chin, Vincent: murder, 45
Chinese: hate crimes against, 70–71; immigration, 67; legal response to, 69–70; media images of, 68; stereotypes, 68, 72
Civil Rights Acts: 1964, 4–5; 1968, 4–5
Colorism, 110–13, 239, 245
Columbus, Christopher, 27
Constitution: amendments, 212, 223, 227, 230–31; state, 2, 151, 160; U.S., 151
Coughlin, Father Charles, 164–65

Council on American-Islamic Relations (CAIR), 172–73

Dabarran, Ahmed, murder, 200
Dearborn Independent, 162–64
Defense of Marriage Act (DOMA), 193–95
Dehumanizing enemies, 24–26, 40–42, 45–47, 237–38
Discourse analysis, 4, 84–85
Disparagement humor, 212–15
Don't Ask, Don't Tell, 189–93
Dower, John: *War Without Mercy*, 24, 41, 44, 59
Dundas, Alan: *Cracking Jokes*, 214–16

Enemies: Arabs, 50–59; Japanese, 40–44; Native Americans, 26–30; Vietnamese, 45–47
Ethnic jokes, 213–15

Farmington, New Mexico: murders, 37–39
Fighting words, 224, 231–32
Film representations: Arabs, 49; Blacks, 113–14, 116–17; Italians, 82; LGBT, 184–86; Native Americans, 34
Ford, Henry, 162
Framing: hate crimes, 203–206; illegal immigrants, 85–87; Muslims, 168–69, 174–75; Other, 237, 240–44
Frank, Leo, 161–62

Gay. *See* LGBT
Gay panic defense, 197–202
Gender-neutral restrooms, 189
Gone with the Wind, 117
Gunn, Sakia: murder, 206

Haditha, 57
Hate crime effects, 39–40, 56, 140–41
Hate crime laws, purpose, 13–14, 15–16
Hate crime legislation: state laws, 13–14; Statistics Act, 1990, 9–10; Prevention Act, 2009, 12–13
Hate groups, 36, 122–24
Hate rock, 123
Hate speech, 224–32; symbolic, 211, 225–26

Hawkins, Yusuf: Bensonhurst, 136–37; bias crime, 7; media response, 7–9, 139; murder of, 5–7
Hennessey, David, 79–81
Holocaust denial, 166–67
Homosexuals. *See* LBGT
Horton, Willie, 114, 118–19
Hose, Sam: lynching, 133
Howard Beach, 142–44

Immigration legislation: Arizona, 91, 97; Barred Zone Act (1917), 65; Chinese Exclusion Act, 65, 67, 70; Emergency Quota Act (1921), 161; Immigration Act (1990), 66; Immigration Restriction Act, 161; Johnson-Reed Act (1924), 65, 161; Naturalization Act (1790), 65, 69, 72; Proposition 187, 88; Reform and Control Act (1986), 66, 83; Reform and Responsibility (1996), 66
Imus, Don, 218
Irish: immigrants, 153–54; stereotypes of, 153–55
Islamaphobia, 172
"Islamic terrorist," 173–75
Italians: hate crimes against, 79–82; immigration, 73–74; lynching, 79–82; race, 74, 77–79; stereotypes of, 75–76, 82

Jackson, Andrew, 31
Japanese: as enemies, 40–44; internment camps, 44–45
Jefferson, Thomas, 30, 151
Jewish: anti-Semitism, 163–67; immigrants, 159, 161; stereotypes of, 160–61, 165–66; students at Harvard, 163
Joke cycles, 215–16

Kearney, Dennis, 69–70
Kennedy, John, 157–58
Kerry, John, 159
Know-Nothing, 154–55
Ku Klux Klan, 37, 123, 126, 155–57, 162, 238

Langer, Elinor: *A Hundred Little Hitlers*, 125–27
Lesbian. *See* LGBT

LGBT: Boy Scouts, 188; in children's literature, 182–84; in film, 184–86; gay panic defense, 197–199; gender neutral restrooms, 189; hate crimes against, 1–2, 10, 192–93, 199–202; media representations of, 182–88; in the military, 193; overkill, 10; press, 204–5; same-sex marriage, 193–96; stereotypes of, 2–3, 183–88; on television, 186–88
Lindbergh, Charles: anti-Semitism, 165; war diary, 43
Lipstadt, Deborah: *Denying the Holocaust*, 167
Love, Gregory: assault, 201
Lynching, 71, 79–82, 93–94, 127–35

Maricopa County, Arizona: racial profiling, 92–93; sheriff's office, 91–93
Media representations: Arabs, 47–53, 56–57; Asians, 40; Blacks, 110–14; Chinese, 68; enemies, 25; immigration, 82–88; Japanese, 41–42; LGBT, 182–88, 202–6, 240–41; lynching, 129–31; Native Americans, 32–34, 36–37; Persian Gulf War, 50–51; September 11, 51–52;
Mexican: hate crime trends, 96–98; immigration, 82–86; lynching, 93–94; removal, 94–95; stereotypes of, 86–88, 97; zoot suit riots, 95–96
Mississippi Burning (MIBURN), 5
Move-in violence, 135–41
Mudin, Gul, murder, 58–59
"Muslim-looking," 55, 245–46
Muslims: anti-Muslim sentiment, 171–72; hate crimes against, 168, 173; stereotypes of, 167–70, 173

Native Americans: hate crimes against, 34–35, 37–39; mascot controversy, 219–21; religion, 27, 151, 219–20; stereotypes of, 32–34; treaty rights, 35–37; war crimes, 28–30
Nativism, 65–66, 74, 76, 88–89
Navajo, assaults and murders of, 38–39
Neal, Claude, lynching, 134
Nguyen, Luyen Phan, murder, 47, 217

Obama, Barack, 170–71
Oklahoma City bombing, 49–50, 167–68
O'Neal, Shaquille, 218
Other: creation, 232, 237–42; definition, 3; dehumanizing, 24; enemy, 23–26, 40–42, 53–54, 59; immigrant, 83, 88, 98, 229–30, 238–39; racial, 77, 144, 239–40; religious, 240

People with disabilities, 215, 242–43
Perry, Barbara, 26, 33–34, 37, 39
Persian Gulf War, 50–51
Political correctness, 221–24
Political rhetoric: Blacks, 118–19; Catholics, 157–59; LGBT, 190, 194, 196; Muslims, 171–73; Native Americans, 30–32
Profiling: Arabs, 54; Blacks, 120–21; Mexicans, 90–93; Muslims, 173
Propaganda, 24–25
Proposition 187, 88

Race: ideological construct, 105–7, 239; Irish, 153–54; Italians, 74, 77–79, 106
Racial zoning, 138–39
Racism, 107–9,
R.A.V. vs. St. Paul, 16, 226
Robles, Joel, murder, 201–2
Roosevelt, Theodore, 31–32, 78

Sand Creek massacre, 29
September 11, 2001: hate crimes as a result of, 52–53; media response to, 51–52
Seraw, Mulugeta, murder of, 124–27
Shepard, Matthew: gay panic defense, 199; media response, 11–12, 202–3, 206; murder, 10–11
Sikhs, 245–46; murders of, 52, 123
Skinheads, 123–25
Smith, Al, 156–57
Southern Poverty Law Center, 126–27
Symbolic language, 211–12

Transgender. *See* LGBT
Trophy taking of: Blacks, 132–34; Japanese, 42–44; Native Americans, 30; Vietnamese, 43–44

Vietnamese: hate crimes against, 47; war crimes against, 45–46, 58

Washington, Jesse: lynching, 133–34
Wisconsin vs. Mitchell, 16
Wounded Knee massacre, 29–30

Zoeller, Fuzzy, 217–18
Zoot suit riots, 95–96

About the Author

VICTORIA MUNRO, PhD, is the coordinator for an undergraduate research grant program at the University of Minnesota. Her published works include "The Murder of Yusuf Hawkins: Bias Crimes and a Neighborhood on Trial" in Greenwood's *Crimes & Trials of the Century* and "Popular Cultural Images of Criminals and Prisoners since Attica" in *Social Justice*. Munro holds a master's degree in criminal justice studies and a doctorate in American studies from the University of Minnesota.